West's Law School Advisory Board

CRITICAL RACE THEORY

CASES, MATERIALS, AND PROBLEMS

Second Edition

By

Dorothy A. Brown
Professor of Law
Washington and Lee University School of Law

AMERICAN CASEBOOK SERIES®

THOMSON
WEST

Mat #40426962

© West, a Thomson business, 2003
© 2007 Thomson/West
      610 Opperman Drive
      P.O. Box 64526
      St. Paul, MN 55164–0526
      1–800–328–9352

Printed in the United States of America

ISBN: 978–0–314–16633–3

 *TEXT IS PRINTED ON 10% POST CONSUMER RECYCLED PAPER*

For my mother, Dorothy Brown,

who prophesied this book into existence.

*

Preface

This book would never have been written without a lot of help. First, I want to thank Dean David Partlett for inviting me to teach a Critical Race Theory Seminar when I visited Washington and Lee in the Fall Semester 2001. I had always wanted to teach a seminar in Critical Race Theory, but never could fit it into my teaching package. So, when Dean Partlett asked, I quickly agreed.

I had several goals for the course. First, I wanted to make sure that my students did not look upon Critical Race Theory as an academic exercise—a theory to be used only in the classroom—something separate from their "regular" law school experience. I wanted them to come away with the view that Critical Race Theory is an analytical tool that can be used to make them more effective lawyers. Second, I wanted to do what no other Critical Race Theory casebook had done and use the case method approach. I wanted to select cases to study that would benefit from a Critical Race Theory perspective, but where race wasn't always an obvious factor. In order to benefit the largest number of students, I decided to examine cases from the first year curriculum. Third, to the extent possible, I wanted to include cases in which courts have acknowledged and applied Critical Race Theory.

The second of the three goals proved the most problematic in this project. Examining cases from the first year curriculum seemed like a great idea, but there was one problem—I DIDN'T TEACH FIRST YEAR COURSES!!! As a result, I spent a considerable time harassing my friends and anyone else that I thought would be able to suggest first-year cases that I could use for my seminar. If it were not for the individuals listed below, I could not have taught the seminar the way I wanted, and this book would never have been written. A special thanks therefore goes to Professors Jody Armour, Margalynne Armstrong, Larry Cata Backer, Taunya Banks, Barbara Bernier, Lisa Ikemoto, Ruth Jones, Betsy Malloy, Deborah Post, Jenny Rivera, Benjamin Spencer, Cheryl Wade, Stephanie Wildman, Keith Wingate, Margaret Woo, and Frank Wu.

I especially want to thank the students in my Critical Race Theory Seminar at Washington and Lee in the Fall 2001. It was the first time I taught the class and you each were and remain an inspiration to me. In alphabetical order—and showing no favoritism—I thank Faiz Ahmad, Andrew Carpenter, Andrea Coleman, Suzanne Cuba, Kelly Jones, Amy King, Audrey Marcello, Anne Musgrove, Christina Pignatelli, Justin Pingel, Pranita Raghavan, Suzanne Takata and Loren Weiss Villa. In addition a special thanks goes to the following students in my Critical Race Theory Seminar in the Fall 2003—in alphabetical order—and again showing no preference—Jennifer Bennett, Les Brock, David Edelstein, Susan Gibbons, Mark Kennedy, Priya Nath, Paul Pittman, Shellie Sewell,

Yetunde Talabi and Ahmed Younis. I would also like to thank all of my other past, present and future students. Your comments can only improve this book and the way I teach the course.

I would like to give a special mention to Cynthia Aninao, the acquisitions librarian at the University of Cincinnati College of Law, for helping me track down the *Madrigal* opinion and any other material that I needed as I put together the first draft of my seminar materials. I am forever in your debt. I also thank the members of the Washington and Lee University School of Law library staff for their cheerful disposition and assistance in completing this project.

I also want to thank the following Washington and Lee colleagues for reading chapters, giving me ideas, and otherwise providing support and encouragement. In alphabetical order—and showing no favoritism—I thank Denis Brion, Darryl Brown, Montré Carodine, David Caudill, Mark Drumbl, Roger Groot, Louise Halper, Ned Henneman, John Keyser, Ron Krotoszynski, Blake Morant, Brian Murchison, David Partlett, Doug Rendleman, Joan Shaughnessy, Scott Sundby, and Melissa Waters.

I also want to thank Ms. Erin Troy and Ms. Kristina Longo for their extraordinary research assistance. I never would have made my deadline without their diligence, dedication and hard work. I want to thank Ms. Diane Cochran, my faculty services assistant, who worked on discrete parts of the manuscript and generally kept me organized. Last, and certainly not least, I want to thank Roxanne Birkel, Pamela Siege Chandler, Heidi Hellekson, Staci Herr, and the group at Thomson West who caught my vision and supported me at every step.

DOROTHY A. BROWN

April 2007

Foreword

Dorothy Brown,
Professor of Law and Director, Frances Lewis Law Center
Washington and Lee University School of Law
Sydney Lewis Hall, Room 3011
Lexington, VA 24450–0303

Dear Professor Brown:

My name is Geneva Crenshaw and I am a central figure in many of Professor Derrick Bell's books, particularly *And We Are Not Saved: The Elusive Quest for Racial Equality*,[1] and *Faces at the Bottom of the Well: The Permanence of Racism*.[2] I just learned that Professor Bell promised months ago that he would write a *Foreword* for the Second Edition of your casebook, *Critical Race Theory: Cases, Materials, and Problems.* Now, with your deadline looming, he has prevailed on me to write something for which he will be all too ready to accept credit. Well, I have reviewed your book and I am certain that its selection of articles and cases on legal subjects generally covered in the first year of law school should prove revelatory for many students and perhaps even reform inspiring for some. I will explain the latter prediction later.

Let me first commend you on your book's impressive effort to inject Critical Race Theory thinking into the hallowed first-year curriculum. It is a much-needed supplement to the traditional courses and is very much in keeping with recommendations in the 2007 Carnegie Foundation report, "Educating Lawyers: Preparation for the Profession of Law."[3] Based on visits to 16 public and private law schools in the United States and Canada that were geographically diverse and varied in selectivity, the Report found that law schools fail to complement the focus on developing skill in legal analyses with effective support for developing ethical standards and practice skills.

Confirming what every law student knows, the Report found that law schools give only casual attention to teaching how to use legal thinking in the complexity of actual law practice. Instead, in the first year of law school, students are often warned not to let their moral concerns or compassion for the people in the cases they discuss "cloud their legal analyses."

---

[1] Basic Books, 1987.

[2] Basic Books, 1992.

[3] See, http://www.carnegiefoundation.org/publications/pub.asp?key=43&subkey=617

This warning, the Report acknowledged, may help students escape the grip of misconceptions about how the law works as they hone their analytic skills. But when the misconceptions are not addressed directly, students have no way of learning when and how their moral concerns may be relevant to their work as lawyers and when these concerns could throw them off track. As a result, students can be left with the impression that ethical and moral concerns about social welfare must be subordinated to legal procedure and doctrine as set out in judicial precedents.

I recall reading an unpublished article, "Training Lawyers Not to Care," by a former law teacher, Sheila Rush, one of the first women to graduate from the Harvard Law School back in the 1960s. For her, the law school experience was marked by a pervasive boredom that stifled the human emotions the cases being studied should have evoked. She wrote:

"Being bored meant that I felt nothing stronger than indifference for a Hawkins and McGee, 'the hairy hand case',[4] that I really didn't care very much about them, or how their case turned out. Being bored meant that I seldom experienced the feelings of concern for people, the expressions of empathy, that are the essence of caring. The casebook people weren't real, of course, but in the pressured atmosphere of law school, where studies and classes consumed most of the day, they were my companions. I interacted with them far more than with their flesh-and blood counterparts. The effect on me, over time, was one of numbing. Feelings (apart from anxiety and fear over 'doing well') just simply weren't a part of the study of law, and mine seemed to atrophy from lack of use, receding, as it were, into the grey dullness of 'legal detriments,' 'consideration,' and 'measure of damages.'

It's possible, I suppose, to be emotionally deprived for the better part of one's day and still remain a concerned, caring person, but I have never been one to compartmentalize. What affects me in one part of my life, affects me in all. In having so few opportunities to experience and express the sentiments of caring as I studied law, in feeling practically nothing for the casebook people while being exposed to their numerous difficulties, in being so numbed that I didn't even attempt the kind of introspective self-criticism that might have given me a better perspective—my overall capacity to care was affected, I became less human."

Thankfully, at most law schools, teaching has improved since Sheila Rush described her first-year ordeal suffered during "The Paper Chase" era. The improvements, though welcome, have not lessened the reasons set out in the Carnegie Foundation report that much more needs to be done.

---

[4] Hawkins v. McGee, 84 N.H. 114, 146 A. 641 (N.H. 1929), is a leading case on damages in contracts handed down by the New Hampshire Supreme Court. It was mentioned in both the book and the film versions of "Tje Paper Chase." See, http://en.wikipedia.org/wiki/Hawkins_v._McGee

Quite recently, for example, a second-year, black student explained why she did not support an electoral reform she felt was clearly needed to remedy long-standing racial discrimination in the election process. She explained: "While I viscerally agreed with the arguments for election reform, I ultimately found myself voting against them. I use the passive voice consciously to emphasize my frustration. In each of my doctrinal courses in law school I found myself asking, ' ... but what about [insert X under-represented group]?' when we are told to accept a certain policy or practice as the legal standard. The law doesn't seem to give us—or when it does, accept as readily—arguments that aren't steeped in case law, supported by longstanding doctrine, etcetera. The Petitioner's points (historical, personal, and commonsensical) are just the sort of arguments I make in my head, but refrain from relying on in my large lecture courses because there doesn't seem to be room for them."

Over the years, frustrations like those expressed by this student have motivated many of her predecessors to forge reforms in curriculum selection, classroom procedures, and final exam alternatives. Many schools now boast of a range of clinical offerings that would likely never have happened without student demands.

And here is the real potential of your book. In area after area, the cases and readings you have selected, the potent questions you raise fill an important void in law students' learning process. While many of the cases involve blacks and other people of color, the cases and articles interpreting those cases reveal how the actual significance of race is often ignored or subordinated to seemingly neutral principles applied in ways that do actual damage to the black parties and can in significant ways be harmful as well to whites.

Many of the articles you use are by black, Latino, and Asian legal scholars whose work is not frequently enough published in the "major" law reviews or cited very often by the "major" names in the field. Law teachers who fear raising issues of race in torts, contracts, and even criminal law classes for fear that they will embarrass black and upset white students, now have cases and writings offering vehicles for such discussions within the existing parameters of the course material.

In short, Professor Brown, through your book you have created the academic equivalent of an Underground Railroad through which students can escape the rigidity of first-year teaching formats and explore with liberated minds and hearts the means for more effective and far more satisfying professional work.

Here, though, you must be prepared for the burdens of your achievement. For, as the old saying warns, "no good deed goes unpunished." I can both imagine and predict that with the growing popularity of your book, some students and then more and more will bring CRT thinking into every aspect of their first-year courses. They will question the application of rules that disadvantage the already disadvantaged regardless of race or sex or sexual orientation. Their critiques will broaden to the selection of cases and the casebooks that contain them. Inevitably, this will lead first to questions and then challenges as to how they are taught and how their performances are graded.

In order to do so effectively, they will begin reading and heeding the works of CRT writers, those cited in the footnotes of the articles you use to be sure, but then branching out to other similar works. Increasingly, students, particularly in the first year, will urge their teachers to abandon Socratic dialogues in the classroom and replace them with pedagogically effective teaching procedures. Their insistence on teaching that builds confidence rather than undermines it will spread from school to school. Students will refuse to subject themselves to final exams with all the inherent unfairness of a grading process that rewards with high grades those with skills of memory and the ability to organize and write effectively not learned in the classroom.

Predictably, those in authority faced with demands for effective teaching will conclude that their positions depend on maintenance of the traditions they know. And rather than even seriously consider new ideas, they will read the calls for reform as revolt and place the blame on you, the reformer's messenger and instigator. As has been the experience of every forward-thinking person since the Old Testament prophets, You will be treated harshly. You can expect little support from even those who heeded your call for they will be too busy—or so they will claim—with their reform efforts to have time to defend you and your by then besmirched character.

Years in the future, the teaching reforms your book promoted will be in place and already somewhat corrupted. At some point, those then in charge will remember the important role you played, and in a major commemoration and in many more silent moments of thanks, you will be remembered and hailed. You may likely no longer be around to hear these tardy acknowledgments. Your absence will spare you the trauma of watching some of those who initially opposed your efforts stepping forward to receive the awards you earned and deserved. That, though, is the lot of the true reformer, who neither resentful nor envious, finds comfort in the knowledge of a challenge recognized and met.

Well done, Professor Brown, well done.

Geneva Crenshaw

Copyright Acknowledgements and Reprint Permissions

I gratefully acknowledge the authors and publishers that have allowed me to reprint copyrighted materials. Excerpts from the following materials appear with the permission of the copyright holders.

Taunya Lovell Banks, Teaching Laws With Flaws: Adopting a Pluralistic Approach to Torts, 57 Mo. L. Rev. 443, 443–445, 448–454 (1992). Copyright 1992 by the Curators of the University of Missouri. Reprinted by permission of the Missouri Law Review and Taunya Banks.

Roy L. Brooks, Critical Race Theory: A Proposed Structure and Application to Federal Pleading, 11 Harv. BlackLetter L. J. 85, 85–86, 87–88, 90–98, 102–112 (1994). Copyright © 1994 by the President and Fellows of Harvard College. Reprinted with permission of the Harvard Blackletter Law Journal and Roy L. Brooks.

Alfred L. Brophy, Integrating Spaces: New Perspectives on Race in the Property Curriculum, 55 J. Legal Educ. 319–320, 322–324 (2005). Reprinted with permission of the Journal of Legal Education and Alfred L. Brophy.

Justice Ming W. Chin, Fairness or Bias?: A Symposium on Racial and Ethnic Composition and Attitudes in the Judicary, 4 Asian L. J. 181, 184, 187–189, 190–191, 192, 193 (1997). Reprinted with permission of the Asian Law Journal and Justice Ming W. Chin.

Eben Colby, Note, What did the Doctrine of Unconscionability Do to the Walker-Thomas Furniture Company?, 34 Conn. L. Rev. 625, 625–627, 646–650, 651–655, 656–660 (2002). Reprinted with permission of the Connecticut Law Review.

Kimberle Williams Crenshaw, Race, Reform, and Retrenchment: Transformation and Legitimation in Antidiscrimination Law, 101 Harv. L. Rev. 1331, 1356–1386 (1988). Copyright © 1988 by the Harvard Law Review Association. Reprinted with permission of the Harvard Law Review and Kimberle Williams Crenshaw.

Linda E. Davila, Note, The Underrepresentation of Hispanic Attorneys in Corporate Law Firms, 39 Stan. L. Rev. 1403, 1403–1405, 1406–1407, 1410–1424, 1431–1432, 1434–1435, 1436–1437 (1987). Reprinted with permission of the Stanford Law Review.

Angela J. Davis, Prosecution and Race: The Power and Privilege of Discretion, 67 Fordham L. Rev. 13, 13–38, 54–67 (1998). Reprinted with permission of the Fordham Law Review and Angela J. Davis.

Cheryl I. Harris, Whiteness as Property, 106 Harv. L. Rev. 1707, 1714–1720, 1721–1724, 1725–1731, 1757–1764 (1993). Copyright ©

1993 by the Harvard Law Review Association. Reprinted with permission of the Harvard Law Review and Cheryl I. Harris.

Kevin R. Johnson, Integrating Racial Justice Into the Civil Procedure Survey Course, 54 J. Legal Educ. 242–247, 253, 259, 263 (2004). Permission of the Journal of Legal Education and Kevin R. Johnson.

Amy Kastely, Out of the Whiteness: On Raced Codes ad White Race Consciousness in Some Tort, Criminal, and Contract Law, 63 U. Cin. L. Rev. 269, 270–271, 280–286, 303–310 (1994). Reprinted with permission of the University of Cincinnati Law Review and Amy H. Kastely.

Charles R. Lawrence III, The Id, the Ego, and Equal Protection: Reckoning with Unconscious Racism, 39 Stan. L. Rev. 317, 321–327, 339–344, 355–358, 369–374, 375, 378–381, 387–388 (1987). Reprinted with permission of the Stanford Law Review and Charles R. Laurence III.

Cynthia Kwei Yung Lee, Race and Self-Defense: Toward a Normative Conception of Reasonableness, 81 Minn. L. Rev. 367, 369–374, 398–452, 495–499 (1996). Reprinted with permission of the Minnesota Law Review and Cynthia Kwei Yung Lee.

Tracey Maclin, Race and the Fourth Amendment, 51 Vand. L. Rev. 333, 333–341, 342–362, 375–393 (1998). Reprinted with permission of the Vanderbilt Law Review and Tracey Maclin.

Muriel Morisey, Teaching Williams v. Walker-Thomas Furniture Co., 3 Temp. Pol. & Civ. Rts. L. Rev. 89, 89–98, 102–104 (1993). This article originally appeared at 3 Temp. Pol. & Civ. Rts. L. Rev. 89 (1993). Reprinted with the permission of the Temple Political & Civil Rights Law Review and Muriel Morisey.

William T. Pizzi, Irene V. Blair, and Charles M. Judd, Discrimination in Sentencing on the Basis of Afrocentric Features, 10 Mich. J. Race & L. 327, 327–329, 330–332, 350–352 (2005). Reprinted with permission of the Michigan Journal of Race and The Law and William T. Pizzi, Irene V. Blair, and Charles M. Judd.

Restatement of the Law Second-Contracts § 208 and Comment. Copyright 1981 by the American Law Institute. Reprinted with permission. All rights reserved.

Joseph William Singer, Legal Theory: Sovereignty and Property, 86 Nw. U. L. Rev. 1, 40–43, 44–47, 50–51 (1991). Reprinted by special permission of Northwestern University School of Law, Law Review and Joseph William Singer.

Uniform Commercial Code § 2–302. Copyright by the American Law Institute and the National Conference of Commissioners on Uniform State Laws. Reproduced with the permission of the Permanent Editorial Board for the Uniform Commercial Code. All rights reserved.

David B. Wilkins and G. Mitu Gulati, Why Are There So Few Black Lawyers in Corporate Law Firms? An Institutional Analysis, 84 Calif. L. Rev. 493, 493–516, 554–584, 585–590, 598–614 (1996). © 1996 by the California Law Review. Reprinted from California Law Review. Vol. 84 No.3, by the permission of the University of California, Berkeley and David B. Wilkins and G. Mitu Gulati.

Neil G. Williams, Offer, Acceptance, and Improper Considerations: A Common-Law Model for the Prohibition of Racial Discrimination in the Contracting Process, 62 Geo. Wash. L. Rev. 183, 201–202, 203–205, 206–207, 218–220, 222–227, 228–229 (1994). Reprinted by permission of the George Washington Law Review and Neil G. Williams.

*

Summary of Contents

_____

Table of Contents

*

Table of Cases

The principal cases are in bold type. Cases cited or discussed in the text are roman type. References are to pages. Cases cited in principal cases and within other quoted materials are not included.

---

*

CRITICAL RACE THEORY

CASES, MATERIALS, AND PROBLEMS

Second Edition

*

Chapter 1

INTRODUCTION TO CRITICAL RACE THEORY

This chapter provides an introduction to Critical Race Theory and the main focus of this book, namely how Critical Race Theory can be a useful tool for case analysis. Critical Race Theory examines the role that race plays in the judicial decision making process. Justice Thurgood Marshall observed:

> What is striking is the role legal principles have played throughout America's history in determining the condition of Negroes. They were enslaved by law, emancipated by law, disenfranchised and segregated by law; and, finally, they have begun to win equality by law.

Thurgood Marshall, *Reflections on the Bicentennial of the United States Constitution*, 101 Harv. L. Rev. 1, 5 (1987). The law has been a significant determinant in the lives of people of color in the United States. Critical Race Theory seeks to use the law as an affirmative tool to improve the lives of people of color.

Critical Race Theory was birthed out of the Critical Legal Studies movement which questioned the objectivity and neutrality of the law. When it was determined that Critical Legal Studies was not taking race into account in a meaningful way, a Critical Race Theory movement began. *See e.g.* Kimberle Williams Crenshaw, *Critical Race Studies: The First Decade: Critical Reflections, or A Foot in the Closing Door*, 49 UCLA L. Rev. 1343 (2002); and Crossroads, Directions, and a New Critical Race Theory xi-xxi (Francisco Valdes et al. eds., 2002) (for a history of the early days of Critical Race Theory.) Professor Cheryl Harris states that in addition to numerous law schools offering Critical Race Theory courses, a growing number of undergraduate and graduate schools are offering Critical Race Theory as well. *See* Cheryl I. Harris, *Critical Race Studies: An Introduction*, 49 UCLA L. Rev. 1215, 1215–1216 (2002). In the Spring of 2000, the UCLA School of Law became the first law school in the country to approve a concentration in Critical Race Studies.

1

Not all scholars are convinced of the merits of Critical Race Theory. *See e.g.* Randall Kennedy, *Racial Critiques of Legal Academia*, 102 Harv. L. Rev. 1745 (1989); Daniel A. Farber & Suzanna Sherry, Beyond All Reason: The Radical Assault on Truth in American Law 52–71 (1997). Not all scholars disagree agreeably. *See* Ilhyung Lee, *Race Consciousness and Minority Scholars*, 33 Conn. L. Rev. 535, 536 (2001) for an insightful description. ("Yet legal scholarship, which calls for reasoned analysis of fact and doctrine, has fared no better in the conversation over the difficult subject of race. There is growing incivility in legal scholarship generally, and when the subject of the discourse has a racial component, the tone becomes sharp, biting, and sometimes personal. As a result, even (and perhaps especially) in legal academia, much of what is written about race in legal academia can be 'dishonest, confused, ill-informed, unhelpful.' ")

SECTION 1. HOW DO YOU DEFINE CRITICAL RACE THEORY?

Consider the following description of Critical Race Theory by Professor Roy L. Brooks.

ROY L. BROOKS

Critical Race Theory: A Proposed Structure and Application to Federal Pleading
11 Harv. BlackLetter L.J. 85, 85–86, 87–88, 90–98 (1994).

Critical Race Theory (CRT) is a collection of critical stances against the existing legal order from a race-based point of view. Specifically, it focuses on the various ways in which the received tradition in law adversely affects people of color not as individuals but as a group. Thus, CRT attempts to analyze law and legal traditions through the history, contemporary experiences, and racial sensibilities of racial minorities in this country. The question always lurking in the background of CRT is this: What would the legal landscape look like today if people of color were the decision-makers?

* * *

II. THE STRUCTURE OF CRITICAL RACE THEORY

To some, the term "CRT" might appear a misnomer. The term might seem to imply falsely that the experiences of people of color are fixed and homogeneous, thereby obscuring important differences in race, color, gender, class, and sexual orientation among people of color. If these differences are not taken into account, the argument might continue, then one would have to conclude that the term "CRT" is meaningless.

In this Article, the term "CRT" is used as an organizational concept, bringing together under a single rub[r]ic various race-based theories, values, and attitudes against the existing legal order. The term suggests that a race-conscious reference point and opposition to the received tradition are the common bonds that hold together certain theories, values, and attitudes in the legal cosmos. Thus, as an organizational concept, the term "CRT" stands for something quite significant.

The theories, values, and attitudes that constitute CRT are organized in this Article around four recurring intellectual themes: common objective; methodology; values and assumptions; and epistemology.

A. Common Objective

Although there are theoretical differences among race crits as to the objectives of CRT, most crits agree that the basic objective of CRT is to use the law to effectuate racial equality. Recognizing that there is a symbiotic relationship between law and society, crits conceptualize the law instrumentally. They maintain that law has several social purposes, one of which should be to effectuate racial equality.

At least one race crit, Professor Derrick Bell, has questioned the extent to which the quest for racial equality through legal reform is elusive. He has gone so far as to suggest that people of color should abandon the notion that the legal system can be used as a vehicle of social transformation. But most race crits continue to argue that the law has the potential to end racial injustice.

B. Methodology

The common objective of CRT is effectuated through a method of legal analysis that encourages judges, legal scholars, and law students to adopt a more critical approach to the law and legal disputes. This methodology—called the "subordination question"—entails a two-pronged inquiry that asks (1) whether a rule of law or legal doctrine, practice, or custom subordinates important interests and concerns of racial minorities and (2) if so, how is this problem best remedied? The subordination question seeks to deconstruct the existing legal order to reveal the ways in which it invalidates or handicaps the claims of people of color.

* * *

C. Values and Assumptions
1. The Concept of "Racism"

The central assumption of CRT is also the most controversial and least understood claim of CRT: namely, that American society and its institutions, including its legal institutions, are fundamentally racist, and that racism is not a deviation from the normal operation of American society. The scholarship of various race crits bears this out.

Professor Derrick Bell, for example, maintains that white racism is hegemonic, which is to say that "all our institutions of education and information—political and civic, religious and creative—either knowingly or unknowingly 'provide the public rationale to justify, explain, legitimize, or tolerate racism.'" Bell concludes from this that racism is permanent.

Professor Charles Lawrence expounds a similar thesis but focuses on unconscious racism. He argues that since racism is so deeply ingrained in our culture and is transmitted by tacit understandings, it is difficult to eradicate. Professor Richard Delgado is also pessimistic about the degree to which racism can be eliminated and questions the claim that there has been a meaningful improvement in America's race relations. According to Delgado, "[t]here is change from one era to another, but the net quantum of racism remains exactly the same, obeying a melancholy Law of Racial Thermodynamics: Racism is neither created nor destroyed." Finally, Professor Kimberle Crenshaw, exploring the "hegemonic role of racism," argues that racism is a central ideological and political pillar upholding existing social conditions.

Notwithstanding these conceptions of racism, it is still not easy to define exactly what constitutes racism—that is, to name racism. Professor Delgado provides the most complete definition. I will quote Delgado at some length here because his definition is simple, yet holistic. Racism, he argues, takes two basic forms, "substantive" and "procedural":

> By substantive racism I mean that which treats blacks and other nonwhite persons as though they were actually inferior to whites. Attitudes and treatment taking this form have flourished at different points in our history; to its shame, the law also fully embraced and accommodated them through such means as sterilization statutes, Jim Crow laws, the separate but equal doctrine, antimiscegenation statutes, and racist immigration laws and policies. During periods when substantive racism is used to subjugate blacks and manage white guilt, media images like Aunt Jemima are used to satisfy whites' need to believe that blacks are happy and content to serve them. At other times, society disseminates images of blacks as primitive and bestial, of Mexicans as lazy, happy-go-lucky, untrustworthy or unclean, of Asians as aloof and manipulative. Although designed to serve different purposes, they all converge on the idea that nonwhites deserve inferior treatment because they are actually inferior. Our society currently appears to be moving into a phase of substantive racism.

> At other times, racism takes on what I call a procedural cast. In these periods, there are fewer images, stories, and laws conveying the idea of black inferiority. That idea is banished, put underground. Instead, we promulgate narratives and rules that invalidate or handicap black claims. We erect difficult-to-satisfy standing requirements of civil rights cases, demand proof of intent, and insist on tight chains of causation. We place limitations on the type and pace of relief that may be ordered. We limit attorneys fees and decrease funding for agencies that litigate nonwhites' cases. We insist that remedies not endanger white well-being; "reverse discrimination" is given a wide berth. We elevate equality of opportunity over equality

of result and reject statistical proof of lack of the former. We use the excuse of "widening the pool" to avoid hiring nonwhites now. Procedural racism puts racial-justice claims on the back burner and makes sure they stay there.

This definition of racism dates back to the 1960s (at least), when scholars such as Anthony Downs defined racism as embracing both a state of mind (the belief in white supremacy)—what is traditionally called "racism"—and facially neutral practices or customs that have a discriminatory effect—what is traditionally called "discrimination."

2.   The Concept of "Racial Equality"

CRT seeks to achieve racial equality through the instrumentalities of law. There is, however, no formal definition of racial equality in the literature on CRT. In this section, I shall speculate on a definition of racial equality that is congruent with CRT's concepts of racism.

There are two models of racial justice to consider—"symmetrical" and "asymmetrical." Symmetrical equality focuses on racial sameness, "denying that there are . . . any significant natural differences between [the races]." This model seeks to construct society such that "the [races] are symmetrically situated with regard to any issue, norm, or rule."

Symmetrical equality can be further divided into two smaller models—"assimilation" and "pluralism." The assimilation model (sometimes called "one-way integration") proceeds from the assumption that nonwhites are basically just like whites (or should be just like whites). Fundamental to this model is the notion that "the law should require social institutions to treat [nonwhites] as they already treat [whites]." Under an assimilation model of racial equality, then, a law school would be required to hire black law professors on the same basis as it employs white law professors—class rank, law review membership, and judicial clerkships—without regard for the social, economical or psychological difficulties that the black law professors might have experienced.

Race crits would undoubtedly reject assimilation as a model of racial equality. They would argue that the assimilation model of racial equality is flawed because it denies significant societal differences—advantages and disadvantages—between whites and nonwhites. Also problematic from a CRT perspective is the fact that the assimilation model is uncritical of the extent to which existing social institutions operate systemically to privilege whites and disadvantage people of color. Notwithstanding these glaring defects, the assimilation model, to a considerable degree, is what informs the judiciary's and the legislature's concept of racial equality.

Like assimilation, pluralism is premised on the belief that nonwhites and whites are essentially the same and have the same desire for success and happiness. But, unlike assimilation, pluralism argues that equality requires institutions to adopt standards that can reasonably accommodate differences that result from the uneven distribution of societal advantages and disadvantages, which are oftentimes racially determined.

Significantly, the pluralistic model of equality does not suggest that people of color appropriate or approximate what constitutes a "white identity." Instead, it attempts to "normalize" racial differences. In the context of faculty hiring a pluralistic rule would look something like the following: if a nonwhite candidate has had to struggle against social or psychological handicaps because of race, if such a candidate has qualifications roughly equal to those of a white male candidate who has not experienced the same difficulties, and if the institution in question is racially imbalanced, then the nonwhite candidate should be preferred.

To some degree, pluralism is incompatible with CRT, although less so than assimilation, because to be effective, pluralistic rules depend on the good intentions of those charged with their implementation—mostly white men. Given the omnipresence and perhaps permanence of racism, race crits would probably not trust white decisionmakers to apply pluralistic rules fairly, or value the special circumstances and experiences of nonwhites. The problem with pluralism, in short, is that it leaves white decisionmakers with too much discretion, allowing them to proffer ostensibly race-neutral rationales for decisions that adversely affect people of color.

In contrast to symmetrical models of racial equality, asymmetrical equality embraces racial differences "[and] rejects the notion that all [racial] differences are likely to disappear, or even that they should." Central to asymmetrical equality is the idea that in order to reach racial balance (i.e., racial equality) a certain amount of racial imbalance must be tolerated. Asymmetrical equality repudiates the notion that African Americans, for example, need to mimic the behaviors, values, and appearances of white Americans in order to succeed in a racially integrated American society. Because asymmetrical equality celebrates racial diversity and multiculturalism and promotes the empowerment of people of color, it is most compatible with the various theories underlying CRT.

With regard to faculty hiring, asymmetrical equality would require universities to use racial quotas, because this would diminish the extent to which university administrators could exercise discretion to deny people of color jobs. The effect of such a rule would be to assure professors of color positions on college faculties.

Proponents of the symmetrical model of racial equality would sharply criticize this rule. Advanced by people of color, the argument would probably include the points that such a rule stigmatizes nonwhite law professors, entrenches social stereotypes about their intellectual capacities, and reinforces racial inequality. A simple rejoinder to these claims is that it is far better to have a job tainted by a racial stigma than to have no job at all because of racial discrimination.

3. Other Values and Assumptions

In addition to an interest in racial equality, CRT is also concerned with rule specificity, legal rights, universal values, and consciousness-raising. Although some of these issues were alluded to in the previous discussion, they are important enough to warrant a brief commentary here.

To ensure racial equality in the dispensation of legal rights, CRT privileges rule specificity and eschews amorphous legal "standards." The latter obscures pretextual racism (racism that does not appear as such on its face), and allows it to go unchecked.

Related to the idea of rule specificity is the notion of rights. Race crits recognize that, to quote Professor Torres, " 'civil rights' law or 'anti-discrimination' law [has] transform[ed] [sic] the beliefs and class structure of contemporary American culture." Moreover, as Professor Williams maintains, rights-based theories have a strong appeal to groups whose historical ties with other groups bear the marks of domination and the denial of rights. Thus, while some white, leftist scholars argue that rights are "contradictory, indeterminate, reified and marginally decisive in social behavior," CRT recognizes that formal equality or the guarantee of legal rights is an important step towards the goal of substantive equality.

Notwithstanding CRT's embrace of rights, it remains critical of the notion that experiences are universal—that whites and nonwhites live similar experiences. As Professor Mari Matsuda points out, unlike white people, people of color "are quick to detect racism, to distrust official claims of necessity and to sense a threat to freedom." Furthermore, people of color experience the institutional effects of racism and understand that the "system" or the "man" functions in a multitude of ways to contribute to their subordination.

In addition to its concern about the universality of values, CRT also seeks to raise the consciousness of people of color and whites alike. It attempts to accomplish this by grounding its analysis on the real, everyday experiences of people of color. Implicit in this approach is the belief that legal analysis can proceed from any number of starting points, and that the conventional method of expository legal writing is not the sole means of legal expression. Accordingly, CRT manifests itself in the form of chronicles, parables, narratives, personal stories, and poems.

The issue of writing style has epistemological implications. If truth and knowledge are acquired through experience, then the conventional form of legal writing, which tends to relegate experience to the sidelines, may not be the best way to convey information. Conversely, if truth and knowledge come only (or mostly) through abstract reasoning and empirical validation, then personal, reflective "legal writing" should not be encouraged.

D. *Epistemology*

In the second and third editions of his book, Race, Racism and American Law, oftentimes referred to as "the CRT casebook," Professor Bell provides a thorough analysis of civil rights law. Reviewing this book, Professor Alan Freeman accurately describes one of its unifying principles as follows:

A major theme is that there is one and only one criterion for assessing the success or failure of civil rights law—results. Bell's approach to legal doctrine is unabashedly instrumental. The only important question is whether doctrinal developments have improved, worsened, or left unchanged the actual lives of American blacks (the book focuses almost exclusively on black/white relationships because it is in that context that most of the doctrine has developed). Bell eschews the realm of abstract, historical, normative debate, he focuses instead on the relationships between doctrine and concrete change, and the extent to which doctrine can be manipulated to produce more change.

As Professor Freeman's commentary suggests, the epistemology of CRT is experiential. It has "a vision of legal knowledge that includes the perspectives and experiences of oppressed people in the critique and reformulation of legal doctrine." At the core of CRT is the claim that truth and knowledge are based in experience (not in mathematical formulas) and it is experience that is alchemical—that has the power of transmutation. No doubt Justice Holmes's famous aphorism that "the life of the law has not been logic; it has been experience" was informed by these realizations.

But (perhaps) unlike Holmes' legal pragmatism, CRT's legal pragmatism is anti-objectionist. The latter, in other words, rejects the notion that law is objective, or value-neutral. This, indeed, is one of the most persistently argued themes in CRT, that the law legitimizes the "perpetrator's" or "insider's" perspective and is constructed by the dominant group to serve its own purpose.

Because the existing legal order, including traditional legal analysis, has a built-in bias in favor of whites, CRT consciously looks at the law from the perspective of nonwhites. It relocates the source of truth and knowledge from the perpetrator to the victim, from the insider to the outsider. Thus, legal analyses presented by race crits are informed by the shared values of people of color.

Some race crits privilege the "victim's story" because they believe that the extent to which white people can understand what it means to be a person of color is limited. It is this belief that informed Professor Bell's indictment of the then-Supreme Court nominee Clarence Thomas (who opposes affirmative action and whose political views contravene those held by most African American politicians) on the ground that "he doesn't think like a black." This concern with experience has implication for legal education as well; white people and people of color oftentimes disagree about what constitutes racism and this disagreement manifests itself in the construction of legal rules, the application of legal principles, and the interpretation of complicated fact patterns. As Professor Delgado observes, "it is possible to compile an a priori list of reasons why we might look with concern on a situation in which the scholarship about group A [nonwhites] is written by members of group B [white man]." One of these reasons is that "those who have experienced discrimination speak with a special voice to which we should listen," that "the victims of racial oppression have distinct normative insights," and that "[t]hose who are oppressed in the present world can speak most eloquently of a better one."

Although accepting the need to advance the nonwhite perspective in legal analysis, other race crits are uncomfortable with racial essentialism, which is at the core of the scholarship of Professors Bell, Delgado, and Matsuda. They argue that race is an underinclusive proxy for truth and knowledge and is not fixed and "transcendent ... but rather particular and fluctuating, constituted within a complex set of social contexts." Being an "African American," "white" or any other race, they argue, "is strictly a matter of social, historical, and cultural construction." From this they conclude that "racial perspectives" can be intellectually accessed transracially.

Of the race crits, Professor Williams comes closest to employing an anti-essentialist epistemology. Her legal analysis is the most contextualized and subjective of the race crits, so much so that it can appropriately be described as "personal." When Williams tells a story, she not only uses allegory, as does Professor Bell, but she also uses dreams, other personal experiences, and the personal experiences of others. She uses these "multiple subjectivities" to demonstrate that we can draw important insights from the experiences of others.

The fact that CRT privileges experiences, however, does not mean that race crits avoid traditional legal analysis altogether. Quite the contrary, race crits often approach legal problems from a rationalist epistemology. Proponents of CRT often push empirical points and resort to arguments and analysis that appeal to abstract reason, deductive logic, and empirical validation. For example, race crits consistently make the empirical point that the dominant culture and even feminist discourse ignore "black voices." Moreover, race crits frequently analyze the logic of cases and legal doctrine, drawing factual distinctions along the way.

But in using the traditional approach to legal problem-solving, race crits do not concede the universality or objectivity of the law. They realize that a rationalist epistemology has limited transformative capabilities, because it does not challenge the normative values underlying much of traditional legal scholarship. Race crits know that, in the end, rationalist arguments do not decide hard cases but only perpetuate the status quo.

* * *

Notes and Questions

1. When was the last time you had a discussion about race with a person of another race?

2. How can you be sure that you were having a discussion with someone of a different race? *See* Nicholas Wade, *For Sale: A DNA Test to*

Measure Racial Mix, N.Y. TIMES, October 1, 2002 (describing a company in Sarasota, Florida., that offers a DNA test that measures a customer's racial ancestry).

3. Professors Juan F. Perea, Richard Delgado, Angela P. Harris and Stephanie M. Wildman provide in their casebook RACE AND RACES: CASES AND RESOURCES FOR A DIVERSE AMERICA 84 (2000):

> Historically, racial classification in America arises out of what is apparently a uniquely "American institution known informally as 'the one-drop rule,' which defines as black a person with as little as a single drop of 'black blood.' This notion derives from a long-discredited belief that each race had its own blood type, which was correlated with physical appearance and social behavior." (citation omitted)

4. Scholars argue that race is a social construction and not biological. *See e.g.* Ian F. Haney López, White By Law (1996); George A. Martinez, The Legal Construction of Race: Mexican–Americans and Whiteness, 2 Harv. Latino L. Rev. 321 (1997); Michael Omi & Howard Winant, Racial Formation in the United States: From the 1960s to the 1980s (1986). Not all scholars agree. *See e.g.* Anthony Appiah, The Uncompleted Argument: Du Bois and the Illusion of Race, in "Race," Writing, and Difference (Henry Louis Gates, Jr., ed., 1986). As you consider the materials in this book, determine which side has the better argument.

5. How would you define Critical Race Theory? Describe CRT themes discussed in the Brooks' excerpt.

6. Do you believe that the judicial system has been used to improve the conditions for people of color? Can you provide specific examples?

7. Do you believe there is at least one area of the law which is currently being used to hurt people of color?

8. Professor Brooks quotes Professor Delgado as he states: "[d]uring periods when substantive racism is used to subjugate blacks and manage white guilt, media images like Aunt Jemima are used to satisfy whites' need to believe that blacks are happy and content to serve them. At other times, society disseminates images of blacks as primitive and bestial, of Mexicans as lazy, happy-go-lucky, untrustworthy or unclean, of Asians as aloof and manipulative. Although designed to serve different purposes, they all converge on the idea that nonwhites deserve inferior treatment because they are actually inferior." What impact does the media have on your perception of group members of your race? What impact does the media have on your perception of group members of different races? *See e.g.* Adeno Addis, *Hell Man, They Did Invent Us: The Mass Media, Law, and African Americans*, 41 Buff. L. Rev. 523 (1993); Dorothy A. Brown, *The Invisibility Factor: The Limits of Public Choice Theory and Public Institutions*, 74 Wash. U. L. Q. 179, 214–222 (1996). The stereotypes are different for each racial and ethnic group. Does that result in a different outcome? *See also* Richard Delgado and Jean Stefancic, *Images of the Outsider in American Law and Culture: Can Free Expression Remedy Systemic Social Ills?*, 77 Cornell L. Rev. 1258, 1262–1275 (1992) (discussing African–Americans, Native Americans, Asian–Americans, and Hispanic–Americans); Ediberto Roman, *Who Exactly Is Living La Vida Loca ?: The Legal and Political Consequences of Latino–*

Latina Ethnic and Racial Stereotypes in Film and Other Media, 4 J. Gender Race & Just. 37, 42–48 (2000) (discussing Latinas and Latinos); Rebecca Tsosie, *Sacred Obligations: Intercultural Justice and the Discourse of Treaty Rights*, 47 UCLA L. Rev. 1615, 1660–1661 (2000) (discussing Hispanic–Americans, and Native Americans); Rhoda J. Yen, *Racial Stereotyping of Asians and Asian Americans and Its Effect on Criminal Justice: A Reflection on the Wayne Lo Case*, 7 Asian L.J. 1, 7–8 (2000) (discussing Asian–Americans); Jessica R. Herrera, *Not Even His Name: Is the Denigration of Crazy Horse Custer's Final Revenge?*, 29 Harv. C.R.-C.L. L. Rev. 175, 188 (1994) (discussing Native Americans).

9. *People v. Hall*, 4 Cal. 399 (1854) provides a glimpse into the racism incurred by Asian Americans. Hall, a free White citizen, appealed his conviction of murder. Hall argued that he was wrongfully convicted because the conviction was based upon the testimony of Chinese witnesses. According to Hall, this testimony was unlawful because the 14th section of the Act of April 16th, 1850, regulating Criminal Proceedings, provides that "No Black or Mulatto person, or Indian, shall be allowed to give evidence in favor of, or against a white man." *Id.* at 399. After examining the language and legislative history of the section, the court concluded that the legislature intended to include Chinese people among those prohibited from testifying in favor of or against a White man. *Id.* at 404. In reversing appellant's conviction, the court held that it would be an anomalous spectacle to allow a race of people whom nature marked as inferior to swear away the life of a citizen. *Id.* at 404. *See* Neil Gotanda, Comparative Racialization: Racial Profiling and the Case of Wen Ho Lee, 47 UCLA L. Rev. 1689, 1695–1696 (2000). (comparing People v. Hall with Dred Scott v. Sandford to illustrate the early ambiguity about the meaning of the term Chinese. According to Professor Gotanda, in the Dred Scott decision, the Supreme Court provided a clear statement which unambiguously created the racial category of Negro. In contrast, the court in *People v. Hall* "suggested that the racialization of the Chinese was ambiguous and incomplete."); *see also* Robert S. Chang, *Toward an Asian American Legal Scholarship: Critical Race Theory, Post–Structuralism, and Narrative Space*, 81 Calif. L. Rev. 1243, 1291 (1993). (using *People v. Hall* as an example of the exclusion of Chinese from legal and political participation that all citizens have the right to enjoy); Richard P. Cole and Gabriel J. Chin, *Emerging from the Margins of Historical Consciousness: Chinese Immigrants and the History of American Law*, 17 Law & Hist. Rev. 325, 327 (1999). ("An infamous example of discriminatory lawmaking was the 1854 decision of the California Supreme Court in *People v. Hall*."); Adrienne D. Davis, *Identity Notes Part One: Playing in the Light*, 45 Am. U.L. Rev. 695, 712 (1996). ("Implicated was not just the value of Chinese lives, but the general availability of the courtroom as a physical and discursive site... access to the courtroom is critical to negotiating civil life in America."); Keith Aoki , *"Foreign-ness" & Asian American Identities: Yellowface, World War II Propaganda, and Bifurcated Racial Stereotypes*, 4 UCLA Asian Pac. Am. L.J. 1, 19 (1996). (using *People v. Hall* to illustrate "the blurring of perceived racial characteristics of the yellow, black, and red races into a single subordinated legal category of 'non-whites' in the nineteenth century American imagination...." Like blacks, the Chinese were characterized as morally inferior, savages and heathens.).

10. Critical Race Theory has recently developed some "branches" that address issues unique to certain racial and ethnic groups. First, Latina/o Critical Theory (LatCrit). *See e.g. Symposium, LatCrit Theory: Naming and Launching a New Discourse of Critical Legal Scholarship*, 2 Harv. Latino L. Rev. 177 (1997); Francisco Valdes, *Barely at the Margins: Race and Ethnicity in Legal Education—A Curricular Study With LatCritical Commentary*, 13 Berkeley La Raza L. J. 119 (2002). Second, Asian American Legal Scholarship. *See e.g.* Mari J. Matsuda, *Voices of America: Accent, Antidiscrimination Law and a Jurisprudence for the Last Reconstruction*, 100 Yale L. J. 1329 (1991); Robert S. Chang, *Toward an Asian American Legal Scholarship: Critical Race Theory, Post–Structuralism, and Narrative Space*, 81 Cal. L. Rev. 1241, 1 Asian L. J. 1 (1994). Third, Critical Race Feminism. *See* Critical Race Feminism: A Reader (Adrien Katherine Wing ed., 1997).

SECTION 2. IS ALL RACISM THE SAME?

CHARLES R. LAWRENCE III

The Id, The Ego, and Equal Protection: Reckoning with Unconscious Racism
39 Stan. L. Rev. 317, 321–327, 339–344, 355–
358, 369–375, 378–381, 387–388 (1987).

* * *

Much of one's inability to know racial discrimination when one sees it results from a failure to recognize that racism is both a crime and a disease. This failure is compounded by a reluctance to admit that the illness of racism infects almost everyone. Acknowledging and understanding the malignancy are prerequisites to the discovery of an appropriate cure. But the diagnosis is difficult, because our own contamination with the very illness for which a cure is sought impairs our comprehension of the disorder.

Scholarly and judicial efforts to explain the constitutional significance of disproportionate impact and governmental motive in cases alleging racial discrimination treat these two categories as mutually exclusive. That is, while disproportionate impact may be evidence of racially discriminatory motive, whether impact or motive is the appropriate focus is normally posed in the alternative: Should racially disproportionate impact, standing alone, trigger a heightened level of judicial scrutiny? Or, should the judiciary apply a deferential standard to legislative and administrative decisions absent proof that the decisionmakers intended a racial consequence? Put another way, the Court thinks of facially neutral actions as either intentionally and unconstitutionally or unintentionally and constitutionally discriminatory.

I argue that this is a false dichotomy. Traditional notions of intent do not reflect the fact that decisions about racial matters are influenced in large part by factors that can be characterized as neither intentional—in the sense that certain outcomes are self-consciously sought—nor unintentional—in the sense that the outcomes are random, fortuitous, and uninfluenced by the decisionmaker's beliefs, desires, and wishes.

Americans share a common historical and cultural heritage in which racism has played and still plays a dominant role. Because of this shared experience, we also inevitably share many ideas, attitudes, and beliefs that attach significance to an individual's race and induce negative feelings and opinions about nonwhites. To the extent that this cultural belief system has influenced all of us, we are all racists. At the same time, most of us are unaware of our racism. We do not recognize the ways in which our cultural experience has influenced our beliefs about race or the occasions on which those beliefs affect our actions. In other words, a large part of the behavior that produces racial discrimination is influenced by unconscious racial motivation.

There are two explanations for the unconscious nature of our racially discriminatory beliefs and ideas. First, Freudian theory states that the human mind defends itself against the discomfort of guilt by denying or refusing to recognize those ideas, wishes, and beliefs that conflict with what the individual has learned is good or right. While our historical experience has made racism an integral part of our culture, our society has more recently embraced an ideal that rejects racism as immoral. When an individual experiences conflict between racist ideas and the societal ethic that condemns those ideas, the mind excludes his racism from consciousness.

Second, the theory of cognitive psychology states that the culture—including, for example, the media and an individual's parents, peers, and authority figures—transmits certain beliefs and preferences. Because these beliefs are so much a part of the culture, they are not experienced as explicit lessons. Instead, they seem part of the individual's rational ordering of her perceptions of the world. The individual is unaware, for example, that the ubiquitous presence of a cultural stereotype has influenced her perception that blacks are lazy or unintelligent. Because racism is so deeply ingrained in our culture, it is likely to be transmitted by tacit understandings: Even if a child is not told that blacks are inferior, he learns that lesson by observing the behavior of others. These tacit understandings, because they have never been articulated, are less likely to be experienced at a conscious level.

In short, requiring proof of conscious or intentional motivation as a prerequisite to constitutional recognition that a decision is race-dependent ignores much of what we understand about how the human mind works. It also disregards both the irrationality of racism and the profound effect that the history of American race relations has had on the individual and collective unconscious.

It may often be appropriate for the legal system to disregard the influence of the unconscious on individual or collective behavior. But where the goal is the eradication of invidious racial discrimination, the law must recognize racism's primary source. The equal protection clause requires the elimination of governmental decisions that take race into account without good and important reasons. Therefore, equal protection doctrine must find a way to come to grips with unconscious racism.

In pursuit of that goal, this article proposes a new test to trigger judicial recognition of race-based behavior. It posits a connection between unconscious racism and the existence of cultural symbols that have racial meaning. It suggests that the "cultural meaning" of an allegedly racially discriminatory act is the best available analogue for, and evidence of, a collective unconscious that we cannot observe directly. This test would thus evaluate governmental conduct to determine whether it conveys a symbolic message to which the culture attaches racial significance. A finding that the culture thinks of an allegedly discriminatory governmental action in racial terms would also constitute a finding regarding the beliefs and motivations of the governmental actors: The actors are themselves part of the culture and presumably could not have acted without being influenced by racial considerations, even if they are unaware of their racist beliefs. Therefore, the court would apply strict scrutiny.

This proposal is relatively modest. It does not abandon the judicial search for unconstitutional motives, nor does it argue that all governmental action with discriminatory impact should be strictly scrutinized. Instead, it urges a more complete understanding of the nature of human motivation. While it is grounded in the Court's present focus on individual responsibility, it seeks to understand individual responsibility in light of modern insights into human personality and collective behavior. In addition, this proposal responds directly to the concern that abandoning the *Washington v. Davis* [426 U.S. 229 (1976)] doctrine will invalidate a broad range of legitimate, race-neutral governmental actions. By identifying those cases where race unconsciously influences governmental action, this new test leaves untouched nonrace-dependent decisions that disproportionately burden blacks only because they are overrepresented or underrepresented among the decision's targets or beneficiaries.

This effort to inform the discriminatory intent requirement with the learning of twentieth century psychology is important for at least three reasons. First, the present doctrine, by requiring proof that the defendant was aware of his animus against blacks, severely limits the number of individual cases in which the courts will acknowledge and remedy racial discrimination.

Second, the existing intent requirement's assignment of individualized fault or responsibility for the existence of racial discrimination distorts our perceptions about the causes of discrimination and leads us to think about racism in a way that advances the disease rather than combatting it. By insisting that a blameworthy perpetrator be found before the existence of racial discrimination can be acknowledged, the Court creates an imaginary world where discrimination does not exist unless it was consciously intended. And by acting as if this imaginary world was real and insisting that we participate in this fantasy, the Court and the law it promulgates subtly shape our perceptions of society. The decision to deny relief no longer finds its basis only in raw political power or economic self-interest; it is now justifiable on moral grounds. If there is no discrimination, there is no need for a remedy; if blacks are

• definition discussed in·class

being treated fairly yet remain at the bottom of the socioeconomic ladder, only their own inferiority can explain their subordinate position.

Finally, the intent doctrine's focus on the narrowest and most unrealistic understanding of individual fault has also engendered much of the resistance to and resentment of affirmative action programs and other race-conscious remedies for past and continuing discrimination. If there can be no discrimination without an identifiable criminal, then "innocent" individuals will resent the burden of remedying an injury for which the law says they are not responsible. Understanding the cultural source of our racism obviates the need for fault, as traditionally conceived, without denying our collective responsibility for racism's eradication. We cannot be individually blamed for unconsciously harboring attitudes that are inescapable in a culture permeated with racism. And without the necessity for blame, our resistance to accepting the need and responsibility for remedy will be lessened. * * *

A crucial factor in the process that produces unconscious racism is the tacitly transmitted cultural stereotype. If an individual has never known a black doctor or lawyer or is exposed to blacks only through a mass media where they are portrayed in the stereotyped roles of comedian, criminal, musician, or athlete, he is likely to deduce that blacks as a group are naturally inclined toward certain behavior and unfit for certain roles. But the lesson is not explicit: It is learned, internalized, and used without an awareness of its source. Thus, an individual may select a white job applicant over an equally qualified black and honestly believe that this decision was based on observed intangibles unrelated to race. The employer perceives the white candidate as "more articulate," "more collegial," "more thoughtful," or "more charismatic." He is unaware of the learned stereotype that influenced his decision. Moreover, he has probably also learned an explicit lesson of which he is very much aware: Good, law-abiding people do not judge others on the basis of race. Even the most thorough investigation of conscious motive will not uncover the race-based stereotype that has influenced his decision.

This same process operates in the case of more far-reaching policy decisions that come to judicial attention because of their discriminatory impact. For example, when an employer or academic administrator discovers that a written examination rejects blacks at a disproportionate rate, she can draw several possible conclusions: that blacks are less qualified than others; that the test is an inaccurate measure of ability; or that the testers have chosen the wrong skills or attributes to measure. When decisionmakers reach the first conclusion, a predisposition to select those data that conform with a racial stereotype may well have influenced them. Because this stereotype has been tacitly transmitted and unconsciously learned, they will be unaware of its influence on their decision.

If the purpose of the law's search for racial animus or discriminatory intent is to identify a morally culpable perpetrator, the existing intent requirement fails to achieve that purpose. There will be no evidence of self-conscious racism where the actors have internalized the relatively new American cultural morality which holds racism wrong or have learned racist attitudes and beliefs through tacit rather than explicit lessons. The actor himself will be unaware that his actions, or the racially neutral feelings and ideas that accompany them, have racist origins.

Of course, one can argue that the law should govern only consciously motivated actions—that societal sanctions can do no more than attempt to require that the individual's Ego act as society's agent in censoring out those unconscious drives that society has defined as immoral. Under this view, the law can sanction a defective Ego that has not fully internalized current societal morality and has, therefore, allowed illegal racist wishes to reach consciousness and fruition in an illegal act. But the law should not hold an individual responsible for wishes that never reach consciousness, even if they also come to fruition in discriminatory acts.

The problem is that this argument does not tell us why the law should hold the individual responsible for racial injury that results from one form of Ego disguise but not the other. I believe the law should be equally concerned when the mind's censor successfully disguises a socially repugnant wish like racism if that motive produces behavior that has a discriminatory result as injurious as if it flowed from a consciously held motive.

* * *

* * * I propose a test that would look to the "cultural meaning" of an allegedly racially discriminatory act as the best available analogue for and evidence of the collective unconscious that we cannot observe directly. This test would evaluate governmental conduct to see if it conveys a symbolic message to which the culture attaches racial significance. The court would analyze governmental behavior much like a cultural anthropologist might: by considering evidence regarding the historical and social context in which the decision was made and effectuated. If the court determined by a preponderance of the evidence that a significant portion of the population thinks of the governmental action in racial terms, then it would presume that socially shared, unconscious racial attitudes made evident by the action's meaning had influenced the decisionmakers. As a result, it would apply heightened scrutiny.

The unconscious racial attitudes of individuals manifest themselves in the cultural meaning that society gives their actions in the following way: In a society that no longer condones overt racist attitudes and behavior, many of these attitudes will be repressed and prevented from reaching awareness in an undisguised form. But as psychologists have found, repressed wishes, fears, anger, and aggression continue to seek expression, most often by attaching themselves to certain symbols in the external world. Repressed feelings and attitudes that are commonly experienced are likely to find common symbols particularly fruitful or productive as a vehicle for their expression. Thus, certain actions, words, or signs may take on meaning within a particular culture as a result of the collective use of those actions, words, or signs to represent or express shared but repressed attitudes. The process is cyclical: The expression of shared attitudes through certain symbols gives symbols cultural meaning, and once a symbol becomes an enduring part of the culture, it in turn becomes the most natural vehicle for the expression of those attitudes and feelings that caused it to become an identifiable part of the culture.

Cognitive theory provides an alternative explanation of why the racial meaning the culture gives an action will be evidence of the actor's unconscious racial motivation. According to cognitive theory, those meanings or values that are most deeply ingrained in the culture are commonly acquired early in life through tacit lessons. They are, therefore, less recognizable and less available to the individual's consciousness than other forms of knowledge. Looked at another way, if the action has cultural meaning, this meaning must have been transmitted to an individual who is a member of that culture. If he professes to be unaware of the cultural meaning or attitude, it will almost surely be operating at an unconscious level.

Thus, an action such as the construction of a wall between white and black communities in Memphis [*City of Memphis v. Greene*, 451 U.S. 100 (1981)] would have a cultural meaning growing out of a long history of whites' need to separate themselves from blacks as a symbol of their superiority. Individual members of the city council might well have been unaware that their continuing need to maintain their superiority over blacks, or their failure to empathize with how construction of the wall would make blacks feel, influenced their decision. But if one were to ask even the most self-deluded among them what the residents of Memphis would take the existence of the wall to mean, the obvious answer would be difficult to avoid. If one told the story leading to the wall's construction while omitting one vital fact—the race of those whose vehicular traffic the barrier excluded—and then asked Memphis citizens to describe the residents of the community claiming injury, few, if any, would not guess that they were black.

The current racial meanings of governmental actions are strong evidence that the process defects of group vilification and misapprehension of costs and benefits have occurred whether or not the decisionmakers were conscious that race played a part in their decision-making. Moreover, actions that have racial meaning within the culture are also those actions that carry a stigma for which we should have special concern. This is not the stigma that occurs only because of a coincidental congruence between race and poverty. The association of a symbol with race is a residuum of overtly racist practices in the past: The wall conjures up racial inferiority, not the inferiority of the poor or the undesirability of vehicular traffic. And stigma that has racial meaning burdens all blacks and adds to the pervasive, cumulative, and mutually reinforcing system of racial discrimination.

* * *

[*Washington v.*] *Davis* presents a more difficult case than *Arlington Heights*. Two unsuccessful black candidates for positions in the District of Columbia Metropolitan Police Department alleged that some of the Department's hiring practices—particularly "Test 21," a written test that blacks failed at a rate roughly four times that of whites—discriminated against blacks and violated the guarantee of equal protection implicit in the fifth amendment's due process clause. "Test 21," which was used throughout the federal civil service, was designed to test verbal ability, vocabulary, reading, and comprehension. While the Court found that the test was a useful indicator of success in police training school, there was no proof that either the test scores or the school's examination scores predicted job performance or measured success in job-related training.

What evidence might the plaintiffs have presented to establish that the government's action in this case had racial meaning? Unlike segregated housing, we do not ordinarily associate the use of civil service exams with race. But an action that has no racial meaning in one context may have significant racial meaning in another. We have seen that human behavior must be examined in context, as it may well derive its meaning from the specific historical and cultural milieu in which it takes place. Despite the race-neutral origins of civil service exams as a generic entity, one has an intuitive sense that their use in this case has racial connotations—that this case is more like the Memphis wall than it is like an increased bus fare or a regressive tax. It is important to pay heed to one's intuitions at this juncture. One individual's gut feeling is hardly conclusive evidence of cultural meaning, but such feelings often derive from feelings that are more widely shared, and they may well indicate that more substantial testimony is available.

At this point, it is helpful to consider the setting in which "Test 21" was employed. Can one identify the contextual elements that have attracted the attention of our intuition? Are there elements not present in other civil service cases, elements that speak in terms of race? The most obvious racial element is the exam's racially disproportionate impact. One can argue that the government's action racially stigmatizes because blacks fail the exam in larger numbers than whites. But not every case of racially disparate impact has racial meaning. An increased bus fare may burden a larger percentage of blacks than whites, but we do not think of the fare increase as a direct stigmatization of blacks. It does not convey a message of racial inferiority. Thus, if the governmental action in *Davis* conveys a racial message, it must derive that meaning from something other than, or in addition to, its racial impact. Like the traffic barrier in *Memphis v. Greene*, there must be something in the particulars of its historical and cultural context that causes us to interpret this action—at least intuitively—in racial terms.

I suggest that there are two such elements. The first involves the nature of the work or activity from which blacks have been excluded: the job of police officer in a predominantly but not entirely black community. The second relates to the reason given for their exclusion: that they failed to demonstrate sufficient proficiency in verbal and written language skills.

It is significant that the challenged action in *Davis* excluded blacks from working as police officers and not as mail carriers or bus drivers. The occupation of police officer has symbolic meaning within our culture. Police officers represent the law as well as enforce it. They are armed and have discretionary authority to use violence. They are charged with protecting the lives and property of some individuals within society and controlling the violent and unlawful behavior of others. If history—the accumulated meaningful behavior of our culture—has taught us to attach significance to race in considering these elements of the job of police officer—authority, control, protection, and sanctioned violence—then an action that determines the racial composition of a police force also has racial meaning.

Furthermore, throughout American history police forces have had a different relationship to black communities than to white communities. In white communities, the police officer is viewed as a public servant. His job is to protect the lives and property of those in the community where he works. But the job of the law enforcement officer in black communities has been to control the communities' inhabitants and to protect the lives and property of whites who perceive blacks as the primary potential source of violence and crime.

For blacks, those entrusted with law enforcement and the firepower that gives them authority have always been servants of the white men in power who exploit blacks economically and demean them socially. Slaves were forbidden to bear arms and a white police force of overseers and sheriffs' posses enforced the master's law. With the abolition of slavery, the use of organized, socially sanctioned violence against blacks increased, and the authority of the sheriff's office was often indistinguishable from that of the Ku Klux Klan. As recently as 1967, there were nearly a dozen major American cities where blacks accounted for over 25 percent of the population that were patrolled by police forces with only a token minority representation. It is not surprising that many black communities continue to view the police as an occupying army.

The fact that police officers are authority figures to white as well as black citizens is also significant in determining the cultural meaning of excluding large numbers of blacks from the D.C. police force. To the extent that our culture attaches specific meaning to the assignment of racial groups to certain occupational and hierarchical roles, behavior that maintains those role assignments will have racial meaning. For example, whites are accustomed to seeing blacks as servants performing menial tasks. Thus, whites are generally neither surprised nor threatened when they see black porters, maids, and janitors. This is not simply a reflection of the fact that many blacks have performed these jobs. It is also indicative of a historical and culturally ingrained system of beliefs that leads us to think of blacks as suited to these jobs, to associate the jobs with blacks.

By contrast, whites are not accustomed to seeing blacks in positions of authority or power. Black managers, black professors, and black doctors are confronted with reactions ranging from disbelief to resistance to concern about their competence. The historical exclusion of blacks from these jobs has been rationalized by a belief in their unsuitability for these roles. What is at issue here is not just occupational stereotypes born out of habit. These stereotypes manifest a larger and more complex ideology that has legitimized the white-over-black authority relationship. Stereotypes are cultural symbols. They constitute our contemporary interpretation of past and present meaningful behavior.

The argument in defense of all-male police forces provides a useful analogue for understanding our less readily apparent attitudes about authority and race. In suits alleging discrimination against women in the selection of patrol officers, police department defendants have argued that women would not make good officers because the job requires an individual who can command respect from the man on the street. Men, they have argued, would not take orders from women, and, therefore, women would be less effective patrol persons. In other words, the departments' discriminatory hiring practices have been defended as a necessary adaptation to the sexist beliefs and practices of the culture.

Whites would be less likely to verbalize the same argument regarding blacks, but the fact remains that many individuals in our culture continue to resist and resent taking orders from blacks. If the court were convinced that the absence or presence of substantial numbers of black police officers on the D.C. force would be interpreted as the maintenance or disestablishment of culturally instilled beliefs about the need to control blacks and the appropriate roles for blacks and whites in authority relationships, then the Civil Service Commission's decision to rely on "Test 21" would have racial meaning.

There is another reason why a significant segment of the culture is likely to view the exclusionary impact of "Test 21" in racially stigmatizing terms. "Test 21" was primarily a test of verbal and written skills. The Civil Service Commission justified its use of the test by noting its desire to upgrade the communication skills of the city's police officers. Our society has increasingly sought to measure intelligence through the use of written tests, and we have come to believe that performance on such tests accurately reflects the whole of our intelligence. Thus, most people are likely to think of those who performed poorly on "Test 21" not simply as lacking in communication skills but as unintelligent. The average person is likely to see the city's use of the test as an admirable and reasonable attempt to insure that the city has smart police officers. If larger numbers of blacks than whites fail the test, this will be seen as proof that blacks are not smart enough for the job.

But evidence of cultural meaning must include more than disproportionate impact. Some whites also performed poorly on the test. Observers of the test's results would not necessarily conclude that, because blacks performed less well on this test, they are intellectually inferior as a group. They might think instead that the blacks who took this test just happened to be a less intelligent group, that less well-educated people performed less well on the test and the blacks who took this test had not on the whole received as good an education as the whites, or that poor people are less intelligent and blacks had done less well because a higher percentage of them were poor.

The cultural meaning test would require the plaintiffs to produce evidence that a substantial part of the population will interpret the disproportionate results of "Test 21" not as the product of random selection or the differential educational background or socioeconomic status of the test takers but as testimony to the inherent intellectual abilities of the racial groups to which the test takers belong. In other words, the government's use of the test has racial meaning if our culture has taught us to believe that blacks that fail the test have done so because they are black.

This is precisely how most Americans will interpret the events in *Davis*. Throughout American history, a cultural myth that describes blacks as an inherently inferior race has justified their economic and social subjugation. At first, the myth found verification in religious doctrine. By the mid-nineteenth century, the dogma of biblical scripture and verse was supplemented by the pseudoscience of biologists and social scientists who found fodder for the myth in craniometry, eugenics, and cultural anthropology. With the introduction of the I.Q. test in the early twentieth century, the psychometricians assumed primary authorship of this Homeric tale of God and nature's differential distribution of intellectual talent among the races. They provided the theory and numbers to prove the veracity of the myth, and the people's bards—the press, popular literature, and the theater—transformed the racism of pseudoscience into a folklore that shaped the nation's consciousness. * * *

Plaintiffs trying *Davis* under the test proposed in this article would present evidence detailing both the history and the contemporary manifestations of this myth. They would seek to convince the court that most people in our culture believe that the average white person is inherently smarter than the average black person and that whites will interpret the racially selective impact of "Test 21" as a confirmation of that belief. If the culture gives the governmental action this kind of racial meaning, the action constitutes a direct racial stigmatization. Like the segregated beach and the Memphis wall, it conveys a message that has its origins in a pervasive and mutually reinforcing pattern of racially stigmatizing actions, and it adds one more stigmatizing action to that pattern. Presumably, the decisionmakers who chose to use "Test 21" were aware of that message and were influenced by it, whether consciously or unconsciously. * * *

One can anticipate several additional difficulties regarding the test's application. I think that none of them are insurmountable. And while their resolution is not within the scope of this article, I will discuss each of them briefly in order to indicate the direction such resolution might take.

An initial difficulty with applying the cultural meaning test arises from the fact that we are not a monolithic culture. There may be instances in which governmental action is given different meanings by two subcultures within the larger culture. For example, the court might find that blacks see the decision to fund AFDC recipients at lower levels than other need-categories in racial terms while whites do not, or the court may find that people in northern urban areas give racial meaning to restrictions on federally funded abortions while people in southern rural areas do not.

The easiest solution to this problem is to acknowledge racial meaning for constitutional purposes only when the evidence indicates that the racial understanding will be widely shared within the predominant culture. This solution is better than the *Davis/Arlington Heights* intent test in that, at a minimum, it will correctly identify unconscious intent in cases like *Memphis v. Greene* or even *Arlington Heights*.

A second difficulty with the cultural meaning test rests in the inevitable cultural biases of judges. Judges are not immune from our culture's racism, nor can they escape the psychological mechanisms that render us all, to some extent, unaware of our racist beliefs.

We must recognize, however, that this difficulty inheres in all judicial interpretation. The advantage of the cultural meaning test is that it makes the issue of culturally induced bias explicit. The judge who is hearing evidence regarding how our history and culture have influenced our racial beliefs is more likely to be made aware of his own heretofore unrecognized biases. Judges continue to come primarily from elite white backgrounds. They undoubtedly share the values and perceptions of that subculture, which may well be insensitive or even antagonistic toward the values, needs, and experiences of blacks and other minorities. The benefit of the cultural meaning test is that it confronts judges with this conflict and forces them to take responsibility for their own biases and preconceptions.

A third difficulty in applying the cultural meaning test arises where the parties, particularly the plaintiffs, create a racial issue where there seemingly was none. How, for example, should a court treat a challenge to a state bar exam where the racial issues were not apparent until mass demonstrations or a media campaign attracted public attention to them? Again, the answer must be found in the sophistication of the interpretive process. Is the new found awareness of the racial issue merely a result of media hype, or has the media campaign succeeded because it has touched a cultural nerve lying just below the surface of our consciousness?

Each of these potential problems indicates that the cultural meaning test will not create an easily recognizable bright line for judges to follow. The test's advantage lies not so much in its ease of application as in its ability to spotlight the source of injury in cases of racial discrimination:

the unconscious racism that continues to pervade our culture and influence our decisionmaking.

* * *

Ultimately, the greatest stumbling block to any proposal to modify the intent requirement will not be its lack of jurisprudential efficacy but the perception among those who give substance to our jurisprudence that it will operate against their self-interest. Derrick Bell has noted that the interests of blacks in achieving racial equality have been accommodated only when they have converged with the interests of powerful whites: The legal establishment has not responded to civil rights claims that threaten the superior societal status of upper and middle class whites. Alan Freeman has argued persuasively for the more radical proposition that antidiscrimination law has affirmatively advanced racism by promoting an ideology that justifies the continued economic subjugation of blacks. The intent requirement is a centerpiece in an ideology of equal opportunity that legitimizes the continued existence of racially and economically discriminatory conditions and rationalizes the superordinate status of privileged whites.

The workings of the unconscious make this dissonance between efforts to achieve full civil rights for blacks and the self-interest of those who are most able to effect change even more difficult to overcome. The ideology of which Freeman speaks is more than a consciously wielded hegemonic tool of domination. It is also an unconscious defense mechanism against the guilt and anxiety of those who hold power and privilege through means and with motives that they cannot acknowledge. Racism continues to be aided and abetted by self-conscious bigots and well-meaning liberals alike.

I do not anticipate that either the Supreme Court or the academic establishment will rush to embrace and incorporate the approach this article proposes. It has not been my purpose to advance an analysis that is attractive for its ease of application or for its failure to challenge accepted and comfortable ways of thinking about equal protection and race. Rather, it is my hope that the preliminary thoughts expressed in the preceding pages will stimulate others to think about racism in a new way and will provoke a discussion of how equal protection doctrine can best incorporate this understanding of racism.

This article has argued that judicial exploration of the cultural meaning of governmental actions with racially discriminatory impact is the best way to discover the unconscious racism of governmental actors. This exploration will be beset by the complexities and inadequacies of social interpretation and buffeted by the head winds of political resistance. Perhaps I am over optimistic in believing that in the process of this difficult exploration we may discover and understand a collective self-interest that overshadows the multitude of parochial self-interests the unconscious seeks to disguise and shield. But of one thing I am certain. A difficult and painful exploration beats death at the hands of the disease.

Notes and Questions

1. Do you believe you hold unconscious racial stereotypes? Take the test at http://www.tolerance.org/hidden_bias/test.jsp?test=race. The test is a web project sponsored by the Southern Poverty Law Center. Did your results surprise you? What category did you fall within?

2. How would you explain the cultural meaning test to someone of a different race? Were you convinced by Professor Lawrence's examples?

3. The LSAT explains more of the variance in first year law school grades than a student's undergraduate grade point average. *See* Lisa C. Anthony, Vincent F. Harris, and Peter J. Pashley, *Predictive Validity of the LSAT: A National Summary of the 1995–1996 Correlation Studies* (LSAC Research Report Series) 1999. In a multivariate analysis, the LSAT explains 16 percent of the difference of why students get the grades they get in their first year of law school. In social science research, explaining 16 percent of the variance makes the LSAT a relatively strong predictive variable. However, the LSAT does not explain a great deal—even the majority—of the variance. *See also* Richard Delgado, *Official Elitism or Institutional Self Interest? 10 Reasons Why UC–Davis Should Abandon the LSAT (and Why Other Good Law Schools Should Follow Suit)*, 34 U.C. Davis L. Rev. 593, 599–600 (2001). ("[T]he LSAT and other standardized tests simply are not very good at doing what they profess to do, namely predict first year grades. The LSAT, for example, correlates with first year grades with a coefficient of about .4, meaning that it predicts only about sixteen percent of the variation in those grades. Other factors, which we could focus on but do not because the test is so simple and convenient, account for the other eighty-four percent. And, a study of minority law students showed a sharp drop off in correlation after the first year—.27 for the second year and .17, barely positive, for the third. That is another way of saying that by year three, test scores were predicting less than three percent of the variation in performance.") One study has shown that "among law school applicants with essentially the same performance in college, students of color encounter a substantial performance difference on the LSAT compared to their White classmates. These gaps are most severe for African American and Chicano/Latino applicants." William C. Kidder, *Does The LSAT Mirror or Magnify Racial and Ethnic Difference in Educational Attainment?: A Study of Equally Achieving "Elite" College Students*, 89 Calif. L. Rev. 1055, 1058 (2001). If prospective law students of color sue law schools that rely on the LSAT in their admissions decisions, under Professor Lawrence's cultural meaning test, should they win?

4. Professor Roithmayr argues that merit standards have been created by those in power who are in power in part because of their race and ethnicity. *See* Daria Roithmayr, *Deconstructing the Distinction Between Bias and Merit*, 85 Cal. L. Rev. 1449 (1997). According to Professor Roithmayr the determination of what constitutes "merit" is subjective and racially biased. *Id.* at 1454. Merit standards she continues "can be redescribed as a form of bias that has come to be socially accepted." *Id.* at 1454–55. Is the LSAT a subjective and racially biased merit standard? Professor Roithmayr suggests that "merit" standards, such as the LSAT, used in law school

admissions violates Title VI in part because those standards disproportionately exclude African–Americans and Latinos/as. *Id.* at 1496–1500.

SECTION 3.   HOW ARE WHITES CENTRAL TO CRITICAL RACE THEORY ANALYSIS?

KIMBERLE WILLIAMS CRENSHAW

Race, Reform, and Retrenchment: Transformation
and Legitimation in Antidiscrimination Law
101 Harv. L. Rev. 1331, 1356–1386 (1988).

* * *

The failure of the [Critical Legal Studies scholars ("the Critics")] to consider race in their account of law and legitimacy is not a minor oversight: race consciousness is central not only to the domination of Blacks, but also to whites' acceptance of the legitimacy of hierarchy and to their identity with elite interest. Exposing the centrality of race consciousness is crucial to identifying and delegitimating beliefs that present hierarchy as inevitable and fair. Moreover, exposing the centrality of race consciousness shows how the options of Blacks in American society have been limited, and how the use of rights rhetoric has emancipated Blacks from some manifestations of racial domination.

A realignment of the Critical project to incorporate race consciousness must begin with beliefs about Blacks in American society, and how these beliefs legitimize racial coercion. Thus, this Part examines the deep-rooted problem of racist ideology—or white race consciousness—and suggests how this form of consciousness legitimates prevailing injustices and constrains the development of new solutions that benefit Black Americans.

Racist ideology provides a series of rationalizations that suppress the contradiction between American political ideals and Black existence under white supremacy. Not only does racism legitimate the oppression of Blacks, it also helps to define and privilege membership in the white community, creating a basis for identification with dominant interests. Racism serves a consensus-building hegemonic role by designating Black people as separate, visible "others" to be contrasted in every way with all other social groups. Although not consenting to domination, Black people are seen as legitimate objects of antipathy and coercion by whites.

* * *

Throughout American history, the subordination of Blacks was rationalized by a series of stereotypes and beliefs that made their conditions appear logical and natural. Historically, white supremacy has been premised upon various political, scientific, and religious theories, each of which relies on racial characterizations and stereotypes about Blacks that have coalesced into an extensive legitimating ideology. Today, it is probably not controversial to say that these stereotypes were developed primarily to rationalize the oppression of Blacks. What *is* overlooked, however, is the extent to which these stereotypes serve a hegemonic function by perpetuating a mythology about both Blacks *and* whites even today, reinforcing an illusion of a white community that cuts across ethnic, gender, and class lines.

As presented by Critical scholars, hegemonic rule succeeds to the extent that the ruling class world view establishes the appearance of a unity of interests between the dominant class and the dominated. Throughout American history, racism has identified the interests of subordinated whites with those of society's white elite. Racism does not support the dominant order simply because all whites want to maintain their privilege at the expense of Blacks, or because Blacks sometimes serve as convenient political scapegoats. Instead, the very existence of a clearly subordinated "other" group is contrasted with the norm in a way that reinforces identification with the dominant group. Racism helps create an illusion of unity through the oppositional force of a symbolic "other." The establishment of an "other" creates a bond, a burgeoning common identity of all non-stigmatized parties—whose identity and interests are defined in opposition to the other.

According to the philosophy of Jacques Derrida, a structure of polarized categories is characteristic of Western thought:

> Western thought ... has always been structured in terms of dichotomies or polarities: good vs. evil, being vs. nothingness, presence vs. absence, truth vs. error, identity vs. difference, mind vs. matter, man vs. woman, soul vs. body, life vs. death, nature vs. culture, speech vs. writing. These polar opposites do not, however, stand as independent and equal entities. The second term in each pair is considered the negative, corrupt, undesirable version of the first, a fall away from it.... In other words, the two terms are not simply opposed in their meanings, but are arranged in a hierarchical order which gives the first term *priority*....

Racist ideology replicates this pattern of arranging oppositional categories in a hierarchical order; historically, whites represented the dominant antinomy while Blacks came to be seen as separate and subordinate. This hierarchy is reflected in the chart below. Note how each traditional negative image of Blacks correlates with a counter-image of whites:

Historical Oppositional Dualities

WHITE IMAGES	BLACK IMAGES
Industrious	Lazy
Intelligent	Unintelligent
Moral	Immoral
Knowledgeable	Ignorant
Enabling Culture	Disabling Culture
Law–Abiding	Criminal
Responsible	Shiftless
Virtuous/Pious	Lascivious

The oppositional dynamic symbolized by this chart was created and maintained through an elaborate and systematic process. Laws and customs helped create "races" out of a broad range of human traits. In the process of creating races, the categories came to be filled with meaning—Blacks were characterized one way, whites another. Whites became associated with normatively positive characteristics; Blacks became associated with the subordinate, even aberrational characteristics. The operation of this dynamic, along with the important political role of racial oppositionalism, can be illustrated through a few brief historical references.

Edmund Morgan provides vivid illustration of how slaveholders from the seventeenth century onward created and politicized racial categories to maintain the support of non-slaveholding whites. Morgan recounts how the planters "lump[ed] Indians, mulattoes, and Negroes in a single slave class," and how these categories became "an essential, if unacknowledged, ingredient of the republican ideology that enabled Virginians to lead the nation." Having accepted a common interest with slaveholders in keeping Blacks subordinated, even whites who had material reasons to object to the dominance over the slaveholding class could challenge the regime only so far. The power of race consciousness convinced whites to support a system that was opposed to their own economic interests. As George Fredrickson put it, "racial privilege could and did serve as a compensation for class disadvantage." *legacy admissions*

Domination through race consciousness continued throughout the post-Reconstruction period. Historian C. Vann Woodward has argued that the ruling plantocracy was able to undermine the progressive accomplishments of the Populist movement by stirring up anti-Black sentiment among poor white farmers. Racism was articulated as the "broader ground for a new democracy." As racism formed the new base for a broader notion of democracy, class differences were mediated through reference to a racial community of equality. A tragic example of the success of such race-conscious political manipulation is the career of Tom Watson, leader of the progressive Populist movement of the 1890's. Watson, in his attempts to educate the masses of poor farmers about the destructive role of race-based politics, repeatedly told Black and white audiences, "You are made to hate each other because upon that hatred is rested the keystone of the arch of financial despotism which enslaves you both. You are deceived and blinded that you may not see how this race antagonism perpetuates a monetary system which beggars you both." Yet, by 1906, Watson had joined the movement to disenfranchise Blacks. According to Woodward, Watson had "persuaded himself that only after the Negro was eliminated from politics could Populist principles gain a hearing. In other words, the white men would have to unite before they could divide."

White race consciousness also played a role in the nascent labor movement in the North. Labor historian Herbert Hill has demonstrated that unions of virtually all trades excluded Black workers from their ranks, often entirely barring Black employment in certain fields. Immi-grant labor unions were particularly adamant about keeping out Black workers; indeed, it was for the precise purpose of assimilating into the American mainstream that immigrant laborers adopted these exclusion-ary policies.

The political and ideological role that race consciousness continues to play is suggested by racial polarization in contemporary presidential politics. Several political commentators have suggested that many whites supported Ronald Reagan in the belief that he would correct a perceived policy imbalance that unjustly benefited Blacks, and some argue further that Reagan made a direct racist appeal to white voters. Manning Marable notes, for example, that "[a]ppeals to the 'race consciousness' of white workers were the decisive factor in Reagan's 1984 victory, especial-ly in the South." Reagan received nearly 70% of the white vote whereas 90% of Black voters cast their ballots for Mondale. Similarly, the vast majority of Blacks—82%—disapproved of Reagan's performance, where-as only 32% of whites did.

Even the Democratic Party, which has traditionally relied on Blacks as its most loyal constituency, has responded to this apparent racial polarization by seeking to distance itself from Black interests. Although it has been argued that the racial polarization demonstrated in the 1984 election does not represent a trend of white defections from the Demo-cratic Party, it is significant that, whatever the cause of the Party's inability to attract white votes, Democratic leaders have expressed a willingness to moderate the Party's stand on key racial issues in at-tempts to recapture the white vote.

The previous section emphasizes the continuity of white race con-sciousness over the course of American history. This section, by contrast, focuses on the partial transformation of the functioning of race con-sciousness that occurred with the transition from Jim Crow to formal equality in race law.

Prior to the civil rights reforms, Blacks were formally subordinated by the state. Blacks experienced being the "other" in two aspects of oppression, which I shall designate as symbolic and material. Symbolic subordination refers to the formal denial of social and political equality to all Blacks, regardless of their accomplishments. Segregation and other forms of social exclusion—separate restrooms, drinking fountains, en-trances, parks, cemeteries, and dining facilities—reinforced a racist ideology that Blacks were simply inferior to whites and were therefore not included in the vision of America as a community of equals.

* * *

Yet the attainment of formal equality is not the end of the story. Racial hierarchy cannot be cured by the move to facial race-neutrality in the laws that structure the economic, political, and social lives of Black people. White race consciousness, in a new form but still virulent, plays an important, perhaps crucial, role in the new regime that has legitimated the deteriorating day-to-day material conditions of the majority of Blacks.

The end of Jim Crow has been accompanied by the demise of an explicit ideology of white supremacy. The white norm, however, has not disappeared; it has only been submerged in popular consciousness. It continues in an unspoken form as a statement of the positive social norm, legitimating the continuing domination of those who do not meet it. Nor have the negative stereotypes associated with Blacks been eradicated. The rationalizations once used to legitimate Black subordination based on a belief in racial inferiority have now been reemployed to legitimate the domination of Blacks through reference to an assumed cultural inferiority.

Thomas Sowell, for example, suggests that underclass Blacks are economically depressed because they have not adopted the values of hard work and discipline. He further implies that Blacks have not pursued the need to attain skills and marketable education, and have not learned to make the sacrifices necessary for success. Instead, Sowell charges that Blacks view demands for special treatment as a means for achieving what other groups have achieved through hard work and the abandonment of racial politics.

Sowell applies the same stereotypes to the mass of Blacks that white supremacists had applied in the past, but bases these modern stereotypes on notions of "culture" rather than genetics. Sowell characterizes underclass Blacks as victims of self-imposed ignorance, lack of direction, and poor work attitudes. Culture, not race, now accounts for this "otherness." Except for vestigial pockets of historical racism, any possible connection between past racial subordination and the present situation has been severed by the formal repudiation of the old race-conscious policies. The same dualities historically used to legitimate racial subordination in the name of genetic inferiority have now been adopted by Sowell as a means for explaining the subordinated status of Blacks today in terms of cultural inferiority.

Moreover, Sowell's explanation of the subordinate status of Blacks also illustrates the treatment of the now-unspoken white stereotypes as the positive social norm. His assertion that the *absence* of certain attributes accounts for the continued subordination of Blacks implies that it is the *presence* of these attributes that explains the continued advantage of whites. The only difference between this argument and the older oppositional dynamic is that, whereas the latter explained Black subordination through reference to the ideology of white supremacy, the former explains Black subordination through reference to an unspoken social norm. That norm—although no longer explicitly white supremacist—remains, nonetheless, a white norm. As Martha Minow has pointed out, "[t]he unstated point of comparison is not neutral, but particular, and not inevitable, but only seemingly so when left unstated."

White race consciousness, which includes the modern belief in cultural inferiority, acts to further Black subordination by justifying all the forms of unofficial racial discrimination, injury, and neglect that flourish in a society that is only formally dedicated to equality. In more subtle ways, moreover, white race consciousness reinforces and is reinforced by the myth of equal opportunity that explains and justifies broader class hierarchies.

Race consciousness also reinforces whites' sense that American society is really meritocratic and thus helps prevent them from questioning the basic legitimacy of the free market. Believing both that Blacks are inferior and that the economy impartially rewards the superior over the inferior, whites see that most Blacks are indeed worse off than whites are, which reinforces their sense that the market is operating "fairly and impartially"; those who should logically be on the bottom are on the bottom. This strengthening of whites' belief in the system in turn reinforces their beliefs that Blacks are *indeed* inferior. After all, equal opportunity *is* the rule, and the market *is* an impartial judge; if Blacks are on the bottom, it must reflect their relative inferiority. Racist ideology thus operates in conjunction with the class components of legal ideology to reinforce the status quo, both in terms of class and race.

To bring a fundamental challenge to the way things are, whites would have to question not just their own subordinate status, but also both the economic and the racial myths that justify the status quo. Racism, combined with equal opportunity mythology, provides a rationalization for racial oppression, making it difficult for whites to see the Black situation as illegitimate or unnecessary. If whites believe that Blacks, because they are unambitious or inferior, get what they deserve, it becomes that much harder to convince whites that something is wrong with the entire system. Similarly, a challenge to the legitimacy of continued racial inequality would force whites to confront myths about equality of opportunity that justify for them whatever measure of economic success they may have attained.

Thus, although Critics have suggested that legal consciousness plays a central role in legitimating hierarchy in America, the otherness dynamic enthroned within the maintenance and perpetuation of white race consciousness seems to be at least as important as legal consciousness in supporting the dominant order. Like legal consciousness, race consciousness makes it difficult—at least for whites—to imagine the world differently. It also creates the desire for identification with privileged elites. By focusing on a distinct, subordinate "other," whites include themselves in the dominant circle—an arena in which most hold no real power, but only their privileged racial identity. Consider the case of a dirt-poor, southern white, shown participating in a Ku Klux Klan rally in the movie *Resurgence,* who declared: "Every morning, I wake up and thank God I'm white." For this person, and for others like him, race consciousness—manifested by his refusal even to associate with Blacks—provides a powerful explanation of why he fails to challenge the current social order. * * *

Some critics of legal reform movements seem to overlook the fact that state power has made a significant difference—sometimes between life and death—in the efforts of Black people to transform their world. Attempts to harness the power of the state through the appropriate rhetorical/legal incantations should be appreciated as intensely powerful and calculated political acts. In the context of white supremacy, engaging in rights discourse should be seen as an act of self-defense. This was particularly true because the state could not assume a position of neutrality regarding Black people once the movement had mobilized people to challenge the system of oppression: either the coercive mechanism of the state had to be used to support white supremacy, or it had to be used to dismantle it. We know now, with hindsight, that it did both.

Blacks did use rights rhetoric to mobilize state power to their benefit against symbolic oppression through formal inequality and, to some extent, against material deprivation in the form of private, informal exclusion of the middle class from jobs and housing. Yet today the same legal reforms play a role in providing an ideological framework that makes the present conditions facing underclass Blacks appear fair and reasonable. The eradication of barriers has created a new dilemma for those victims of racial oppression who are not in a position to benefit from the move to formal equality. The race neutrality of the legal system creates the illusion that racism is no longer the primary factor responsible for the condition of the Black underclass; instead, as we have seen, class disparities appear to be the consequence of individual and group merit within a supposed system of equal opportunity. Moreover, the fact that there are Blacks who are economically successful gives credence both to the assertion that opportunities exist, and to the backlash attitude that Blacks have "gotten too far." Psychologically, for Blacks who have not made it, the lack of an explanation for their underclass status may result in self-blame and other self-destructive attitudes.

Another consequence of the formal reforms may be the loss of collectivity among Blacks. The removal of formal barriers created new opportunities for some Blacks that were not shared by various other classes of African–Americans. As Blacks moved into different spheres, the experience of being Black in America became fragmented and multifaceted, and the different contexts presented opportunities to experience racism in different ways. The social, economic, and even residential distance between the various classes may complicate efforts to unite behind issues as a racial group. Although "White Only" signs may have been crude and debilitating, they at least presented a readily discernible target around which to organize. Now, the targets are obscure and diffuse, and this difference may create doubt among some Blacks whether there is enough similarity between their life experiences and those of other Blacks to warrant collective political action.

Formal equality significantly transformed the Black experience in America. With society's embrace of formal equality came the eradication of symbolic domination and the suppression of white supremacy as the norm of society. Future generations of Black Americans would no longer be explicitly regarded as America's second-class citizens. Yet the transformation of the oppositional dynamic—achieved through the suppression of racial norms and stereotypes, and the recasting of racial inferiority into assumptions of cultural inferiority—creates several difficulties for the civil rights constituency. The removal of formal barriers, although symbolically significant to all and materially significant to some, will do little to alter the hierarchical relationship between Blacks and whites until the way in which white race consciousness perpetuates norms that legitimate Black subordination is revealed. This is not to say that white norms alone account for the conditions of the Black underclass. It is instead an acknowledgment that, until the distinct racial nature of class ideology is itself revealed and debunked, nothing can be done about the underlying structural problems that account for the disparities. The narrow focus of racial exclusion—that is, the belief that racial exclusion is illegitimate only where the "White Only" signs are explicit—coupled with strong assumptions about equal opportunity, makes it difficult to move the discussion of racism beyond the societal self-satisfaction engendered by the appearance of neutral norms and formal inclusion.

Rights have been important. They may have legitimated racial inequality, but they have also been the means by which oppressed groups have secured both entry as formal equals into the dominant order and the survival of their movement in the face of private and state repression. The dual role of legal change creates a dilemma for Black reformers. As long as race consciousness thrives, Blacks will often have to rely on rights rhetoric when it is necessary to protect Black interests. The very reforms brought about by appeals to legal ideology, however, seem to undermine the ability to move forward toward a broader vision of racial equality. In the quest for racial justice, winning and losing have been part of the same experience.

The Critics are correct in observing that engaging in rights discourse has helped to deradicalize and co-opt the challenge. Yet they fail to acknowledge the limited range of options presented to Blacks in a context where they were deemed "other," and the unlikelihood that specific demands for inclusion and equality would be heard if articulated in other terms. This abbreviated list of options is itself contingent upon the ideological power of white race consciousness and the continuing role of Black Americans as "other." Future efforts to address racial domination, as well as class hierarchy, must consider the continuing ideology of white race consciousness by uncovering the oppositional dynamic and by chipping away at its premises. Central to this task is revealing the contingency of race and exploring the connection between white race consciousness and the other myths that legitimate both class and race hierarchies. Critics and others whose agendas include challenging hierarchy and legitimation must not overlook the importance of revealing the contingency of race.

Optimally, the deconstruction of white race consciousness might lead to a liberated future for both Blacks and whites. Yet, until whites recognize the hegemonic function of racism and turn their efforts toward neutralizing it, African–American people must develop pragmatic political strategies—self-conscious ideological struggle—to minimize the costs of liberal reform while maximizing its utility. A primary step in engaging in self-conscious ideological struggle must be to transcend the oppositional dynamic in which Blacks are cast simply and solely as whites' subordinate "other."

The dual role that rights have played makes strategizing a difficult task. Black people can afford neither to resign themselves to, nor to attack frontally, the legitimacy and incoherence of the dominant ideology. The subordinate position of Blacks in this society makes it unlikely that African–Americans will realize gains through the kind of direct challenge to the legitimacy of American liberal ideology that is now being waged by Critical scholars. On the other hand, delegitimating race consciousness would be directly relevant to Black needs, and this strategy will sometimes require the pragmatic use of liberal ideology.

* * *

Notes and Questions

1.   Professor Crenshaw states "[e]xposing the centrality of race consciousness is crucial to identifying and delegitimating beliefs that present hierarchy as inevitable and fair." What is she talking about?

2.   Does racism affect all African–Americans the same? Are there class differences? How does Professor Crenshaw describe those differences?

3.   What about other racial groups? Professor Frank Wu writes: "Anyone who studies Asian Americans knows about the model minority myth….this ubiquitous superminority image has suggested that Asian Americans achieve economic success and gain societal acceptance through conservative values and hard work. The image is a myth because Asian Americans have not achieved economic success except in a superficial sense. Comparing equally educated individuals, whites earn more money than Asian Americans. Qualifications count less than race, in a pattern of regular discrimination, not so-called 'reverse' discrimination." Frank H. Wu, *Changing America: Three Arguments About Asian Americans and the Law*, 45 Am. U. L. Rev. 811, 813–814 (1996).

4.   Does racism operate differently with different racial and ethnic groups? Consider another quote from Professor Wu. "Everyone should know that the model minority myth is deployed in ways that expose the insincerity of its goodwill. The myth is used to denigrate other racial minorities. It is used to ask African Americans, rhetorically, 'Well, the Asian Americans succeeded; why can't you?'" *See* Frank H. Wu, *Changing America: Three Arguments About Asian Americans and the Law*, 45 Am. U. L. Rev. 811, 814 (1996). *See also* Robert S. Chang, *Toward an Asian American Legal Scholarship: Critical Race Theory, Post–Structuralism, and Narrative Space*, 81 Cal. L. Rev. 1241, 1260 (1993) ("At its surface, the label 'model minority' seems like a compliment. However, once one moves beyond this complimentary façade, one can see the label for what it is–a tool of oppression which works a

dual harm by (1) denying the existence of present-day discrimination against Asian Americans and the present-day effects of past discrimination, and (2) legitimizing the oppression of other racial minorities and poor whites.") Professors Delgado and Stefancic write regarding Mexican–Americans: "[i]mages of Mexican–Americans ('Chicanos') fall into three or four well-delineated stereotypes—the greaser, the conniving, treacherous bandido, the happy-go-lucky shiftless lover of song, food, and dance, and the tragic, silent 'Spanish' tall, dark, and handsome type of romantic fiction—which change according to society's needs. As with blacks, Asians, and Indians, most Americans have relatively few interpersonal contacts with Mexican–Americans; therefore, these images become the individual's only reality. When such a person meets an actual Mexican–American, he or she tends to place the other in one of the ready-made categories. Stereotyping thus denies members of both groups the opportunity to interact with each other on anything like a complex, nuanced human level." *See* Richard Delgado and Jean Stefancic, *Images of the Outsider in American Law and Culture: Can Free Expression Remedy Systemic Social Ills?*, 77 Cornell L. Rev. 1258, 1273 (1992).

5. *See* Chapter 6 *infra* for a discussion of how different stereotypes impact the application of self-defense.

6. How would you explain the complexity of race in America to someone from another planet? Doesn't that presuppose that you understand the complexity of race in America?

7. Assuming you have concluded that there is more learning that needs to take place on your part, where would you start? Where do you usually start when you're trying to master a subject you want to learn more about? What kind of attitudes do you usually bring to such an endeavor? How is learning about race different than learning about those other subjects?

8. How is talking about race different than talking about other subjects? Harvard Sociology Professor Orlando Patterson has stated: "[t]he language of race itself is loaded, and it is so often the case that in a conversation, as soon as race is introduced, it changes everything. It introduces a new dimension that makes it very nearly impossible to think straight about the subject." Orlando Patterson, *The Nexus Between Race and Policy: Interview with Orlando Patterson, Professor of Sociology at Harvard University*, 4 Geo. Public Pol'y Rev. 107, 108 (1999). Should you drop the course?

9. For an excellent discussion of the classroom dynamics when race is included, *see* Kimberle Williams Crenshaw, *Foreword: Toward a Race–Conscious Pedagogy in Legal Education*, 11 Nat'l Black L. J. 1 (1989).

10. As difficult as conversations about race are to have, I believe the rewards far outweigh the challenges. As a country we haven't made a lot of progress understanding each other. Numerous polls demonstrate the racial divide in this country. Conversations that you will begin in your classes and continue over lunch or dinner will bridge at least part of that gap. As Frederick Douglass has said: "[I]f there is no struggle there is no progress." Frederic Douglass, Two Speeches by Frederick Douglass; West India Emanci-

pation. And the Dred Scott Decision, The Frederick Douglass Papers at the Library of Congress 22 (1998). Cf. Dorothy A. Brown, *Fighting Racism in the Twenty-First Century*, 61 Wash. & Lee L. Rev. 1485 (2004) ("Twenty-first century racism, on the other hand, is more subtle. It is harder to prove intentional racial discrimination today, and as a result, its existence is widely disputed.")

Chapter 2

CRITICAL RACE THEORY AND THE LEGAL PROFESSION

This chapter will address issues that attorneys of color face in the workplace as well as those issues faced by litigants of color in the judicial system. It begins with an employment discrimination case that resulted when an African–American attorney sued his former employer. It is then followed by article excerpts that discuss the obstacles faced by African–American and Hispanic attorneys in large corporate law firms. This chapter concludes with an excerpt that addresses the lack of racial diversity in the judiciary. Assuming that you wish to work towards eradicating all barriers faced by attorneys and litigants of color, what can you—the most junior associate in your firm—do?

SECTION 1. IS LITIGATION AN EFFECTIVE STRATEGY?

MUNGIN v. KATTEN MUCHIN & ZAVIS

116 F.3d 1549 (D.C.Cir. 1997).

RANDOLPH, CIRCUIT JUDGE:

In July 1994, Mark Dombroff left the law firm that bore his name—Katten Muchin Zavis & Dombroff—the Washington, D.C., branch of Chicago's Katten Muchin & Zavis. Principally because of Dombroff's departure, defections and terminations reduced the number of lawyers in the D.C. office from 42 to 14. Lawrence Mungin, an associate in the D.C. office, was among the lawyers who left the firm. He departed on July 25, 1994.

In September 1994, Mungin filed a racial discrimination charge with the EEOC. The EEOC took no action on his claim. Mungin then sued the firm and several of its current and former partners, asserting violations of 28 U.S.C. § 1981, Title VII, and the D.C. Human Rights Act. Pretrial proceedings eliminated the individual defendants from all claims and narrowed Mungin's § 1981 claim (but not his coextensive claims under Title VII and the D.C. statute) to the firm's failure to consider him for partnership the year before his departure. By special verdict, a jury found for Mungin, imposing liability on the firm for (1) race-based constructive discharge; and (2) racially discriminatory treatment with respect to (a) Mungin's starting salary, (b) his 1994 salary, (c) his work assignments, and (d) his consideration for partnership.

The jury awarded Mungin $1 million in compensatory damages, and an additional $1.5 million in punitive damages. After the district court entered judgment, and denied Katten's motion for judgment as a matter of law, *see Mungin v. Katten Muchin & Zavis*, 941 F.Supp. 153, 155 (D.D.C. 1996), the firm filed this appeal.

I. Factual Background

A 1983 Harvard Law School graduate, Mungin had worked at several firms. Immediately before his move to Katten, he was an associate in the D.C. office of Powell, Goldstein, Frazer & Murphy.[1] When the Powell firm began experiencing financial difficulties it froze associate salaries. At the time, Mungin was making $87,000 per year. In February 1992 Mungin informed the Powell firm of his plan to leave that May. In March 1992, a legal headhunter sent Mungin's resume to Dombroff, who was both the hiring partner and managing partner of Katten in D.C. Accompanying the resume was the headhunter's note pitching Mungin: not only would Mungin bring with him a $250,000 to $500,000 book of business, but "he is a minority." Letter from Peter Yenne, Keith Ross & Associates, Inc., to Mark Dombroff (Mar. 20, 1992).

When he interviewed with Dombroff in April, Mungin said he was interested in bankruptcy work and "was looking for a law firm with an established practice, because," contrary to headhunter's note, he "didn't have a book of business of" his "own." Trial Transcript at 147. Mungin also wanted to be considered for partnership the following year. Dombroff allayed Mungin's concerns. He told Mungin that he, as the biggest rainmaker at the firm, generated work, as did a new partner in the D.C. office, Jeff Sherman. Combined with the possibility of doing work with Katten's offices in Chicago and Los Angeles, Mungin "would be more than busy." *Id*. On the spot, Dombroff offered Mungin a position as a sixth-year associate, with annual pay of $91,000. As was the firm's policy, Mungin could be considered for partnership the following year.

Before accepting the offer, Mungin met with Jeff Sherman, the only bankruptcy partner in Washington. Sherman told Mungin that "there was plenty of bankruptcy" work in Washington, generated by Sherman himself, as well as by Dombroff, and that he "was hoping to get work from Chicago." *Id*. at 151. Mungin accepted the position at the Katten firm, contingent on being able to visit the firm's home office. Chicago was the headquarters of the firm's Finance and Reorganization department, the department encompassing the bankruptcy lawyers in Washington. Mungin joined the firm on May 1, 1992, and visited Chicago on June

---

1. Except where otherwise indicated, the facts presented in this introductory section are those that Mungin conveyed in his testimony at trial.

3, 1992. In Chicago, Mungin met one of the two heads of the Finance Department, Laurie Goldstein; the other department head, Vince Sergi, was not available. Mungin's starting salary was $92,000, an amount he negotiated after the firm's initial offer of $91,000.

In the beginning, Mungin kept busy, receiving his work almost exclusively through Jeff Sherman and Mark Dombroff, with Sherman serving as Mungin's supervisor and mentor. Then the bankruptcy work started drying up. In February 1993, Sherman left the firm along with Stuart Soberman, the only other bankruptcy associate in Katten's D.C. office. Mungin thus wound up as the only bankruptcy attorney in the D.C. office.

Concerned about his partnership chances in an office without the work he was trained to perform or attorneys to supervise him, Mungin traveled to Chicago in February 1993 to meet more members of the Finance and Reorganization department. Mungin hoped his trip would result in the Chicago office referring more work to him. Although Vince Sergi was too busy to meet with Mungin, Mungin did meet with several attorneys and attended a department meeting where he was introduced to everyone.

The intra-firm marketing with the Chicago, as well as Los Angeles and Milan attorneys, proved unsuccessful. To keep Mungin busy, in April 1993 Sergi recommended that Mungin handle work then being done by a first-year associate in Chicago. Patricia Gilmore, a D.C. partner who worked closely with Dombroff, lowered Mungin's billing rate (which imperfectly reflected the level of responsibility with which he was entrusted) to $125 per hour, down from $185 per hour.

Meanwhile, it was coming time for Mungin's annual performance review. But at the designated time—October 1993—nothing happened. Mungin kept quiet, wanting to lie low while the firm accepted nominations for partnership. Although there was a buzz in the office about who was being considered for partnership, no partners told Mungin they would sponsor him for partnership.

Also in autumn 1993, the firm made its compensation decisions. Mungin received an annual bonus, in the amount of $4,000. His base salary for 1994 remained unchanged from 1993. Mungin asked the firm's human resources director why he had not received a raise; the director told him to talk to Sergi. If the firm's failure to give him a raise was not some sort of oversight, it made Mungin want the performance evaluation that much more: without an explanation of why the firm thought his performance sub-par, Mungin thought that he risked being denied a raise for the following year. Mungin scheduled a meeting for December 6, 1993, with Sergi and the new co-head of the department, David Heller.

When Mungin arrived in Chicago on December 6, Sergi was there, Heller was not. Sergi presented Mungin with the two performance reviews partners had prepared, one by Dombroff, the other by Gilmore; the other partners for whom Mungin had worked had not filled out the evaluation forms. Gilmore's evaluation was positive overall:

Much of Larry's time is consumed by routine tasks, such as drafting status letters to our client. Occasionally we receive a challenging assignment from AIG [a large client], which Larry accomplishes with great skill. AIG is a very difficult client and Larry's ongoing efforts to coordinate with me have made a potentially troublesome situation, relatively easy. I do not believe that, for the most part, AIG offers challenging work to Larry. Larry nonetheless accomplishes the tasks for AIG with a helpful attitude and a willingness to tackle the unique problems this client presents.

Plaintiff's Exhibit II, *reprinted in* Joint Appendix 213. Sergi saw this not as a substantive evaluation—that is, a description of Mungin's skills and weaknesses—but as a testament to his affability. Sergi also stated that Gilmore was not respected by the firm, and that her opinions would not help Mungin achieve partnership. Dombroff's evaluation said that he was "not in a position to judge the quality of Larry's work," but that Mungin "has always appeared cooperative and willing to get the job done." Plaintiff's Exhibit HH, *reprinted in* Joint Appendix 209. Mungin gave Sergi the names of the other partners for whom he had worked so that Sergi could solicit evaluations from clients with whom Mungin had contact.

Mungin asked Sergi why he had not received a raise. Sergi responded that his name just had not come up in connection with compensation discussions or, for that matter, partnership considerations. Sergi told Mungin that although he had not been considered for partnership in 1993, he would still be eligible the following year. Mungin also asked Sergi for a marketing allowance, a perquisite usually reserved for partners seeking to recruit clients. Mungin never received the allowance. After the meeting the quality of work assigned to Mungin did not improve. He found himself still doing work he believed less-experienced attorneys could have performed. But on December 10, 1993, the firm did raise Mungin's salary to $108,000, retroactive to October 1, 1993.

Effective July 15, 1994, Dombroff and Gilmore would leave the Katten firm to form their own firm, Dombroff & Gilmore, P.C. In May 1994, Sergi called Mungin and asked him what he expected to do in the wake of Dombroff's and Gilmore's departure. Mungin was surprised by Sergi's question since he had assumed that in light of the departures, the firm would, as a matter of course, more closely integrate him into the Chicago bankruptcy practice. Instead, Sergi asked Mungin if he would consider moving to Katten's New York office. Mungin did not find this option appealing because the firm had no bankruptcy lawyers in New York. Mungin did not reject the New York option outright. Instead, he asked about the firm's severance policies so that he could compare the benefits and drawbacks of leaving the firm with the alternative of moving to New York.

Shortly thereafter, Mungin spoke with Dick Waller, an attorney who had become an administrator in the Chicago office. Waller offered Mungin the additional option of relocating to Chicago. Mungin felt this option was not attractive since Sergi, in whose department Mungin would be working in Chicago, did not advance that option himself. On July 7, 1994, Mungin sent the following electronic mail message to Waller:

> Unfortunately, due to personal constraints and other considerations I cannot possibly move to New York or Chicago at this time. Because you have made it clear that there is not enough work in the D.C. office to keep me busy and that my only alternative is to be laid off, I would like to discuss an appropriate amount of time to search for a job and an appropriate departure date.

Electronic Mail Message from Lawrence Mungin to Richard Waller (July 7, 1994). Mungin arranged his severance with Waller: he would be terminated on July 25, 1994, and would receive severance pay through October 25, 1994.

After the EEOC failed to pursue Mungin's claim, on October 19, 1994, the firm reiterated its offer to transfer Mungin to either Chicago or New York, and for the first time offered to transfer him to Katten's Los Angeles office. The firm made clear that it would reimburse Mungin for any costs incurred in connection with a transfer, and that he would "continue to be considered for salary increases and partnership on the same basis as other associates." Letter from Allan B. Muchin, Managing Partner, Katten Muchin & Zavis, to Lawrence D. Mungin 1 (Oct. 19, 1994). The firm anticipated "that the work available in any of the other three offices" would put it "in a position to consider [Mungin] for partnership within a year." *Id.* at 2. Mungin thought these were not *bona fide* offers, and pursued the litigation that is now before us.

II. STANDARD OF REVIEW

Title VII of the Civil Rights Act of 1964 makes it "an unlawful employment practice for an employer ... to discharge any individual, or otherwise discriminate against any individual with respect to his compensation, terms, conditions, or privileges of employment, because of," among other protected categories, "such individual's race, [or] color." 42 U.S.C. § 2000e–2(a). District of Columbia law proscribes the same conduct. *See* D.C. CODE § 1–2512(a). If the firm discriminated against Mungin by not considering him for partnership—thus depriving him of the opportunity to enter a new contractual relationship with the firm, as partner—it violated 42 U.S.C. § 1981(a), which guarantees that all persons within the United States shall have the same right "to make and enforce contracts." *See Patterson v. McLean Credit Union*, 491 U.S. 164, 185, 105 L.Ed.2d 132, 109 S.Ct. 2363 (1989). The burdens of persuasion and production for claims raised under § 1981 or under the D.C. law are identical to those for claims alleging discriminatory treatment in violation of Title VII. *See Patterson*, 491 U.S. at 186–87 (42 U.S.C. § 1981); *American Univ. v. D.C. Comm'n on Human Rights*, 598 A.2d 416, 422 (D.C. 1991) (D.C. CODE § 1–2512(a)(1)).

Under the Title VII scheme first described in *McDonnell Douglas Corp. v. Green*, 411 U.S. 792, 802, 36 L.Ed.2d 668, 93 S.Ct. 1817 (1973), the burdens of production shift from employee to employer. The plaintiff "must first establish, by a preponderance of the evidence," a prima facie case of racial discrimination. *St. Mary's Honor Ctr. v. Hicks*, 509 U.S. 502, 506, 125 L.Ed.2d 407, 113 S.Ct. 2742 (1993). If the employee succeeds, the employer must introduce evidence of "some legitimate, nondiscriminatory reason" for its purportedly discriminatory action, *McDonnell Douglas*, 411 U.S. at 802, evidence "legally sufficient to justify a judgment for the" employer, *Texas Dep't of Community Affairs v. Burdine*, 450 U.S. 248, 255, 67 L.Ed.2d 207, 101 S.Ct. 1089 (1981). If the employer does so, "the presumption raised by the prima facie case is rebutted." *Id*. The burden of persuasion, having "at all times" been borne by the employee, then requires the employee to show that the employer's "proffered reason was not the true reason for the employment decision," *Hicks*, 509 U.S. at 508 (quoting *Burdine*, 450 U.S. at 256 "and that race was," *Hicks*, 509 U.S. at 508). Thus, "where the defendant has done everything that would be required of him if the plaintiff had properly made out a prima facie case, whether the plaintiff really did so is no longer relevant." *U.S. Postal Serv. Bd. of Governors v. Aikens*, 460 U.S. 711, 715, 75 L.Ed.2d 403, 103 S.Ct. 1478 (1983).

Once the case has been fully tried, and the plaintiff and defendant have satisfied their burdens of production, "the *McDonnell Douglas* framework—with its presumptions and burdens—is no longer relevant." *Hicks*, 509 U.S. at 510. We therefore turn to the question whether Mungin met his burden of persuasion—that is, whether a reasonable juror could find that the firm discriminated against him on the basis of his race. *See Barbour v. Merrill*, 310 U.S.App.D.C. 419, 48 F.3d 1270, 1276 (D.C.Cir. 1995).

III.   Mungin's Claims of Discrimination

We will examine each of Mungin's claims roughly in chronological order: first his 1992 salary; then his 1994 salary; the quality of his work assignments; partnership consideration; and finally, his discharge.

A.   *Starting Salary*

In support of his argument that his $92,000 starting salary was discriminatorily low, Mungin demonstrated that every sixth-year associate enjoyed a salary ranging from $95,000 to $102,000, that they were white and that he is black. The evidence showed, however, that Katten offered to associates who are lateral hires from firms paying less, salaries midway between the associate's former salary and the salary Katten pays its current associates.

Mungin never carried his burden of explaining how the firm's actual decision in his case was based on race. Not "all of the relevant aspects of" his "employment situation were 'nearly identical' to those" of the associates to whom he compared himself. *Neuren v. Adduci, Mastriani, Meeks & Schill*, 310 U.S.App.D.C. 82, 43 F.3d 1507, 1514 (D.C.Cir. 1995) (quoting *Pierce v. Commonwealth Life Ins. Co.*, 40 F.3d 796, 802 (6th Cir. 1994)); *see also Byrd v. Ronayne*, 61 F.3d 1026, 1032 (1st Cir. 1995). Mungin's mistake was comparing himself to homegrown associates, rather than to lateral entries like himself. Mungin offered nothing to show that the firm's reason for hiring him at $92,000 was pretextual. On appeal, he argues that Katten "never demonstrated that such a policy was ever consistently and systematically enforced." Supplemental Final Brief of the Appellee at 17. If this were so, we would have expected Mungin to point our attention to other associates to whom this policy was not enforced. He has not. Since it is Mungin's burden of persuasion, his argument without evidence fails to prove that the firm's reason was pretextual.

Mungin offers another reason for finding the firm's policy pretextual: "his base salary never caught up with the salary levels of Caucasian attorneys in his class." Supplemental Final Brief of the Appellee at 17. We fail to see what this has to do with his starting salary. While it is potentially evidence of the firm's later discrimination—discrimination with respect to Mungin's 1994 salary, for instance—it brings nothing to bear on whether the firm engaged in racial discrimination by starting him at $92,000.[2] *See Price Waterhouse v. Hopkins*, 490 U.S. 228, 241, 104 L.Ed.2d 268, 109 S.Ct. 1775 (1989) (noting that the "critical inquiry" is whether discrimination "was a factor in the employment decision at the moment it was made").

B. 1994 Salary

As to Mungin's 1994 salary, he not only asserts that $108,000 was discriminatorily low, but he also complains that he had to ask for a raise. The firm, he says, did not provide him with the compensation review which would have led to his salary being raised *sua sponte*. The problem for Mungin is that he introduced no evidence that he was underpaid relative to his peers. He claims to have shown that the average base salary in 1994 for the 1986 class was $116,000, while he ultimately received $108,000. Mungin does not explain where the $116,000 figure comes from and we understand why. When the average base salaries of all associates are calculated—those in Washington, Chicago, and Los Angeles—we arrive at $116,000. But this calculation includes the mean salary in Los Angeles of $121,250, and in Chicago of $115,370. *See* Plaintiff's Exhibit 3, *reprinted in* Joint Appendix 142–45; Defendant's Exhibit K2, *reprinted in* Joint Appendix 228–31. The mean salary in Washington, excluding Mungin's, was $108,800. *See id., reprinted in* Joint Appendix 230. Mungin's unstated assumption must be that the firm's D.C. associates should receive the same salaries as those in the other cities. But he offered no proof of this and he did not give the jury any basis to conclude that these D.C. attorneys were similarly situated to their Chicago or Los Angeles counterparts.

---

2. In any event, as we shall soon see, by 1994 Mungin did catch up.

Mungin also states that three of his colleagues in D.C., Dane Jacques, Jonathan Stern, and John Henderson, received base salaries of $120,000. Supplemental Final Brief of the Appellee at 11. Two of these individuals, Jacques and Stern, became partners during 1994, and their salaries were increased accordingly. Both made $120,000 in 1994. *See* Trial Transcript at 891. Mungin's situation is not comparable; he takes issue with his 1994 base salary as an associate, not a partner. Jacques's base salary as an associate was $115,000; Stern's was $117,000. *See* Plaintiff's Exhibit 3, *reprinted in* Joint Appendix 144; Defendant's Exhibit K2, *reprinted in* Joint Appendix 230. As to Henderson, Mungin cites no evidence to back up his claim that Henderson made $120,000; the record indicates that Henderson received $104,000. *Id.* When we use these salaries—Jacques's $115,000, Stern's $117,000, and Henderson's $104,000—along with those of the two other associates in D.C., Judith Rayner and John Enerson (each earning $104,000), we arrive at the figure we mentioned earlier—$108,800, nearly identical to the salary Mungin received.

Thus, Mungin's 1994 salary was not discriminatorily low, and the district court recognized as much, stating in its Memorandum Opinion that "with respect to his salary for 1994, plaintiff has not shown and does not argue that his 1994 salary level was below that of similarly situated white lawyers." *Mungin*, 941 F.Supp. at 155. The only possible basis for inferring discrimination, then, deals with Mungin's seeking (and getting) a raise for 1994. The firm's putting him in the position of having to ask for a salary increase, Mungin asserts, discriminated against him on account of race.

At oral argument (and somewhat less clearly in its briefs), the Katten firm argued that in light of *Milton v. Weinberger*, 225 U.S.App. D.C. 12, 696 F.2d 94, 99 (D.C.Cir. 1982), the fact that Mungin ultimately received his raise eliminated any potential liability for discrimination. As *Milton* makes clear, however, the no-harm no-foul rule discussed in the opinion, a rule derived from *Day v. Mathews*, 174 U.S.App.D.C. 231, 530 F.2d 1083 (D.C.Cir. 1976) (per curiam), "has nothing to do with whether a defendant is guilty of discrimination, but instead focuses on the question of remedy." *Milton*, 696 F.2d at 98. Furthermore, shortly after we decided *Milton*, we expressly rejected the application of *Day v. Mathews* to cases, such as this, alleging disparate treatment of an individual employee rather than of a group of employees pursuing litigation through a class action. *See Toney v. Block*, 227 U.S.App.D.C. 273, 705 F.2d 1364, 1368 (D.C.Cir. 1983) (Scalia, J.); *see also Johnson v. Brock,* 258 U.S.App.D.C. 100, 810 F.2d 219, 224 (D.C.Cir. 1987).

Katten is on more solid ground in observing that other circuits have reached the conclusion it seeks: that "interlocutory or mediate decisions having no immediate effect upon employment ... were not intended to fall within the direct proscriptions of ... Title VII." *Page v. Bolger*, 645 F.2d 227, 233 (4th Cir. 1981) (en banc); accord *Dollis v. Rubin*, 77 F.3d 777, 781–82 (5th Cir. 1995). *But see Hayes v. Shalala*, 902 F.Supp. 259, 266–67 (D.D.C.1995); cf. *Harris v. Forklift Systems, Inc.*, 510 U.S. 17, 22,

126 L.Ed.2d 295, 114 S.Ct. 367 (1993). We have never decided the issue, however, and we do not need to do so here.

Mungin never proved that in failing to receive a performance review or a raise the firm treated him differently than other associates. One year earlier, Stuart Soberman, the white bankruptcy associate in the D.C. office, failed to receive a raise, and had to pursue the same sort of recourse Mungin did. Mungin also never showed that the firm's failure to give him a substantive evaluation was unusual. Although it was the firm's formal "policy" to provide substantive reviews semiannually, *see* Katten Muchin & Zavis Firm Reference Manual § 2.5 (Aug. 1991), an "employer's failure 'to follow its own regulations and procedures, alone, may not be sufficient to support' the conclusion that its explanation for the challenged employment action is pretextual." *Fischbach v. D.C. Dep't of Corrections,* 318 U.S.App.D.C. 186, 86 F.3d 1180, 1183 (D.C.Cir. 1996) (quoting *Johnson v. Lehman,* 220 U.S.App.D.C. 100, 679 F.2d 918, 922 (D.C.Cir. 1982)). When an employer's "departure from the prescribed procedure" has become "the norm," that departure "lends no support at all to the plaintiff's inference that" the employer's departure "is a pretext." *Fischbach,* 86 F.3d at 1183. Mungin presented no evidence that the firm ever consistently abided by its policy. The uncontroverted evidence in the record is that the firm at best sporadically provided substantive evaluations. The witnesses—whether put on the stand by Mungin or Katten—uniformly testified that they never received regular or formal reviews; the reviews they did receive amounted to no more than a pat on the back. *See* Trial Transcript at 597 (testimony of defense witness Mark Thomas); *id.* at 735 (testimony of defense witness Stuart Soberman); *id.* at 799 (testimony of plaintiff's witness Charles Thomson). As against this, Mungin presented nothing. We suppose he could have offered testimony of finance and reorganization attorneys who received the sort of meaningful review Mungin claims he was denied. But Mungin directs our attention to no such testimony, and scouring the record, we find none.

The only witness even arguably in Mungin's favor was Elaine Williams. She was a young partner who switched from Katten's corporate department to the finance and reorganization department in 1990. As an associate, she was never reviewed by anyone in the finance and reorganization department, and as a partner she could not recall Chicago lawyers ever reviewing D.C. attorneys. Having presented no evidence to cast doubt on the firm's legitimate nondiscriminatory reasons, we conclude that no reasonable juror could find that the firm denied Mungin a review on the basis of his race.

C. *Work Assignments*

Mungin's next complaint is that the firm discriminated against him by providing him with unchallenging work on the basis of his race. Katten conceded that Mungin received "routine bankruptcy work," and not the more sophisticated work for which he was hired. Brief for the Appellant, Final Version, at 26. But the firm showed that after the D.C.

office's bankruptcy work dried up, causing Sherman and Soberman to depart in February 1993, it was left with no other bankruptcy lawyers in the D.C. office except Mungin, and with little bankruptcy work.

Mungin tells us that to show pretext, he presented evidence of "numerous occasions where complex bankruptcy work originated from" Katten's "D.C. office only to be assigned to other" Katten "offices around the country." Supplemental Final Brief of the Appellee at 22. No such evidence exists. Mungin only introduced proof of one assignment rerouted from D.C. to Chicago—a matter in Chicago bankruptcy court handled by a partner and associate in Chicago who already had successfully handled a major, similar matter for the same client. Trial Transcript at 600–01, 808–09. This single instance is grossly insufficient to constitute a plausible discrimination claim. In an analogous context, we recently noted that the factfinder "may not 'second-guess an employer's personnel decision absent demonstrably discriminatory motive.'" *Fischbach,* 86 F.3d at 1183 (quoting *Milton v. Weinberger,* 696 F.2d at 100). Thus, when an employer makes a hiring decision, "short of finding that the employer's stated reason was indeed a pretext ... the court must respect the employer's unfettered discretion to choose among qualified candidates." *Fischbach,* 86 F.3d at 1183. The same standard holds true when an employer decides which of several qualified employees will work on a particular assignment. Perhaps in recognition of the judicial micromanagement of business practices that would result if we ruled otherwise, other circuits have held that changes in assignments or work-related duties do not ordinarily constitute adverse employment decisions if unaccompanied by a decrease in salary or work hour changes. *See, e.g., Kocsis v. Multi–Care Mgmt.,* 97 F.3d 876, 886–87 (6th Cir. 1996); *Crady v. Liberty Nat'l Bank & Trust Co.,* 993 F.2d 132, 136 (7th Cir. 1993); *see also Williams v. Bristol–Myers Squibb Co.,* 85 F.3d 270, 274 (7th Cir. 1996). An employer has discretion to assign work to equally qualified employees so long as "the decision is not based upon unlawful criteria." *Burdine,* 450 U.S. at 259. The jury had no basis for thinking the Chicago attorneys who staffed the one matter Mungin identified were any less qualified than he, or that race played a factor in the firm's decision to staff the Chicago bankruptcy matter with attorneys in Chicago.

[handwritten margin note: "judicial micro-mgmt of biz practices"]

D.   Partnership Consideration

Next comes Mungin's claim that the firm unlawfully failed to consider him for partnership in the summer of 1993 and thus deprived him of the remunerative and other rewards partnership brings. Mungin does not argue that the firm must make every eligible associate a member of the firm's partnership. Instead, he claims that he "was unquestionably qualified to at least be considered for partnership pursuant to" Katten's "procedures," and that "he was the only eligible associate who was not formally evaluated." Supplemental Final Brief of the Appellee at 24.

Mungin introduced evidence that department heads would confer with the other partners in their departments to recommend particular associates for partnership. The recommendations then passed through several more committees—the committee comprised of all the department heads, the partnership review committee, the executive committee, and finally the board of directors—with names being screened out along the way.

The firm presented evidence to establish that Mungin's lack of sophisticated bankruptcy experience and that the disappearance of bankruptcy work for which he was hired precluded him from qualification for partnership.[3] As in the case of Mungin's 1994 pay, we need not decide whether an "interlocutory or mediate decision[ ] having no immediate effect on employment"—here the partnership nomination that would not have resulted in Mungin's becoming a partner—"falls within the direct proscriptions of ... Title VII" or, for that matter, § 1981 or the D.C. statute. *Page,* 645 F.2d at 233.

Mungin never contested the fact that associates are screened out from consideration at the first round, when the department head and/or the partners in that department decide not to nominate certain associates to the committee of department heads. It was well within Sergi's authority to decline to recommend finance and reorganization department associates for partnership. Sergi testified that no one in his department could recommend Mungin for partnership, so no one did. Trial Transcript at 971. Mungin found himself in a bind. The insurance group headed by Dombroff tried to build a bankruptcy practice of its own, but failed. Mungin was left trying to secure partnership from a department in which no one had worked extensively with him. Mungin offered absolutely nothing that would have permitted a reasonable jury to conclude that the firm discriminated against him when it failed to consider him for partnership. He tried to establish that the insurance group headed by Dombroff had certain procedures for recommending partners. But the partnership decisions were made by departments, and in Mungin's case, by the finance and reorganization department, not the insurance department. Without any evidence that this department—the one that chose not to nominate him—acted discriminatorily, Mungin failed to prove a claim.   ⁀ INTENT

E. Constructive Discharge

Mungin's last ground to support the verdict is his alleged constructive discharge. He claims the firm's offers to transfer him to New York, Chicago, or Los Angeles, were not *bona fide,* and that he deserved a more genuine offer to transfer to those offices, and more information so that he could make an informed decision whether to move. With respect to the computation of back pay, however, the district court concluded that Mungin "had no reasonable expectation of continued employment in Katten Muchin's Washington office after October 1994." *Mungin,* 941 F.Supp. at 156. The court based this decision on the following reasons:

---

3. Katten also argued that Mungin's low billable hours explained why he was not considered for partnership. The facts on this subject were disputed, and we therefore assume that the jury did not credit the firm's explanation.

In July 1994, Katten, Muchin decided to close down the insurance practice that had provided work for plaintiff and a number of other lawyers in its Washington office. Between July and November 1994, defections and terminations reduced the number of lawyers in Katten, Muchin's Washington office from 42 to 14. The firm terminated all five of the Washington office associates whose work had been supported by Mark Dombroff's insurance clients but who were left behind by Dombroff's departure.

Id. We agree with the district court that Mungin had no reasonable expectation of continued employment, but unlike the district court, we find that this prevents Mungin from having any basis for a constructive discharge claim.

Even without the district court's finding, we would conclude that there was no constructive discharge. Circuit law is clear that a "finding of constructive discharge depends on whether the employer deliberately made working conditions intolerable and drove the employee" out. *Clark v. Marsh,* 214 U.S.App.D.C. 350, 665 F.2d 1168, 1173 (D.C.Cir. 1981) (internal citations and modifications omitted). Constructive discharge thus requires a finding of discrimination and the existence of certain "aggravating factors." *Id.* at 1174; *see also Dashnaw v. Pena,* 304 U.S.App.D.C. 247, 12 F.3d 1112, 1115 (D.C.Cir. 1994). (These "aggravating factors" are those things that would force an employee to leave. *Clark,* 665 F.2d at 1174.) Having rejected all of Mungin's disparate treatment claims, we are left without any discriminatory acts upon which Mungin could rest his constructive discharge claim. And, as the district court said, Mungin ultimately was treated better than his peers, for unlike the four white associates who, after Dombroff's departure, were terminated without the opportunity to relocate, Mungin had a chance to stay with the firm. We therefore conclude that the jury had no basis for a finding of constructive discharge.

DELIBERATE

IV. CONCLUSION

Because the evidence was insufficient "for a reasonable jury to have reached the challenged verdict," the judgment of the district court is reversed and the case is remanded for entry of a judgment for the defendant.[4] *Barbour v. Merrill,* 310 U.S.App.D.C. 419, 48 F.3d 1270, 1276 (D.C.Cir. 1995); *Kolstad v. American Dental Ass'n,* 108 F.3d 1431, 1436 (D.C.Cir. 1997), reh'g en banc granted (May 28, 1997) (Nos. 96–7030 & 96–7047).

Reversed and remanded.

---

4. Our holding is not affected by this court's decision in *Aka v. Washington Hospital Center,* 116 F.3d 876, 1997 U.S.App.LEXIS 14890, No. 96–7089 (D.C.Cir. June 20, 1997), slip op. at 9–12, which dealt with the question whether plaintiffs need to show more than pretext in rebutting an employer's legitimate nondiscriminatory reasons. *Aka* held that no such extra showing is required. *See id.* In this case, however, Mungin either failed to establish a *prima facie* case or failed to offer *any* evidence showing that Katten's nondiscriminatory reasons were pretextual.

EDWARDS, CHIEF JUDGE, concurring in part and dissenting in part: I dissent from the majority's reversal of the jury finding of discrimination. Although a close question, there was sufficient evidence for a reasonable jury to have concluded that Katten Muchin intentionally discriminated against Mungin on the basis of race.

I agree, however, that there was insufficient evidence to support a finding of "constructive discharge." * * * Thus, I would reverse on the basis that no reasonable jury could have found that Mungin was constructively discharged. Because the compensatory and punitive damages were based in part on this finding, I would remand the damage awards to the District Court.

Notes and Questions

1. U.S. District Court Judge James Robertson wrote in Mungin v. Katten Muchin & Zavis, 941 F.Supp. 153, 155 (D.D.C.1996):

> Plaintiff is an African–American lawyer. He was hired in 1992, in part because of his race, to do bankruptcy work at Katten, Muchin & Zavis's Washington, D.C. office. He was well qualified for that work. Nevertheless: (i) his starting salary was less than the average salary of white associates having similar seniority and expertise; (ii) a white associate from Katten, Muchin's Chicago office was given bankruptcy work originating in the D.C. office for which plaintiff was qualified; (iii) plaintiff "fell between the cracks" when he first became eligible for partnership, and his name was not considered with those of white lawyers in the firm's evaluation process and (iv) he was again overlooked when it was time for his annual pay adjustment in 1994 and did not receive the raise given to white associates until he asked for it. Those facts were established by plaintiff's case-in-chief and were sufficient to make out a prima facie case of disparate treatment. (citation omitted)

> Katten, Muchin & Zavis introduced evidence of legitimate, nondiscriminatory reasons for what plaintiff saw as discrimination: (i) that the starting salary was set by the marketplace; (ii) that the Chicago associate had previously worked with the client and on the D.C. matter; (iii) that plaintiff was indeed "considered" for partnership, by his department head, who decided not to send his name forward; and (iv) that plaintiff's 1994 salary was adjusted promptly, and to his satisfaction, as soon as the oversight was brought to the firm's attention. The Jury evidently rejected the law firm's nondiscriminatory reasons. That rejection permits a finding of racial discrimination * * * (citations omitted) The jury's verdict was not irrational or unsupported by the record, and defendant's motion for judgment as a matter of law must be denied.

What did the jury and Judge Robertson see that the appellate court did not see? How important was witness credibility in this case? Should the appellate court have reversed the jury's finding of race discrimination?

2. How would the application of Professor Lawrence's cultural meaning test change the result in the appellate decision?

3. Was Katten Muchin & Zavis a poorly run firm, or was it poorly run with respect to Lawrence Mungin?

4. Racial facts: There were six jurors and two alternates that were allowed to deliberate and vote. Seven of those jurors were African–American. Paul M. Barrett, The Good Black: A True Story of Race in America 175–176 (1999); Judge Harry Edwards is African–American and Judge Robertson is White. *Id.* at 276. *See* http://www.dcd.uscourts.gov/robertson-bio.html for a picture and a brief biography of Judge Robertson.

5. Consider the following quote: "Roberts was a prominent criminal defense attorney in Washington, and she was also black. . . . The defense side had grown worried about pale Michael Warner standing in front of a predominantly black Washington jury, questioning Mungin's character and veracity. So [Katten Muchin] launched a search for a local black lawyer willing to lend his or her complexion to the defendants' cause." Paul Barrett, The Good Black: A True Story of Race in America 166–167 (1999). Larry Mungin's lawyer, Abbey Hairston, was African–American as well. *Id.* at 137. What do you think of Katten Muchin specifically seeking an African–American attorney for this case? Should an African–American agree to be hired under these circumstances? For a discussion of these issues *see* Margaret M. Russell, *Beyond "Sellouts" and "Race Cards": Black Attorneys and the Straitjacket of Legal Practice*, 95 Mich. L. Rev. 766, 772 (1997) ("Unlike white attorneys, who have the relatively luxurious comfort of invisibility and transparency in raising issues of race in the lawyering process, Black attorneys must always brace themselves to have *their* racial, professional, and personal identities placed in issue as well. This additional layer of scrutiny and suspicion may in turn raise for the Black attorney difficult professional and personal questions of identity, autonomy, authenticity, and loyalty.")

6. Larry Mungin's ordeal was written about by his law school roommate, Wall Street journalist Paul M. Barrett. *See* The Good Black: A True Story of Race in America (1999). For an excellent book review read Harvard law professor David B. Wilkins' book review in 112 Harv. L. Rev. 1924 (1999). *See also* Paul M. Barrett and Suzanne J. Schmitz, *When Playing by the Rules Did Not Work: The Good Black: A True Story of Race in American*, 25 S. Ill. U. L. J. 563 (2001). For additional articles discussing the *Mungin v. Katten Muchin & Zavis* decision, *see* Kenji Yoshino, *Covering* 111 Yale L. J. 769, 879–888 (2002); Clark Freshman, *Whatever Happened to Anti–Semitism? How Social Science Theories Identify Discrimination and Promote Coalitions Between "Different" Minorities*, 85 Cornell L. Rev. 313, 356–357 (2000).

7. Consider the next excerpt as you try to reconcile the two decisions in *Mungin v. Katten Muchin & Zavis*.

SECTION 2. FACTS AND FIGURES...

DAVID B. WILKINS and G. MITU GULATI

Why Are There So Few Black Lawyers in Corporate
Law Firms? An Institutional Analysis
84 Calif. L. Rev. 493, 496–498, 501–513, 554–
582, 585–587, 588–590, 613–614 (1996).

* * *

Although the number of black students graduating from law schools has increased significantly in recent decades, blacks still make up a very small minority of the lawyers working in large corporate law firms. Available data indicate that these firms hire few blacks, and that those they do hire are more likely than their white peers to leave the firms before becoming partners. Conventional explanations blame the under-representation of blacks in corporate firms on either the racism of firms and their clients, or a shortage of qualified, interested black candidates. While acknowledging that in some instances these factors may help to explain the problem, this Article looks behind them to examine institutional factors that tend to perpetuate the existing underrepresentation. Specifically, the Article shows how the ways in which large corporate firms recruit and train lawyers tend both to shield discriminatory choices between black and white candidates from any competitive disadvantage, and to discourage black law students and lawyers from investing in skills that will enable them to succeed within corporate firms. Thus, the Article argues, firms' hiring and training decisions both shape and are shaped by the strategic choices of black candidates, with the net effect of keeping all but a few blacks from being hired and succeeding in the firm setting. * * *

This Article addresses what for many is an uncomfortable reality: Despite a substantial increase in the number of black students attending law school over the last forty years, African Americans still constitute only a tiny percentage of the associates and partners working in the nation's largest corporate law firms. Given the legal profession's role in championing the principles of non-discrimination and equality of opportunity, this reality is particularly troubling. More generally, however, the fact that blacks have had little success breaking into the upper echelons of the elite bar is emblematic of a deeper and more intractable set of problems facing those interested in workplace integration.

Forty years after the Supreme Court's landmark decision in Brown v. Board of Education, society has made substantial progress toward eradicating the kind of overtly racist policies that excluded blacks from virtually every desirable sector of the economy. For many blacks, these changes have produced a dramatic growth in income and opportunity. In recent years, however, it has become painfully clear that simply dismantling America's version of apartheid has not produced economic parity between blacks and whites. Although poor blacks have benefited the least from the civil rights revolution, "high level" jobs in business and the professions have also proved surprisingly resistant to change. The fact that blacks have made so little progress in breaking into the corporate law firm elite—particularly at the partnership level—fits this larger pattern.

Commentators generally offer one of two explanations for this "glass ceiling" effect. The first, generally proffered by firms, posits a shortage of black applicants with both the qualifications and the interest necessary to succeed in the demanding world of elite corporate practice. The second, most often articulated by blacks, blames the slow progress on continued racism both inside corporate firms and among the clients upon whom these entities depend for their livelihood.

As we argue below, both the "pool problem" and continuing racism against blacks play important roles in determining the employment opportunities available to African American lawyers. Standing alone, however, each explanation begs important questions. The "pool problem" explanation begs the question of whether the existing hiring and promotion criteria utilized by elite law firms to determine who is in the pool fairly and accurately predict future productivity. The racism story, on the other hand, fails to explain why firms that discriminate by refusing to hire or promote qualified black lawyers do not suffer a competitive disadvantage when those workers are employed by their competitors.

In order to arrive at a more thorough understanding, we must move beyond this familiar dichotomy. We do so by taking a closer look than either of the standard explanations at how corporate firms structure, and are structured by, the relevant markets for labor and clients. Our interest in this neglected institutional dimension is the product of our prior work on race, professionalism, and markets. One of us is engaged in the ongoing study of the legal profession with particular attention to the experiences of black lawyers. The other is studying how particular market conditions allow firms to insulate some kinds of discriminatory decisionmaking from the disciplining effects of competition. In this Article, we seek to combine these two perspectives by offering a preliminary account of how corporate firms recruit and retain lawyers and why these practices may adversely affect the employment prospects of black lawyers. * * *

As the Article's title implies, two assumptions underlie our analysis. First, we assume that blacks are underrepresented in corporate law firms. Second, we hypothesize that this underrepresentation is due in part to the way in which the structural characteristics of corporate firms shape the strategic choices of black lawyers. * * *

One's feeling about the progress made by large corporate law firms in hiring and retaining black lawyers is likely to be influenced by the time frame one selects to examine the problem. Looking from the perspective of the corporate bar in the late 1960s, the numbers might look relatively good. Thus, when Erwin Smigel conducted his famous study of Wall Street firms in the 1960s, he reported that "in the year and a half that was spent interviewing, I heard of only three Negroes who had been hired by large law firms. Two of these were women who did not meet the client." Integration did not come much sooner in other parts of the country. Compared to this dreary portrait, recent numbers seem impressive. For example, the National Law Journal reports that as of 1995 there were more than 1,641 blacks working in the nation's 250 largest firms, of whom 351 were partners.

Viewed against the rapid expansion in corporate firms during the last twenty-five years and the dramatic growth in the number of women lawyers working in this area, the foregoing numbers are a good deal less inspiring. Thus, **although there has been a significant growth in the absolute number of black lawyers in corporate firms, the percentages remain microscopically small.** The same 1996 National Law Journal survey reveals that blacks constituted just 2.4% of the lawyers in corporate firms, and, more importantly, just over one percent of the partners. These percentages have remained relatively constant for the last 15 years. Moreover, these percentages lag behind those achieved by other legal employers. For example, minorities constitute 17.2% of the lawyers employed by federal, state, and local government agencies in the Chicago metropolitan area, as compared to the 3.6% of the attorneys in large Chicago firms. At higher levels, the comparison is even more lopsided. Minority lawyers occupy 19.5% of the supervisory positions in these government offices as compared to 1.6% of the partnerships at large Chicago firms. Indeed, although the contrast is less dramatic, law firms have also failed to equal the success achieved by some of their corporate clients. Blacks occupy 2.5% percent of all of the executive or management level jobs in private sector industries—still well below the percentage of blacks in the general population, but more than double the percentage of blacks who are partners in elite firms. In certain industries, black men and women have done significantly better. For example, in the communications industry, black men hold 3.7% of all executive, administrative, and managerial positions, while black women occupy an additional 4.9%, bringing the total black participation to 8.6%.

Standing alone, however, statistics can not answer the question of whether blacks are underrepresented in corporate firms. To reach an informed judgment on this issue, one must have some idea about the number of blacks in the pool of people who are qualified to become corporate lawyers. Once again, one's vantage point is key. For example, if the relevant pool is all law school graduates, there is little doubt that blacks are seriously underrepresented in corporate firms, particularly at the partnership level. Since the mid–1970s, blacks have consistently constituted more than six percent of the students enrolled in law school—a percentage far higher than the current African American representation among law firm associates and partners cited above, even if one adjusts for the time it took for these newcomers to enter the system.

Many would assert, however, that the population of all law school graduates is not the relevant pool. Traditionally, corporate firms have hired most of their incoming associates from elite law schools, such as Harvard and Yale. In addition, those who secure jobs in this sector often have other traditional signals of academic success, such as high grades, law review memberships, and judicial clerkships.

* * * [T]he claim that law firms have always employed a set of meritocratic hiring criteria that limit the eligible pool to elite law school graduates at the top of their class is belied by the historical record. Even if one accepts this basic definition of the relevant pool, however, blacks may still be underrepresented. Thus, Robert Nelson reported in 1988 that the percentage of minority students attending the leading law schools from which corporate firms generally recruit "is considerably higher than the proportion of minorities among even the youngest cohorts of lawyers in firms."

More importantly, whatever the traditional patterns of law firm recruitment were, the tremendous growth in the size of these institutions during the last twenty-five years has resulted in a significant expansion in the schools from which firms interview and recruit. For example, in Nelson's study of Chicago corporate firms, only 18.4% of incoming associates between 1970 and 1974 graduated from local or regional law schools. Between 1975 and 1988, that number had more than doubled to 37.5%. Today, the hiring needs of elite corporate firms are so great that their demand probably could not be satisfied if they hired every graduate in the top half of the class from the nation's top twenty law schools. A definition of the pool that includes only those with "traditional" credentials, therefore, understates the relevant employment market.

Finally, even if we could accurately identify the criteria that law firms actually employ in choosing among prospective applicants, these criteria would only define the pool of qualified applicants (as opposed to the pool of applicants with a realistic chance of being selected) to the extent that there is a relatively tight correlation between these signals and the skills that are necessary to perform the job proficiently. It is precisely this linkage, however, that many critics bitterly attack. * * * As a result, we assume that the pool of "qualified" applicants is larger than current hiring practices would lead one to believe, and, correspondingly, that blacks are in fact underrepresented. * * *

One can usefully divide the **competing explanations** for black underrepresentation in corporate firms into three categories: (1) that blacks and whites have differential abilities; (2) that blacks are less interested in corporate work; and (3) pervasive racism on the part of individuals within the firms or of the firms themselves. Although each of these theories advances our understanding of the variation we see between the success rates of blacks and whites in these institutions, each begs important questions that must be answered if one is to have a full explanation of this phenomenon. The institutional perspective we advocate helps to fill in these crucial gaps. It also responds to the concerns of those scholars and policy makers who are skeptical that race continues to be a significant obstacle for black Americans, and who doubt the efficacy of group-based policies to promote workplace integration.

Those who emphasize the importance of the traditional credentials for being hired by a corporate law firm often implicitly rely on empirical assumptions about the differential abilities of black and white applicants. These arguments come in two quite different forms. The first claims that blacks are inherently inferior to whites in terms of one or more attributes, for example intelligence, necessary for success in a corporate firm. The second approach rejects the claim that blacks are fundamentally inferior to whites (genetically or otherwise), but asserts that they nevertheless have acquired less of the human capital assets (that is, education, work skills, etc.) that it takes to succeed in this environment than their white peers.

Like most others of good will, we reject the first of these arguments. Although a complete statement of the fallacy of this position is beyond the scope of this Article, as others have demonstrated in painstaking detail, the argument for innate or even deeply embedded racial differences in intelligence or any other relevant quality is based on either pseudo-science or quasi-racist premises. As we indicate below, however, the persistent myth of black intellectual inferiority continues to play an important role in shaping both the opportunities available to and the choices made by black lawyers.

* * * [T]here is little reliable information on the relative attributes and performance of black and white law students and lawyers. Nevertheless, there is reason to suspect that black law school graduates may on average have fewer of the traditional markers of academic success than their white counterparts. Once again, it remains an open question whether these differences in credentials reflect actual differences in human capital that are likely to affect performance. But even assuming that there is a significant correlation, we still need to know why blacks invest less in their own development. We posit that the answer to this question is likely to depend upon the opportunities black lawyers face and the likelihood that investing in certain kinds of human capital will significantly improve those opportunities. In the world that we study, this opportunity calculus will be filtered through the institutional practices of large law firms. Understanding these practices is therefore a necessary component of any theory that seeks to explain racial differences in employment on the basis of a non-biological theory of differential ability.

This explanation offers an alternative account of why blacks do not invest in succeeding at corporate law firms, one based in preferences rather than incentives. According to this line of argument, many black students are uninterested in the work done by corporate law firms. Consequently, they are less likely to apply to these institutions and, if they do, leave after a relatively short time. Once again, there are reasons to suspect that this factor plays a contributing role. Black lawyers are disproportionately concentrated in the government and the not-for-profit sector. In addition, given the historical connection between the black bar and the struggle for racial justice, many blacks come to law school intending to use their new skills to advance the interests of the African American community. Corporate law firms are not the obvious arena in which to pursue that goal.

Nevertheless, the claim that blacks are uninterested in corporate law firms is not supported by the available data. In their study of the first job choices of New York University and University of Michigan graduates, Kornhauser and Revesz discovered that after adjusting for grades, loans, law school activities, and even stated preferences, blacks were more likely to take jobs at corporate law firms than their white counterparts. If anything, blacks appear to be more interested in starting work at a corporate firm than whites.

Moreover, as Vicki Schultz has observed, one should be skeptical of claims that a particular group is underrepresented because of their lack of interest—especially where the group has previously faced express discriminatory barriers to entry and the job in question is both prestigious and high paying. As Schultz demonstrates, firms can construct their use of labor in ways that will discourage applicants from certain groups from seeking these positions. An understanding of these institutional practices is therefore a necessary precondition to explaining why blacks "choose" careers other than corporate law practice.

To say that firms "construct" their use of labor in a manner that disadvantages blacks sounds as if this conduct is merely racism in a more sophisticated form. Critics of the slow progress towards integration in various sectors of the economy frequently make precisely this charge. Although many of these critics do not equate "institutional racism" with the intentional racism of individuals, the two are nevertheless often closely intertwined. Thus, scholars who discuss institutional racism generally assert that those who design and run institutions either fail to police discriminatory conduct by their subordinates and/or adopt facially neutral practices with at least the implicit knowledge (if not the express intent) that these practices will disadvantage blacks.

Undoubtedly, there is merit in the institutional racism story. As study after study demonstrates, there are still a substantial number of whites who hold (consciously or unconsciously) discriminatory and/or stereotypical views about blacks. Scholars have put forward a plethora of theories to explain this continuing phenomenon, including, inter alia, that certain whites have an exogenous "taste" for discrimination, that whites employ biased stereotypes when evaluating blacks and whites, that whites judge individual blacks on the basis of the average statistical achievements of blacks as a group, that the preferences of customers and/or workplace culture impose additional costs on firms that hire and promote black workers, and that individual whites reward actions that reinforce the dominant status of whites as a group. Regardless of the cause, however, unless we have reason to believe that corporate law firms are immune to attitudes and beliefs prevalent in the rest of society, it is likely that a non-trivial number of whites working in these institutions hold some of these views. As a result, one does not have to believe that overt racism is widespread in elite firms to conclude that these often subtle predispositions are sufficient to provide the grist for the dynamic described by institutional racism theories. Moreover, to the extent that some of the hiring and promotion policies followed by certain corporate firms bear little or no relation to the substantive qualifications of performing the job of a corporate lawyer, one can legitimately ask whether these practices actually serve a more invidious purpose.

Nevertheless, the institutional racism story, at least in the relatively straightforward terms in which it is usually presented, is at best incomplete. As a preliminary matter, this account is in tension with the widely accepted fact that overt racist attitudes are on the decline, particularly among highly educated and economically successful whites. Nor does it explain why many firms have adopted voluntary affirmative action programs or taken other steps to increase the number of black lawyers.

More fundamentally, the institutional racism story does not explain why firms neither change institutional practices in the face of evidence that they disproportionately burden blacks. Nor, in a world without de jure barriers to hiring blacks, can these theories explain why firms do not suffer a significant competitive disadvantage as a result of their failure to utilize black workers who, although not meeting the "discriminatory" traditional criteria, are nevertheless fully competent to perform the job. In order to answer these questions, one must construct a richer account of the actual structure and operation of corporate law firms than the ones generally offered by institutional racism theorists. As we explain below, continuing racism—as well as a host of other attitudes, dispositions, and beliefs that tend to make it more difficult for whites and blacks to live and work together as equals—is an important component of this account. These individual attitudes, however, are at least in part the product of the manner in which firms hire, train, and monitor their employees. It is in the interplay between these structual [sic] factors and background assumptions about race and merit, we assert, that one must look for the answer to the question posed in this Article.

Notwithstanding the evidence cited in the preceding Section, many academics and policymakers are skeptical about claims that race continues to play a significant role in impeding the progress of black Americans. Building on the indisputable evidence that outright racial prejudice is on the wane, these skeptics are inclined to attribute disparities between blacks and whites to a lack of effort on the part of blacks. As a result, those who hold these views tend to oppose public and private efforts to redress racial imbalance on the grounds that these initiatives are both unnecessary, since blacks could solve their own problems by working harder to conform to traditional American values, and costly, because they will inevitably lower standards in a manner that decreases productivity and increases costs.

The institutional analysis we propose speaks directly to these concerns. * * * [W]e begin by accepting two central premises generally associated with conservative thought: that the practices and policies of elite corporate firms are a rational response to the market conditions within which these firms compete for labor and clients, and that individuals within firms (and those considering joining them) respond rationally to the incentives created by these institutional structures. We hope to demonstrate, however, that these institutional structures are less directly connected to productivity than conservatives seem to believe, and that they create incentives for blacks that are contrary to the values and objectives that conservatives wish to further. Such a showing, we believe, should help to move the debate over black participation in elite sectors of the economy away from the current impass created by conclusory charges about whether racism is or is not widespread in contemporary American society. In order to do so, however, we must temporarily bracket the most contentious issue in this debate—affirmative action.

[handwritten margin notes: INSTITUTIONAL / INDIVIDUAL / "these institutional structures... create incentives for blacks that are contrary to the values and objectives that conservatives wish to further."]

Any examination of black underrepresentation in corporate firms must inevitably confront the issue of affirmative action. This is true for two reasons. First, the level of affirmative action in law school admissions, law review memberships, firm hiring, and other relevant decisions affects the definition of the pool of qualified applicants. Second, judgments about this first issue are likely to be affected by normative and factual claims about the fairness and/or efficacy of various affirmative action policies.

Judgements about both of these issues have become increasingly controversial. As to the first, perceptions vary widely about the degree to which schools, organizations, firms, and other relevant decision makers actually give some form of preference to black applicants, with some claiming that such preferences are pervasive while others assert that affirmative efforts to help blacks are much more apparent than real. Indeed, there is very little consensus on what constitutes "affirmative action" or whether policies that might fall under this rubric are properly considered as a "preference" for black applicants as opposed to a mechanism for giving blacks the same "preferences" as whites. This last debate merely underscores the deep divisions in the American public over whether affirmative action policies are a proper response to past and/or present racism or an illegitimate racial spoils system that inevitably ends up harming everyone including its intended beneficiaries.

[handwritten margin notes: like this; this reflects my argument; in-class discussion re: current v. historical racism]

Given this construction the debate is irresolvable. There is very little reliable data on the actual extent of affirmative action (however defined) in corporate firms. Moreover, so long as this empirical question is tied to background assumptions about the extent to which blacks are disproportionately disadvantaged (or whites are unfairly advantaged) by other aspects of the system, the information that does exist is unlikely to sway those who hold different normative presuppositions.

* * *

b/c social markers v. abilities

"human capital strategies"?

In the absence of countervailing policies, we predict that blacks will be disadvantaged by recruiting practices * * *. First, since firms have little incentive to investigate the actual quality of their potential employees, average blacks are less likely to be hired than average whites. Second, because black applicants are aware of their reduced employment prospects, they have an incentive to adopt human capital strategies that, on average, decrease their overall prospects for success. The following examination of how blacks have fared in the recruiting process supports both predictions.

The fact that firms rely on a few objective signals to identify qualified applicants at the visible stage and reserve the right to go behind these credentials to make judgments about personality and fit at the invisible stage doubly disadvantages black applicants. As others have documented, by relying on sorting devices such as law school status, grades, and law review membership, firms systematically exclude the majority of black applicants, who do not have these standard signals. Thus, although blacks may be more likely to attend higher status law schools than whites, the schools with the largest black populations are not ones from which large firms typically recruit. Even black students with superstar credentials from lower status schools have little or no chance of being hired by a large firm. Those blacks who do attend elite schools face recognized barriers (e.g., poor primary and secondary school education, diminished expectations, hostile environments, and part-time work) to performing well in the classroom or in extra-curricular activities such as law review. Given these added pressures, it is plausible, as both conservative critics of affirmative action in elite schools and supporters of historically black schools frequently assert, that some black students who are currently admitted to elite schools would be more successful (both academically and personally) if they did not attend these academic institutions. However, given the nearly dispositive role that the status of an applicant's law school plays in the recruiting process, black students who want to have the option of working at an elite firm have little incentive to choose this option. Those who have problems at elite institutions, however, risk being branded as unacceptable by prospective employers.

Indeed, to the extent that firms make hiring decisions based on signals such as grade point averages, as opposed to the substantive content of the courses a student has taken or other indicia of the skills that the candidate has acquired in law school, black applicants have an incentive to structure their education so as to maximize the former at the expense of the latter. For example, it is widely believed that certain advanced corporate courses, such as corporate tax, commercial transactions, and securities regulation, are among the most difficult in the law school curriculum, particularly for students who have little or no prior background (academic or otherwise) in these areas. If this is true, and if black students are less likely to have the kind of background knowledge that increases their chance of doing well in these subjects, then they will have an incentive to avoid these difficult, but potentially useful, courses in favor of classes where they stand a better chance of getting a good grade.

— It is my impression that most students engage in this calculus

At the same time, the emphasis on /personality and fit| at the invisible stage can disadvantage black applicants with traditional signals. Like the general population from which they come, law firm interviewers hold a variety of conscious and unconscious stereotypes about black law students. Although incidents such as the 1989 debacle involving a partner from Chicago's Baker & McKenzie, who demanded to know a black female applicant's high school grade point average and how she would react to being called a "black bitch" or "nigger" are undoubtedly rare, they underscore the fact that outright prejudice against blacks still exists at elite firms. Sexual harassment and other forms of overt discrimination against women mean that black women face a double burden. Such outright prejudice is no longer condoned and, when detected, is sanctioned. The subtler forms of bias or preferencing, however, are more pervasive and difficult to pin down.

For example, a consistent line of empirical research demonstrates that when whites evaluate blacks, they frequently attribute negative acts "to personal disposition, while positive acts are discounted as the product of luck or special circumstances." Empirical and anecdotal accounts of the experiences of black and white applicants in the interviewing process confirm that this phenomenon negatively affects employment opportunities for black lawyers. Pervasive myths about black intellectual inferiority combined with lower average levels of achievement in areas such as grades and test scores tend to make white interviewers question the credentials of blacks more than those of whites. In addition, interviewers generally expect to feel less comfortable when interviewing blacks. Similarly, as we note above, interviewers frequently tend to believe that blacks are "uninterested" in corporate practice. Black women are particularly vulnerable to this "lack of interest" stereotype in light of the persistent belief that women place family responsibilities above professional commitments.

Given that firms collect little information about an applicant's actual skills, it is not surprising that interviewers are affected by such stereotypes. Since race is costless to observe, it provides a convenient mechanism, much like "personality" and "fit," for sorting applicants. The fact that it does not correlate to the ability to practice law is irrelevant from the point of view of firm profits, so long as the only consequence of error is that average whites are hired in the place of average blacks.

"costless"?

Moreover, blacks on average have less access to influential contacts and other informal networks that allow some other candidates to bypass the formal screening requirements. Consider the experiences of two students at the University of Virginia law school reported in a recent story in the American Lawyer. Both students—Jay, a white male and Jennifer, a black female—had grades in the B-minus/C range. As a result, although both have strong personal qualities and extra-curricular activities, neither was able to secure an interview with a large firm in their respective cities of choice (Richmond for Jay, Atlanta for Jennifer) through the normal UVA process. Nevertheless, by the end of the story, Jay is headed for three promising interviews with Richmond firms while Jennifer has no such prospects. Why? Because Jay was able to call a friend "with considerable influence in Richmond." Jennifer had no similar connections.

This story also highlights another way in which the interplay between formal and informal criteria disadvantages blacks. Although her grades were uninspiring, Jennifer was a member of the UVA law review and had worked for two small firms during prior summers, including one in Atlanta. Law review membership and prior work experience are the kind of easily observable signals upon which firms generally rely, but Jennifer appears to be getting less mileage out of these signals than one might expect. Although there may be many explanations for this result, one possible explanation is that even traditional signals such as good grades and law review membership count less for blacks than they do for whites.

Even black superstars can fall victim to this phenomenon. A firm does suffer an efficiency loss if it consistently fails to hire blacks who fall into the superstar category. Nevertheless, the bias against average blacks also makes it more difficult for black superstars to be regarded as such. Because employers know that blacks have an incentive to signal themselves as superstars when they are in fact average, and that this strategy (if successful) will be difficult to detect, firms have an incentive to discount indicia of accomplishment as false positives. Since hiring partners know that criteria such as grades are fuzzy, lawyers who are predisposed to believe that blacks are less likely to be superstars than whites can justify looking beyond the usual signals to reach a more subjective evaluation of the candidate's quality. Anecdotal evidence suggests that this occurs with some frequency. At a minimum, this possibility must be counted against the potential, documented by Stephen Carter, for whites, because of their diminished expectations of black performance to accord superstar status to average blacks because they are the "best black" in the group.

Together, the fact that firms prefer average whites over average blacks and the corresponding tendency for these employers to discount the credentials of blacks who signal themselves to be superstars make it harder for blacks to be hired by elite law firms. This state of affairs is self-perpetuating, since firms that substitute average whites for average blacks suffer no competitive disadvantage. Once we take into account the additional fact that the number of black lawyers already working in a particular firm is positively correlated with that firm's likelihood of hiring additional black attorneys, the chances of moving beyond this equilibrium seem daunting.

Ironically, these structural features of the recruiting process also lead us to predict that the blacks who are hired will tend, on average, to be clustered in the superstar range. In light of the rampant discrimination during the "golden age," it is not surprising that the few black lawyers who were hired during this period had superstar qualifications. We suspect, however, that something similar may be continuing today.

In order to investigate this proposition, we asked 250 elite firms to tell us the law school attended by each member of their most recent entering class of associates and to indicate which of these lawyers is black. The results of this survey, although far from conclusive, suggest that the blacks who are hired by elite firms tend to come from the superstar end of the distribution in terms of the key variable of law school status. The percentage of black associates identified by this survey who were graduates from elite schools is only 5% higher than the percentage for non-black associates. However, the black associates tend to come from schools at the top of the elite range. Thus, graduates from Harvard Law School constituted 24% of all of the blacks in our law firm survey. Even if we limit the universe of qualified African–American applicants to the graduates of the schools from which the firms in our survey actually hired during the year in question, this percentage is nearly four times greater than the percentage of black Harvard graduates in the available pool.

The numbers are even more striking in New York and Washington, the two cities with the largest concentration of elite firms. In New York, Harvard graduates constitute 15.6% of the total number of black associates hired. However, when we add black graduates from Columbia and New York University, the percentage rises to 51.1. Similarly, in Washington, D.C., black Harvard graduates account for 32% of the total blacks hired. When we include black graduates from Georgetown, these two schools account for 52% of the total.

Admittedly, there are problems with this data, as well as alternative hypotheses that can also explain these results. Only one-third of the firms responded to our survey (although the response rates in New York and Washington, D.C. were 51% and 50% respectively). In addition, the number of blacks in the survey is small, and the results are only for one year. Moreover, because of affirmative action in law school admissions, it is possible that Harvard and other similar schools have a disproportionate share of the talented black students. Although this would still mean that firms tend to hire blacks from the superstar end of the distribution, it would weaken the corresponding implication that the black graduates from other elite schools that are less well represented are being unfairly overlooked in favor of white graduates from those same institutions. For affirmative action in law school admissions to account for these differentials, however, the gap between the quality of black students from, for example, Harvard and the University of Michigan or the University of Pennsylvania (two elite schools that contributed only two black associates apiece to our sample), must be substantially larger than that between white students from these same institutions. So far as we know, there is no evidence to support the existence of a gap of this magnitude.

Moreover, to the extent that these considerations overstate the importance of top echelon schools like Harvard in our sample, there are other forces that seem likely to pull in the opposite direction. For example, a comparison between the percentage of black associates in our sample and the latest information about blacks in corporate firms suggests that the firms that chose to respond to our survey have more blacks than average. In addition, given recent initiatives to increase minority hiring undertaken by bar associations around the country (including those in New York and Washington, D.C.), it seems likely that firms responding to our survey have engaged in more affirmative action in hiring this class of incoming associates than in previous years. Both of these factors seem likely to increase the chances that average blacks, that is, those without superstar credentials like attending an elite law school, would make it into our sample.

Indeed, when we look back to a period when by all accounts there was less affirmative action than there is today, we find evidence that going to an elite law school was even more important for blacks. * * * The results [of our data] suggest that the current generation of black partners are much more likely to have graduated from an elite law school then their white counterparts. Thus, 77% of all black partners attended one of the eleven elite law schools where corporate law firms have traditionally done most of their recruiting. In contrast, the combined percentage of elite graduates at five of the nation's most elite firms is 70%, with firms such as Atlanta's Kirkpatrick and Cody drawing less than half of their partners from these schools. When we narrow our focus to graduates from Harvard and Yale, the two schools generally considered to be at the top of the status hierarchy, the results are even more dramatic. Forty-seven percent of the black partners at elite firms attended Harvard or Yale, a percentage only surpassed by Boston's Ropes & Gray. None of the other firms has more than 41% of its partners from these two institutions, and the average for the five firms is only 33%. More importantly, if we remove graduates of Howard Law School from the percentage of black partners from non-elite schools, a reasonable supposition in light of the unique position that Howard holds for black lawyers, the likelihood of a black partner attending a non-elite school is approximately a third less than that for the general population of partners at the sampled firms.

Once again, this comparison is not definitive. To highlight the most obvious complication, we do not know whether the population of black partners is representative of the other blacks who might have been hired at the same time but who did not win the tournament. Nevertheless, the fact that so many of the current generation of black partners attended elite schools at a time when law school affirmative action policies were less entrenched then they are today suggests that the similar effects we observed in our survey of associates reflect a tendency for the black associates who are hired by elite firms to come disproportionately from the superstar end of the distribution. Anecdotal descriptions of the recruiting process by some black partners provide further support for this assessment. If this is correct, however, it brings up a further paradox: if black associates are disproportionately clustered in the superstar range, why are there so few black partners? This brings us the question of retention.

Virtually all the blacks who start at a given elite law firm leave before becoming partner. In this Section, we examine how the institutional characteristics of elite firms—high salaries, pyramiding, and tracking—affect a black associate's partnership prospects. Unlike others who have addressed this issue, however, we concentrate on more than partnership rates. To understand why there are so few black partners, one must investigate what happens both before and after the partnership decision—and what opportunities are available for those who leave.

Elite firms make few formal distinctions among entering associates. The implication is that associates in a class are part of a unified group operating on a level playing field. * * * Although firms maintain few formal distinctions, the inevitable scarcity of training opportunities pushes associates along informal, but nevertheless identifiable, career paths almost from the moment they arrive. The few associates who get on the training track will receive interesting work, meaningful training, supervision, and supportive mentors. The others will end up as flatliners drowning in a sea of routine paperwork.

Empirical and anecdotal reports about the practices of elite law firms support this account. From the "golden age" forward, associates have been lured to join big firms by the promise of excellent training. For the reasons outlined above, these promises are difficult to keep. As a result, "associates voice strong concerns about the lack of on-the-job training, delegation, supervision, and feedback."

These complaints, although pervasive, are not uniform even among associates at a single firm. Instead, some associates report that they receive valuable training opportunities while others do not. In addition, once an associate acquires a reputation as being well-trained, she will continue to receive training in the form of demanding work. Although managing partners understandably continue to deny that firms track incoming associates, more detached observers, as well as partners in more candid moments, report the contrary.

An associate's perception about which track she is on will have a substantial impact on how long she decides to stay with the firm. Associates know that firms look for two things when they select partners: legal ability and marketing potential. An associate who has not been trained cannot credibly signal either of these capacities. Training is the Royal Jelly that enables associates to develop the job-related skills partners expect to see in those who will be elevated to their rank. Similarly, although an associate may have business contacts independent of the firm, the most likely way for an associate to demonstrate her rainmaking skills is through contact with the firm's existing clients. Such contact is one of the commodities that training can help an associate accrue.

The effect on lateral movement is equally plain. The implicit promise that big firm associates are well trained lies at the heart of their marketability. Associates therefore work to avoid sending any signal that might tend to refute this presumption. Being fired is, of course, the ultimate negative signal, but failing to receive the same training opportunities as one's peers may also adversely affect one's lateral mobility. The fact that others are getting better work experience will not only lead an associate to doubt her own partnership chances, but may also lead her to believe that she will have less success in signaling to other potential employers that she is well-trained. Whether or not these fears are justified, they are likely to increase the pressure to look for another job.

Associates who do not find themselves on the training track have three options: (i) they can leave immediately; (ii) they can attempt to move themselves onto the training track; or (iii) they can stay at the firm but invest their time and energy in developing non-firm-specific skills that will help them get another job. Which of these strategies a given associate will pursue depends upon both the likelihood that she can change her reputation within the firm and her prospects in the external employment market. We believe that African–American associates face important barriers on both of these fronts. We therefore turn our attention to the particular experiences of black lawyers.

Black associates face three significant barriers to getting on the training track. First, they are less likely than whites to find mentors who will give them challenging work and provide them with advice and counseling about how to succeed at the firm. Second, they face higher costs from making mistakes than their white peers. Third, their future employment prospects with other elite firms diminish more rapidly than those of similarly situated associates.

In order to get on the training track, an associate has to have mentors among the firm's partners or senior associates who can provide the Royal Jelly of good training. Blacks consistently report that they have difficulty in forming these supportive relationships. For example, in our survey of black Harvard Law School graduates, less than 40% of those surveyed, and only 24% of the pre–1986 graduates, stated that a partner had taken interest in their work or their career. Sixty-eight percent of those who did not find a mentor, including 79% of the post–1986 graduates, stated that this was a significant factor in their decision to leave the firm. Although we do not have comparable data on white associates, our hypothesis that blacks have an especially difficult time finding mentors is consistent with the views of others who have examined the issue. There is reason to believe that the situation is even bleaker for black women, who confront gender as well as racial barriers to forming meaningful mentoring relationships.

A number of factors contribute to this problem. Chief among them is the bias that potential mentors have for proteges who remind them of themselves. Studies of cross-racial and cross-gender mentoring relationships in the workplace repeatedly demonstrate that white men feel more comfortable in working relationships with other white men. Anecdotal evidence suggests that white partners in law firms are no different. This natural affinity makes it difficult for blacks to form supportive mentoring relationships.

These problems are magnified in a low-monitoring environment. Because partners have little information about a new associate's actual skills, the decision about who is a superstar worthy of training will be made as an initial matter in the same way as it is done at the recruiting stage—based on a few easily observable signals such as law school status, academic honors, and grades. Indeed, since partners not on the recruiting committee will probably not have met the great majority of incoming associates (nor seen their credentials) decisions about which of these lawyers are superstars will be even more loosely correlated with these signals than typical hiring decisions. Under these circumstances, background prejudices and preconceptions can lead white partners to believe that black associates are more likely to be average or perhaps even unacceptable.

As indicated above, blacks may also suffer from a general perception that they are "less interested" in corporate work than other lawyers. This sentiment may be reinforced by the fact that black associates appear to be more likely than their white peers to do more than the average amount of pro bono work, to hold skeptical views about the social utility of some of the goals of their corporate clients, and to leave corporate practice for jobs in the public sector. As with recruiting, black women face an additional hurdle, since partners frequently believe that family responsibilities will inevitably reduce the number of hours these associates are willing to commit to the firm. The fact that these generalizations say almost nothing about any individual black associate's level of interest or commitment to the firm is unlikely to dissuade partners from relying on such gross statistical correlations when deciding whom to mentor.

Finally, black associates will have difficulty getting onto the training track precisely because the generation of black associates before them did not. Partners have less incentive to invest scarce training resources in associates who they think are unlikely to be at the firm long enough for them to recoup their investment. Not only are black associates less likely to make partner, but their average tenure may also be shorter than that of their white peers. As a result, black associates are doubly penalized for the firm's failure to retain and promote black lawyers.

Sociologists contend that when a group's representation in the workforce is small, individual members face increased pressures to perform and conform. Although these pressures can work to the "token's" advantage, the dominant tendency is for them to magnify the cost of making mistakes. Reports by black associates lend credence to this hypothesis.

Black associates frequently state that they are judged more harshly when they make mistakes than their white contemporaries. For example, over 40% of our survey respondents reported that they were criticized more than white associates for making similar mistakes. Even if these respondents are mistaken about this, the fact that they believe it to be true may induce some black associates to embark on the counterproductive career strategies we describe below. There is reason to suspect, however, that these reports are not simply a product of the black associates' collective imagination. A low-monitoring environment amplifies negative signals. For black associates the problem is exacerbated by expectations. If, for the reasons outlined above, partners expect black associates to be average or unacceptable, then any mistake will be seen as confirming this initial assessment. Mistakes by whites, on the other hand, are more likely to be dismissed as "aberrational" or "growing pains," since these associates are presumed competent in the absence of conclusive evidence to the contrary.

Finally, small numbers also increase the probability that group members will be tied together in the minds of members of the dominant group. To the extent that white partners think (consciously or unconsciously) that "we had a [black] once and he didn't work out," the chances of any other black lawyer having a successful career at the firm are correspondingly reduced.

Collectively, these aspects of tokenism encourage black associates to think about outside job possibilities. What they see when they examine the lateral job market, however, is likely to make them even more concerned about their future.

The pyramid structure of the elite law firm ensures that the vast majority of associates leave without becoming partners. When they leave, however, depends in part on their perceptions about the lateral market. Lawyers wishing to move laterally face conflicting incentives. On one hand, the longer they stay, the more they can claim to have accumulated valuable skills. On the other, the closer they are to partnership, the greater the danger that potential employers may presume that they are leaving because they are not "good enough" to make partner.

For black associates, the decision is less complex but more draconian. It is less complex because blacks may not receive the beneficial presumption that comes from length of service. Length of service is only positively correlated with skill if an associate has been trained. Since making quality judgments is difficult in the lateral market, firms are likely to rely on statistical approximations. To the extent that firms are aware of the barriers faced by black associates regarding getting on the training track, employers looking for lateral hires may be less likely to believe that a black lawyer has been well trained (even if he has been). Given the large number of lateral applicants, a firm that hires fewer average black laterals will not suffer a competitive disadvantage. As a result, a black lawyer will expect more difficulty in moving laterally to another large law firm than will his white counterparts.

Our survey of black Harvard graduates provides some support for this conclusion. Only 15% of the black lawyers who had left their first elite firm went to another one. Instead, the majority went into either government (33%), corporate legal departments (20%), or small non-elite firms (17%). This distribution appears to be significantly different from that for whites.

Given this distribution, we hypothesize that the optimal time for black associates to leave firms is earlier than that for white associates because whites do not face the general market presumption that they have not been trained. Within the first few years, the common perception is that no one has received much training, so blacks suffer no particular disadvantage. Indeed, the only significant new signal potential lateral employers have to look at is the fact that the associate was hired by his first firm and has been at least minimally competent. (If a black associate were not minimally competent, he would have been fired.) This additional credential, may be even more valuable for blacks, since the second firm can rely on the first firm to screen out those blacks who are in the unacceptable range.

Blacks, therefore, have an incentive to make decisions about moving laterally even more quickly than whites. This incentive in turn affects the choices these associates make while at the firm. On average, the strategies black lawyers are likely to pursue will decrease their chances of succeeding at the firm even further.

Black associates find themselves in a double bind. On one hand, they understand that they are less likely to get on the firm's training track. On the other, they face diminishing opportunities in the lateral job market the longer they stay at the firm. This combination produces a level of fear and anxiety about the future that is, even from the firm's perspective, sub-optimally high. * * * [E]lite firms rely on the fear of job loss or diminished partnership prospects as a means of inducing associates to work hard at low monitoring costs. Like all motivational tools, however, fear has its own rate of diminishing marginal utility. When fear levels are sub-optimally low (in a low monitoring world), associates and partners have an incentive to shirk. When levels are sub-optimally high, lawyers have an incentive to adopt career strategies that reduce their benefit to the firm.

For the forgoing reasons, black associates are especially vulnerable to these pressures. As a result, they have strong incentives to choose career strategies that either minimize the danger of sending a negative signal or, conversely, maximize their opportunity for being regarded as superstars. Both strategies, however, can end up diminishing a black associate's long term chances for success at the firm.

An associate wishing to reduce the chance of making mistakes can either steer clear of demanding assignments (because of either the difficulty of the work or the level or intensity of the scrutiny likely to be given by the partner) or take fewer risks in completing the work. There is some evidence to suggest that black associates disproportionately pursue both of these strategies.

Considering the choice of specialty, many observers believe that corporate practice in general (as opposed to litigation), and related specialties such as tax, securities, and banking in particular, require higher levels of substantive legal knowledge and technical skill than other fields of practice. Moreover, these areas (particularly specialties such as tax) tend to have lower associate-to-partner ratios. Consequently, associates in these areas are more closely supervised, thereby increasing the odds that mistakes will be detected.

Blacks appear to be underrepresented in these high-level corporate areas. In our survey of Harvard black alumni, only 32% (24% of the pre–1986 graduates) worked in corporate practice. Similarly, our review of the classes of 1981–1982 and 1987–1988 revealed a similar pattern: those in corporate practice accounted for 25% and 27% of the total number who were in elite firms. Of those who were in corporate practice, few worked in specialty departments such as tax. The distribution of black partners confirms this trend. Only 14% of black partners work in general corporate practice, and less than 11% specialize in technical fields such as banking (6%), bankruptcy (2%), and tax (1%).

Undoubtedly, there are many reasons why blacks do not go into these areas, ranging from a genuine lack of interest to the very real possibility that many black associates believe that specializing in other areas (particularly litigation) will improve their chances in the lateral job market. Nevertheless, just as the draconian consequences of sending a negative signal during the recruiting process can lead black students to avoid advanced corporate courses in law school, the problems associated with being a token in a particularly difficult area of practice is likely to produce a similar pattern of avoidance when blacks join firms.

Anecdotal evidence also suggests that black associates may, on average, be overly cautious when performing their work. Thus, those who study law firm interactions report that many black associates tend to speak less in meetings (particularly with clients), ask more clarifying questions when receiving work, are more likely to check (and recheck) assignments before handing them in, are more reluctant to disagree with partners or express criticism of their peers, and construe their assignments more narrowly than their white peers.

From a black associate's perspective, both of these risk-averse strategies are rational responses to his environment. Given the inherent subjectivity of "good judgment," a risky action can be interpreted as either a sign of innovativeness and independence or a mark of stupidity and an inability to follow instructions. Since black associates have reason to fear that they are more likely to be branded with the negative description and that this characterization will be more difficult to shake, it is not surprising that they tend to be overly cautious in their choices.

Nevertheless, both of these risk-averse strategies reduce the gains (in terms of retention and promotion) that black associates can expect to receive from their work. Successfully completing "difficult" work assignments is the best way for an associate to signal her quality and therefore to demonstrate that she is worthy of training. Since partners are looking for associates who can work effectively with relatively little supervision, traits such as initiative, creativity, speed, and confidence are highly valued. The more risk-averse one is, however, the more difficult it is to signal that one has these qualities.

At the opposite extreme, a black associate may seek out demanding assignments in order to overcome the presumption that she is "only" average—or worse. For example, a black lawyer might volunteer to work with a particularly demanding partner or take on a large number of assignments. To the extent that a black associate successfully completes these projects, she has a better chance of signaling that she is a superstar and therefore worthy of training. The risks, however, are also high. If the project is particularly difficult or the partner especially demanding, the black associate who is in fact "average" has a greater chance of failing—and failing big. Similarly, the high effort strategy of taking on a large number of assignments can also fail if the projects suddenly become due at once.

Our research suggests that a large number of black associates are engaged, albeit unwittingly, in a particular variant of this strategy. Black associates are disproportionately concentrated in litigation departments. For example, 45% of the respondents to our survey, including 52% of the pre–1986 graduates, specialize in litigation. Our examination of the classes of 1981–1982 and 1987–1988 produced comparable numbers (50% and 39%, respectively). These data are consistent with the results of other studies. * * * Just as with the shortage of blacks in high-level corporate areas of practice, many factors contribute to this over-concentration. One factor that is frequently overlooked, however, is that going into litigation is a plausible strategy for maximizing a black lawyer's career prospects. As an initial matter, litigation has been the most successful avenue to partnership for black lawyers. Fifty-six percent of the black partners at elite firms specialize in this area. Moreover, the fact that law schools tend to concentrate on teaching litigation related skills may make black lawyers feel better prepared to become litigators. To the extent that a black student seeks to acquire additional signals to overcome the presumption against average blacks, the ones most readily available (such as moot court, clerkships, and clinical placements) also tend to be connected to litigation. Finally, black associates might plausibly believe that litigation practice provides good opportunities for them to demonstrate their talents. Even the largest firms generally have a range of cases in their litigation departments, including some number of smaller cases that are being handled pro bono or at reduced rates as favors for important clients. Doing something visible in one of these cases might seem like a good way to get noticed.

In addition to these benefits to an associate's career in the firm, litigation may also appear to be the best way for black lawyers to develop marketable skills. Although many kinds of corporate work are handled exclusively by elite firms, litigators are needed in many different set-tings, including government, small firms, solo practice, and in-house legal departments. As we reported earlier, blacks are more likely to go into these areas when they leave corporate firms. Our survey indicates that for a substantial number of black associates, the possibility of acquiring marketable skills is an important reason for choosing litigation in the first instance.

Unfortunately, what look like advantages can turn out to have negative repercussions for a black associate's prospects at the firm. The lower levels of scrutiny in litigation increase the risk that an associate will fall through the cracks. On the typical case, there is a substantial amount of routine low visibility work. Because the teams are big, it is more difficult for partners to get any real sense of the quality of junior associates. Moreover, because clients tend to want "name" litigators arguing their cases, and because many of these litigators are recruited laterally, litigation associates have less opportunity to develop their skills and signal their quality to partners. These factors combine to make litigation one of the least likely routes to partnership for associates as a whole. The prospects are worse for black associates, given the likelihood that certain clients will feel less comfortable entrusting their cases to a black lawyer. Black women probably face even steeper odds.

Moreover, the pro bono and other small cases in which a black associate might be given major responsibility often do not generate the kind of positive feedback that might justify the risk and effort. Although many firms view pro bono projects as "training vehicles" for young lawyers, this work is often not supervised closely by partners. Thus, even a good job frequently goes unnoticed. Should the case become a serious problem for the firm, however, it is the junior associate who is likely to be blamed. Moreover, as we indicated above, black lawyers who do significant amounts of pro bono work run the risk of being viewed as uninterested in the firm's paying clients, further reducing the probability that a partner will see the black associate as one worth training.

Finally, litigation is generally less stable than corporate work. Liti-gation is a very costly way for corporations to resolve their problems. Not surprisingly, corporate general counsel look for ways to reduce these expenses. When litigation projects end, the client is likely to go too (or at least to leave the litigation department and move to the corporate side). Moreover, although some kinds of litigation are repetitive (e.g., antitrust and securities) a good deal of the work done by junior associates involves mastering the facts of the case and doing research on fact-specific legal issues. Unlike mastery of the details of a particular kind of corporate transaction, this dispute-specific knowledge is less transferable to future cases. This makes it harder for a litigation associate to become expert in a particular substantive field and therefore to provide valuable services to the firm during lean economic times.

Given this dynamic between the structural features of elite firms and the strategic choices of black lawyers, it is not surprising that the turnover rate among these associates appears to be especially high. Because they are less likely to receive the Royal Jelly of good training in core areas of the firm's practice, black lawyers legitimately fear that they will become flatliners with no future at the firm. As these lawyers increasingly focus on their lives after the firm, however, they simultaneously hasten their own departure. Not only is there likely to be a divergence between what is likely to make a black lawyer more marketable outside the firm (e.g., litigation training) and what leads to success within the firm (e.g., working for partners in the core areas of firm growth), but by contracting the time frame within which they must decide whether to stay or go, black associates often forfeit the opportunity to be "discovered" by partners with an interest in the firm's productivity. In a forthcoming study of successful minority managers in corporations, David Thomas concludes that even those who ultimately make it into the top ranks do not have the same smooth linear progression as their white peers. Instead, minority managers frequently suffer periods during which their careers stall, only to jump ahead when a senior manager notices their talents. This pattern of slow growth (and even periods of no progress) followed by relatively dramatic jumps in position is difficult enough in the general up-or-out world of elite law firms; it is virtually impossible in a world in which both firms and associates make important career decisions within the first one to two years.

There is, however, a way in which black lawyers have been able to replicate the success patterns Thomas outlines within the context of the current trend towards decreasing associate tenure. Ironically, it involves leaving the firm. A substantial percentage of all black partners in our data set worked in government (37%), in-house counsel's office (28%), and/or academia (11%) before becoming partners. Similarly, in our survey, all four black Harvard graduates who had become partners in major firms left their first firms and went into either government (3) or a small firm (1) before becoming partners. This suggests that one way for black lawyers to accumulate the kind of human capital and name recognition that law firms look for when making partners is by going outside the firm where they may have better opportunities to develop their talents. The continuing success of this strategy, however, depends upon the criteria that firms are likely to employ in making partnership decisions. * * *

* * *

Many commentators have documented the difficulty of applying Title VII and other similar anti-discrimination laws to high-level jobs in which quality judgments are inherently subjective. Neither disparate treatment nor disparate impact analysis is well suited to rooting out the kind of adverse employment practices we describe. For the most part, the lawyers who prefer average whites to average blacks have no discriminatory animus as that term has been traditionally defined. Indeed, other things being equal, they would probably prefer to hire and/or promote (and indeed probably have hired and promoted) superstar blacks over average whites. Nor are the institutional practices that tend to keep blacks off the training track likely to be condemned under a disparate impact analysis, given that changing these practices would involve a fundamental restructuring of the way corporate firms do business. Not surprisingly, when they have been presented with claims of this type, courts have generally refused to second guess the subjective decision making of partners in the absence of clear evidence of discrimination.

* * *

Applying objective standards to the partnership decision would be even more complex. By the time a black associate comes up for partner, she may very well be less "qualified" precisely because she has not received the Royal Jelly that would allow her to develop these qualifications. In order to be effective, therefore, the requirement that firms objectively justify choices between average whites and average blacks would have to be applied to every staffing and mentoring decision made throughout the firm. Even if such a requirement were not per se unadministrable, which it probably is, it would undermine the kind of collegiality and informal working relationships that are essential elements of the practice of law.

Nevertheless, it is important that law firms do not feel that they are immune from anti-discrimination laws. The threat of liability undoubtedly encourages firms to pay more attention to their employment practices than they otherwise would. This vigilance may help to prevent some of the more egregious instances of discriminatory conduct. In addition, discrimination lawsuits can sometimes make "visible" the largely "invisible" process by which firms choose partners.

* * *

* * *Nevertheless, by shining light on the normally invisible world of law firm staffing and work assignment decisions, [Lawrence] Mungin's case may encourage firms to pay more attention to whether black associates are getting access to challenging and productive work.

There may, however, be other consequences. As Mungin's case suggests, the threat of litigation probably decreases a black associate's chances of being fired. Firms face both defense and reputation costs from being accused of discrimination even if the suit is ultimately unsuccessful. These costs, in addition to the firm's desire to have at least one senior black associate "visible" to the outside world (even if he was "invisible" to the firm's partners when it came to assigning work) may have been what stopped Katten from firing Mungin when a white seventh year associate who could only be billed out at second or third year rates probably would have been let go.

The fact that anti-discrimination law decreases a black lawyer's chances of being fired will have mixed effects on her opportunities at the firm. Given this phenominon [sic], firms may be less likely to hire average black associates, and/or more inclined to flatline those who are hired, thereby inducing them to leave "voluntarily." * * *

For all of these reasons, it is not surprising that anti-discrimination cases are rarely brought in this area and even more rarely won. Moreover, even if courts were more hospitable to such lawsuits, the practical consequnces [sic] of applying anti-discrimination law in this area might be less than the proponants [sic] of this strategy tend to believe. * * *

* * *

Nevertheless, one final aspect of the legal profession's past makes us cautiously optimistic about the ability to make progress on these difficult issues. Few would dispute that the campaign to end legal segregation culminating in Brown v. Board of Education is the legal profession's finest accomplishment—just as the profession's complicity in the regime that this campaign demolished was its darkest hour. The fact that the country's most prestigious law firms are nearly as segregated today as the entire legal system was forty years ago stands as a constant rebuke to the profession's attempt to claim the noble side of this heritage. At the same time, initiatives such as the Minority Counsel Demonstration Program and the efforts by state and local bar associations to promote workplace diversity demonstrate that the ideals captured by Brown can still energize lawyers to work for institutional change. As the legal profession confronts the uncertainties of the next millennium, it is this energy that holds the best hope for charting a new path that connects the profession's future to the best of its past.

Notes and Questions

1. Did Lawrence Mungin's experiences fit the profile explained by Wilkins and Gulati? Explain.

2. Why aren't there more lawsuits against law firms due to racial discrimination? *But see* Rhonda Wills v. Vinson & Elkins, which was a lawsuit filed by an African–American female associate against her firm alleging race and gender discrimination as well as sexual harassment. Shortly before trial was to begin, the lawsuit settled for an undisclosed amount. *Cf* Wendy Parker, *Lessons in Losing: Race Discrimination in Employment*, 81 NOTRE DAME L. REV. 889 (2006) where author discusses the barriers to success in Title VII lawsuits, especially where unconscious racism could have been a factor. In addition, she examines empirical data showing the low success rate of plaintiffs in race-based employment discrimination claims and argues that the strongest cases often settle.

3. How many lateral moves did Mungin make? During which years in his career? Did they help or hurt Mungin? Would Wilkins and Gulati have recommended those lateral moves?

4. Who would Mungin describe as his mentor when he arrived at Katten, Muchin & Zavis?

5. How well informed do you think Mungin was about the types of issues that Wilkins and Gulati discuss? Can you give specific examples to support your answer?

6.   How did Mungin's choice of bankruptcy law help or hurt his career? According to Wilkins and Gulati would litigation have been a preferable specialty for Mungin?

7.   What do you think would have happened to Mungin if he were White instead of African–American? Is retention only an issue for African–American lawyers? Professor Wilkins in an interview in The Washington Lawyer stated "I think that if the firms had listened to what black lawyers were saying back in the 1980s, they might have learned something that would have helped them before the crisis in retention hit. After all, black lawyers weren't working in different law firms from their white counterparts. They were working in the same law firms. Race may have made some problems more pronounced..., but the reality was those problems were there for everybody." Tim Wells, *A Conversation with David Wilkins*, THE WASHINGTON LAWYER, 22 Dec. 2002.

8.   For an additional study of elite law firms *see* Elizabeth Chambliss, *Organizational Determinants of Law Firm Integration*, 46 Am. U. L. Rev. 669 (1997). (Professor Chambliss studied ninety-seven elite law firms for the purpose of identifying law firm characteristics that lead to increased gender and race integration.)

9.   Once African–Americans become partners, their workplace problems are not over. In many ways, they are just beginning. *See* David B. Wilkins, *Partners Without Power? A Preliminary Look at Black Partners in Corporate Law Firms*, 2 J. Inst. Stud. Leg. Eth. 15 (1999). In that article Professor Wilkins makes it clear that "treating the partnership decision as the end of the diversity analysis is a mistake." *Id*. First, becoming a partner doesn't mean staying a partner given the current competitive environment. As Professor Wilkins puts it "[P]artnership is no longer the equivalent of tenure." *Id*. Second, some law partners are more equal than others. At many firms there are equity partners who divide the profits–and share in the liabilities–of the firm and there are non-equity partners who are salaried employees like associates. Professor Wilkins describes growing evidence that partners of color are concentrated in income rather than equity partnerships and even where they are equity partners are found most often at the bottom of the "point" scale for determining not only income but influence. *Id*. at 16–17. Professor Wilkins concludes by noting that "if firms do not begin to address the powerlessness of the average black partner, they are likely to lose these lawyers as fast (or faster) than they are willing to promote them to partnership." *Id*. at 48.

See e.g. Alex M. Johnson, Jr. *Representing Race: The Underrepresentation of Minorities in the Legal Profession: A Critical Race Theorist's Perspective*, 95 Mich. L. Rev. 1005 (1997) (calls on the legal profession to use affirmative action to increase the number of attorneys of color at elite law firms); J. Cunyon Gordon, *Painting By Numbers: "And, Um, Let's Have A Black Lawyer Sit At Our Table,"* 71 Fordham L. Rev. 1257 (2003) (discusses how corporate clients "encourage" diversity hiring by letting law firms know that one factor in deciding whether or not to retain them as outside counsel is the extent to which they have a diversified work force). See also Leonard Baynes, Falling Through the Cracks: Race and Corporate Law Firms, 77 St. John's L. Rev. 785 (2003).

10. For the first hundred year history of black lawyers, *See* J. Clay Smith's Emancipation: The Making of the Black Lawyer, 1844–1944 (1993). *See also* Dorothy A. Brown, *Faith or Foolishness*, 11 Harv. BlackLetter L.J. 172 (1994) (book review). *See also*, Kenneth Mack, *A Social History of Everyday Practice: Sadie T.M. Alexander and the Incorporation of Black Women into the American Legal Profession* 1925–60, 87 Cornell L.Rev. 1405 (2002)(for a discussion of Black female lawyers).

11. Wal–Mart Stores has decided not to continue using certain law firms as outside counsel because of their lack of diversity. Karen Donovan, *Pushed by Clients, Law Firms Step Up Diversity Efforts*, N.Y. Times, July 21, 2006, at C6. Could client "pressure" prove more effective than lawsuits in integrating law firms?

LINDA E. DAVILA

Note, The Underrepresentation of Hispanic Attorneys in Corporate Law Firms
39 Stan. L. Rev. 1403, 1403–1405, 1406–1407, 1410–
1424, 1431–1432, 1434–1435, 1436–1437 (1987).

The law firm is a meritocracy: If you perform well, there are no 'unique barriers" for minorities.

> Hispanic graduate of Stanford Law School, Class of 1981, currently employed in a corporate law firm.

The law is the most bigoted profession.

> Hispanic graduate of Stanford Law School, Class of 1975, formerly employed in a corporate law firm.

The attorneys quoted above apparently have had very different experiences in corporate law firms. But which quotation more closely represents the experiences of most Hispanics? Many commentators would argue that the latter quotation is more appropriate because of the small percentage of Hispanics and other minority attorneys in the offices of our more prestigious law firms. In fact, some observers have described the underrepresentation of minority attorneys in corporate law firms as a "serious indictment of [the legal] profession. . . . Law is a profession which by its nature should be a model of opportunity for all."

This indictment is ironic in view of the legal profession's integral role in the civil rights movement of the 1960s. This movement awoke the country to the wide array of discriminatory practices inflicted upon members of minority groups; it also helped create the political climate needed to pass federal and state legislation outlawing many of these practices. Equally important, the civil rights movement helped foster an ethical environment that condemned overt discrimination and recognized the idea of equal opportunity for minorities.

Despite many advances, minority representation in the legal profession, as in most prestigious fields, is still not proportionate to the minority presence in the general population. But even within the legal world, corporate law firms have been slower than other professional groups in moving toward a more proportionate racial balance. Indeed, the number of Hispanic attorneys working for corporations is 50 percent greater than the number of Hispanic associates in corporate law firms. One survey reported that Hispanics represent less than 1 percent of the attorneys in the 151 biggest law firms in the United States.

This note examines the underrepresentation of Hispanic attorneys in corporate law firms. Admittedly, all minority groups and women may confront similar barriers in pursuing professional careers in fields such as law. However, while various commentators have addressed the specific experiences of blacks and women, the experiences of Hispanic professionals have not received similar treatment. Rather, commentators have only discussed the problems faced by Hispanics in articles about minorities in general or in opinion pieces. Although Hispanics may share many of their experiences with other minorities, it is valuable to examine any perceived or actual differences between those experiences. The rapidly increasing population growth of Hispanics in the United States further underscores the need to study Hispanics as a group. Moreover, Hispanic experiences in the United States are somewhat unique among those of other minority groups. For example, Hispanics apparently hold on to their original culture and identity more tenaciously than do other ethnic groups. A separate examination of Hispanics may lead to a better understanding of their particular problems and thus may increase their presence in the private legal community. For these reasons, this note specifically addresses the status of Hispanics in corporate law firms.

In an effort to explore more fully the reasons and possible solutions for Hispanic underrepresentation, the *Stanford Law Review* conducted a survey in connection with this note. The survey, distributed to 272 Hispanic and nonHispanic alumni/ae from Stanford Law School, questioned these attorneys on their opinions and experiences regarding Hispanics in corporate law firms. Obviously, Stanford Law School graduates are not representative of all American lawyers, and consequently their responses must not be unduly generalized. Nevertheless, the survey responses are useful in pinpointing problems faced by Hispanics and in posing suggestions for increasing the number of Hispanics in corporate law firms. In addition, this note makes use of the survey responses to substantiate, supplement, or refute the existing literature on this topic.
* * *

Minority representation in the legal profession rose from 1.3 percent to 4.2 percent between 1973 and 1983.

Total minority representation in the legal profession was less than one-fifth of the percentage of racial minorities in the nation's population in 1983. * * *

Minority representation in the partner and associate ranks of large corporate law firms is even more dismal. In particular, Hispanic attorneys are represented in very small numbers in these firms. For example, in 1982, three-fourths of the nation's largest firms had no Hispanic partners and more than half of the firms had no Hispanic lawyers at all on their rosters. Although one may be tempted to attribute these figures to geographic factors, a survey conducted by the National Law Journal found that, in California, which has a larger Hispanic population than any other state, only two of 530 partners in eight of the largest firms were Hispanic.

As the statistics above show, Hispanics are underrepresented in corporate law firms partly because they are underrepresented in the legal profession in general. Moreover, Hispanics may face additional obstacles to joining corporate law firms. * * *

At the interviewing stage of the hiring process, Hispanics confront difficulties not encountered by their white peers. * * * [O]ver half of the Hispanic survey respondents disagreed with the statement that race and ethnicity are *not* significant factors when interviewing for corporate law firm positions. At the interviewing stage, Hispanics are aware that they must confront the preconceptions many interviewers will have of them, preconceptions of which whites might not even be aware. Hispanic students are often stereotyped as being oriented more to public service careers than to careers with corporate law firms. Perhaps this stereotype is founded on the fact that Hispanics in the past have generally gravitated toward government jobs, poverty law, or legal services. But even if in the past Hispanics were reluctant to associate with the large law firm establishment, this is no longer the case. Today, Hispanics are looking for careers in this field. * * *

Overcoming preconceptions about the kind of law Hispanics want to practice is not the only problem Hispanics face during a corporate law firm interview. All law students face the problem that hiring partners often are not trained interviewers. But opportunities for Hispanics may be reduced as a result, because nonprofessional interviewers are likely to choose lawyers who they perceive as fitting their own patterns of behavior. Since these interviewers—who are mostly white males—may not see Hispanics as fitting the patterns of behavior of white males, they will look instead for someone who will. In essence, these interviewers try to "hire themselves." As one Hispanic attorney stated, "I do not believe there is much conscious discrimination. Instead, people tend to attract and be more comfortable with others similar to themselves."

Hispanic law school graduates also face a double academic standard. Major law firms are gradually opening up opportunities for minorities, but they usually only hire minority students with outstanding academic records who have worked on law review and attended top law schools. According to the American Bar Association Journal, "often white law students with average backgrounds are considered for positions when minority students with similar backgrounds are not." The result is that a Hispanic must surpass the accomplishments of his white colleagues before he is considered their equal. Gloria Pyszka, former director of Stanford Law School's Career Placement Office, said that a minority law student in the top 10 percent of his class can "write his own ticket. Conversely, if you are at the bottom of the class it can be a lot harder for a minority than [for a nonminority student]."

Several Hispanic survey respondents shared Pyszka's assessment. Thirty percent of the Hispanics asserted that preconceived notions and stereotypes of Hispanics created a situation in which Hispanics had to surpass nonminority performance to be viewed equally. One Hispanic attorney was particularly explicit in this belief: "[A] tougher hiring standard is applied to minority recruits—a grudging 'As long you're *better* than our average hire, we'll put up with your being different and we can justify it to our friends.'"

Understandably, many Hispanics are hesitant to arrange interviews with corporate law firms. Law firms are viewed as possessing "personalities," and a personality perceived as racially biased will very likely lessen Hispanic interest. It is difficult to face the notion of being the first minority hired at a firm or having to break the ethnic barrier. As one Hispanic survey respondent commented about succeeding in corporate law firms: "Anyone can do it . . . [but w]e need to support each other. It is lonely to be the 'only one.' We have to change that."

Another commentator, Ed Cray, asserts that "assimilation of minority lawyers into prestigious firms has been slowed by 'mutual deselection.'" Cray uses this term to describe the phenomenon created by the tendency of minorities to choose to work where ethnic status is not perceived as a barrier *and* the tendency of lawyers in law firms to select attorneys "like themselves." When faced with the choice of assimilation with a white-dominated, establishment firm or separatism with a "hardy band of brothers," Cray asserts that a minority lawyer may be strongly motivated to go where he will not risk rejection by mere virtue of being different and will not have to cope with the daily pressure of being *the* Hispanic in the office. Cray surmises that these factors have compelled minorities to choose other career options. Minority firms may be smaller and pay less, but Hispanics "know they are welcome there." This process of mutual deselection has, of course, led to fewer minorities moving into established corporate law firms.

The problems Hispanics face in getting jobs at corporate law firms do not end with the first job after law school. Having been barred from entry level positions at corporate law firms, Hispanics are effectively prevented from joining firms later as lateral hires. The problem Hispanics have had with lateral promotions is that few Hispanics have substantial legal experience in corporate fields. So long as Hispanics have difficulty entering these firms at entry levels, the number of Hispanics gaining corporate experience will continue to be minimal. The firms, however, will not hire lawyers without corporate experience. Thus, Hispanic representation in corporate firms is not likely to be improved through lateral hiring. As for the Hispanic attorney, he is caught in a vicious cycle.

A handful of Hispanic attorneys have overcome the entry barriers and have joined corporate law firms. Even for these attorneys, however, their ethnicity may continue to disadvantage them within the firms by creating additional barriers or increased pressures. * * *

One factor affecting some Hispanic attorneys is a sense of isolation within the firm. In fact, 44 percent of the responding Hispanics stated that they have experienced a sense of isolation at work that they attributed to being Hispanic. One commentator suggested that perhaps in some cases this results from looking "different." Large law firms can be intimidating to Hispanics because Hispanics perceive themselves (or are perceived) as being or looking different from everyone else. Breaking the racial barriers of a firm by being the first or only Hispanic attorney is not an easy task, and it can be even more difficult if the attorney feels lonely or isolated. Also, if a Hispanic perceives that a firm is geared toward white interests, the process of integrating with the firm becomes more difficult.

Various survey respondents agreed that isolation may be a major reason why Hispanics have difficulty in the corporate law firm setting. They indicated that this sense of isolation may be rooted in the fact that the Hispanic attorneys' backgrounds and value systems differ so radically from those of their white counterparts. They noted that, unlike many white associates, few Hispanics were raised in middle-class or wealthy homes or have families involved in legal careers. In fact, one commentator has noted that, unlike whites and other minorities, Hispanics come from homes that instilled family loyalty and spiritual values rather than more materialistic ones. Thus, fewer Hispanics have been exposed to the materialistic value systems that pervade corporate law firms and they may feel isolated and uncomfortable as a result. One Hispanic noted, "With Latinos/-as, there is an uneasiness about buying into the corporate culture. It is a real concern that takes extra effort to allay. You don't have this with typical white males and most Anglo women. They sell themselves harder because they want the corporate culture." A nonHispanic noted that coming from noncorporate, nonlegal backgrounds is a disadvantage to Hispanics because they don't share the same set of expectations as people from "that world.... It's a culture shock, in that norms, communication patterns, etc. are all different. That is not unique to Latinos and not all Latinos face this." While not all Hispanics face this so-called "culture shock," the recurrence of this idea throughout the responses indicates that it may be a common experience.

Isolation may be enhanced by a lack of Hispanic mentors. Mentors serve as role models and advisors, and many attorneys feel that the lack of minority mentors hurts their progress within the firm. Another factor affecting Hispanics is a sense of tokenism. Many Hispanics who enter corporate law firms want to be involved in all aspects of corporate law. Unfortunately, Hispanics have commented that some firms do not rotate Hispanic lawyers into all areas of law. Thus, Hispanics in these positions may experience frustration due to their limited assignments and the feeling of tokenism. Being treated in this manner may motivate some Hispanics to look for work elsewhere, away from corporate law firms.

Generally, however, the Stanford survey respondents did not perceive their firms as assigning them work in a discriminatory fashion.

* * * [O]ver 90 percent of the Hispanic respondents agreed that minority and nonminority attorneys are given comparable assignments. Perhaps Stanford alumni/-ae don't experience this type of tokenism very frequently because they are perceived as better qualified than Hispanics from other law schools. Alternatively, once a firm hires an attorney, the firm may be economically limited in its discretion to assign work. In other words, it may not be able to afford to hire an attorney and not require that attorney to perform work comparable with that of other attorneys in his class.

Tokenism may also result in the "window dressing" syndrome. This term describes the feeling some lawyers have of always being on display. One Hispanic alumnus surveyed stated that, at his firm, "sometimes women or minorities were given assignments because of their high profile—to affect the client, judge, [or] opposition ... in some subtle way." Whether or not this is a true picture, the feelings are nonetheless real, particularly if the lawyer is the only minority at the firm.

According to the Stanford survey respondents, tokenism is encountered less frequently than isolation. Twenty-seven percent of the Hispanic attorneys indicated that they had experienced a sense of tokenism that they attributed to being a minority. As previously noted, 44 percent responded that they had experienced a sense of isolation at their firms. Because the respondents do not perceive the firms as assigning work in a discriminatory manner, this may reduce any sense of tokenism that exists. Isolation may occur more frequently because of the strength of the Hispanic culture in affecting acculturation to corporate settings.

Isolation and tokenism may be demoralizing and affect Hispanics' performances, thus impeding their advancement. These are not, however, the only difficulties faced by Hispanics in corporate law firms. Some literature suggests that Hispanics also face greater difficulty getting clients. Bringing in business may be harder for Hispanics for several reasons. Clients generally make contact with lawyers in social circles, and because Hispanics are often excluded from these circles, they have fewer opportunities to make the contacts. Also, some lawyers feel that because they are Hispanic, the general public questions their legal skills and qualifications and, therefore, fails to seek them out as legal counselors when the need arises.

Even the growth of Hispanic businesses and communities has not created a substantial amount of new business for Hispanic attorneys. In the Hispanic culture, the lawyer is not often viewed as a business advisor, and thus he is not consulted on many business decisions. As a result, the increased presence of Hispanics in the business world has not substantially assisted Hispanic lawyers in getting clients. Contrary to these findings, the survey respondents overwhelmingly asserted that one advantage firms believe they will garner if they hire Hispanics is the ability to develop Spanish-speaking client bases.

Interestingly, the survey respondents generally split over the question of whether Hispanics have trouble attracting clients. * * *

Finally, the survey indicates that the major obstacle Hispanics face within corporate law firms is overcoming preconceptions. Thirty percent of the Hispanic respondents stated that a presumption exists that Hispanics are not qualified. This belief was reinforced by the fact that various nonHispanics, at firms with no Hispanic attorneys, responded that Hispanic attorneys probably face a problem in their ability to communicate due to deficiencies in the English language. This preconception is likely to occur because, as one respondent said, "Many minorities carry the extra baggage of racial stigma. That is, many colleagues assume that minorities get their jobs primarily because they're minorities." Another commented, "[There exist] distorted perceptions and misplaced generalities about Latino articulateness, intelligence, work ethics, etc."

Another recurring comment, particularly among nonHispanics, was that Hispanics may be disadvantaged by client prejudices. Thus, firms may be concerned that Hispanics will not be accepted by their clients, and the result may be different treatment of Hispanic attorneys. One Hispanic responded:

> I have found the profession of law to be the most open to diverse backgrounds with distinctions based more on ability than on background. Some corporate law firms could be accused of discrimination, but I have found this generally to be a reflection of their client base rather than a consciously chosen practice.

Despite recognition by most survey respondents that many Hispanics have faced different experiences in the legal profession from those of most white, middle- and upper-class attorneys, some attorneys firmly asserted that no differences exist. These comments were based on profitability. For instance, one Hispanic respondent reasoned, "In the private sector, the lawyer who performs the best legal service for the least amount of money is going to win in the long run. Both hostile discrimination and benign tokenism are expensive luxuries in the legal marketplace, where the bottom line is increasingly important as competition increases." Another attorney, answering the question of what problems or obstacles Hispanics face, more directly asserted: "None, so long as you make money for the firm."

Notwithstanding the fact that, as one attorney put it, "[g]reen is the universal color," the surveys and research confirm that some Hispanic attorneys have had to cope with experiences that middle- and upper-class white attorneys have not. As the following section discusses, some commentators have suggested that these problems or obstacles are the result of unconscious biases. These theories may further explain why Hispanics are underrepresented in corporate law firms.

One commentator has suggested that a cause of Hispanic underrepresentation in corporate law firms is the perpetuation of an elitist mentality in the firms. Jerold Auerbach asserts that the history of the legal profession led to the development of a stratified bar that differentiated lawyers on the basis of ethnicity and class. The lawyers constituting the elite class were able to maintain control over the legal profession and its development. These lawyers came to represent the bar and were thus able to establish rules and guidelines affecting the entire legal community. In particular, they were able to limit participation by defining the qualifications for admission to the bar. Auerbach suggests that this elite group wanted to use the legal profession to maintain the status quo. Therefore, the entire structure of the profession was designed to promote certain political views and to resist change that was viewed as threatening.

Auerbach surmises that despite external influences, the legal profession—specifically the part of the profession practicing in corporate law firms—continues to be strongly influenced by this elitist ideology. Hispanic lawyers do not necessarily share the values and preferences of the elite corporate lawyers. They are therefore a threat to the status and privileges that the elite now enjoy.

The perpetuation of racism has also been explained by Derrick Bell as arising from white self-interest. "Self-interest has been described . . . as the most basic and important force underlying whites' policies and actions vis-a-vis minorities." In other words, whites will act against racism only when it is in their best interest. Bell recognizes that values and morals may at times cause some people to act against their self-interest, but he concludes that these factors are insufficient to overcome the strength of most whites' self-interested behavioral patterns. "A racist culture, then, can move to eradicate or make racism ineffective only when racism itself becomes a serious threat to the culture and its bearers."

Other theories of contemporary racism may also help explain what is happening in corporate law firms. Some commentators suggest that overt racism has merely been replaced by "a more subtle, insidious" form of racism. Today, blatant race discrimination is illegal and not widely accepted, but attitudes and generalizations based on race and ethnicity persist.

Gordon Allport's explanation for the continued existence of racial and ethnic prejudice is based on the notion that the human mind relies on generalizations for convenience. For example, if a person meets someone who has blue eyes and is intelligent, he may generalize the experience and assume that everyone who has blue eyes is also intelligent. Such generalizations are unavoidable because there is a tendency for the human mind to form categories in order to facilitate the thinking process. Furthermore, when people have different backgrounds, finding out whether a generalization holds true in a particular case can be extremely difficult. As a result, Allport concludes that people are more likely to stereotype people who are different than to stereotype people with similar backgrounds and beliefs. This kind of stereotyping is perpetuated because people are prone to interact with those most similar to themselves: This requires the least effort and expresses pride in their own culture.

Other commentators, principally Joel Kovel, describe the attitudes of some whites toward minorities as "aversive." Aversive racists have conflicting feelings toward minorities. On the one hand, they are aware of a desire to disassociate themselves from negative concepts such as racism and prejudice. At the same time, they hold negative feelings toward minorities which very often are not conscious feelings. Researchers have found that aversive racists may often be well-intentioned. However, their need to avoid a racist self-image negatively affects their interaction with minorities. The result is that aversive racists avoid interracial interaction but when forced to interact, "instead of responding spontaneously and naturally [they] are motivated primarily to avoid acting inappropriately."

Although both blatant and unconscious racism can hold Hispanics back, neutrality is also seen as an obstacle. A University of Texas sociologist has noted:

> Those managers and executives who are the biggest problem are not the overt racial bigots. They are people who see discrimination but remain neutral and do nothing about it. These are the people who let racially motivated behavior go unnoticed, unmentioned, or unpunished. These are the people who won't help.

All of the factors discussed in this section have likely played some role in the underrepresentation of Hispanics in corporate law firms. Historically, legislative and judicial efforts have been made to minimize or eliminate disadvantages that may arise because of such factors. Although these remedies have been successful in some areas, for the most part they have failed to redress the underrepresentation of Hispanics in corporate law firms. Examining historical remedies for inequality and discrimination provides a basis from which to evaluate suggestions for reducing Hispanic underrepresentation in law firms. * * *

Law firms should put pressure on law schools to recruit Hispanic students more effectively and should support programs such as the Council on Legal Education Opportunity ("CLEO"). Many survey respondents recognized Hispanic student recruitment as a key factor to increasing the numbers of Hispanics in law firms. * * * [A] majority of the respondents believed that affirmative action in law schools is still needed in order to promote racial equality. Thus, putting pressure on law schools is of utmost importance if the pool of Hispanic attorneys is to increase.

Besides putting pressure on law schools, corporate law firms should modify their recruiting practices to promote racial equality within their profession. Recruiters must educate themselves about what life is like for Hispanics in the geographic regions in which they are trying to recruit new Hispanic lawyers. This can be done by contacting regional Hispanic bar associations. Firms should strive to foster commitment from and frequent contacts with members of such organizations. Such action may make firms aware of the "personality" that Hispanics associate with particular firms. One respondent suggested that firms should approach law school Hispanic groups for qualified candidates. By tuning in to the needs and concerns of Hispanics, law firms can recruit more effectively.

Another productive step would be to identify schools with large percentages of Hispanic students and recruit there. By looking beyond the major law schools, firms can uncover a whole new pool of talent. This does not suggest that firms lower their standards, but only that they open their eyes to the larger applicant pool. Survey respondents strongly endorsed this idea. In particular, respondents noted that firms should look beyond numbers to the individual's determination and potential. One attorney stated that firms should tolerate diversity and not merely look positively at those Hispanics who conform completely to the corporate image. Another Hispanic elaborated on this theme by stating that firms should encourage ethnic identification.

Recruiting efforts can also be enhanced by using Hispanics to recruit Hispanics in much the same way that most firms strategically use attorneys to recruit at their alma maters. Hispanics can reassure prospective lawyers about a firm's commitment to racial and ethnic equality and its practice of treating all associates equally. In fact, Hispanic partners should ideally recognize an obligation as attorneys and as members of a minority group to assist society in achieving equality. In addition, since there are so few Hispanic partners, their firms should take this obligation into account in assigning work and in assessing the performance of Hispanic firm members.

* * *

In addition to making concerted efforts to encourage Hispanics to enter the profession, law firms can take concrete steps to retain Hispanics. The presence of more than a token group within a firm will help convince Hispanic lawyers that the firm is sincerely committed to racial equality and will encourage Hispanics to remain with the firm. One attorney cited a need for hiring attorneys at all partnership levels and recommended that firms look seriously at attorneys who follow different career paths as potential laterals. * * *

Law firms must avoid enhancing any sense of tokenism whenever possible. For instance, assigning Hispanics work in "traditional" minority areas of law such as civil rights, employment discrimination, or community relations promotes feelings of tokenism. Instead, law firms should involve Hispanics in all kinds of positions and treat them with equal respect. These goals can be achieved by assigning major clients and mainstream matters to Hispanics. Several nonHispanic survey respondents suggested that Hispanic attorneys be introduced to existing clients in order to foster confidence in Hispanic attorneys. This is particularly important if client prejudices have been a problem for Hispanics. Only when Hispanics are truly treated as equals will their frustration and sense of isolation be eliminated.

Furthermore, the few Hispanics who have become partners not only have an obligation to assist in the recruiting process, they must also be involved in guiding new associates. This includes fostering a mentorprotege system that will help Hispanic attorneys to avoid early mistakes. Because mentors can be so important, Hispanic partners should make their presence known to new associates as soon as possible.

Apparently, some firms have taken very positive steps toward increasing Hispanic representation. One survey respondent reported that a **Washington, D.C., firm runs a prelaw preparation class** each summer for minority students about to enter law school. This program has been successful in helping students to do well in their first year and thereby establish a solid career foundation. The basic problem for law firms is that they do not see enough minority applicants that are "qualified" according to traditional standards. Wider support for these types of programs may help to minimize this problem.

* * *

Hispanic law and prelaw student associations should be actively involved in recruiting efforts to increase the number of Hispanic students who actually enroll in law school. They must also encourage admissions policies that will result in greater Hispanic representation in law schools. In addition, Hispanic students should provide academic and personal support to one another. Peer support can be invaluable, particularly in the first year of law school. By encouraging others to attend law school, by helping to bring about favorable admissions policies, and by helping each other get through law school, Hispanic law students can play a key role in increasing their numbers in the legal profession.

Hispanic bar associations can also make significant contributions. Hispanic lawyers have formed their own bar associations to foster professional and social fellowship and to address professional, social, and political concerns of special interest to them and their communities. The Mexican American Bar Association in Los Angeles, for example, has worked hard to increase the number of Hispanic judges. Hispanic bar associations must focus attention on the inequities in the legal profession in order to increase Hispanic representation.

Bar associations should also encourage Hispanics to become law professors. The number of full time minority faculty in ABA-approved law schools is very low. As of June 1980, the presence of Hispanic, black, and Asian faculty in our nation's law schools totaled 293 out of a roster of 5226 law school teachers. Hispanic professors serve as role models and important sources of support for Hispanic students. Increasing the number of Hispanic faculty members should help reduce attrition among Hispanics.

As mentioned, Hispanic associates and partners can help increase Hispanic representation by being actively involved in the recruiting process. They can also be helpful by serving as mentors for new associates. The Hispanic legal community must be willing to help its members out. Whether at the student, associate, or partner level, Hispanics can commit themselves to assisting other Hispanics to become attorneys.

Everyone must be involved if the goal of racial equality in the profession is to be attained.

Notes and Questions

1. Do Hispanics and other persons of color experience race discrimination because discrimination exists or because they expect to experience it? Which comes first, the expectation or the discrimination?

2. The survey respondents thought they were given work assignments comparable to their White counterparts. Is that the end of the analysis?

3. What stereotypes do Hispanic attorneys face? How do they compare with those faced by African–American lawyers?

4. What role do White attorneys have in eliminating workforce discrimination?

5. Have you ever seen discrimination—in any sphere—and done nothing about it? How did it make you feel? How many people paid a price for your silence?

6. Is racial diversity a significant factor in your employment decisions?

7. Are law firms the only institutions that need to address racial discrimination issues? Consider the next excerpt dealing with the judiciary.

SECTION 3.   WHY DIVERSITY IN THE LEGAL PROFESSION MATTERS

JUSTICE MING W. CHIN

Fairness or Bias?: A Symposium on Racial and Ethnic
Composition and Attitudes in the Judiciary
4 Asian L.J. 181, 184, 185–186, 187–189, 190–191, 192, 193 (1997).

* * * As we look forward to the next millennium, we must continue to improve our legal system. We must continue to build a system of justice without bias, without prejudice, and without bigotry. Even though we can say that Asian–Americans and other minority groups are enjoying opportunities that did not exist a mere generation ago, ethnic and racial biases are still with us. The subject, as it always has been, is highly volatile. Despite that—or perhaps because of that—we must continue to address bias wherever found, particularly in our justice system.

In 1991, former Chief Justice Malcolm Lucas recognized the importance of addressing bias in the California judiciary. He created the Advisory Committee on Racial and Ethnic Bias in the Courts. I was fortunate to serve on the Committee. * * *

The Committee's work was focused on three areas: first, to study the treatment of ethnic and racial minorities in California's courts; second, to ascertain public perceptions on the fairness or lack of fairness in the judicial system; and third, to make recommendations on reforms and remedial programs in response to what the Committee found.

* * *

First, we can look to statistics illustrated in the report that show us one origin of perceived bias. For example, even though minorities make up an increasingly greater percentage of the state's population, statistics show that the number of minority judges remains low. Currently, 57 percent of California's population is Caucasian, and 43 percent of the population is part of a minority group. Asians and Pacific Islanders make up about 9 percent of California's population and are expected to be almost 12 percent in 2020. But when you look to the municipal courts, 84 percent of the judges in these courts are Caucasian. Asian–Americans hold only 2.9 percent of these positions. Moving up to the next level, there are 768 superior court judges in California; of these, 89 percent are Caucasian. Of the superior court judges, 2.3 percent are Asian–Americans. At the appellate level, you find that three California Supreme Court justices are from ethnic minority groups, two of us Asian–American. But there are only two Asian–Americans total in California's other appellate districts.

Other areas of our justice system appear to lack diversity as well. Eighty-five percent of California's district attorneys and eighty percent of our public defenders are Caucasian. In private practice, minority groups account for only 2.8 percent of the partners in the nation's major law firms. When we look at statistics like these, we must remember that statistics do not always tell the whole story. Nevertheless, they are a source of the public's view that there is bias in the justice system.

A second source of the public's perception of bias has to do with what the general public sees in our courts. We can look to the personal experiences of people who have participated in the court system. A judge in Alameda County was publicly reprimanded for a racist remark to a Japanese–American attorney. Testimony at some of the Committee hearings revealed that people with limited English speaking skills or those who speak with accents experienced insensitivity in court or felt they were given less credibility than other people. Some Asian–American litigants who were not familiar with the court system felt they were treated arrogantly by court personnel. For litigants already bewildered by the court system and perhaps not fluent in English, lack of patience by court personnel can certainly affect their perception of the court's fairness in dealing with them. Personal experiences especially can shape negative perceptions of the courts by Asian–Americans because, according to a survey cited in the Committee's report, Asian–Americans have significantly less experience with the courts than other groups. When we view these statistics and anecdotal personal experiences together, the fact that that there is a perception of bias in the judiciary is no surprise.

* * *

A major source of the perception of bias is the lack of diversity among those who play key roles in the justice system. The report acknowledges that diversity is a particularly important issue because the legal system depends on the public's trust in it. A perceived lack of diversity leads to a lack of confidence in the system. California is an extremely diverse state and will continue to become more diverse. By the year 2020, people of color—together—will form a majority of California's population. With growing diversity in the general population, there will be a need for increased diversity in our courts.

* * *

The availability of court interpreters is another important issue, particularly with the Asian–American community, where so many languages may be spoken. In fact, nine of the fourteen most commonly used languages in the California courts are Asian languages. This state is unique in its language diversity, with an estimated 224 languages currently used by residents in this state. California's growing population will increase the need for interpreters in our courts, as the number of languages spoken in California will surely exceed its current level. Because the effective administration of justice requires effective communication, removing language barriers is essential to providing fairness in our courts. Sentencing, jury selection, language barriers, and other related topics addressed by the report are also important issues to examine.

I would like to turn our focus for a moment to a cornerstone issue that substantially affects our entire system: the question of diversity among our judges on the California bench. * * *

The report shows from an historical standpoint that Asian–Americans are making headway in the number of judicial appointments. For example, from 1953 to the present in Los Angeles County, there has been an increase in the numbers of Asian–American judges serving on the Bench:

From 1953 to 1973: 2 Asian–Americans were appointed to the superior court;

From 1973 to 1981: 9 Asian–Americans were appointed to the superior court and 14 to the municipal court;

From 1982 to 1996: 13 Asian–Americans were appointed to the superior court and 16 to the municipal court.

Los Angeles County has had one Asian–American on the appellate court. Statewide, four Asian–Americans sit on appellate courts. On the whole, 12 of 89 appellate court justices come from ethnic minority groups in general.

Twenty-nine Asian–American judges have been appointed to the Bench in the last fifteen years. That is more than the number of Asian–American judges appointed in the 30 years prior to that.

There are a couple of ways to look at these statistics: on one hand, they are encouraging because they show progress for Asian–Americans obtaining positions on the bench. On the other hand, one may wonder why more Asian–American lawyers have not become judges. Despite statistical increases, the percentage increase and the actual number of appointments of minority judges is necessarily dependent on the number of minorities available for appointment. Thus, we can infer a lot from statistics like these, but it is important to remember what these statistics do not show. The report is not, and I am not, suggesting that the absence of diversity is proof of intentional bias in our justice system. I have great respect for the judges of California. I am personally familiar with the work of most of them, and I can assure you that most are hardworking, dedicated professionals. Most work diligently to improve the legal system. Most would agree with me that bias and prejudice have no place in our judicial system.

The statistics are also not meant to suggest that a change in the current configuration of the courts alone will ensure greater fairness. That is too simplistic. We would be remiss if we emphasized only the numbers and blindly aimed for certain percentages of ethnic minorities on the courts. The quality of our judges is just as important as their ethnic composition.

Having said what the Report does not show, let's look at what the Report does suggest. The statistics about the racial configuration of the bench in California are one reason for the public's perception and concern that the bench does not reflect California's diversity. * * *

There are ways we can improve diversity on the bench in California. But I firmly believe that it must start with you—minority law students and minority members of the Bar. Last summer, I spoke at the Conference of Minority Partners. I told them that when I began practicing law 26 years ago, if a meeting of minority partners was called, we could have held the meeting in a telephone booth. I was glad to see so many of them at that conference, and I hope the numbers of minority partners will continue to grow as more ethnic minorities seek to enter private practice. Years ago, a meeting of a Bay Area Asian–American Bar Association would not have drawn very much attention or response. Today, the Asian–American Bar Association of the Greater Bay Area is helping to sponsor an event like this symposium here today at one of the finest law schools in the country. And with more Asian–American law school graduates, I am sure the organization can be confident that its membership will grow with talented young people like those in the audience here today.

At this time, the number of minority judges is certainly not what it should be. But we cannot complain about the lack of diversity in our courts if our talented minority lawyers are not willing to assume the responsibilities of judicial office. What is exciting is the fact that the number of minority law school graduates and the number of minority attorneys eligible for appointment to the bench has increased dramatically, particularly in the last ten years.

Statistics from the American Bar Association reveal that the number of minority law school graduates nearly doubled from 1984 to 1994, jumping to 15.5 percent of total graduates. Asian–Americans enjoyed the most dramatic increase of any minority group—in 1994, Asian–Americans accounted for 4.5 percent of the total number of law school graduates, jumping from just 1.5 percent in 1984. Scholarly publications like Asian Law Journal here at Boalt Hall reflect the increased presence of Asian–Americans on our law school campuses.

The growth in minority law school graduates has led to a growth in the number of minority attorneys eligible for appointment as judges. To be eligible for appointment to municipal court, a lawyer must have five or more years of active membership in the State Bar. The figure is ten years for appointment to a superior court judgeship. The Committee found that between 1984 and the present, the pool of minority attorneys with more than five and ten years of experience has grown and will continue to grow. What this means is that in the next century, a greater number of qualified applicants will increase the available applicant pool for potential judicial appointments.

I encourage you actively to seek judicial positions. Your efforts are increasingly important because, frankly, the people of California want their judges to reflect more closely the diversity they see every day in the general population. And so the quest for diversity on the bench begins with you. Keep in mind that the opportunities are there. We have almost 1,600 judges in California—just last July, twenty-one new trial court judgeships were created along with five new seats on appellate courts. We have one of the largest, if not the largest, judicial system in the world. We even exceed the size of the federal judiciary.

* * *

Another solution to the lack of diversity is in the hands of the minority judges who are now on the bench. When I was appointed to the Committee on Racial and Ethnic Bias in the Courts, I looked around the room. I took particular note that among the other Committee members were some very fine judges. I expressed to them my belief that the best thing we could do for diversity on the bench would start with each of our courtrooms. If we judge well, and if we are respected by our colleagues and our communities, then the stature of minority judges will improve, and the opportunities for future judicial appointees from a qualified pool of ethnic minority candidates will be greater. Those of us on the bench must lead by example. Perhaps we can remove some of the obstacles and clear a path for other minority judges to follow.

* * *

If our bench becomes more diverse, other areas of the judiciary are inevitably affected. This, in turn, may instill more confidence in the judiciary in the public's mind. For example, public perception of bias in the judiciary extends not only to the judges, but also to the personnel throughout the legal system. Statistics support this view—Caucasians, for example, hold 78 percent of the court reporter positions, 68 percent of the courtroom clerk positions, and 81 percent of the official and manager positions in the state superior courts. Again, this does not indict our judges for intentional bias; it is, however, the public's perception, based on what they see in our courts. If the bench becomes more diverse, however, the chances are likely to increase that these judges will, in turn, contribute to more diversity in their appointments of court personnel. This, of course, will also help to improve the perception of bias in the courts.

key assumption —"public" perception of bias in the courts.

* * *

The California Report illustrates, in great detail, a crisis of confidence in our court system. One important source of that lack of confidence is that our judiciary does not reflect California's changing population. The Chinese word for crisis contains two characters—one meaning "danger" and the other meaning "opportunity." California's judicial family must respond to this crisis directly and squarely. The danger is clear from the negative public perception of the courts. But we also have an opportunity—an opportunity to address the dangers based on the positive recommendations in the committee report. We must not only follow the recommendations of this report; we must also continue our conversation on the subject of fairness and bias to find the right answers to critical questions.

* * *

Notes and Questions

1. Justice Chin believes that as more minority attorneys seek judicial positions, the perceived racial bias of the judiciary will disappear. Do you agree or disagree?

2. What stereotypes are faced by Asian–Americans in this country? How do those stereotypes impact Asian–American lawyers and judges?

3. Recall on April 4, 1995, then Senator Alfonse D'Amato (a Republican Senator from New York) went on a radio show mid-way through the O.J. Simpson trial and "imitated" Judge Ito by speaking with a heavy Asian accent. Judge Ito has no such accent. *See e.g.* Lawrence Van Gelder, *D'Amato Mocks Ito and Sets Off Furor*, N.Y. Times, Apr. 6, 1995, at B1; Melinda Hennenburger, *D'Amato Gives a New Apology on Ito Remarks*, N.Y. Times, Apr. 7, 1995, at A1.

4. Professor Ifill states that the judiciary remains "a powerful tenured institution that is overwhelmingly white, male, and upper-middle class." *See* Sherrilyn A. Ifill, *Racial Diversity on the Bench: Beyond Role Models and Public Confidence*, 57 Wash. & Lee L. Rev. 405, 407 (2000). Professor Ifill argues racial diversity on the bench encourages judicial impartiality by ensuring that a single set of values or a single set of views do not dominate judicial decision-making. *Id.* at 405. But she also raises the issue whether the constitutionally mandated judicial impartiality precludes judges of color from consciously including minority community perspectives and values in their decision-making. *Id.* at 413. Does impartiality require the absence of perspective? Do White judges lack a perspective?

5. Professor Krotoszynski argues that the presence of racial minorities on the bench would encourage members of those racial minority groups to have greater faith in the judiciary. He makes an analogy between excluding

judges of color from the bench and excluding people of color from jury duty. *See* Ronald J. Krotoszynski, Jr., *The New Legal Process: Games People Play And The Quest For Legitimate Judicial Decision Making*, 77 Wash. U. L. Q. 993, 1051 (1999) ("Just as the systematic exclusion of racial minorities from juries delegitimized the deliberative process of juries, so too the relative absence of cultural minorities on the bench raises questions about the basic fairness of the public courts.") Do you agree? Do all judges of color think alike? Do all White judges think alike? Do you think that race can be a proxy for analysis? Is this stereotyping by a different name?

6. **Judge Harry T. Edwards,** an African–American judge on the U.S. Court of Appeals for the D.C. Circuit had this to say about the issue: "I don't know how to quantify these racial differences; but I am convinced that they exist and should be given voice in our judicial deliberations. If I sometimes bring unique perspectives to judicial problems—perspectives that are mine in whole or in part because I am black—that is a good thing. It is good because it is inevitable that judges' different professional and life experiences have some bearing on how they confront various problems that come before them. And in a judicial environment in which collegial deliberations are fostered, diversity among the judges makes for better-informed discussion. It provides for constant input from judges who have seen different kinds of problems in their pre-judicial careers, and have sometimes seen the same problems from different angles. A deliberative process enhanced by collegiality and a broad range of perspectives necessarily results in better and more nuanced opinions—opinions which, while remaining true to the rule of law, over time allow for a fuller and richer evolution of the law." Harry T. Edwards, *Race and the Judiciary*, 20 Yale L. & Pol'y 325, 329 (2002). Recall Judge Edwards dissented in part in Mungin v. Katten Muchin, & Zavis, *supra* at 48.

7. For an example of a less than collegial judicial exchange about race compare the following excerpts about whether a judge should have recused himself from a case involving a White police officer, Thomas Moran, who was found guilty by the Board of Police Commissioners of failing to exercise his authority to prevent the beating of Gregory Bell, a mentally impaired African–American teenager. When Officer Moran was suspended without pay and demoted to a patrolman, he sued. In the course of the trial Officer Moran's attorney filed a motion asking U.S. District Court Judge Charles Shaw to recuse himself because he knew the President of the Board of Police Commissioners. He denied the motion which was appealed and the Eighth Circuit remanded back to Judge Shaw with instructions that he "revisit and more thoroughly consider and respond to Moran's recusal request." *Moran v. Clarke*, 247 F.3d 799, 806 (8th Cir. 2001) After the remand, Judge Shaw stated that he was "left with the deeply troubling impression that had I been white, or had plaintiff Moran been African–American, and all the other facts of this 'hard case' remained the same, the [Eighth Circuit's] majority's opinion on the recusal issue would have been significantly different." *Moran v. Clarke*, 213 F.Supp.2d 1067, 1075 (E.D.Mo.2002). *See Moran v. Clarke,* 309 F.3d 516 (8th Cir. 2002) for the Eighth Circuit's response. The Court in a per curiam opinion stated "[h]owever, instead of recognizing that this court was giving the district court the opportunity on remand to make the record it should have made, the district court instead concluded, with absolutely no basis at all to do so, that the decision to remand the recusal

issue for further consideration was based on his race, the race and sex of the judges of this court who joined the majority opinion, and the race of the plaintiff. The district court gratuitously describes the judges in the majority as "a majority of six white men" and the judges who dissented as "two white men, one white woman, and an African–American man." While the observations are accurate, they are wholly irrelevant and, in our view, were calculated to impugn the integrity of this court in the eyes of the public." *Id.* at 517. Is this what either Judge Edwards or Justice Ming had in mind?

8. There have been a number of race and gender diversity task forces documenting race and gender bias in the courts. *See* Report of the Working Committees to the Second Circuit Task Force on Gender, Racial and Ethnic Fairness in the Courts, 1997 Ann. Surv. Am. L. 11, 43 (1997) (reporting that "far more women and minority men than white men reported observing biased conduct based on gender and that far more minorities than whites reported observing biased conduct based on race or ethnicity"); *see also* Special Committee on Race and Ethnicity, Report of the Special Committee on Race and Ethnicity to the D.C. Circuit Task Force on Gender, Race, and Ethnic Bias, 64 Geo. Wash. L. Rev. 189, 268–69 (1996) (finding "pro se filers are 18 percent white, 78 percent black, 0.4 percent American Indian, 1.2 percent Asian, and 5 percent Hispanic" and "when compared with the general population (66% black, 30% white), blacks are overrepresented (78% of petitioners) and whites underrepresented (18%) among bankruptcy court pro se petitioners"); John C. Coughenour, et. al., *The Effects of Gender in The Federal Courts: The Final Report of The Ninth Circuit Gender Bias Task Force*, 67 S. Cal. L. Rev. 745, 811 (1994) (excerpting remarks from Sandra Day O'Connor announcing the findings of the task force that "gender adds an extra dimension to courtroom and law firm interactions, a dimension that is often discomforting and sometimes destructive to female counsel and perhaps to their clients"); *But see* Commission on Gender & Commission on Race & Ethnicity, Report of the Third Circuit Task Force on Equal Treatment in the Courts, 42 Vill. L. Rev. 1355, 1382 (1997) (finding that "large majorities of all groups agreed that they had not suffered or observed adverse treatment based upon race, ethnicity or gender").

9. Why is a diverse judiciary an important societal goal?

Chapter 3

CRITICAL RACE THEORY
AND TORTS

This chapter considers the doctrine of consent, contributory negligence and assault and battery in the context of cases that you are probably familiar with from your first-year Torts classes. Professor Frank McClellan states:

> My hypothesis is that the race problem impacts on every aspect of a tort claim, adversely affecting lawyers, clients, and the public conception of justice. Moreover, the approach of pretending that race has nothing to do with tort law compounds the evil by allowing private bias to control.... We need to go beneath the doctrine to gain a better appreciation of the scope and depth of the influence of race on decision making in torts cases.

Frank M. McClellan, *The Dark Side of Tort Reform: Searching For Racial Justice*, 48 Rutgers L. Rev. 761, 772–73 (1996). As you read this chapter, see if you agree with him.

SECTION 1. THE DOCTRINE OF CONSENT

O'BRIEN v. CUNARD S.S. CO., LTD.

154 Mass. 272, 28 N.E. 266 (1891).

OPINION: KNOWLTON, J.

This case presents two questions: first, whether there was any evidence to warrant the jury in finding that the defendant, by any of its servants or agents, committed an assault on the plaintiff; secondly, whether there was evidence on which the jury could have found that the defendant was guilty of negligence towards the plaintiff. To sustain the first count, which was for an alleged assault, the plaintiff relied on the fact that the surgeon who was employed by the defendant vaccinated her on shipboard, while she was on her passage from Queenstown to Boston. On this branch of the case the question is whether there was any evidence that the surgeon used force upon the plaintiff against her will. In determining whether the act was lawful or unlawful, the surgeon's conduct must be considered in connection with the circumstances. If the plaintiff's behavior was such as to indicate [consent] on her part, he was justified in his act, whatever her unexpressed feelings may have been. In determining whether she consented, he could be guided only by her overt acts and the manifestations of her feelings. *Ford* v. *Ford*, 143 Mass. 577, 578. *McCarthy* v. *Boston & Lowell Railroad*, 148 Mass. 550, 552. It is undisputed that at Boston there are strict quarantine regulations in regard to the examination of immigrants, to see that they are protected from small-pox by vaccination, and that only those persons who hold a certificate from the medical officer of the steamship, stating that they are so protected, are permitted to land without detention in quarantine or vaccination by the port physician. It appears that the defendant is accustomed to have its surgeons vaccinate all immigrants who desire it, and who are not protected by previous vaccination, and give them a certificate which is accepted at quarantine as evidence of their protection. Notices of the regulations at quarantine, and of the willingness of the ship's medical officer to vaccinate such as needed vaccination, were posted about the ship, in various languages, and on the day when the operation was performed the surgeon had a right to presume that she and the other women who were vaccinated understood the importance and purpose of vaccination for those who bore no marks to show that they were protected. By the plaintiff's testimony, which in this particular is undisputed, it appears that about two hundred women passengers were assembled below, and she understood from conversation with them that they were to be vaccinated; that she stood about fifteen feet from the surgeon, and saw them form in a line and pass in turn before him; that he "examined their arms, and, passing some of them by, proceeded to vaccinate those that had no mark"; that she did not hear him say anything to any of them; that upon being passed by they each received a card and went on deck; that when her turn came she showed him her arm, and he looked at it and said there was no mark, and that she should be vaccinated; that she told him she had been vaccinated before and it left no mark; "that he then said nothing, that he should vaccinate her again"; that she held up her arm to be vaccinated; that no one touched her; that she did not tell him that she did not want to be vaccinated; and that she took the ticket which he gave her certifying that he had vaccinated her, and used it at quarantine. She was one of a large number of women who were vaccinated on that occasion, without, so far as appears, a word of objection from any of them. They all indicated by their conduct that they desired to avail themselves of the provisions made for their benefit. There was nothing in the conduct of the plaintiff to indicate to the surgeon that she did not wish to obtain a card which would save her from detention at quarantine, and to be vaccinated, if necessary, for that purpose. Viewing his conduct in the light of the circumstances, it was lawful; and there was no evidence tending to show that it was not. The ruling of the court on this part of the case was correct.

The plaintiff contends that, if it was lawful for the surgeon to vaccinate her, the vaccination, as alleged in the second count, was negligently performed. "There was no evidence of want of care or precaution by the defendant in the selection of the surgeon, or in the procuring of the virus or vaccine matter." Unless there was evidence that the surgeon was negligent in performing the operation, and unless the defendant is liable for this negligence, the plaintiff must fail on the second count.

Whether there was any evidence of negligence of the surgeon, we need not inquire, for we are of opinion that the defendant is not liable for his want of care in performing surgical operations. The only ground on which it is argued that the defendant is liable for his negligence is, that he is a servant engaged in the defendant's business, and subject to its control. We think this argument is founded on a mistaken construction of the duty imposed on the defendant by law. By the act of Congress of August 2, 1882, § 5, it is provided that "every steamship or other vessel carrying or bringing emigrant passengers, or passengers other than cabin passengers, exceeding fifty in number, shall carry a duly qualified and competent surgeon or medical practitioner, who shall be rated as such in the ship's articles, and who shall be provided with surgical instruments, medical comforts, and medicines proper and necessary for diseases and accidents incident to sea voyages, and for the proper medical treatment of such passengers during the voyage, and with such articles of food and nourishment as may be proper and necessary for preserving the health of infants and young children; and the services of such surgeon or medical practitioner shall be promptly given, in any case of sickness or disease, to any of the passengers, or to any infant or young child of any such passengers, who may need his services. For a violation of either of the provisions of this section the master of the vessel shall be liable to a penalty not exceeding two hundred and fifty dollars."

Under this statute it is the duty of ship-owners to provide a competent surgeon, whom the passengers may employ if they choose, in the business of healing their wounds and curing their diseases. The law does not put the business of treating sick passengers into the charge of common carriers, and make them responsible for the proper management of it. The work which the physician or surgeon does in such cases is under the control of the passengers themselves. It is their business, not the business of the carrier. They may employ the ship's surgeon, or some other physician or surgeon who happens to be on board, or they may treat themselves, if they are sick, or may go without treatment if they prefer; and if they employ the surgeon, they may determine how far they will submit themselves to his directions, and what of his medicines they will take and what reject, and whether they will submit to a surgical operation or take the risk of going without it. The master or owners of the ship cannot interfere in the treatment of the medical officer when he attends a passenger. He is not their servant, engaged in their business and subject to their control as to his mode of treatment.

They do their whole duty if they employ a duly qualified and competent surgeon and medical practitioner, and supply him with all necessary and proper instruments, medicines, and medical comforts, and have him in readiness for such passengers as choose to employ him. This is the whole requirement of the statute of the United States applicable to such cases, and if, by the nature of their undertaking to transport passengers by sea, they are under a liability at the common law to make provision for their passengers in this respect, that liability is no greater. It is quite reasonable that the owners of a steamship used in the transportation of passengers should be required by law to provide a competent person to whom sick passengers can apply for medical treatment, and when they have supplied such a person, it would be unreasonable to hold them responsible for all the particulars of his treatment, when he is engaged in the business of other persons in regard to which they are powerless to interfere.

The reasons on which it is held, in the courts of the United States and of Massachusetts, that the owners are liable for the negligence of a pilot in navigating the ship, even though he is appointed by public agencies, and the master has no voice in the selection of him, do not apply to this case. *The China*, 7 Wall. 53, 67. *Yates v. Brown*, 8 Pick. 23. The pilot is engaged in the navigation of the ship, for which, on grounds of public policy, the owners should be held responsible. The business is theirs, and they have certain rights of control in regard to it. They may determine when and how it shall be undertaken, and the master may displace the pilot for certain causes. But in England it has been held that even in such cases the owners are not liable. *Carruthers* v. *Sydebotham*, 4 M. & S. 98. The Protector, 1 W. Robinson 45. *The Maria*, 1 W. Robinson 95.

The view which we have taken of this branch of the case is fully sustained by a unanimous judgment of the Court of Appeals of New York, in *Laubheim* v. *De Koninglyke Stoomboot Co.* 107 N.Y. 228. *See also Secord* v. *St. Paul, Minneapolis, & Manitoba Railway*, 18 F. 221; *McDonald* v. *Massachusetts General Hospital*, 120 Mass. 432. We are of opinion that on both parts of the case the rulings at the trial were correct.

The evidence which was excepted to, consisting of the printed quarantine regulations above referred to, and of testimony that only the steerage passengers holding a surgeon's certificate were allowed to land, all others being vaccinated by the port physician or detained at quarantine, was rightly admitted.

Exceptions overruled.

Notes and Questions

1. Mary O'Brien was an Irish woman. How does Critical Race Theory apply to her?

2. The court early in the decision states "[i]f the plaintiff's behavior was such as to indicate consent on her part, he was justified in his act,

whatever her unexpressed feelings may have been. In determining whether she consented, he could be guided only by her overt acts and the manifestations of her feelings." Doesn't that statement determine the outcome? What has the court assumed away?

3. The Restatement (Second) of Torts provides that the plaintiff has the burden of proof in a lack of consent to an invasion of their person, but not to an invasion of their property. Does the law have an unconscious bias in favor of property protection?

4. Do you think Mary O'Brien believed she could refuse the vaccination? Should that make a difference to the court's analysis?

5. If the vaccination policy was to prevent the spread of disease, why were only those in steerage required to get the vaccination?

6. Consider the next case which provides a more recent look at the issue of doctor-patient consent.

MADRIGAL v. QUILLIGAN

No. CV 75–2057–JWC (1978) (C.D. Cal.).

JUDGE CURTIS.

This is a civil rights action brought pursuant to Title 42, U.S.C. § 1983, by ten Mexican women claiming violations of their constitutional rights. Specifically, they charge that they were surgically sterilized at the USC–Los Angeles County General Medical Center, allegedly without their voluntary and informed consent.

STATE ACTION

Since the Medical Center is owned and largely funded by the County of Los Angeles and all defendant doctors were either employees of the hospital or working under the direction and control of the hospital staff, there can be little doubt but that the State action requirements of Section 1983 have been satisfied. *See McCabe v. Nassau County Medical Center*, 453 F.2d 698 (2d Cir. 1971). *Compare Chrisman v. Sisters of St. Joseph of Peace*, 506 F.2d 308 (9th Cir. 1974).

MAINTAINABILITY OF ACTION UNDER § 1983

It is also clear that procreation is a fundamental constitutional right, *Roe v. Wade*, 410 U.S. 113 (1973); *Griswold v. Connecticut*, 381 U.S. 479 (1965); *Skinner v. Oklahoma*, 316 U.S. 535 (1942), and a person being deprived of this right is entitled to relief under Section 1983.

* * *

CONCERTED ACTION

The rather subtle but underlying thrust of plaintiffs' complaint appears to be that they were all victims of a concerted plan by hospital attendants and doctors to push them, as members of a low socio-economic group who tend toward large families, to consent to sterilization in order to accomplish some sinister, invidious, social purpose. A careful search of the record fails to produce any evidence whatever to support this contention. It did appear that the hospital had received funds for the establishment of a family planning program, and that discussion and encouragement of alternative methods of birth control, including sterilization, were carried on in the outpatient prenatal care clinic. In the obstetrics ward, however, whenever a sterilization procedure was suggested or advised, it was done on the initiative of the individual employee. There was no hospital rule or instruction directed to these employees relative to the encouragement of patients to be sterilized and there was no evidence of concerted or conspiratorial action.

Consequently, this case in its present posture consists of ten separate and distinct claims against the individual doctors who actually performed the sterilization, and the liability of each must be determined by his own conduct.

ACTIONABLE CONDUCT UNDER § 1983

* * *

On its face, the statute creates a species of tort liability that admits of no immunities. *Imbler v. Pachtman*, 424 U.S. 409, 417 (1976). * * * [The court then explains how the Supreme Court has carved out exceptions of absolute immunity from Section 1983 liability for legislators, judges, and prosecutors for acts performed in their official capacities and "qualified" immunity for certain State officers. The court then describes how appellate court decisions have extended the qualified immunity to a variety of state officials including State doctors.]

* * *

* * *In the *Downs* case the court was presented with precisely the type of "informed consent" to sterilization problem with which we are faced in the instant case. The court ruled there that in order for the defendant physician to be liable the absence of free and informed consent must be intelligibly communicated to the doctor. If he

> "negligently interpreted plaintiff's communications to indicate she consented to the operation, he is not liable under the standards enunciated in *Wood*, even if plaintiff did not intend to consent."

Liability, in this context, is predicated upon some conduct which is either malicious or is in wanton disregard of constitutional rights. There would be liability

> "... if ... [the doctor] determined that sterilization of the plaintiff was for her own good or the good of society and as a consequence of that belief ignored indications from the plaintiff that she did not consent to the operation, or if ... he attempted to take advantage of her mental and communication limitations to unduly influence her decision...." (Citations omitted)

[handwritten margin note: must be wanton violation of CR]

With these legal principles in mind we turn to a consideration of the facts.

COMMUNICATION BREAKDOWN

This case is essentially the result of a breakdown in communication between the patients and the doctors. All plaintiffs are Spanish speaking women whose ability to understand and speak English is limited. This fact is generally understood by the staff at the Medical Center and most members have acquired enough familiarity with the language to get by. There is also an interpreter available whose services are used when thought to be necessary. But even with these precautions misunderstandings are bound to occur.

Furthermore, the cultural background of these particular women has contributed to the problem in a subtle but very significant way. According to the plaintiffs' anthropological expert, they are members of a traditional Mexican rural subculture, a relatively narrow spectrum of Mexican people living in this country whose lifestyle and cultural background derives from the lifestyle and culture of small rural communities in Mexico. He further testified that a cultural trait which is very important with this group is an extreme dependence upon family. Most come from large families and wish to have large families for their own comfort and support. Furthermore, the status of a woman and her husband within that group depends largely upon the woman's ability to produce children. If for any reason she cannot, she is considered an incomplete woman and is apt to suffer a disruption of her relationship with her family and husband. When faced with a decision of whether or not to be sterilized, the decision process is a much more traumatic event with her than it would be with a typical patient and, consequently, she would require greater explanation, more patient advice, and greater care in interpreting her consent than persons not members of such a subculture would require.

But this need for such delicate treatment is not readily apparent. The anthropological expert testified that he would not have known that these women possessed these traits had he not conducted tests and a study which required some 450 hours of time. He further stated that a determination by him based upon any less time would not have been worth "beans." It is not surprising therefore that the staff of a busy metropolitan hospital which has neither the time nor the staff to make such esoteric studies would be unaware of these atypical cultural traits.

It is against this backdrop therefore that we must analyze the conduct of the doctors who treated the plaintiffs in this case.

DOCTOR'S CUSTOM AND PRACTICE

Since these operations occurred between 1971 and 1974 and were performed by the doctors operating in a busy obstetrics ward, it is not surprising that none of the doctors have any independent recollection of the events leading up to the operations. They all testified, however, that it was their custom and practice not to suggest a sterilization procedure unless a patient asked for it or there were medical complications which would require the doctor, in the exercise of prudent medical procedures, to make such suggestion. They further testified that it was their practice when a patient requested sterilization to explain its irreversible result and they stated that they would not perform the operation unless they were certain in their own mind that the patient understood the nature of the operation and was requesting the procedure. The weight to be given to such testimony and the inferences to be drawn therefrom will be determined in the light of all the testimony relating to each doctor's conduct.

Guadalupe Acosta and Rebecca Figueroa

These two plaintiffs have sued Edward I. Cohen, M.D., a resident physician at the Medical Center at the time the operation was performed. Dr. Cohen was never served and these plaintiffs assert no claim or right to recovery against any other party defendant except the defendant E.J. Quilligan, M.D., against whom this action was dismissed. Therefore, since there is no basis upon which these plaintiffs may succeed in this action, their causes of action are dismissed.

Dolores Madrigal

The plaintiff Madrigal was born in a small town in Mexico and attended school there through the sixth grade. She does not read or speak English fluently. She had two children and after the birth of her second child she underwent a tubal ligation performed by Dr. Rutland. The medical file contains an early note that Mrs. Madrigal wished a tubal ligation. If this were so, she apparently changed her mind as she refused the suggestion several times prior to the operation. Presumably such a procedure was suggested because Mrs. Madrigal had suffered from a placenta previa during heir first pregnancy and from toxemia during her second. During labor, and having indicated that she did not wish a tubal ligation, her husband was called to the hospital. She overheard an interpreter telling him that because of the complications she might die in the event of a future pregnancy. She was then told that her husband had agreed to the operation and she was again presented with a consent form which she signed, inserting in her own handwriting therein a statement that she understood she was not going to have any more children. She complains that some pressure was put upon her to sign the consent, although Nurse Lang, who witnessed the signature, testified that she would not have witnessed a consent for sterilization if the patient had not verified her understanding of the nature of the operation and its consequences. In any event, there is no evidence that Dr. Rutland, who performed the operation, had any part in any overzealous solicitation for the sterilization, even if it had occurred. Dr. Rutland, on the other hand, testified that he speaks some Spanish and in accordance with his custom and practice would have explained the nature of the procedure, its permanency and its risks through an interpreter. In any event, he had before him the medical file which indicated an earlier desire on the part of the plaintiff for a tubal ligation and her written consent with the insertion of her own handwriting that she understood that the operation would prevent her from having children ever again.

I find that under the circumstances Dr. Rutland performed the operation in the bona fide belief that Mrs. Madrigal had given her informed and voluntary consent, and that his belief was reasonable.

Maria Hurtado

Mrs. Hurtado is a forty-two year old Mexican–American born in Mexico and has a sixth grade education. She has five living children and gave birth to three more who were born dead. She has had three cesarean sections and was given a tubal ligation by Dr. Neuman after the birth of her last child. Mrs. Hurtado contends that she was never informed about the nature and effect of the tubal ligation and nothing was ever said about it until she was in labor. She further states that the consent forms were brought to her during labor and she was not aware that she was signing a consent for tubal ligation. Although Mrs. Hurtado denies it, the hospital records indicate that she had made a request to the intern in the clinic some time before that she desired a tubal ligation. A similar note appeared in the medical record made by another doctor during another one of Mrs. Hurtado's clinical visits. At the time of her admission, she was examined by still another doctor to whom she again indicated her desire to have no more children. Consequently, consent forms were prepared and were signed by her before she had had any medication and before she was in active labor. Dr. Neuman, who performed the operation, testified that it was his custom and practice to always ask a patient who had indicated that she wanted a tubal ligation to again express her consent. In the light of the contrary evidence, Mrs. Hurtado's statement that she did not remember signing the consent for tubal ligation and had not been informed of its nature and results is simply not credible.

I find therefore that the evidence is insufficient to rebut the inferences drawn from the record, and that in any event Dr. Neuman was acting in a bona fide belief that Mrs. Hurtado had consented to the operation and that such belief was reasonable.

Jovita Rivera

This plaintiff was born in Mexicali, Mexico, in 1946 and came to the United States to live in 1968. She neither speaks nor understands the English language well. There have been five children of the marriage, one of whom was born dead. Mrs. Rivera obtained prenatal care at the Medical Center. At the time of her admission to the hospital she told the admitting doctor that she wanted her tubes tied. She had previously agreed with her husband that she would have her tubes tied after the fourth child. She understood, however, from her sister-in-law that this operation was reversible and that, at a later date if she decided she wanted more children, she could have tubes untied. She did not tell anyone at the hospital of this belief. While in labor, an emergency situation arose in which it became apparent that Mrs. Rivera could not deliver normally and a cesarean section was necessary within the next ten minutes in order to save the baby's life. Because of the emergency, a resident physician was called in to perform the operation. He again asked the plaintiff if she intended to have her tubes tied and she answered in the affirmative. Because of the emergency nature of the matter, no written consent was obtained from the plaintiff, but as a part of the cesarean section a tubal ligation was performed.

The doctor testified that it was not his practice to ask a patient about a sterilization procedure unless it was suggested by the patient herself or unless some medical reason for doing so arose. After it was determined that a cesarean section would have to be performed on Mrs. Rivera, and seeing the note in the hospital record indicating that she had previously asked to have her tubes tied, he again mentioned it to her and got an affirmative answer. The doctor further testified that he would never have performed a tubal ligation had he not fully believed that the plaintiff specifically asked for it.

From these facts, I conclude that the doctor was acting in good faith believing that he had an unequivocal consent and that such belief was reasonable under the circumstances.

Maria Figueroa

Mrs. Figueroa is a thirty-one year old Mexican woman, the mother of three children, all of whom were delivered by cesarean section. At the time of the birth of the first child both Mrs. Figueroa and her husband had executed a consent form for a possible emergency tubal ligation or hysterectomy prior to the delivery of the child by cesarean section. However, this was not necessary and no such operation was performed. At the time of the birth of her last child, Dr. Kreitzer attempted a low transverse cesarean section which he was compelled to abandon in favor of a classical cesarean section when he encountered dense adhesions affecting the uterus and bladder rendering it impossible to mobilize the bladder. The excessive scarring and adhesions and the additional incisions significantly increased the risk in the event of a subsequent pregnancy, including uterine rupture. At the time of her most recent previous cesarean section, multiple adhesions between the interior abdominal wall omentum and uterus were also noted and the lower uterine segment was described as very thin. Since Mrs. Figueroa was already in surgery when these conditions were revealed, her husband was called and the increased risks were discussed with him. He consented to the tubal ligation for his wife and signed a consent for sterilization form and Dr. Kreitzer and senior resident William E. Merritt executed a physician's certificate of emergency certifying that the delay necessary to obtain complete consent for treatment would endanger the patient's life or chance of recovery. Mrs. Figueroa now believes that the operation was unnecessary.

I find that Dr. Dreitzer performed the operation in the bona fide belief that Mrs. Figueroa would have consented had she been able, since she had done so once before when a cesarean procedure seemed imminent. This belief was further supported by the written consent form signed by the husband after the risks had been explained to him. Such a belief I find to be reasonable.

Helena Orozco

Helena Orozco was born in Forth Worth, Texas, and speaks both English and Spanish. She has had four children by a previous marriage and two by her present marriage. She has, in addition, one adopted daughter. She received her prenatal care at the Medical Center and was, on many occasions, advised by personnel that she should have her tubes tied so that she would not have any more children because she had already had "too many cesarean sections." Her condition was further complicated by a ruptured hernia which someone attending her indicated would be a serious problem in the event of another pregnancy. She at first indicated that she did not want a tubal ligation but did consent to the cesarean. At a later time, however, she did sign her written consent because, she says, of the insistence of some member of the staff. The defendant Robert Yee performed the cesarean section, bilateral tubal ligation, and umbilical hernia repair, in reliance upon the written consent found in the file. There is no evidence which indicates that Dr. Yee was present or participated in obtaining the written consent, nor that he was aware that the plaintiff was in any way unwilling to have the operation. In fact, he testified that he would not have performed the sterilization procedures if he had any reason whatever to doubt the validity of the written consent.

I conclude therefore as to this defendant, Dr. Yee, that he was acting in the bona fide belief that he had the plaintiff's consent and that this belief was reasonable.

Georgina Hernandez

Mrs. Hernandez is a thirty-eight year old Mexican–American woman who understands some English and who had no prenatal care at the Medical Center. She first came to the hospital with complications as she was already bleeding and experiencing labor pains. As she progressed it became apparent that a cesarean section was necessary at which time the doctor asked her about having her tubes tied. He told her the Mexican people were very poor and that she should not have any more children because she could not support them. She does not remember signing any consent form although there is one in the file. Plaintiff contends that her handwriting on this consent form shows indications of medication and traumatic shock, especially so when compared with other signatures of hers appearing in the file. The handwriting expert believed this signature was written under abnormal conditions. He testified that this could have been caused in one of several ways. One of these possibilities was that she was in severe labor pains and another possibility, which seems to me to be more credible, was that the consent was signed while she was lying in her hospital bed. In any event, there was nothing about this signature which would suggest to the surgeon that her consent was equivocal. The doctor testified that Mrs. Hernandez had been offered a sterilization operation at the time of her admission but had refused. As the time for delivery arrived and it became apparent that a cesarean section would be required, he again discussed the sterilization process with Mrs. Hernandez, at which time she signed the consent for cesarean but was not yet willing to consent to the sterilization. Shortly before she was going in to the operating room, she indicated the decision to have the operation and this was noted in the file. The doctor denied that at any time he had made the statement that she should not have any more children because the Mexican people were too poor to support them. He also states that such a remark is entirely out of character and that he was certain he did not make it. He further stated that the consent was obtained before any anesthetic was applied and before she had been given any medication which would affect her ability to make a decision. He said that it was his custom and practice never to perform such an operation without a clear, voluntary consent by the patient, and that he would not have performed such an operation on this occasion had he not believed that she had voluntarily consented to it.

I find therefore that in performing a tubal ligation upon this plaintiff, Dr. Mutch was acting in the bona fide belief that he had the voluntary and knowing consent of the plaintiff, and that such a belief was reasonable.

CONSUELO HERMOSILLO

This plaintiff was born in 1949 in Vera Cruz, Mexico, where she was educated through the eighth grade. She had three children, all born by cesarean section. It was at the birth of her third child that a tubal ligation was performed. She had received prenatal care at a County clinic where she was informed that it was advisable, after her third cesarean, to have a sterilization operation because of the risk of serious complications in further pregnancies. She testified that she did not want to give up having more children and that because of this advice given her at the clinic often came home crying. She then discussed the matter with her sister-in-law who told her that she had had her tubes tied and that she thought she could later have them untied. Such a belief was never mentioned to anyone at the hospital. In the early states of labor it appeared that Mrs. Hermosillo might be able to deliver normally but as the delivery progressed it became apparent that a cesarean section would be necessary, at which time she apparently signed a consent form for tubal ligation. Neither she nor the doctors have any specific recollection of what occurred at the time the consent was actually signed. The form, however, did contain a statement in her own handwriting in Spanish to the effect that she understood the nature of the operation. Both Dr. Muth, who performed the tubal ligation, and the senior resident physician, Allen Luckman, M.D., who assisted in the surgery, both testified that they would not have performed the sterilization process had they not believed that Mrs. Hermosillo had given a free and voluntary consent as indicated by the written form in the hospital record. The evidence amply supports the inference that Mrs. Hermosillo was thoroughly acquainted with the nature of the operation, except possibly for the undisclosed belief that despite what doctors told her she could have her tubes untied.

I conclude therefore that Mrs. Hermosillo was fully aware of the nature and effect of the tubal ligation although she had hoped for a normal delivery in which event such an operation would not have been done. But when it became apparent that a cesarean section was necessary she changed her mind and voluntarily consented and, in doing so, signed a consent form upon which the surgeon relied. I find that Dr. Muth performed the tubal ligation in the bona fide belief that Mrs. Hermosillo had consented and that his belief was reasonable under the circumstances.

Estela Benavides

This plaintiff was born in 1942 in the State of Michoacan, Mexico. She does not either speak or read English and has only a sixth grade education in Mexican schools. She and her husband have three children, the first two of which were born normally. When her third child was expected she developed complications which started with profuse bleeding and she eventually asked to be delivered by cesarean section. She was asked by the doctors if she wanted a tubal ligation in view of the potential high risk of future cesarean deliveries. She first refused, but after some persuasion she signed a written consent for she was fearful that if she should become pregnant again she might die and her children would be left alone with no one to care for them. In her written consent, she wrote in Spanish in her own handwriting the phrase, "I understand that I will not have any more children after this operation."

I find that the plaintiff was well aware of the nature and effect of the tubal ligation, and the consent form was signed by her after weighing all considerations. I further conclude that the doctor performing the tubal ligation did so in the bona fide belief that the plaintiff had given her free and knowing consent and that this belief was reasonable.

A Woman's Decision While in Labor

The plaintiffs have placed great reliance upon a New York psychiatrist who stated unequivocally that it would be impossible for a woman in labor, after suffering her first pain, to give an intelligent and knowing consent to a sterilization operation. Such a statement completely defies common sense. I prefer as more credible the testimony of the other doctors to the effect that whether a consent represented an informed and voluntary decision depended upon many facts, that a judgment could best be made by someone present at the moment the decision is made. One doctor testified that the fact that a woman was in labor might or might not affect her decision, depending upon the circumstances. There was further evidence that the attending physician was probably in the best position to make a judgment since he would be acutely aware of the necessity of having the patient's consent.

CONCLUSION

This case has not been an easy one to try for it has involved social, emotional and cultural considerations of great complexity. There is no doubt but that these women have suffered severe emotional and physical stress because of these operations. One can sympathize with them for their inability to communicate clearly, but one can hardly blame the doctors for relying on these indicia of consent which appeared to be unequivocal on their face and which are in constant use in the Medical Center.

Let judgment be entered for the defendants.

Notes and Questions

1.   Once the Court states that the case is "essentially the result of a breakdown in communication between the patients and the doctors," the reader suspects that the plaintiffs will lose. Do you agree with the court's analysis? *Madrigal* was affirmed on appeal. *See Madrigal v. Quilligan*, 639 F.2d 789 (9th Cir. 1981).

2.   How carefully did the Court consider the circumstances surrounding when consent was given? Do you get the sense that the Court had any empathy for the plaintiffs? Was that a function of their gender? race? class status?

3.   How did the Court take into account the power differential between the plaintiffs and the doctors?

4.   Plaintiffs had the burden of proof. What additional evidence would they have needed to present in order to prevail in this Court?

5.   An anthropologist who was an expert witness in *Madrigal v. Quilligan*, wrote about the trial. *See* Carlos G. Velez–I, *The Nonconsenting Sterilization of Mexican Women in Los Angeles* in TWICE A MINORITY: MEXICAN AMERICAN WOMEN 235–248 (1980). He described the judge as a Nixon appointee who was "a white-haired 70–year-old" who "seemed like the stereotype of the paternalistic figure" with a "[f]irm-jawed, angular face[], with piercing blue eyes set beneath profuse eyebrows that moved in unison in mostly frowns." *Id*. at 243–244. Judge Curtis, the description continues, was a "conservative judge who lived aboard his yacht in Newport Beach, one of the most prestigious areas in Southern California." *Id*. at 244. The plaintiffs' two attorneys—one male, one female—were "Chicano lawyers [who] came from the local poverty legal centers...." *Id*. at 243. The defendants' two attorneys—one male, one female—were White—and "from one of the more prestigious Beverly Hill law firms" who "seemed quite relaxed ... in the courtroom." *Id*. at 243. The defendants were described as follows: "at the time of sterilization the mean age ... was 32.6 years with a range of 24 to 39 years; they had 3.6 mean number of children and a mean income of $9,500 per year, which was the median family income for that of the total United

States population; a mean education of 8.5 years which is only .6 years below that of the median Mexican females in the United States; and stable housing and employment characteristics." *Id.* at 238–239. The hospital was "in the middle of the largest Mexican barrio outside Mexico City." *Id.* at 246.

6. Much has been written about the analysis of legal decisions based upon the empathy the judge has for those litigants who come seeking justice. *See e.g.* Lynne N. Henderson, *Legality and Empathy*, 85 Mich. L. Rev. 1574 (1987); Toni M. Massaro, *Empathy, Legal Storytelling, and the Rule of Law: New Words, Old Wounds?* 87 Mich. L. Rev. 2099 (1989); Sophie H. Pirie, John T. Noonan, *As Judge: What Can Empathic Judging Mean For Women?*, 12 J. L. & Religion 541 (1995–96); John T. Noonan, Jr., Persons and Masks of the Law (1976). Can you point to portions of *Madrigal v. Quilligan* to show that the Judge was not empathetic towards the plaintiffs? Can you point to portions of *Madrigal v. Quilligan* to show that the Judge was empathetic towards the plaintiffs? Consider the following excerpt from the Court's opinion: "[t]he plaintiffs have placed great reliance upon a New York psychiatrist who stated unequivocally that it would be impossible for a woman in labor, after suffering her first pain, to give an intelligent and knowing consent to a sterilization operation. Such a statement completely defies common sense."

7. For an example of a judge who "appreciates the importance of [a litigant's] perspective" and who seemed "to understand that an important part of his job is to try, to the best of his ability, to imagine their situations" *see* Catherine Gage O'Grady, *Empathy and Perspective in Judging: The Honorable William C. Canby*, Jr., 33 Ariz. St. L. J. 4, 6 (2001).

8. Reread the following excerpt from the Court. Where is the burden placed? Why do the doctors escape liability?

According to the plaintiffs' anthropological expert, they are members of a traditional Mexican rural subculture, a relatively narrow spectrum of Mexican people living in this country whose lifestyle and cultural background derives from the lifestyle and culture of small rural communities in Mexico. He further testified that a cultural trait which is very important with this group is an extreme dependence upon family. Most come from large families and wish to have large families for their own comfort and support. Furthermore, the status of a woman and her husband within that group depends largely upon the woman's ability to produce children. If for any reason she cannot, she is considered an incomplete woman and is apt to suffer a disruption of her relationship with her family and husband. When faced with a decision of whether or not to be sterilized, the decision process is a much more traumatic event with her than it would be with a typical patient and, consequently, she would require greater explanation, more patient advice, and greater care in interpreting her consent than persons not members of such a subculture would require.

But this need for such delicate treatment is not readily apparent. The anthropological expert testified that he would not have known that these women possessed these traits had he not conducted tests and a study which required some 450 hours of time. He further stated that a determination by him based upon any less time would not have been worth "beans." It is not surprising therefore that the staff of a busy metropolitan hospital which has neither the time nor the staff to make such esoteric studies would be unaware of these atypical cultural traits.

The hospital was "in the middle of the largest Mexican barrio outside Mexico City." Shouldn't the doctors have been more aware of the effect that sterilization would have on their patients? Is being busy a legally valid excuse for improper patient care? What kind of information should doctors be required to obtain before sterilizing women, some of whom were only 24 years old? Notice how the fact that the plaintiffs' anthropology expert spent 450 hours studying the plaintiffs and their community was used against the plaintiffs.

9. Consider the following excerpt by Professor Taunya Banks who discusses the court's decision in *O'Brien v. Cunard Steamship Company* as well as *Madrigal v. Quilligan*.

TAUNYA LOVELL BANKS

Teaching Law With Flaws: Adopting A Pluralistic Approach to Torts
57 Mo. L. Rev. 443, 443–445, 448–454 (1992).

It is important to say at the outset that this discussion about one case, *O'Brien v. Cunard Steamship Co.*, would not have been as rich without access to the pleadings and trial record in the case. For example, much of Professor Bourne's discussion of *O'Brien* relies heavily on information not contained in the published case. As I explained in this essay, most casebooks contain appellate cases where the stories of the parties have been distilled; the extent to which the full story is told falls to the law teacher.

Too often we teach law courses as perspectiveless, adopting an analytical approach that consciously acknowledges no specific cultural, political, or class characteristics, but which is decidedly male, white and elitist. We ignore personal baggage both judges and litigants bring with them to the courtroom. But many of our students are not fooled.

Today's law school classroom is more diverse both as to gender, race, and class, than ten or twenty years ago. This more diverse student body enters law school with life experiences and perspectives not fully reflected in our legal textbooks. However, we law teachers tend to acknowledge these differences, if at all, only in the margins of our courses.

Data I collected from law schools indicate that large numbers of law students, especially white women and people of color, feel alienated in law school. Many students believe that law and the legal system are not neutral, but reflect only the values and perspectives of a white male dominated society. This dominant society also assumes incorrectly, that all people in America share their values and perspectives.

* * *

It is undisputed that Mary O'Brien did not verbally say she wanted to be vaccinated, but according to the appellate court, her conduct also did not suggest lack of consent. Specifically, Mary testified, and the court accepts, that she told the physician she had already been vaccinated. It is undisputed that the physician found no mark on her arm, but it also is undisputed that the physician told Mary she should be vaccinated again. Finally, it is undisputed that Mary continued to hold her arm up toward the doctor after he made the remark and the doctor vaccinated her. So the legal question is whether in light of the facts supplied by the appellate court and the court's legal definition Mary O'Brien "consented" to be vaccinated.

When you read the case, whether in the textbook or the reporter, the court's decision seems very clear cut. The court's operational definition of consent is the failure to indicate verbally or by conduct lack of consent. The court reasons that Mary's consent was implied by her conduct. According to the court, a reasonable person would conclude from this conduct that Mary consented to be vaccinated.

Although the case seems very clear cut and many in the class agree with the court that she did consent, some students still have questions. Students might claim that Mary's actions were ambiguous. She may have been holding out her arm to refute the physician's claim that she needed to be vaccinated. Perhaps the physician should have affirmatively asked Mary if she wanted to be vaccinated. It seems a case can be made that her conduct is not as clear as the court suggests. However, as Professor Bourne points out, it is the "objective" not the "subjective" perspective that counts here. These questions are all valid, and might be raised in any torts class.

There are other dimensions to this case which display some of the inherent biases in the law and raise some larger issues. Unfortunately, students are denied the information to make a truly informed choice about the wisdom of the decision. Only by reading the trial record and briefs in the appellate court, do you get a more complete picture of the circumstances surrounding this controversy.

This problem is not unique to the Henderson and Pearson casebook, but is a problem of casebooks generally. Critics of the casebook approach to law teaching question the use of appellate cases to teach subjects like torts where factual distinctions are so important. Henderson and Pearson at least put students on notice by occasionally providing them with a more complete picture. Once a more complete record is provided a very different picture emerges. Whether this additional information changes the outcome is a matter of dispute. However, these additional facts force students to understand that the judges were operating from a perspective that was quite different from that of the plaintiff Mary O'Brien. Students will see that this difference in perspective may significantly have affected the outcome of the case.

The plaintiff's brief and bill of exceptions indicated that Mary O'Brien was a 17–year-old Irish woman traveling with her recently widowed father and younger brother in steerage from Queenstown in Ireland to Boston. This means while not illiterate, she was poor, unsophisticated, and perhaps, easily intimidated by the authority of the ship's crew. In addition, she was working-class Irish, as opposed to English, a significant difference. Mary had never left home before, and except for the vaccination process had remained with her family during the voyage.

The men who judged her conduct most likely were upper class Anglo–Saxons, so there were some cultural and class differences between the parties. The appellate court concludes that Mary understood the importance and purpose of a vaccination for those who had not been vaccinated. But the trial record does not clearly support this conclusion.

Mary O'Brien testified that she learned once she was in line that she would be vaccinated if she had no vaccination mark. She waited until last before approaching the physician because she had no vaccination mark, but knew from her dead mother that she had been vaccinated as a child. There was no other way back to the deck where she left her family except the door on the elevated platform where the male steerage steward stood. Even though Mary O'Brien could read the signs posted around the ship those signs used the terms "quarantine" and "vaccinate" and the trial record suggests she did not understand the meaning of those terms.

Thus the real issue here is whether Mary consented, or merely submitted to the vaccination. There is a difference, because submission under duress may not be effective consent to battery. The full court record raises the question of whether there was some miscommunication of Mary's wishes because of differences in culture, gender, class, or all these factors and whether the doctor or the steamship company was obligated to do more than was done to ascertain consent.

The question of miscommunication from gender, culture, or class differences are additional concerns, not usually covered in traditional first year subject casebooks. For example, in determining whether a reasonable person would have construed Mary O'Brien's actions as evidence of consent no serious attempt was made by the appellate court to consider the different power dynamics between the parties that resulted from the traditional subordination of women. No attention is paid to the fact that Mary O'Brien, as a person seeking entry into this country, and that the fear of exclusion from the United States has a powerfully coercive aspect. Henderson and Pearson, in their teaching manual raise the class issue by asking whether an upper class or aristocratic English woman would have been treated the same way. It is doubtful since this policy of compelled vaccinations only applied to passengers traveling in steerage, obviously a class distinction.

The record and pleadings also suggest that Mary O'Brien's "silent consent" was either coerced or uninformed. In light of this new information, students are forced to consider whether consent *really* is legally effective if you believe that it would be useless to resist. According to traditional tort law principles the answer is yes. Legally effective consent can be manifested through silence and inaction even where there is no willingness to incur an invasion of the person, because the defendant is entitled to rely upon what a reasonable "man" would understand from the plaintiff's conduct. In addition, under the Restatement (Second) of Torts the plaintiff has the burden of proving lack of consent to a personal invasion, but not to an invasion of property. Thus tort law principles concerning consent either presuppose equal power between individuals on a personal level or are derogatory of the power imbalances that result from differences in gender, class, or culture. But these assumptions are not made when property as opposed to personal invasions are claimed. To some students this distinction between consent to personal as opposed to property invasions may suggest a conscious choice to protect a point of view and power relationship long enjoyed by wealthy propertied men in England and this country.

These are important issues in consent cases both in 1891 and today. In *O'Brien* you have a plaintiff and defendants who are dissimilar based on gender, class, and culture. It is very hard pedagogically to determine whether the defendant doctor could reasonably assume Mary consented. One recurring question is which party should bear the burden of proof on this point and whether the relationship of the parties matters when making this determination. Students would be forced to question the Restatement's position on this issue. Another question is whether the burden of proof in such cases should be viewed as part of the plaintiff's prima facie case, or whether the defendant should have to prove a reasonable belief that plaintiff consented.

There are public policy questions raised by the record in this case. For example, whether the ship owners can argue that the compelled vaccination policy while "uncivilized," was necessary to protect the health of the people already in America. Some students suggest that the public health argument is a sufficiently compelling argument to justify the personal invasion in *O'Brien*. However, others argue that poor people and other subordinated groups are most likely to be adversely affected by coercive public health policies.

All of these questions raise issues of class, gender, and culture, all factors which directly or indirectly influenced the decision in *O'Brien*. I contend it is not enough to raise the class issues, as Henderson and Pearson do in their teacher's manual. The *O'Brien* case illustrates that the gender, class, and cultural differences are so intertwined that each cannot be discussed in isolation because all three are crucial in understanding the true nature of Mary O'Brien's conduct.

One recurring question is whether Mary O'Brien's case would be decided the same way today. There are some analogous modern cases involving gender, class, and cultural miscommunication on this issue of consent. For example, plaintiffs in an unreported 1978 federal district court case from California, *Madrigal v. Quillian*, [sic] alleged that ten Mexican–American women were sterilized without their informed consent by doctors at the University of California at Los Angeles hospital. During the trial, a cultural anthropologist testified for the plaintiffs that the women did not understand the irreversible consequences of sterilization surgery primarily because of a language barrier between the women and the physicians. The district court acknowledged that there was some miscommunication, but concluded that busy physicians do not have the time to deal with more precise language or cultural concerns. The trial judge blamed the women for their inability to communicate more effectively with the physicians.

There are some striking parallels between *Madrigal* and *O'Brien*. In both cases you have busy physicians handling large numbers of poor women. In both you also have poor women whose culture is different from both the defendants and the judge who are interpreting the women's conduct. But in *Madrigal* there is a new complication, language, and more obvious ethnic differences. All of these factors are interrelated to both the harm claimed by the plaintiffs and the way the court resolved the issue of consent. However, in both *O'Brien* and *Madrigal* the unconsenting women lose, and the legal and human issues are whether they should.

The race, culture, gender, and class issues flow naturally from the *O'Brien* trial record, a record usually unavailable to students in the casebooks. Both *O'Brien* and *Madrigal* demonstrate the richness we can bring to our classes when we go beyond the casebooks, and often beyond the recorded cases to supply our students with the whole story. These whole stories more accurately reflect the law as it has always been structured and applied. Laws with flaws, constructed and applied by flawed people. Our goal in legal education should be to learn from these past mistakes and teach our students how to make the laws work for all segments of society.

Notes and Questions

1. How does Professor Banks address the empathy issue between the Court and Mary O'Brien?

2. For an excellent description of how to teach the *O'Brien* decision from a critical perspective, *see* Jody Armour, NEGROPHOBIA AND REASONABLE RACISM: THE HIDDEN COSTS OF BEING BLACK IN AMERICA 84–89 1997. Professor Armor describes the value of providing the additional facts that the court's opinion leaves out. "My students learn early the power of narrative and the capacity of courts to achieve a desired outcome by manipulating the terms of narrative. The notion of law as a body of universal rules that determine the outcomes of disputes dissolves when they see that the framing of legal narrative determines these outcomes at least as much as the underlying substantive rules." *Id.* at 89.

3. As you read the next case, ask yourself why the Court included the race of the attacker in the decision, but not the victim. Was the attacker's race relevant to the Court's decision?

SECTION 2. CONTRIBUTORY NEGLIGENCE: WHAT'S RACE GOT TO DO WITH IT?

WASSELL v. ADAMS

865 F.2d 849 (7th Cir. 1989).

POSNER, CIRCUIT JUDGE.

The plaintiff, born Susan Marisconish, grew up on Macaroni Street in a small town in a poor coal-mining region of Pennsylvania—a town so small and obscure that it has no name. She was the ninth of ten children, and as a child was sexually abused by her stepfather. After graduating from high school she worked briefly as a nurse's aide, then became engaged to Michael Wassell, also from Pennsylvania. Michael joined the Navy in 1985 and was sent to Great Lakes Naval Training Station, just north of Chicago, for basic training. He and Susan had decided to get married as soon as he completed basic training. The graduation was scheduled for a Friday. Susan, who by now was 21 years old, traveled to Chicago with Michael's parents for the graduation. The three checked into a double room at the Ron–Ric motel, near the base, on the Thursday (September 22, 1985) before graduation. The Ron–Ric is a small and inexpensive motel that caters to the families of sailors at the Great Lakes Naval Training Station a few blocks to the east. The motel has 14 rooms and charges a maximum of $36 a night for a double room. The motel was owned by Wilbur and Florena Adams, the defendants in the case.

Four blocks to the west of the Ron–Ric motel is a high-crime area: murder, prostitution, robbery, drugs—the works. The Adamses occasionally warned women guests not to walk alone in the neighborhood at night. They did not warn the Wassells or Susan.

Susan spent Friday night with Michael at another motel. On Saturday the Wassells checked out and left for Pennsylvania, and at the Wassells' suggestion Susan moved from the double room that she had shared with them to a single room in the Ron–Ric. Michael spent Saturday night with her but had to return to the base on Sunday for several days. She remained to look for an apartment where they could live after they were married (for he was scheduled to remain at the base after completing basic training). She spent most of Sunday in her room reading the newspaper and watching television. In the evening she went to look at an apartment.

Upon returning to her room at the motel, she locked the door, fastened the chain, and went to bed. She fell into a deep sleep, from which she was awakened by a knock on the door. She turned on a light and saw by the clock built into the television set that it was 1:00 a.m. She went to the door and looked through the peephole but saw no one. Next to the door was a pane of clear glass. She did not look through it. The door had two locks plus a chain. She unlocked the door and opened it all the way, thinking that Michael had come from the base and, not wanting to wake her, was en route to the Adamses' apartment to fetch a key to the room. It was not Michael at the door. It was a respectably dressed black man whom Susan had never seen before. He asked for "Cindy" (maybe "Sidney," she thought later). She told him there was no Cindy there. Then he asked for a glass of water. She went to the bathroom, which was at the other end of the room, about 25 feet from the door (seems far—but that was the testimony), to fetch the glass of water. When she came out of the bathroom, the man was sitting at the table in the room. (The room had a screen door as well as a solid door, but the screen door had not been latched.) He took the water but said it wasn't cold enough. He also said he had no money, and Susan remarked that she had $20 in her car. The man went into the bathroom to get a colder glass of water. Susan began to get nervous. She was standing between the bathroom and the door of her room. She hid her purse, which contained her car keys and $800 in cash that Michael had given her. There was no telephone in the room. There was an alarm attached to the television set, which would be activated if someone tried to remove the set, but she had not been told and did not know about the alarm, although a notice of the alarm was posted by the set. The parking lot on which the motel rooms opened was brightly lit by floodlights.

A few tense minutes passed after the man entered the bathroom. He poked his head out of the doorway and asked Susan to join him in the bathroom, he wanted to show her something. She refused. After a while he emerged from the bathroom—naked from the waist down. Susan fled from the room, and beat on the door of the adjacent room. There was no response. The man ran after her and grabbed her. She screamed, but no one appeared. The motel had no security guard; the Adamses lived in a basement apartment at the other end of the motel and did not hear her screams.

The man covered Susan's mouth and dragged her back to her room. There he gagged her with a wash cloth. He raped her at least twice (once anally). These outrages occupied more than an hour. Eventually Susan persuaded the rapist to take a shower with her. After the shower, she managed to get out of the bathroom before he did, dress, and flee in her car. To save herself after the rapes, she had tried to convince him that she liked him, and had succeeded at least to the extent that his guard was down. The Adamses' lawyer tried halfheartedly to show that she had consented to the rapes, but backed off from this position in closing argument.

The rapist was never prosecuted; a suspect was caught but Susan was too upset to identify him. There had been a rape at the motel several years previously (a sailor had opened the door of his room to two men who said they were "the management," and the men raped his wife). There had also been a robbery, and an incident in which an intruder kicked in the door to one of the rooms. These were the only serious crimes committed during the seven years that the Adamses owned the motel.

Susan married Michael, but the rape had induced post-trauma stress that has, according to her testimony and that of a psychologist testifying as her expert witness, blighted her life. She brought this suit against the Adamses on January 21, 1986. It is a diversity suit that charges the Adamses with negligence in failing to warn Susan or take other precautions to protect her against the assault. The substantive issues are governed by the law of Illinois. A jury composed of four women and three men found that the Adamses had indeed been negligent and that their negligence had been a proximate cause of the assault, and the jury assessed Susan's damages at $850,000, which was the figure her lawyer had requested in closing argument. But in addition the jury found that Susan had been negligent too—and indeed that her negligence had been 97 percent to blame for the attack and the Adamses' only 3 percent. So, following the approach to comparative negligence laid down in *Alvis v. Ribar*, 85 Ill.2d 1, 421 N.E.2d 886, 52 Ill.Dec. 23 (1981)—the decision in which the Supreme Court of Illinois abolished the common law rule that contributory negligence is a complete bar to a negligence suit—the jury awarded Susan only $25,500 in damages. This happens to be approximately the midpoint of the psychologist's estimate—$20,000 to $30,000—of the expense of the therapy that the psychologist believes Susan may need for her post-traumatic stress.

Susan's lawyer asked the district judge to grant judgment in her favor notwithstanding the verdict, on the ground either that she had been nonnegligent as a matter of law or that her negligence was immaterial because the Adamses had been not merely negligent but willful and wanton in their disregard for her safety. In the alternative, counsel asked the judge to grant a new trial on the ground that the jury's apportionment of negligence was contrary to the manifest weight of the evidence. There were other grounds for the motion, but they have been abandoned. The judge denied the motion, and Susan appeals.

Had she filed her suit after November 25, 1986, she could not have recovered any damages, assuming the jury would have made the same apportionment of responsibility between her and the Adamses. Illinois' new comparative negligence statute (Ill. Rev. Stat. ch. 110, para. 2–1116; *see also* para. 2–1107.1) bars recovery in negligence (or strict liability product) cases in which the plaintiff's "fault . . . is more than 50 percent of the proximate cause of the injury or damage for which recovery is sought." But as her suit was filed before that date, the new statute is inapplicable. *See* Ill. Rev. Stat. ch. 34, para. 429.7 Historical Note.

Susan Wassell's counsel argues that the jury's verdict "reflected a chastened, hardened, urban mentality—that lurking behind every door is evil and danger, even if the guest is from a small town unfamiliar with the area." He takes umbrage at the defendants' argument that Susan's "antennae" should have been alerted when she didn't see anyone through the peephole. He rejects the metaphor, remarking unexceptionably that human beings do not have antennae and that this case is not a Kafka story about a person who turned into an insect (i.e., is not *The Metamorphosis*). He points out that a person awakened from a deep sleep is not apt to be thinking clearly and that once Susan opened the door the fat was in the fire—if she had slammed the door in the rapist's face he might have kicked the door in, as had happened once before at this motel, although she didn't know that at the time. The Adamses' counsel argued to the jury (perhaps with the wisdom of hindsight) that Susan's "tragic mistake" was failing to flee when the man entered the bathroom. Susan's counsel insists that Susan was not negligent at all but that, if she was, she was at most 5 percent responsible for the catastrophe, which, he argues, could have been averted costlessly by a simple warning from the Adamses. To this the Adamses' counsel replies absurdly that a warning *would* have been costly—it might have scared guests away! The loss of business from telling the truth is not a social loss; it is a social gain.

The common law refused to compare the plaintiff's and the defendant's negligence. *See* 4 Harper, James & Gray, The Law of Torts § 22.1 (1986). The negligent plaintiff could recover nothing, unless the defendant's culpability was of a higher degree than simple negligence. *See id.*, §§ 22.5, 22.6, and the discussion of "degrees" of negligence in *Alvis v. Ribar, supra*, 85 Ill.2d at 9–10, 421 N.E.2d at 889–90. Susan argues that the defendants were willful and wanton, which, she says, would make her negligence as irrelevant under a regime of comparative negligence as it would be in a jurisdiction in which contributory negligence was still a complete defense. *See id.*, 85 Ill.2d at 10, 421 N.E.2d at 890; 4 Harper, James & Gray, *supra*, § 22.6.

Both the premise (that the Adamses were willful and wanton) and the conclusion (that if so, her own negligence was irrelevant) are wrong. As we guessed in *Davis v. United States*, 716 F.2d 418, 429 (7th Cir. 1983), that it would, Illinois appears to be lining up with the states that allow the plaintiff's simple negligence to be compared with the defendant's "willful and wanton conduct," *see State Farm Mutual Automobile Ins. Co. v. Mendenhall*, 164 Ill.App.3d 58, 517 N.E.2d 341, 115 Ill.Dec. 139 (1987); *see also Bofman v. Material Service Corp.*, 125 Ill.App.3d 1053, 466 N.E.2d 1064, 81 Ill.Dec. 262 (1984); *Soucie v. Drago Amusements Co.*, 145 Ill.App.3d 348, 495 N.E.2d 997, 99 Ill.Dec. 262 (1986). We say "appears to be" because only *Mendenhall* discusses the issue and it is not a decision of the Illinois Supreme Court, and because a critical premise of the decision may be shaky. That is the proposition that "willful and wanton" under Illinois law denotes merely a heightened form of negligence, so that there is only a small difference between simple negligence and willful and wanton misconduct despite the ominous sound of the words "willful" and "wanton." *See* 164 Ill.App.3d at 61, 517 N.E.2d at 343–44; *Davis v. United States, supra*, 716 F.2d at 425–27. As we noted in *Davis*, there are two lines of "willful and wanton" decisions in Illinois. One, which seemed to be in the ascendancy when we wrote *Davis*, and is the position taken in section 342 of the Second Restatement of Torts (1965), indeed regards "willful and wanton" as merely a heightened form of "negligent." Section 342 requires only that the defendant "knows *or has to reason to know* of the [dangerous condition of his premises] and *should* realize that it involves an unreasonable risk of harm" (emphasis added). But the cases since Davis appear to have swung round to the narrower concept, under which willful and wanton conduct denotes "conscious disregard for ... the safety of others," *Rabel v. Illinois Wesleyan University*, 161 Ill.App.3d 348, 356, 514 N.E.2d 552, 558, 112 Ill.Dec. 889 (1987), or "knowledge that [the defendant's] conduct posed a high probability of serious physical harm to others." Albers v. Community Consolidated #204 School, 155 Ill.App.3d 1083, 1085, 508 N.E.2d 1252, 1254, 108 Ill.Dec. 675 (1987). *See also Soucie v. Drago Amusements Co., supra*, 145 Ill.App.3d at 352, 495 N.E.2d at 999. These formulations come close to—perhaps duplicate—the standard of recklessness that we limned in *Duckworth v. Franzen*, 780 F.2d 645, 652 (7th Cir. 1985), a prisoners' suit involving a claim that reckless disregard for prisoners' safety violates the Eighth Amendment's prohibition against cruel and unusual punishments. *Bresland v. Ideal Roller & Graphics Co.*, 150 Ill.App.3d 445, 457, 501 N.E.2d 830, 839, 103 Ill.Dec. 513 (1986), describes willful and wanton misconduct as "so close to ... intentional misconduct that a party found liable on that basis should not be able to obtain contribution [from his joint tortfeasors]."

If the more recent formulations are authoritative, this would undermine the argument in *Davis* and *Mendenhall* for allowing a plaintiff's simple negligence to be compared with a defendant's willful and wanton misconduct. But it would not help Susan Wassell win her case. No rational jury could find that the Adamses *consciously* disregarded a high probability of serious physical harm. Cf. *Doe v. United States*, 718 F.2d 1039 (11th Cir. 1983). If the laxer version of "willful and wanton" is used, Susan's argument against permitting the jury to compare her culpability with that of the Adamses falls, yet she might seem in that event to have a powerful fallback position. The laxer the standard for "willful and wanton," the stronger the inference that the Adamses were willful and wanton—and if so, surely Susan's own negligence was not so great as to outweigh theirs by a factor of more than 30. But as we shall see in a moment, the defendants' negligence in this case was at most simple, not aggravated, negligence. Indeed, the jury may not have thought the defendants negligent at all.

The district judge was right to deny Susan's request for judgment notwithstanding the verdict. But was he right to deny her request for a new trial? This court treats the question as one of federal law, even in a diversity case. *Davlan v. Otis Elevator Co.*, 816 F.2d 287, 289 (7th Cir. 1987); *see also Abernathy v. Superior Hardwoods, Inc.*, 704 F.2d 963, 971 (7th Cir. 1983). And the federal standard is that "a new trial can be granted only when the jury's verdict is against the clear weight of the evidence," *Davlan v. Otis Elevator Co., supra*, 816 F.2d at 289, and we can reverse only when persuaded that in applying this standard the district judge abused his discretion, *id.; see also Foster v. Continental Can Corp.*, 783 F.2d 731, 735 (7th Cir. 1986); *Babb v. Minder*, 806 F.2d 749, 752 (7th Cir. 1986). The Illinois approach to these questions is similar. * * * [citations omitted]. So Susan has a tough row to hoe to get the district court's refusal to grant her a new trial reversed.

The old common law rule barring the contributorily negligent plaintiff from recovering *any* damages came eventually to seem too harsh. That is why it has been changed in most jurisdictions, including Illinois. It was harsh, all right, at least if one focuses narrowly on the plight of individual plaintiffs, but it was also simple and therefore cheap to administer. The same cannot be said for comparative negligence, which far from being simple requires a formless, unguided inquiry, because there is no methodology for comparing the causal contributions of the plaintiff's and of the defendant's negligence to the plaintiff's injury. In this case, either the plaintiff or the defendants could have avoided that injury. It is hard to say more, but the statute requires more—yet without giving the finder of facts any guidance as to how to make the apportionment.

We have suggested in previous cases, such as *Davis v. United States, supra,* 716 F.2d at 429, that one way to make sense of comparative negligence is to assume that the required comparison is between the respective costs to the plaintiff and to the defendant of avoiding the injury. If each could have avoided it at the same cost, they are each 50 percent responsible for it. According to this method of comparing negligence, the jury found that Susan could have avoided the attack at a cost of less than one thirty-second the cost to the Adamses. Is this possible?

It is careless to open a motel or hotel door in the middle of the night without trying to find out who is knocking. Still, people aren't at their most alert when they are awakened in the middle of the night, and it wasn't crazy for Susan to assume that Michael had returned without telling her, even though he had said he would be spending the night at the base. So it cannot be assumed that the cost—not to her (although her testimony suggests that she is not so naive or provincial as her lawyer tried to convince the jury she was), but to the reasonable person who found himself or herself in her position, for that is the benchmark in determining plaintiff's as well as defendant's negligence, *see, e.g., Blacconeri v. Aguayo,* 132 Ill.App.3d 984, 988, 478 N.E.2d 546, 549–50, 88 Ill.Dec. 231 (1985); 4 Harper, James & Gray, *supra,* § 22.10, at pp. 334–38—was zero, or even that it was slight. As innkeepers (in the increasingly quaint legal term), the Adamses had a duty to exercise a high degree of care to protect their guests from assaults on the motel premises. * * * [citations omitted]. And the cost to the Adamses of warning all their female guests of the dangers of the neighborhood would have been negligible. Surely a warning to Susan would not have cost the Adamses 32 times the cost to her of schooling herself to greater vigilance.

But this analysis is incomplete. It is unlikely that a warning would have averted the attack. Susan testified that she thought the man who had knocked on the door was her fiance. Thinking this, she would have opened the door no matter how dangerous she believed the neighborhood to be. The warning that was not given might have deterred her from walking alone in the neighborhood. But that was not the pertinent danger. Of course, if the Adamses had told her not to open her door in the middle of the night under any circumstances without carefully ascertaining who was trying to enter the room, this would have been a pertinent warning and might have had an effect. But it is absurd to think that hoteliers are required to give so *obvious* a warning, any more than they must warn guests not to stick their fingers into the electrical outlets. Everyone, or at least the average person, knows better than to open his or her door to a stranger in the middle of the night. The problem was not that Susan thought that she *should* open her bedroom door in the middle of the night to anyone who knocked, but that she wasn't thinking clearly. A warning would not have availed against a temporary, sleep-induced lapse.

Giving the jury every benefit of the doubt, as we are required to do especially in a case such as this where the jury was not asked to render either a special verdict or a general verdict with answers to written interrogatories (Fed. R. Civ. P. 49), we must assume that the jury was not so muddle-headed as to believe that the Adamses negligence consisted in failing to give a futile warning. Rather, we must assume that the jury thought the Adamses negligence consisted in failing to have a security guard or telephones in each room, or alarms designed to protect the motel's patrons rather than just the owners' television sets. (The Adamses did, however, have an informal agreement with the local police that the police would cruise through the parking lot of the Ron–Ric whenever they drove down the street at night—and this was maybe three or four times a night.) The only one of these omitted precautions for which there is a cost figure in the record was the security guard. A guard would have cost $50 a night. That is almost $20,000 a year. This is not an enormous number. The plaintiff suggests that it would have been even lower because the guard would have been needed only on busy nights. But the evidence was in conflict on whether the Sunday night after a Friday graduation, which is the night that Susan was attacked, was a busy night. And the need for a security guard would seem to be greater, the less busy rather than the busier the motel; if there had been someone in the room adjacent to Susan's, she might have been saved from her ordeal. In any event the cost of the security guard, whether on all nights or just on busy nights—or just on unbusy nights—might be much greater than the monetary equivalent of the greater vigilance on the part of Susan that would have averted the attack.

The assumption that the jury was clear-thinking and instruction-abiding is artificial, of course. During its deliberations, the jury sent the judge a question about the duty to warn (the judge did not answer it). This is some indication that the jury thought that the Adamses' negligence consisted in failing to warn Susan. But it is equally plausible that the jury didn't think the Adamses were negligent at all toward Susan, but, persuaded that she had suffered terribly, wanted to give her a token recovery. Concern with sympathy verdicts appears to lie behind Illinois' new statute barring the plaintiff from recovering any damages if he is more than 50 percent negligent. "The adoption of the pure comparative negligence doctrine [the doctrine, adopted in *Alvis v. Ribar*, that allows the plaintiff to recover something however great his negligence was relative to the defendant's] was thought to have increased a plaintiff's chances for winning at trial from about 50 percent to 60 percent, even though at the same time it tended to reduce the amount of the damage awards made at trial." Smith–Hurd Ill. Ann. Stat. ch. 110, para. 2–1116 Historical Note. It may be more than coincidence that the jury awarded Susan just enough money to allow her to undertake the recommended course of psychological therapy. We are not supposed to speculate about the jury's reasoning process, *see, e.g.*, Fed. R. Evid. 606(b), and we have just seen that it would not necessarily strengthen Susan's case if we did. The issue for us is not whether this jury was rational and law-abiding but whether a rational jury could, consistently with the evidence, have returned the verdict that this jury did.

If we were the trier of fact, persuaded that both parties were negligent and forced to guess about the relative costs to the plaintiff and to the defendants of averting the assault, we would assess the defendants' share at more than 3 percent. But we are not the trier of fact, and are authorized to upset the jury's apportionment only if persuaded that the trial judge abused his discretion in determining that the jury's verdict was not against the clear weight of the evidence. We are not so persuaded. It seems probably wrong to us, but we have suggested an interpretation of the evidence under which the verdict was consistent with the evidence and the law. And that is enough to require us to uphold the district judge's refusal to set aside the verdict.

AFFIRMED.

Notes and Questions

1. What do you think Judge Posner meant when he wrote: "[I]t was a respectably dressed black man whom Susan had never seen before"? What do you think Susan's race was?

2. Judge Posner's decision declares that "[e]veryone, or at least the average person, knows better than to open his or her door to a stranger in the middle of the night." Is the Court correct in its assertion? Was Susan Marisconish the average person?

3. What do you think Judge Posner was referring to when he wrote "although her testimony suggests that she is not so naïve or provincial as her lawyer tried to convince the jury she was"?

4. Why was Susan Marisconish found 97 percent liable for her injuries?

5. Continue thinking about *Wassell* as you read the next excerpt.

AMY H. KASTELY

Out of the Whiteness: On Raced Codes and White Race Consciousness
in Some Tort, Criminal, and Contract Law
63 U. Cin. L. Rev. 269, 270–271, 280–286 (1994).

* * *

A crucial part of many operas is the recitatif, or recitative, which traditionally is sung in simple style, using everyday words, with minimal instrumental accompaniment. Simplicity is valued because the function of the recitatif is to inform the audience about characters, situations, and developments in the plot. It is important that listeners understand each word of the recitatif so they may follow the story told in the opera.

Toni Morrison's short story, "Recitatif," draws attention to ways that race functions for informative purposes in contemporary written texts, as readers give significance to racial identification in matters of character, situation, and narrative movement and as they unconsciously or uncritically locate themselves in relation to race consciousness in the text. "Recitatif" invites readers to pay attention to the complex arrangements of raced and gendered tropes and codes that are, or are expected to be, quite clear to contemporary readers and to look closely at the construction of race we bring or perform as readers.

* * *

Lawyers have uncovered and analyzed assumptions of race, gender, class, and heterosexual hierarchy underlying particular legal rules and judicial opinions and have explored the ways in which "facially neutral" rules of law operate to maintain these social hierarchies. My purpose here is to explore how race, in particular, is used as a persuasive tool—as rhetorical trope—to structure thought directed to judgment about contested matters within current legal practice.

Race-coded references function as tools of persuasion in a number of different ways. This part focuses on two: the communication of raced "information" and the creation of bonds with and among white readers. Racial codes convey information in alarmingly efficient fashion. The name "Quota Queen," applied to Lani Guinier and Norma Cantu, was read by some as very informative: it conveyed much information about Professor Guinier's and Assistant Secretary Cantu's political commitments and professional interests, information, however, that was false. I call this usage "efficient" because so much information can be conveyed in just a few words. It is also "effective" because the very encoding of this large amount of information both shields it from direct challenge (in order to contest each piece of information, one must first uncover it) and renders it "deniable," in the sense that the writer or his or her defenders can claim that the writer did not intend the encoded message.

At the same time, race-coded references create bonds between and among writer and readers that consist of both the security—or thrill?—

of shared knowledge and the consolidation—or exhilaration?—of power displayed.

Wassell v. Adams

In January of 1986, Susan Wassell filed suit in the United States District Court for the Northern District of Illinois, alleging that Wilber and Florena Adams, doing business as Ron–Ric Motel, had negligently failed to warn or protect her when she stayed as a guest in the motel in September of 1985, and that she was raped as a consequence, causing her severe and lasting injury. A jury found that the Adamses were negligent. The jury also found, however, that Wassell was negligent, and that her negligence was 97% responsible for the attack, while the Adamses' negligence was only 3% responsible. The district court entered judgment in accordance with this finding, and Wassell appealed.

Wassell's attorney argued first that she had been nonnegligent or minimally negligent, as a matter of law, and, second, that the Adamses had been willful and wanton in their disregard for her safety. These arguments depended upon an assessment of what each party knew or had reason to know about the danger of rape in the particular circumstances at the Ron–Ric Motel in September of 1985. The Ninth Circuit affirmed the lower court's entry of judgment, in an opinion written by Judge Richard Posner.

Judge Posner began the opinion with this description of Wassell: "The plaintiff, born Susan Marisconish, grew up on Macaroni Street in a small town in a poor coal-mining region of Pennsylvania—a town so small and obscure that it has no name. She was the ninth of ten children, and as a child was sexually abused by her stepfather." Judge Posner did not explicitly mention the plaintiff's race. Translating Posner as he translated a white norm, I assume that she is white.

Judge Posner then described the defendants' motel:

a small and inexpensive motel that caters to the families of sailors at the Great Lakes Naval Training Station a few blocks to the east. The motel has 14 rooms and charges a maximum of $36 a night for a double room.... To the west of the Ron–Ric motel is a high-crime area: murder, prostitution, robbery, drugs—the works.

Translating Posner's translation, I understand that the neighborhood close to the motel, and particularly that to the west, is predominantly black and generally low-income. Judge Posner's dismissive, disrespectful description of the neighborhood is striking. I wonder in anger if I am implicated as an "ideal reader" of this text. I read Posner's description as an invitation to some readers to join in this public exhibition—celebration?—of white, class-privileged power, to appreciate the display of scorn for poor and working-class black people * * * and as a warning to other readers that judicial power includes the power to hate.

After recounting that Susan Wassell was staying at the Ron–Ric Motel with the parents of her then-fiance, Michael Wassell, in order to attend his graduation from basic training, and that Michael stayed with her for the first two nights that she was in North Chicago, Judge Posner described the events preceding the rape on the third night at the Ron–Ric Motel:

> She was awakened by a knock on the door. She turned on a light and saw by the clock built into the television set that it was 1:00 a.m. She went to the door and looked through the peephole but saw no one. Next to the door was a pane of clear glass. She did not look through it. The door had two locks plus a chain. She unlocked the door and opened it all the way, thinking that Michael had come from the base and, not wanting to wake her, was en route to the Adamses' apartment to fetch a key to the room. It was not Michael at the door. It was a respectably dressed black man whom Susan had never seen before. He asked for "Cindy".... She told him there was no Cindy there.

The man asked for a glass of water and then assaulted Wassell; she ran out of the room; he ran after her, dragged her back into the room, and raped her.

Evaluating Wassell's behavior, Judge Posner wrote: "It is careless to open a motel or hotel door in the middle of the night without trying to find out who is knocking." Why was it careless to open the door? When would it ever be careless or negligent to open a door? Surely it would be careless only if she had some knowledge that danger would result. What did Wassell know about the risks of opening the door?

Apparently responding to this question, Judge Posner mentioned her lawyer's argument that Wassell was "naive and provincial." What might naivete and provincialism have to do with her opening the door? Was it that her level of understanding was determined by naivete and provincialism? What information might she have missed or failed properly to comprehend? A "naive" woman might fail to know the risk of rape? And a "provincial" white woman might fail to fear black men?

After posing this possibility, Judge Posner dismissed it: "Her testimony suggests that she is not so naive or provincial...." Judge Posner does not elaborate or justify this conclusion, so he must assume its self-evidence. I wonder to what in her testimony Judge Posner referred—was it that she was sexually assaulted as a child?—or that she was sexually active as an adult? Is that why Judge Posner mentioned this history so prominently in his description of Wassell? Raped as a child and sexually active as an adult, Wassell was, by definition, not "naive" (virginal?) and, thus, should have understood the risk of rape to an adult woman? Again Judge Posner seems to invite the reader to engage unstated assumptions, here in the construction and dismissal of this woman as the object and creation of male sexuality.

Struggling against my own hurt and resistance, I work harder to understand the recitatif in Judge Posner's opinion. And I do not get it yet. Some crucial event or twist of character is missing. It is not enough to say that Wassell knew about male violence and, therefore, should have known not to open the door. Judge Posner's conclusion depends on something more. It depends upon an image of violence awaiting Wassell on the other side of the motel-room door. If it was not dangerous outside, then it could not have been careless to have opened the door. Is every outside dangerous? I have opened doors late at night; I have even opened motel-room doors late at night. Was I negligent in each case? Is it negligent to think that the person waiting outside is your lover and not your rapist? What information was Judge Posner assuming Wassell had that would move this story forward in a coherent way? Where is the recitatif?

Judge Posner's opinion makes sense only if the reader assumes that Wassell imagined or should have imagined that the area outside her room was dangerous. And why should she have imagined this? How could the court be confident in concluding that she should have imagined this? There is no evidence in the record that Wassell had any specific information about the history or future likelihood of criminal activity at the motel. Upon what basis was she to form an apprehension of danger outside her room? Only race, class, and gender. Wassell saw black people in the neighborhood surrounding the motel. She saw that some of the buildings were run down, that there were bars in the area, and that it was not an affluent white residential neighborhood. She knew that she was a white woman. Translating Posner, these stand as indicia of danger that were available to Wassell. From these marks of race, class, and gender, Judge Posner implied, she should have concluded that there was danger outside her motel door.

Judge Posner described the neighborhood close to the motel as "a high-crime area: murder, prostitution, robbery, drugs—the works." Whatever basis this metonymy may have in the frequency of crime in that neighborhood, Judge Posner did not claim that Wassell had any specific information about a historical record of crime. Instead, in the raced recitatif of this opinion, this description functions to name this neighborhood as black. Having been told this, the reader is invited to conclude that Wassell knew that the neighborhood surrounding the motel was black and, therefore, that Wassell knew that the area outside her room was dangerous, or at least was a place in which the "average person" (translation: a white middle class person) would be afraid and, thus, would exercise extreme caution. By this decision—this exercise of judicial power—Wassell and others are compelled to accept the racist presumptions that Judge Posner employed, and by this opinion—this contribution to legal discourse—readers and others who participate in this discursive practice are required to understand and to reproduce these presumptions. To understand this opinion, I must read through the lens of patriarchal white supremacy. To understand and obey the law that it announces, I must engage in racist practice.

* * *

Notes and Questions

1. Are you persuaded by Professor Kastely's analysis of *Wassell v. Adams*?

2. Was race relevant? What other code words or phrases can you find in the opinion?

3. Professor Mari Matsuda wrote: "In the law of torts, if a woman is raped, we look to the rapist for recourse. He is subject to the narrow criminal and civil sanctions of the law. Others in a position to predict and prevent rape—such as law enforcement officers, parole boards, landlords, hotel operators, and security firms—are typically absolved of responsibility. The law calls this 'no duty.' No duty means that even if there are reasonable things one could do to prevent rape, the law will not require the doing of those things." Mari Matsuda, *On Causation*, 100 Colum. L. Rev. 2195, 2202–2203 (2000). She proposes as a solution that we "take the harm and figure out who is in the best position to prevent it. The person in the best position to prevent the harm is the logical person to hold accountable for the harm." *Id*. at 2211. Isn't she right? What reasonable thing could the Adams have done to prevent Susan Wassell's rape?

4. Consider the different approaches by the courts as you read the next two cases.

SECTION 3.   ASSAULT AND BATTERY: A TORT BY ANY OTHER NAME . . .

FISHER v. CARROUSEL MOTOR HOTEL, INC.

414 S.W.2d 774 (Tex.Civ.App.1967).

McDonald, Chief Justice.

This is an appeal by plaintiff Fisher from a take-nothing judgment in a suit for damages for an alleged assault on plaintiff by defendant's employee.

Plaintiff sued Carrousel Motor Hotel, Inc., the Brass Ring Club, Inc., and R. W. Flynn, alleging plaintiff was invited to dinner by third parties at the Brass Ring Club, operated by defendant Carrousel; that plaintiff was standing in the serving line holding his dinner plate when "plaintiff was assaulted by defendant Flynn, Manager of said Brass Ring Club, who walked over to plaintiff, seized his dinner plate, and violently tore it out of his hand. At the same time, Flynn shouted in a loud and offensive manner that plaintiff, a Negro, could not be served there." Plaintiff alleged as a result of Flynn's conduct, "plaintiff suffered great mental anguish and humiliation."

Defendant Carrousel answered by general denial; defendant Flynn was deceased at time of trial; and the trial proceeded against Carrousel and the Brass Ring.

Trial was to a jury which found:

1) Flynn forcibly dispossessed plaintiff of his dinner plate.

2) Plaintiff was humiliated and subjected to indignity by the actions of Flynn in dispossessing plaintiff of his dinner plate.

3) Flynn shouted in a loud and offensive manner that plaintiff could not be served at the Brass Ring Club.

4) Plaintiff was humiliated and subjected to indignity by actions of Flynn in so shouting.

5) Flynn was acting within course and scope of his employment by Carrousel Motor Hotel.

6) $400 will compensate plaintiff for the humiliation and indignity he suffered caused by Flynn's conduct.

7) Flynn acted maliciously with wanton disregard of plaintiff's rights and feelings.

8) Carrousel Motor Hotel did not authorize or approve the conduct of Flynn.

9) $500 will compensate plaintiff for the malicious act and wanton disregard of plaintiff's feelings and rights committed by Flynn.

Plaintiff moved for judgment on the verdict; and defendant moved for judgment that plaintiff take nothing, asserting that as a matter of law the acts complained of by plaintiff, committed by Flynn, do not constitute an assault or other actionable cause.

The trial court overruled plaintiff's motion for judgment; and granted defendant's motion N.O.V. that plaintiff take nothing.

Plaintiff appeals, contending the trial court erred:

1) In denying plaintiff's motion for judgment; and

2) In granting defendant's motion for judgment non obstante.

The record reflects plaintiff came into the Brass Ring with others and picked up a plate at the serving line. Flynn approached plaintiff and took the plate from his hand and told him he could not be served. Plaintiff testified that Flynn *did not physically touch him*. There is no evidence plaintiff ever suffered any fear or apprehension, or that he suffered any resulting physical injury. Plaintiff testified he was highly embarrassed and humiliated.

Article 1138 Texas Penal Code provides:

> "The use of any unlawful violence upon the person of another with intent to injure him, whatever be the means or the degree of violence used, is an assault and battery. Any attempt to commit a battery, or any threatening gesture showing in itself or by words accompanying it, an immediate intention, coupled with an ability to commit a battery, is an assault."

Under the undisputed factual situation, we think no assault was committed by Flynn on plaintiff. *Texas Bus Lines v. Anderson*, CCA (n.r.e.), 233 S.W.2d 961.

Mental anguish and mental suffering without proof of resulting physical injury will not support a recovery of damages. *Harned v. E–Z Finance Co.*, Sup. Ct., 151 Tex. 641, 254 S.W.2d 81.

Absence an assault or resulting physical injury plaintiff cannot recover for the embarrassment and humiliation suffered as a result of Flynn's conduct.

We think Flynn's conduct did not constitute an assault, and since no resulting physical injuries were alleged or proved, plaintiff has proven no cause of action.

The judgment of the trial court is correct. Plaintiff's points are overruled.

AFFIRMED.

Notes and Questions

1. Why did the Court cite the Texas Penal Code given that this is a Tort action, not a criminal prosecution?

2. Did the appellate court consider this a case of intentional infliction of emotional distress? Did the plaintiff allege that there was an intentional infliction of emotional distress? Consider the following language found in the opinion "[m]ental anguish and mental suffering without proof of resulting physical injury will not support a recovery of damages. Absence an assault or resulting physical injury plaintiff cannot recover for the embarrassment and humiliation suffered as a result of Flynn's conduct." (citation omitted).

3. Compare this Court's analysis with that of the Texas Supreme Court's analysis upon appeal.

FISHER v. CARROUSEL MOTOR HOTEL, INC.

424 S.W.2d 627 (Tex.1967).

GREENHILL, JUSTICE.

This is a suit for actual and exemplary damages growing out of an alleged assault and battery. The plaintiff Fisher was a mathematician with the Data Processing Division of the Manned Spacecraft Center, an agency of the National Aeronautics and Space Agency, commonly called NASA, near Houston. The defendants were the Carrousel Motor Hotel, Inc., located in Houston, the Brass Ring Club, which is located in the Carrousel, and Robert W. Flynn, who as an employee of the Carrousel was the manager of the Brass Ring Club. Flynn died before the trial, and the suit proceeded as to the Carrousel and the Brass Ring. Trial was to a jury which found for the plaintiff Fisher. The trial court rendered judgment for the defendants notwithstanding the verdict. The Court of Civil Appeals affirmed. 414 S.W.2d 774. The questions before this Court are whether there was evidence that an actionable battery was committed, and, if so, whether the two corporate defendants must respond in exemplary as well as actual damages for the malicious conduct of Flynn.

The plaintiff Fisher had been invited by Ampex Corporation and Defense Electronics to a one day's meeting regarding telemetry equipment at the Carrousel. The invitation included a luncheon. The guests were asked to reply by telephone whether they could attend the luncheon, and Fisher called in his acceptance. After the morning session, the group of 25 or 30 guests adjourned to the Brass Ring Club for lunch. The luncheon was buffet style, and Fisher stood in line with others and just ahead of a graduate student of Rice University who testified at the trial. As Fisher was about to be served, he was approached by Flynn, who snatched the plate from Fisher's hand and shouted that he, a Negro, could not be served in the club. Fisher testified that he was not actually touched, and did not testify that he suffered fear or apprehension of physical injury; but he did testify that he was highly embarrassed and hurt by Flynn's conduct in the presence of his associates.

The jury found that Flynn "forceably [sic] dispossessed plaintiff of his dinner plate" and "shouted in a loud and offensive manner" that Fisher could not be served there, thus subjecting Fisher to humiliation and indignity. It was stipulated that Flynn was an employee of the Carrousel Hotel and, as such, managed the Brass Ring Club. The jury also found that Flynn acted maliciously and awarded Fisher $400 actual damages for his humiliation and indignity and $500 exemplary damages for Flynn's malicious conduct.

The Court of Civil Appeals held that there was no assault because there was no physical contact and no evidence of fear or apprehension of physical contact. However, it has long been settled that there can be a battery without an assault, and that actual physical contact is not necessary to constitute a battery, so long as there is contact with clothing or an object closely identified with the body. 1 Harper & James, The Law of Torts 216 (1956); Restatement of Torts 2d, §§ 18 and 19. In Prosser, Law of Torts 32 (3d Ed. 1964), it is said:

> "The interest in freedom from intentional and unpermitted contacts with the plaintiff's person is protected by an action for the tort commonly called battery. The protection extends to any part of the body, or to anything which is attached to it and practically identified with it. Thus contact with the plaintiff's clothing, or with a cane, a paper, or any other object held in his hand will be sufficient; ... The plaintiff's interest in the integrity of his person includes all those things which are in contact or connected with it."

Under the facts of this case, we have no difficulty in holding that the intentional grabbing of plaintiff's plate constituted a battery. The intentional snatching of an object from one's hand is as clearly an offensive invasion of his person as would be an actual contact with the body. "To constitute an assault and battery, it is not necessary to touch the plaintiff's body or even his clothing; knocking or snatching anything from plaintiff's hand or touching anything connected with his person, when done in an offensive manner, is sufficient." *Morgan v. Loyacomo*, 190 Miss. 656, 1 So.2d 510 (1941).

Such holding is not unique to the jurisprudence of this State. In *S. H. Kress & Co. v. Brashier*, 50 S.W.2d 922 (Tex.Civ.App.1932, no writ), the defendant was held to have committed "an assault and trespass upon the person" by snatching a book from the plaintiff's hand. The jury findings in that case were that the defendant "dispossessed plaintiff of the book" and caused her to suffer "humiliation and indignity."

The rationale for holding an offensive contact with such an object to be a battery is explained in 1 Restatement of Torts 2d § 18 (Comment p. 31) as follows:

"Since the essence of the plaintiff's grievance consists in the offense to the dignity involved in the unpermitted and intentional invasion of the inviolability of his person and not in any physical harm done to his body, it is not necessary that the plaintiff's actual body be disturbed. Unpermitted and intentional contacts with anything so connected with the body as to be customarily regarded as part of the other's person and therefore as partaking of its inviolability is actionable as an offensive contact with his person. There are some things such as clothing or a cane or, indeed, anything directly grasped by the hand which are so intimately connected with one's body as to be universally regarded as part of the person."

We hold, therefore, that the forceful dispossession of plaintiff Fisher's plate in an offensive manner was sufficient to constitute a battery, and the trial court erred in granting judgment notwithstanding the verdict on the issue of actual damages.

In *Harned v. E–Z Finance Co.*, 151 Tex. 641, 254 S.W.2d 81 (1953), this Court refused to adopt the "new tort" of intentional interference with peace of mind which permits recovery for mental suffering in the absence of resulting physical injury or an assault and battery. This cause of action has long been advocated by respectable writers and legal scholars. *See*, for example, Prosser, Insult and Outrage, 44 Cal. L. Rev. 40 (1956); Wade, Tort Liability for Abusive and Insulting Language, 4 Vand. L. Rev. 63 (1950); Prosser, Intentional Infliction of Mental Suffering: A New Tort, 37 Mich. L. Rev. 874 (1939); 1 Restatement of Torts 2d § 46(1). However, it is not necessary to adopt such a cause of action in order to sustain the verdict of the jury in this case. The *Harned* case recognized the well established rule that mental suffering is compensable in suits for willful torts "which are recognized as torts and actionable independently and separately from mental suffering or other injury." 254 S.W.2d at 85. Damages for mental suffering are recoverable without the necessity for showing actual physical injury in a case of willful battery because the basis of that action is the unpermitted and intentional invasion of the plaintiff's person and not the actual harm done to the plaintiff's body. Restatement of Torts 2d § 18. Personal indignity is the essence of an action for battery; and consequently the defendant is liable not only for contacts which do actual physical harm, but also for those which are offensive and insulting. *Prosser, supra; Wilson v. Orr*, 210 Ala. 93, 97 So. 133 (1923). We hold, therefore, that plaintiff was entitled to actual damages for mental suffering due to the willful battery, even in the absence of any physical injury.

We now turn to the question of the liability of the corporations for exemplary damages. In this regard, the jury found that Flynn was acting within the course and scope of his employment on the occasion in question; that Flynn acted maliciously and with a wanton disregard of the rights and feelings of plaintiff on the occasion in question. There is no attack upon these jury findings. The jury further found that the defendant Carrousel did not authorize or approve the conduct of Flynn. It is argued that there is no evidence to support this finding. The jury verdict concluded with a finding that $500 would "reasonably compensate plaintiff for the malicious act and wanton disregard of plaintiff's feelings and rights ..."

* * *

[The court then considered the question of whether the defendant corporations were liable for damages and found that they were.]

The judgments of the courts below are reversed, and judgment is here rendered for the plaintiff for $900 with interest from the date of the trial court's judgment, and for costs of this suit.

Notes and Questions

1.   Why did the plaintiff's attorney choose to sue for the tort of assault and battery and not the intentional infliction of emotional distress? Why didn't the attorney sue under the public accommodation section of the Civil Rights Act of 1964? Texas courts did not permit recovery for the tort of intentional infliction of emotional distress without some proof of physical injury, as the opinions make clear. As you recall, Mr. Fisher had no physical injuries. Had plaintiff's attorney sued under the Civil Rights Act of 1964, he would have only received declaratory relief—but not money damages. So if Mr. Fisher wanted to be compensated for his troubles, the tort of assault and battery was his only alternative. (This series of questions were prompted by Professor Taunya Banks.)

2.   Consider the following hypothetical presented by Professor Jerome Culp in his Torts Class:

> As an undergraduate at the University of Chicago, I asked my girlfriend to accompany me to Evanston, Illinois. We got off the train from downtown Chicago with our very long and newly-hip Afros and began walking around Evanston. Near the train station we saw an old white woman. As my girlfriend and I approached the woman, she began to shake. The closer we came to her the more she shook... I remember as clearly as I can taste my last cup of coffee the old white woman turning her back and assuming a pseudo-fetal posture as we approached her. I could read that situation as clearly as any other: for the old white woman, the black revolution had come to Evanston. She saw us not as the well-dressed black college students that we were, but as mythic black revolutionaries. In her mind, she knew we were Black Panthers

who had come to Evanston to do her harm. I ask my class whether it would have been an assault for me to lean over and to whisper "boo" to that old woman. Jerome McCristal Culp, Jr., *Autobiography and Legal Scholarship and Teaching: Finding the Me in the Legal Academy*, 77 Va. L. Rev. 539, 552–553 (1991).

Would Professor Culp be liable for assault if he says boo? In the article, Professor Culp describes the benefit that his students receive from his use of the hypothetical. "By raising an explicit racial situation, I hope to free my black students to include their experiences in the classroom, and to inform the non-black students that other ways of looking at issues are possible and necessary." *Id.* at 553–554.

3. Several Torts scholars have suggested that the use of the reasonable person standard is an example of gender bias, and a preferable analysis would be to use a reasonable woman standard. *See e.g.* Leslie Bender, *A Lawyer's Primer on Feminist Theory and Tort*, 38 J. Legal Educ. 3 (1988); Leslie Bender, *An Overview of Feminist Torts Scholarship*, 78 Cornell L. Rev. 575 (1993); Linda M. Finley, *A Break in the Silence: Including Women's Issues in a Torts Course*, 1 Yale J. L. & Fem. 41 (1989); Ronald K. L. Collins, *Language, History and the Legal Process: A Profile of the Reasonable Man*, 8 Rut. Cam. L. J. 311 (1977); Caroline Forell, *Essentialism, Empathy, and the Reasonable Woman*, 1994 U. Ill. L. Rev. 769. For an excellent overview and assessment of the scholarship addressing the reasonable woman standard, *see* Gary T. Schwartz, *Tort Law: Feminist Approaches to Tort Law*, 2 Theoretical Inq. L. 175, 179–193 (2001). Should there be a reasonable person of color standard?

4. Several scholars have advocated that a tort be recognized for racial slurs and other "words that wound." *See e.g.* Richard Delgado, *Words that Wound: A Tort Action for Racial Insults, Epithets, and Name–Calling*, 17 Harv. C.R.-C.L. L. Rev. 133,150 (1982) where he observes that "[m]any of the arguments for a cause of action for racial insults are similar to the policies underlying causes of action for assault, battery, intentional infliction of emotional distress, defamation, and various statutory and constitutional causes of action." Professor Delgado observes how the facts in *Fisher* show the "inadequacies of the doctrines of assault and battery" in protecting the victims of racial insults. *Id.* at 151. "If the plate had not been snatched from plaintiff's hand, but he had been insulted until he put down the plate and left, or before he picked up the plate, he could not have recovered in battery. And because the employee's words did not put the plaintiff in fear of physical injury or touching, the plaintiff could not have recovered in assault." *Id. See also* Okianer Christian Dark, *Racial Insults: "Keep Thy Tongue From Evil"*, 24 Suffolk U. L. Rev. 559 (1990). In this article Professor Dark argues that victims of "words that wound" should be compensated under the theory of intentional infliction of mental distress. Professor Dark also discusses the *Fisher* decision. *Id.* at 577–578. *See also* Carlos Villarreal, *Culture in Lawmaking: A Chicano Perspective*, 24 U.C. Davis L. Rev. 1193, 1232–1235 (1991) (where author describes several cases where plaintiffs were successful in recovering damages for racial insults.)

5. Is a decision to take into account the racial sensitivities of people of color the solution to the problem? How would you respond to the following quote which was made about Chicanos, but is equally applicable to all racial and ethnic groups: "Chicanos are a heterogeneous group. This diversity

within the group leads to the question of the role of culture in defining the legal relationships between members of the group. Indeed, often the diversity of the group will be the source of conflict." Villareal, at 1235–1236. If members of racial and ethnic groups cannot agree on a solution, or would react differently under the circumstances, what is a judicial system supposed to do?

6.   In calculating damages, consider the following quote from Professor Martha Chamallas: "[r]eliance on race-based and gender-based economic data to determine lost earning capacity is bad social policy. The use of race-based and gender-based tables assumes that the current gender and racial pay gap will continue in the future, despite ongoing legal and institutional efforts to make the workplace more diverse and less discriminatory. The use of these data allows discrimination in one area—the setting of pay rates—to influence valuations in another area—the calculation of personal injury awards." Martha Chamallas, *Questioning the Use of Race–Specific and Gender–Specific Economic Data in Tort Litigation: A Constitutional Argument*, 63 Fordham L. Rev. 73, 75 (1994).

7.   Professor McClellan states "[p]roperly tailored, empirical studies may shed light on the effects of 'raced' decision making on parties and counsel, as well as on the outcome of the case." Frank M. McClellan, *The Dark Side of Tort Reform: Searching For Racial Justice*, 48 Rutgers L. Rev. 761, 772–73 (1996). Professor McClellan proposes several questions for further empirical analysis: 1. frequency and extent to which people of color are persuaded to settle their cases for less than white people would settle their cases for, based on the fear of the impact of racism on the decision-making process; 2. frequency and extent to which insurance companies factor in race to reduce their settlement offers; 3. frequency and extent to which trial judges and magistrates factor in race in making their assessments of the value of a personal injury case; 4. frequency and extent to which expert witnesses factor in race in making their assessments of the value of a personal injury case; 5. the effect of the racial makeup of a potential jury pool on the lawyer's/adjuster's assessment of the value of a case and willingness to settle; 6. the effect of the race of a party's attorney on how participants in torts cases value the case; and, 7. the extent to which juries place lower value on the dignitary and serious physical injury or death claims of people of color than they place on similar claims of White plaintiffs. *Id.* at 773 Although the empirical research to answer these questions is not available, Professor McClellan concludes that outcomes of tort litigation are influenced by race and that people of color fare worse than their White counterparts. *Id.* at 773–774. Having considered the data presented in this chapter, are you persuaded?

8.   See Jennifer Wriggins, Torts, Race, and the Value of Injury, 1900–1949, 49 Howard L. J. 99 (2005) (historical analysis of tort cases in the first half of the twentieth century documenting disparity in treatment received by black plaintiffs when compared with white plaintiffs.)

Chapter 4

CRITICAL RACE THEORY AND CONTRACTS

Instead of being the vehicle by which ideals of liberty, equality, and autonomy could be fostered, the courts and dominant constructions of contract law became the means by which African–Americans became inalienably disempowered; outsiders to the system of justice and equitable economic opportunity.

Anthony R. Chase, *Race, Culture, and Contract Law: From the Cottonfield to the Courtroom*, 28 Conn. L. Rev. 1, 5–6 (1995). Economic empowerment can come as a result of entering into a contract. The ability to enter into a contract is something that everyone over the age of 18 takes for granted. During slavery, African–Americas were the subject of contracts, yet were unable to enter into contracts. *Id*. at 12, 23–24. Now that slavery has been abolished, have things changed or does contract law today continue to disempower African–Americans and other people of color?

Professor Neil Williams advocates using contract law as a means to eliminate racial discrimination. *See* Neil G. Williams, *Offer, Acceptance, and Improper Considerations: A Common–Law Model for the Prohibition of Racial Discrimination in the Contracting Process*, 62 Geo. Wash. L. Rev. 183 (1994).

SECTION 1. A CONTRACT LAW SOLUTION TO MODERN DAY RACIAL DISCRIMINATION

NEIL G. WILLIAMS

Offer, Acceptance, and Improper Considerations: A Common–Law Model For the Prohibition of Racial Discrimination in the Contracting Process
62 Geo. Wash. L. Rev. 183, 201–202, 203–205, 222–227 (1994).

* * *For present purposes, three doctrines are especially important stepping stones in contract law's evolution towards the recognition of a norm prohibiting racial discrimination in the formation, performance, enforcement, or termination of contracts. They are the duty-to-serve doctrine, the unconscionability doctrine and the duty of good faith and fair dealing.

A central proposition of classical contract law was that parties had an unfettered right to choose the parties with whom they contract. As demonstrated in the prior section, even though neoclassical contract law has evolved to the point of imposing some obligations on parties who have negotiated with one another, it generally has stopped short of requiring that parties negotiate or contract with one another. Notwithstanding, the recognition of an antidiscrimination norm applicable in the period prior to the formation of a bargain contract would not be unprecedented. The duty-to-serve doctrine, a legal tenet predating the classical model (it is traceable to the fifteenth century), has long placed limitations on the right of certain parties to choose the persons with whom they contract. Applicable to "public-service companies," i.e., those parties who have elected to engage in a "public calling," this common-law doctrine requires that all members of the public be served, without distinction, unless there are reasonable grounds for not so doing. In fact, the common-law duty-to-serve doctrine can and has been used on a few occasions to provide protection to victims of racial discrimination, though most of the cases interpreting the scope of the doctrine have involved arbitrary refusals to serve for reasons unconnected with race.

* * *

* * * The evolution of the duty-to-serve doctrine demonstrates the willingness of common-law courts to prohibit discrimination prior to bargain contract formation in circumstances deemed appropriate in the light of social values prevailing at a given time.

One of the most important developments in modern contract law has been the resurgence of the unconscionability doctrine. As earlier noted, under the classical model courts generally did not concern themselves with the fairness of an exchange or the fairness of the process through which an agreement was reached, as long as the parties refrained from engaging in gross misconduct rising to the level of fraud or duress. The unconscionability doctrine, however, openly and explicitly is geared toward these types of fairness determinations.

As Judge Skelly Wright noted in *Williams v. Walker–Thomas Furniture Co.*, unconscionability consists of "an absence of meaningful choice on the part of one of the parties together with contract terms which are unreasonably favorable to the other party"; that is, unconscionability provides a defense to a defendant in cases in which an unfair process of agreement gives rise to unfair terms. Following the lead of Professor Arthur Leff, courts and scholars often label unfairness in the process through which an agreement is reached as "procedural unconscionability" and unfairness in the actual terms reached as "substantive unconscionability." Generally, in order for limitations to be placed on the enforceability of an agreement, courts insist that there be both procedural and substantive unconscionability.

Procedural unconscionability, in turn, may be further subdivided into two recognized types: that which arises when one party exploits another party's "lack of knowledge" and that which arises when one party exploits another party's "lack of voluntariness." A "lack of knowledge" occurs when, in Judge Wright's words, a party is not afforded "a reasonable opportunity to understand the terms of the contract." A party may be deprived of this reasonable opportunity, for example, when she lacks the education required to understand terms of a contract or when terms are presented in such a way that they are not likely to come to her attention. "Lack of voluntariness" arises as a result of "a gross inequality of bargaining power," i.e., in cases in which a party has no meaningful opportunity to negotiate the terms of an agreement. For purposes of this Article, the unconscionability doctrine is important for a variety of reasons. The doctrine provides one of the clearest instances of what Professor Robert Summers has termed "contractual morality"; it is a paradigmatic example of the behavior of contracting parties being openly and explicitly subjected to community standards of fairness and decency. Moreover, in its focus on the fairness of the process through which an agreement is reached, the unconscionability doctrine allows courts to police the behavior of contracting parties during the period prior to the formation of a bargain contract. Accordingly, this doctrine constitutes an important precedent for courts using the common law of contracts to advance important community goals by placing limitations on the conduct of parties in the period prior to contract formation. It would be consistent with this general pattern for the common law to prohibit racial discrimination in contract formation.

doesn't this open the "floodgates"- a whole new line of litigation

A closer examination of the unconscionability doctrine demonstrates that it is capable of supporting the latter proposition even more directly. *Williams* and *Jones v. Star Credit Corp.*, another leading case widely taught in American law schools to illustrate the doctrine, both involve instances in which merchants exploited underprivileged members of African American communities. One undeniable consequence of the ravages of racial discrimination in this society is that disproportionately large numbers of minority citizens have neither the economic means (resulting in a "lack of voluntariness") nor the access to education (resulting in a "lack of knowledge") needed to avoid hard bargains in many cases. There can be no doubt that concerns about racism percolate beneath the surfaces of *Williams* and *Jones*, although the courts in both cases were confined to dealing with symptoms of that disease (substantive and procedural unconscionability) rather than directly confronting the disease itself. It would be a natural step in the progression of the common law for tools to be developed for dealing with racial discrimination more overtly. The unconscionability doctrine, therefore, represents an important bridge to the recognition of a broad contractual antidiscrimination norm * * *.

good application

[Professor Williams discusses the duty each party to a contract has to operate in good faith which will be excerpted *infra* at 161–164.]

* * *

Contract law's embrace of an antidiscrimination requirement would be perfectly compatible with its natural, orderly evolution in this century. Indeed, the *Reid* and *Ricci* cases [discussed *infra* at 164–172] provide evidence that some courts, if confronted with the appropriate case, may well be prepared at least to acknowledge that contract law prohibits racial discrimination by parties who have entered into contracts. One prominent jurist, however, refused to recognize a common-law right to be free from racial discrimination when confronted with the issue. In *McKnight v. General Motors Corp.*, Judge Richard Posner made the following observations in rejecting an African American's argument that his employment contract incorporated an antidiscrimination norm:

> If what McKnight is trying to argue is that public policy reads into every such contract a contractual duty not to discriminate on racial grounds, this would imply that every victim of racial discrimination in employment has a claim for breach of contracts as well as a claim under the statutes forbidding such discrimination. That would be extravagant. . . .

Judge Posner appears to argue that the enactment of the antidiscrimination statutes somehow renders it improper for contract law to prohibit racial discrimination. He concedes, however, that state antidiscrimination laws (which would include, to the extent recognized, a common-law prohibition of racial discrimination) generally are not preempted by federal law. In any event, the Supreme Court closed the door on such an argument when it acknowledged in *Patterson v. McLean Credit Union* that states are free to expand their common law of contracts to provide protection against discrimination beyond any protection available under federal statutes. Nor is there a sufficient basis for asserting that the common law should not prohibit racial discrimination because it would thereby undermine basic policies underlying federal antidiscrimination statutes.

Underlying Judge Posner's "extravagance" argument is a perception that the recognition of a common-law antidiscrimination norm is unnecessary because it merely would duplicate the protection available under antidiscrimination statutes (even though in McKnight the relief then available under federal statutes clearly was inadequate to redress harm caused by proven discriminatory misconduct). That this perception does not justify a refusal to recognize a common-law antidiscrimination norm becomes apparent when Judge Posner's logic is extended to comparable contexts. For example, it is well-recognized that victims of securities fraud may bring common-law misrepresentation claims in addition to claims seeking relief under various federal and state statutes. In these cases, courts have not concluded that the common-law claims of victims of securities fraud should not be recognized because doing so would be "extravagant." Moreover, the evolution of statutory regimes to deal with increasingly sophisticated modes of fraudulent misconduct has not deterred the common law from developing along parallel lines. Another instance of this phenomenon is the warm reception that common-law courts have given to the unconscionability doctrine and the duty of good faith and fair dealing. Courts have not been reluctant to include these doctrines in the general law of contracts once state

[handwritten margin note: ?? in what way? is it really extrav... to afford each member of our society a certain automatic amt. of dignity?]

legislatures have rendered them applicable to sales contracts by adopting Article Two of the Uniform Commercial Code. In fact, they have been more willing to incorporate these doctrines into a state's general contract law once the doctrines received the imprimatur of a legislature.

* * *

Furthermore, the common law's incorporation of a broad, internally generated antidiscrimination norm would provide a foundation for the antidiscrimination statutes at the most fundamental moral and intellectual level. By recognizing the antidiscrimination principle as one of its fundamental paradigms, the common law can assist the antidiscrimination statutes in ridding society of the harms caused by racial discrimination. In particular, such an evolution of general contract law will enhance our country's moral development by allowing the message that it is just plain wrong to discriminate on the basis of race to penetrate even more deeply into the core of society. An acceptance of a common-law antidiscrimination norm would lead (we can hope) to an increase in the number of cases in which people conform their behavior to the antidiscrimination norm voluntarily.

One also must not undervalue the influence of the perceived core values of contract law on future generations of lawyers by virtue of its being at the very heart of the first-year curriculum. To the extent law students no longer are taught uncritically that the common law of contracts and the prohibition of racial discrimination are at odds, those who will be charged with the future administration of our legal system will not be indoctrinated into thinking that societal norms of racial justice are alien invaders to our legal shores whose presence can be sanctioned only by the Constitution or a statute.

By evolving to reflect contemporary society's disdain for racial discrimination, the common law of contracts will also benefit. As long as general contract law lags behind prevailing mores, the pace at which it is displaced by statutory regimes undoubtedly will quicken. As we become more a society of minorities, a body of law cannot be expected to endure if it is perceived as a rigid relic of a past that systematically undermined the interests of those who have been historically oppressed. Accordingly, by applying an evolved common law that reflects the values of contemporary society, jurists may be able to help ensure the survival of the common law of contracts as a vital legal presence.

Moreover, a common-law prohibition of racial discrimination in the contracting process need not be limited to mere duplication of protection that is already available through statutes. A common-law antidiscrimination norm has the potential to bolster the fight against discrimination in this society by supplementing shortcomings that have developed in statutory protections. Initially, the forces fighting discrimination appropriately sought to wrest gains at the federal level. This strategy was a coup de maitre; it was much more effective to concentrate energies on national law than to try to win simultaneous battles on fifty state fronts. Even when attention could be diverted toward seeking changes at the

[Handwritten margin note, left side, upper:] "moral" dvpmt? whose morality?

[Handwritten margin note, left side, lower:] I think he over-generalizes. I am just cynical enough to believe that any "disdain" is reserved for OVERT racial discrimination - in part, b/c it is obvious -most majority prefer transparency

state level, it clearly made more sense to lobby legislatures for state statutes similar to federal antidiscrimination statutes than to hope that inspired advocacy might convince a state supreme court to jettison hostile common-law precedent. Given the current political trend of restricting (rather than expanding) rights, it is unlikely that federal statutory protection against racial discrimination will be enhanced any time soon. Moreover, a conservative federal judiciary can be expected to continue interpreting federal antidiscrimination statutes narrowly.

which is the "prevailing norm"? this could represent the "prevailing norm" [restricting rights is in line w/ beginning of the Christian Right movement...]

* * *

Notes and Questions

1. Professor Williams suggests that the doctrine of unconscionability and the duty to bargain in good faith should be useful tools in combating race discrimination. Each doctrine will be considered in the following two sections.

2. Professor Williams comments on Judge Posner's refusal to recognize an antidiscrimination norm. Recall that Judge Posner was the author of the *Wassell v. Adams* decision discussed *supra* at 114. Does Judge Posner have a problem where race is concerned? Professor Jerome Culp of Duke Law School thinks the answer is yes. *See* Jerome McCristal Culp, *Posner on Duncan Kennedy and Racial Difference: White Authority in the Legal Academy*, 41 Duke L. J. 1095, 1097 (1992) ("Judge Posner's defense of neutral and objective standards in legal scholarship fails to acknowledge that facially objective and disinterested standards in fact serve the interests of the white majority. . ."); Jerome McCristal Culp, *To the Bone: Race and White Privilege*, 83 Minn. L. Rev. 1637, 1661 (1999)("The reason I note Judge Posner's racism is to contend that it is possible for good people and—I assume that Judge Posner is such a good person—to commit racist acts.")

SECTION 2.   WHAT IS UNCONSCIONABILITY?

This section will begin with the Restatement's position on unconscionable contracts followed by UCC § 2–302 which deals with unconscionable contracts.

Restatement of the Law Second—Contracts

§ 208.   Unconscionable Contract Or Term

If a contract or term thereof is unconscionable at the time the contract is made a court may refuse to enforce the contract, or may enforce the remainder of the contract without the unconscionable term, or may so limit the application of any unconscionable term as to avoid any unconscionable result.

Comment:

a. Scope. Like the obligation of good faith and fair dealing (§ 205), the policy against unconscionable contracts or terms applies to a wide variety of types of conduct. The determination that a contract or term is or is not unconscionable is made in the light of its setting, purpose and effect. Relevant factors include weaknesses in the contracting process like those involved in more specific rules as to contractual capacity, fraud, and other invalidating causes; the policy also overlaps with rules which render particular bargains or terms unenforceable on grounds of public policy. Policing against unconscionable contracts or terms has sometimes been accomplished "by adverse construction of language, by manipulation of the rules of offer and acceptance or by determinations that the clause is contrary to public policy or to the dominant purpose of the contract." Uniform Commercial Code § 2–302 Comment 1. Particularly in the case of standardized agreements, the rule of this Section permits the court to pass directly on the unconscionability of the contract or clause rather than to avoid unconscionable results by interpretation. Compare § 211.

the court may "pass directly" on unconscionability

b. Historic standards. Traditionally, a bargain was said to be unconscionable in an action at law if it was "such as no man in his senses and not under delusion would make on the one hand, and as no honest and fair man would accept on the other;" damages were then limited to those to which the aggrieved party was "equitably" entitled. *Hume v. United States*, 132 U.S. 406 (1889), quoting *Earl of Chesterfield v. Janssen*, 2 Ves.Sen. 125, 155, 28 Eng.Rep. 82, 100 (Ch.1750). Even though a contract was fully enforceable in an action for damages, equitable remedies such as specific performance were refused where "the sum total of its provisions drives too hard a bargain for a court of conscience to assist." *Campbell Soup Co. v. Wentz*, 172 F.2d 80, 84 (3d Cir.1948). Modern procedural reforms have blurred the distinction between remedies at law and in equity. For contracts for the sale of goods, Uniform Commercial Code § 2–302 states the rule of this Section without distinction between law and equity. Comment 1 to that section adds, "The principle is one of the prevention of oppression and unfair surprise (Cf. Campbell Soup Co. v. Wentz, ...) and not of disturbance of allocation of risks because of superior bargaining power."

c. Overall imbalance. Inadequacy of consideration does not of itself invalidate a bargain, but gross disparity in the values exchanged may be an important factor in a determination that a contract is unconscionable and may be sufficient ground, without more, for denying specific performance. *See* §§ 79, 364. Such a disparity may also corroborate indications of defects in the bargaining process, or may affect the remedy to be granted when there is a violation of a more specific rule. Theoretically it is possible for a contract to be oppressive taken as a whole, even though there is no weakness in the bargaining process and no single term which is in itself unconscionable. Ordinarily, however, an unconscionable contract involves other factors as well as overall imbalance.

Uniform Commercial Code

Article 2. Sales

§ 2–302. Unconscionable Contract or Clause.

(1) If the court as a matter of law finds the contract or any clause of the contract to have been unconscionable at the time it was made the court may refuse to enforce the contract, or it may enforce the remainder of the contract without the unconscionable clause, or it may so limit the application of any unconscionable clause as to avoid any unconscionable result.

(2) When it is claimed or appears to the court that the contract or any clause thereof may be unconscionable the parties shall be afforded a reasonable opportunity to present evidence as to its commercial setting, purpose and effect to aid the court in making the determination.

Notes and Questions

1. The Comment to the Restatement says that a contract can be found unconscionable where the court "determin[es] that the clause is contrary to public policy." What do you think the drafters meant? Are you surprised that race discrimination was not mentioned in the comment?

2. Assuming that race discrimination is contrary to public policy, if an automobile dealership charges a higher price to Black women than White men, should that contract be found unconscionable, assuming that you could prove it? *See e.g.* Ian Ayres, *Fair Driving: Gender and Race Discrimination in Retail Car Negotiations*, 104 Harv. L. Rev. 817 (1991); Ian Ayres, *Further Evidence of Discrimination in New Car Negotiations and Estimates of Its Cause*, 94 Mich. L. Rev. 109 (1995). Professor Emily Houh puts it this way: "Black or female consumers who have negotiated contracts for the purchase of new cars may believe that the particular contracting process is infected with bad faith conduct, while their White and male counterparts may disagree." Emily M.S. Houh, *Critical Interventions: Towards an Expansive Equality Approach to the Doctrine of Good Faith in Contract Law*, 88 Cornell L. Rev. 1025, 1052 (2003).

3. *See also* Steven W. Bender, *Consumer Protection For Latinos: Overcoming Language Fraud and English–Only in the Marketplace*, 45 Am. U. L. Rev. 1027, 1030 (1996) (author proposes a "comprehensive strategy of reform that involves the legislatures, administrative agencies, and courts, as well as nonprofit organizations" for non-English speaking consumers.)

4. Are you concerned that if contracts can be declared unconscionable, when race discrimination is present, that certain people won't be able to enter into contracts?

5. Imagine a client comes to you with a contract that contains the following provision:

The contract further provided that the amount of each periodical installment payment to be made by [purchaser] to the Company under this present lease shall be inclusive of and not in addition to the amount of each installment payment to be made by [purchaser] under such prior leases, bills or accounts; and all payments now and hereafter made by [purchaser] shall be credited pro rata on all outstanding leases, bills and accounts due the Company by [purchaser] at the time each such payment is made.

How would you explain this clause to your client? How does it operate?

6.   Consider the *Williams v. Walker–Thomas Furniture Company* decision.

WILLIAMS v. WALKER–THOMAS FURNITURE CO.

350 F.2d 445 (D.C.Cir.1965).

J. SKELLY WRIGHT, CIRCUIT JUDGE:

Appellee, Walker–Thomas Furniture Company, operates a retail furniture store in the District of Columbia. During the period from 1957 to 1962 each appellant in these cases purchased a number of household items from Walker–Thomas, for which payment was to be made in installments. The terms of each purchase were contained in a printed form contract which set forth the value of the purchased item and purported to lease the item to appellant for a stipulated monthly rent payment. The contract then provided, in substance, that title would remain in Walker–Thomas until the total of all the monthly payments made equaled the stated value of the item, at which time appellants could take title. In the event of a default in the payment of any monthly installment, Walker–Thomas could repossess the item.

The contract further provided that "the amount of each periodical installment payment to be made by [purchaser] to the Company under this present lease shall be inclusive of and not in addition to the amount of each installment payment to be made by [purchaser] under such prior leases, bills or accounts; *and all payments now and hereafter made by [purchaser] shall be credited pro rata on all outstanding leases, bills and accounts* due the Company by [purchaser] at the time each such payment is made." (Emphasis added.) The effect of this rather obscure provision was to keep a balance due on every item purchased until the balance due on all items, whenever purchased, was liquidated. As a result, the debt incurred at the time of purchase of each item was secured by the right to repossess all the items previously purchased by the same purchaser, and each new item purchased automatically became subject to a security interest arising out of the previous dealings.

On May 12, 1962, appellant Thorne purchased an item described as a Daveno, three tables, and two lamps, having total stated value of $391.10. Shortly thereafter, he defaulted on his monthly payments and appellee sought to replevy all the items purchased since the first transaction in 1958. Similarly, on April 17, 1962, appellant Williams bought a stereo set of stated value of $514.95.[1] She too defaulted shortly thereaf-

---

1.   At the time of this purchase her account showed a balance of $164 still owing from her prior purchases. The total of all the purchases made over the years in question came to $1,800. The total payments amounted to $1,400.

ter, and appellee sought to replevy all the items purchased since December, 1957. The Court of General Sessions granted judgment for appellee. The District of Columbia Court of Appeals affirmed, and we granted appellants' motion for leave to appeal to this court.

Appellants' principal contention, rejected by both the trial and the appellate courts below, is that these contracts, or at least some of them, are unconscionable and, hence, not enforceable. In its opinion in *Williams v. Walker–Thomas Furniture Company*, 198 A.2d 914, 916 (1964), the District of Columbia Court of Appeals explained its rejection of this contention as follows:

> "Appellant's second argument presents a more serious question. The record reveals that prior to the last purchase appellant had reduced the balance in her account to $164. The last purchase, a stereo set, raised the balance due to $678. Significantly, at the time of this and the preceding purchases, appellee was aware of appellant's financial position. The reverse side of the stereo contract listed the name of appellant's social worker and her $218 monthly stipend from the government. Nevertheless, with full knowledge that appellant had to feed, clothe and support both herself and seven children on this amount, appellee sold her a $514 stereo set."

[margin note: ★ I feel uncomfortable w/ the paternal tone of his analysis. Obviously she has done just fine so far!]

> "We cannot condemn too strongly appellee's conduct. It raises serious questions of sharp practice and irresponsible business dealings. A review of the legislation in the District of Columbia affecting retail sales and the pertinent decisions of the highest court in this jurisdiction disclose, however, no ground upon which this court can declare the contracts in question contrary to public policy. We note that were the Maryland Retail Installment Sales Act, Art. 83 §§ 128–153, or its equivalent, in force in the District of Columbia, we could grant appellant appropriate relief. We think Congress should consider corrective legislation to protect the public from such exploitive contracts as were utilized in the case at bar."

[margin note: — b/c the court does not find a statute, the court doesn't grant relief]

We do not agree that the court lacked the power to refuse enforcement to contracts found to be unconscionable. In other jurisdictions, it has been held as a matter of common law that unconscionable contracts are not enforceable.[2] While no decision of this court so holding has been found, the notion that an unconscionable bargain should not be given full enforcement is by no means novel. In *Scott v. United States*, 79 U.S. (12 Wall.) 443, 445, 20 L.Ed. 438 (1870), the Supreme Court stated:

[margin note: D.C.Cir. finds unconscionability in the common law]

> " * * * If a contract be unreasonable and unconscionable, but not void for fraud, a court of law will give to the party who sues for its

2. *Campbell Soup Co. v. Wentz*, 3 Cir., 172 F.2d 80 (1948); *Indianapolis Morris Plan Corporation v. Sparks*, 132 Ind.App. 145, 172 N.E.2d 899 (1961); *Henningsen v.* *Bloomfield Motors, Inc.*, 32 N.J. 358, 161 A.2d 69, 84–96, 75 A.L.R.2d 1 (1960). Cf. 1 Corbin, Contracts § 128 (1963).

breach damages, not according to its letter, but only such as he is equitably entitled to. * * * "[3]

Since we have never adopted or rejected such a rule,[4] the question here presented is actually one of first impression.

Congress has recently enacted the Uniform Commercial Code, which specifically provides that the court may refuse to enforce a contract which it finds to be unconscionable at the time it was made. 28 D.C.CODE § 2–302 (Supp. IV 1965). The enactment of this section, which occurred subsequent to the contracts here in suit, does not mean that the common law of the District of Columbia was otherwise at the time of enactment, nor does it preclude the court from adopting a similar rule in the exercise of its powers to develop the common law for the District of Columbia. In fact, in view of the absence of prior authority on the point, we consider the congressional adoption of § 2–302 persuasive authority for following the rationale of the cases from which the section is explicitly derived.[5] Accordingly, we hold that where the element of unconscionability is present at the time a contract is made, the contract should not be enforced.

classic def'n from Williams

Unconscionability has generally been recognized to include an absence of meaningful choice on the part of one of the parties together with contract terms which are unreasonably favorable to the other party.[6] Whether a meaningful choice is present in a particular case can only be determined by consideration of all the circumstances surrounding the transaction. In many cases the meaningfulness of the choice is negated by a gross inequality of bargaining power.[7] The manner in which the

3. *See Luing v. Peterson*, 143 Minn. 6, 172 N.W. 692 (1919); *Greer v. Tweed*, N.Y.C.P., 13 Abb.Pr., N.S., 427 (1872); *Schnell v. Nell*, 17 Ind. 29 (1861); and *see generally* the discussion of the English authorities in *Hume v. United States*, 132 U.S. 406, 10 S.Ct. 134, 33 L.Ed. 393 (1889).

4. While some of the statements in the court's opinion in *District of Columbia v. Harlan & Hollingsworth Co.*, 30 App.D.C. 270 (1908), may appear to reject the rule, in reaching its decision upholding the liquidated damages clause in that case the court considered the circumstances existing at the time the contract was made, *see* 30 App.D.C. at 279, and applied the usual rule on liquidated damages. *See* 5 Corbin, Contracts §§ 1054–1075 (1964); Note, 72 YALE L.J. 723, 746–755 (1963). Compare *Jaeger v. O'Donoghue*, 57 App.D.C. 191, 18 F.2d 1013 (1927).

5. *See* Comment, § 2–302, Uniform Commercial Code (1962). Compare Note, 45 Va.L.Rev. 583, 590 (1959), where it is predicted that the rule of § 2–302 will be followed by analogy in cases which involve contracts not specifically covered by the section. *Cf.* 1 State of New York Law Revision

Commission, Report and Record of Hearings on the Uniform Commercial Code 108–110 (1954) (remarks of Professor Llewellyn).

6. *See Henningsen v. Bloomfield Motors, Inc., supra* Note 2; *Campbell Soup Co. v. Wentz, supra* Note 2.

7. *See Henningsen v. Bloomfield Motors, Inc., supra* Note 2, 161 A.2d at 86, and authorities there cited. Inquiry into the relative bargaining power of the two parties is not an inquiry wholly divorced from the general question of unconscionability, since a one-sided bargain is itself evidence of the inequality of the bargaining parties. This fact was vaguely recognized in the common law doctrine of intrinsic fraud, that is, fraud which can be presumed from the grossly unfair nature of the terms of the contract. *See* the oft-quoted statement of Lord Hardwicke in *Earl of Chesterfield v. Janssen*, 28 Eng.Rep. 82, 100 (1751):

"* * * [Fraud] may be apparent from the intrinsic nature and subject of the bargain itself; such as no man in his senses and not under delusion would make * * *."

contract was entered is also relevant to this consideration. Did each party to the contract, considering his obvious education or lack of it, have a reasonable opportunity to understand the terms of the contract, or were the important terms hidden in a maze of fine print and minimized by deceptive sales practices? Ordinarily, one who signs an agreement without full knowledge of its terms might be held to assume the risk that he has entered a one-sided bargain.[8] But when a party of little bargaining power, and hence little real choice, signs a commercially unreasonable contract with little or no knowledge of its terms, it is hardly likely that his consent, or even an objective manifestation of his consent, was ever given to all the terms. In such a case the usual rule that the terms of the agreement are not to be questioned[9] should be abandoned and the court should consider whether the terms of the contract are so unfair that enforcement should be withheld.[10]

In determining reasonableness or fairness, the primary concern must be with the terms of the contract considered in light of the circumstances existing when the contract was made. The test is not simple, nor can it be mechanically applied. The terms are to be considered "in the light of the general commercial background and the commercial needs of the particular trade or case."[11] Corbin suggests the test as being whether the terms are "so extreme as to appear unconscionable according to the mores and business practices of the time and place." 1 Corbin, *op. cit. supra* Note 2.[12] We think this formulation correctly states the test to be applied in those cases where no meaningful choice was exercised upon entering the contract.

Because the trial court and the appellate court did not feel that enforcement could be refused, no findings were made on the possible unconscionability of the contracts in these cases. Since the record is not

---

And *cf. Hume v. United States, supra* Note 3, 132 U.S. at 413, 10 S.Ct. at 137, where the Court characterized the English cases as "cases in which one party took advantage of the other's ignorance of arithmetic to impose upon him, and the fraud was apparent from the face of the contracts." *See also* Greer v. Tweed, *supra* Note 3.

8. *See* Restatement, Contracts § 70 (1932); Note, 63 Harv.L.Rev. 494 (1950). *See also Daley v. People's Building, Loan & Savings Ass'n*, 178 Mass. 13, 59 N.E. 452, 453 (1901), in which Mr. Justice Holmes, while sitting on the Supreme Judicial Court of Massachusetts, made this observation:

"* * * Courts are less and less disposed to interfere with parties making such contracts as they choose, so long as they interfere with no one's welfare but their own. * * * It will be understood that we are speaking of parties standing in an equal position where neither has any oppressive advantage or power * * *."

9. This rule has never been without exception. In cases involving merely the transfer of unequal amounts of the same commodity, the courts have held the bargain unenforceable for the reason that "in such a case, it is clear, that the law cannot indulge in the presumption of equivalence between the consideration and the promise." 1 Williston, Contracts § 115 (3d ed. 1957).

10. See the general discussion of "Boiler–Plate Agreements" in Llewellyn, The Common Law Tradition 362–371 (1960).

11. Comment, Uniform Commercial Code § 2–307.

12. *See Henningsen v. Bloomfield Motors, Inc., supra* Note 2; *Mandel v. Liebman*, 303 N.Y. 88, 100 N.E.2d 149 (1951). The traditional test as stated in *Greer v. Tweed, supra* Note 3, 13 Abb.Pr. N.S., at 429, is "such as no man in his senses and not under delusion would make on the one hand, and as no honest or fair man would accept, on the other."

sufficient for our deciding the issue as a matter of law, the cases must be remanded to the trial court for further proceedings.

So ordered.

DANAHER, CIRCUIT JUDGE (dissenting):

* * *

My view is thus summed up by an able court which made no finding that there had actually been sharp practice. Rather the appellant seems to have known precisely where she stood.

There are many aspects of public policy here involved. What is a luxury to some may seem an outright necessity to others. Is public oversight to be required of the expenditures of relief funds? A washing machine, e.g., in the hands of a relief client might become a fruitful source of income. Many relief clients may well need credit, and certain business establishments will take long chances on the sale of items, expecting their pricing policies will afford a degree of protection commensurate with the risk. Perhaps a remedy when necessary will be found within the provisions of the "Loan Shark" law, D.C.CODE §§ 26–601 et seq. (1961).

I mention such matters only to emphasize the desirability of a cautious approach to any such problem, particularly since the law for so long has allowed parties such great latitude in making their own contracts. I dare say there must annually be thousands upon thousands of installment credit transactions in this jurisdiction, and one can only speculate as to the effect the decision in these cases will have.[1]

I think that is exactly the point!

Notes and Questions

1. Judge Skelly Wright wrote "[b]ut when a party of little bargaining power, and hence little real choice, signs a commercially unreasonable contract with little or no knowledge of its terms, it is hardly likely that his consent, or even an objective manifestation of his consent, was ever given to all the terms." Do you think Ora Lee Williams understood the terms of the agreement?

2. The dissent seems concerned about the impact that this decision will have on whether the Walker–Thomas Furniture Co. will change its business practices in a way detrimental to the Ora Lee Williams' of the world. Is the majority as concerned?

3. Is this case about unconscionability or capacity? Could the court's decision be read to suggest that Ora Lee Williams was incapable of entering into this contract? Are the Ora Lee Williams' of the world unable to contract?

the intermediate court's decision reflected more on capacity, but still ruled in favor of the furniture store

4. What happened on remand? Both Ora Lee Williams and the Thornes' settled for the value of the seized items. *See* Pierre E. Dostert, *Appellate Restatement of Unconscionability: Civil Legal Aid at Work*, 54

---

1. However the provision ultimately may be applied or in what circumstances, D.C.CODE § 28–2–301 (Supp. IV, 1965) did not become effective until January 1, 1965.

A.B.A. J. 1183, 1186 (1968). In that article, Mr. Dostert who represented William and Ruth Thorne and was very familiar with the facts of Ora Lee Williams wrote about the case in significant detail. He failed to mention the race of the parties describing them generally as "poor and less-educated members of the community." *Id.* at 1183.

5. Consider the following three excerpts concerning the *Williams* decision.

AMY H. KASTELY

Out of the Whiteness: On Raced Codes and White Race Consciousness
in Some Tort, Criminal, and Contract Law
63 U. Cin. L. Rev. 269, 305–310 (1994).

* * *

Williams v. Walker–Thomas Furniture Co. is featured in current unconscionability doctrine. In part, this reflects high regard for Judge Skelly Wright; there is more, however: the case neatly encapsulates a sympathetic, yet uncritical, attitude toward race, class, gender, and contract. *Williams v. Walker–Thomas* involved enforcement of a crosscollateral clause in a series of contracts by which Ora Lee Williams had purchased various household goods. Williams' attorney argued that the cross-collateral clause was unconscionable and, therefore, unenforceable. The lower courts rejected this argument. Judge Wright, writing for the United States Court of Appeals, briefly described the cross-collateral clause included in Walker–Thomas' printed contracts, the items purchased by Williams, and her default in payment. * * *

Following this quotation, **Judge Wright** reasoned that courts do have the power to refuse enforcement of unconscionable contracts, and he enumerated **factors** that might lead a court to conclude that a contract was unconscionable: "gross inequality of bargaining power"; "obvious education or lack of it"; "reasonable opportunity to understand the terms of the contract"; and the use of "fine print" or "deceptive sales practices." * * *

By failing to include further detail about the contracts between Walker–Thomas and Williams and by resting instead on the vague and broadly associated listing of limited power, little knowledge, limited education, and lack of choice, Judge Wright's opinion allows—even invites—the reader to use raced tropes linking poverty, lack of education, single parenthood, and lack of capacity with black women and to disregard the connection between white racism and exploitative pricing and collection practices. If the reader does not translate the text to mean that Williams is black, living in highly segregated, racially exploitative Washington, D.C., then the grounds for finding unconscionability are vague and so broad as to reach most contracts, or at least most involving a printed form. To conclude that Williams is black, however, and that her life is constrained by racially determined barriers and burdens, the reader must accept and think within these raced tropes. Having taken this step, the reader is left with the vague impression that the uncon-

[handwritten margin note: I really took it to mean installment rent-a-center contracts]

scionability doctrine operates to relieve those who are socially and economically disadvantaged; but, at the same time, Judge Wright's opinion invites the reader to anticipate lack of understanding, education, and sophistication as significant factors. In this way, the opinion leads readers to see Williams and other members of subordinated groups as defective and to ignore the fact of racism and other systems of social oppression.

It seems clear that Judge Wright did consider this case to involve the exploitation of low-income people of color by merchants who charge high prices and engage in harsh collection techniques, enabled in part by racist barriers, which prevent many people of color from shopping at less expensive stores, and in part by burdens of transportation, child-care, and ill-health, which are aggravated by racially unfair systems of public transportation, child-care, and medical service. Officially sanctioned racial segregation prevailed in almost every aspect of commercial and social life in Washington, D.C., until the early 1950s, and de facto segregation continued in most commercial and social activities during the period of Williams' purchases from Walker–Thomas, 1957 to 1962. Judge Wright was involved personally in the extended litigation over racial segregation in the District of Columbia public schools. The Civil Rights Act of 1964 declared many forms of overt racial segregation illegal, but racist barriers and burdens continue to effect the lives and commercial choices of black people in the District of Columbia.

By failing to name these racist barriers and burdens, or even to name Williams' race, Judge Wright's opinion leaves readers with nothing but the vague sense that Williams, a black woman receiving welfare, was incompetent and in need of charity from honorable people, a sense given form and credibility only because of its correspondence with racist stereotypes of black women.

Judge Danaher, although dissenting from the majority's decision, did not dispute the stereotypes in Judge Wright's opinion. Instead, his disagreement with the majority was over the appropriate response of the law to the stereotyped construction of Williams' life. Rather than give Williams special excuse from the obligations imposed by the objective interpretation of her contract, Judge Danaher suggested, the law should have held her responsible for her own good * * *

This is the way of the world. Poor people do have to pay more, Judge Danaher maintained, but it is wrong not to hold them to their choices and wrong to treat them as less competent than class-privileged white men. Judge Danaher and Judge Wright both reached decisions based upon submerged, raced-coded logic. They differed merely on the legal conclusions that flowed from this logic in particular cases. Judge Wright responded with paternalistic charity, Judge Danaher with patriarchal discipline; both viewed Williams through the lens of white race consciousness.

Judge Wright could have taken greater care in his analysis and explanation; he could have written a recitatif less dependent on racial stereotype. More detail might have shifted Judge Wright's analytic attention from assumed defects in Williams' cognitive abilities to the racist barriers and burdens that restrained her actions, and it might have allowed his reader to see Williams as a responsible, intelligent actor making choices in the best interests of her family. Some information from the trial record was included in the District of Columbia Court of Appeals opinion: over a five-year period, in fourteen different transactions, Williams purchased many household items from Walker–Thomas, including sheets, curtains, rugs, chairs, a chest of drawers, beds, mattresses, a washing machine, and a stereo. Most of the purchases were from a salesman who came to her home. There is no indication that any other store in her neighborhood sold furniture on any different terms than Walker–Thomas offered or that Walker–Thomas ever agreed to changes in its printed form contract.

I thought that this was why the opinion was so important - to protect people of limited means & choices

For each purchase, the salesman required Williams to sign a document that was six inches in length and described the transaction as a "lease." One paragraph of the form, written in very small print, included a sentence saying in obscure phrasing that payments would be "credited pro rata on all outstanding leases, bills and accounts." Another part of the document said that Walker–Thomas would retain title in the item until the total of all payments equaled the stated value of the item. Blanks in the form documents were not filled in, and Williams was not given copies of them.

The total cost, including finance charges, of these fourteen purchases was $1,800. The court opinions do not mention the market value of these items, but other sources report that Walker–Thomas refused to sell for cash and that its credit sale prices were much higher than the normal retail price of the items. Williams had already paid $1,400 by the time she defaulted in 1962. Walker–Thomas then sought to repossess all of the home furnishings that Williams had purchased in all fourteen transactions. Williams testified at trial that she understood the contracts to mean that when her payments were sufficient to cover the amount due on an individual item, then the item became hers. No mention was made of any evidence establishing a different understanding of the contract terms except the documents. Walker–Thomas apparently relied on the documents alone; it did not present evidence of any conversation about pro rata payments, cross-collateral, or any specific information that Williams had or was given about Walker–Thomas' interpretation of the contract or practices regarding repossession.

In Judge Wright's opinion, the background information was little more than the linking of race, gender, and poverty, and the narrative was individual incompetence. Judge Wright portrayed Williams as not like "ordinary" agreement signers, who assume the risk embodied in the document with the knowledge and ability to undertake the obligation. Unlike "ordinary" people, Williams probably lacked power, education, knowledge, and capacity. Walker–Thomas should not have sold her a stereo.

Reading this opinion, one can barely glimpse the people involved. One glaring inconsistency in Judge Wright's account of this case was that Williams' understanding of the contract reflected a general understanding of credit sales among people outside the credit industry. Her understanding was one that many people would have, unless of course they assumed that the contract would always be unfair to poor people. Williams' failure, if it was one, was in not foreseeing that a seller would—or effectively could—change the legal significance of her understanding merely by requiring her to sign a printed form with blanks left unfilled, without giving her an opportunity to read the form or to talk about the unusual arrangement that Walker–Thomas had buried in the document. A "reasonable person" apparently would be constantly suspicious, alert to the possibility of such devious moves, and would have a cynical view of the law, thinking that courts would give effect to such practices. Are these grounds upon which to characterize Williams as incompetent? Is it not true rather than the objective theory is seriously flawed? Is it just to honor this doctrine that so entwines meaning with subordination and control?

* * *

Notes and Questions

1. Is Professor Kastely correct when she says that "Judge Wright's opinion leaves readers with nothing but the vague sense that Williams, a black woman receiving welfare, was incompetent and in need of charity from honorable people, a sense given form and credibility only because of its correspondence with racist stereotypes of black women." and that "Judge Danaher, although dissenting from the majority's decision, did not dispute the stereotypes in Judge Wright's opinion."

2. What did Ora Lee Williams purchase? "Williams began her purchases in 1957 by ordering two pairs of draperies at a cost of $12.95. Over the course of the next five years, Williams purchases: one wallet, one apron set, one pot holder set, one set of rugs, one more pair of draperies, one 2 x 6 foot folding bed, one chest, one 9 x 12 foot linoleum rug, two pairs of curtains, four sheets, one WS20 portable fan, two more pairs of curtains, one Royal portable typewriter, two gun and holster sets (presumably toys), one metal bed, one inner spring mattress, four chrome kitchen chairs, one bath mat set, shower curtains, one Speed Queen washing machine, and one (now infamous) Admiralty stereophonic radio." Eben Colby, Note: *What Did the Doctrine of Unconscionability Do to the Walker–Thomas Furniture Company?*, 34 Conn. L. Rev. 625, 647 (2002). What do her purchasing habits tell you about her? Does it signal a problem on Ms. Williams' part or on society's part?

3. What is Professor Kastely's primary complaint with Judge Skelly Wright's opinion? How would she solve the problem?

4. Did the court's decision in *Williams v. Walker–Thomas Furniture Co.* solve the problem?

EBEN COLBY

Note: What Did the Doctrine of Unconscionability Do
to the Walker–Thomas Furniture Company?
34 Conn. L. Rev. 625, 625, 652, 653–655, 657–660 (2002).

It was barely an hour after the news that the Rev. Martin Luther King Jr. had been killed in Memphis when a brick crashed through the window of the Peoples Drug Store at 14th and U streets NW.... [Soon], there were the looters, hustling home with anything from fake zebra sofas out of Roessler's furniture store to shopping carts full of soft drinks from Safeway. There was the woman yelling at looters in the Walker–Thomas furniture store, noted for its high-interest charge accounts, to "Get the books! Get the books!" [fn1 William Raspberry, The Day the City's Fury Was Unleashed: Lessons of the Riots, WASH. POST, Apr. 3, 1988, at A1.]

* * *

The *Williams* decision seems to emphasize that customers of the furniture store probably did not know or understand the terms of the contract. But it is not absolutely clear that the low education level of the furniture company's customers meant that they were entirely unaware of what the contract contained. Ora Lee Williams testified that she did not understand the actual contracts; but this statement does not preclude the possibility that she knew from her life experience what the consequences of default were. At least one commentator has noted that it "might be that her long experience with such stores ... [left] her acutely 'street wise' about how such stores work. She might even [have] known people who [had] had their belongings repossessed by the same store." This seems more likely in light of the fact that the Walker–Thomas Furniture Company had filed approximately one hundred writs of replevin each year for many years preceding Williams's litigation and appears to have acquired a reputation for its actions. Think, for example, of the rioters after the death of Martin Luther King, Jr. While not sure about Ora Lee Williams in particular, an attorney that has represented the furniture company is of the opinion that many of the people in the neighborhood, and many customers of the store, were familiar with the repercussions of not making timely payments—specifically that the company would repossess all items sold to that customer.

* * *

While it is difficult to assess how much of the furniture company's form contract customers understood, it is easy to see that the *Williams* decision did not stop the furniture company from attempting to obfuscate some of the terms of its contract after the decision. This is demonstrated by the 1977 case *Blackmond v. Walker–Thomas Furniture Co.* Beckita Blackmond sued the furniture company in United States District Court for the District of Columbia for violating the Truth in Lending Act. Granting summary judgment for Blackmond, the court found that the furniture company violated the Truth in Lending Act by not providing a clear description of the property subject to a security interest. The court included in its decision a detailed description of the contract, which can be compared to the contract that the furniture company was using in *Williams*. The face of the contract in the 1977 case contained the statutorily required Truth in Lending disclosure statement, but it only listed the last item purchased as being subject to the security interest. Alas this was not the case. "No specific statement on the front side directs pointed attention to the further and more crucial security statement on the reverse side." And even if an alert buyer were to notice the clause on the back, it was not necessarily easy to understand. The clause on the back of the contract does not point out that it modifies the deceptively simple security interest statement on the front of the agreement. It is written in confusing and complicated "legalese:"

> Whenever subsequent purchases have been added and consolidated in a new balance, the payment provided herein on the new balance shall be considered allocated to the first purchase, and, in order, to each subsequent purchase. Each purchase will be considered a single unit for the purposes of each allocation, thereby each purchase unit will be completely paid for in order of seniority, the seller retaining title only to those purchases not completely paid for on this allocation. The amount of any down payment on a subsequent purchase shall be allocated in its entirety to such subsequent purchase. In the case of items purchased on the same date, the lowest priced shall be deemed first paid for.

The court assessed that there was "no clear way" that the buyer could determine which items had been paid for and released from security interests, and in fact it would be impossible without a copy of each of the contracts previously signed by the buyer. Additionally, the payments did not distinguish between principal and interest, complicating matters further. The court wrote that "where each of the six prior transactions was itself a consolidation, the confusion makes the language quoted less and less intelligible as time goes on. Few consumers have the capability to make the computations this so-called 'disclosure' involves. . . ."

While it was no longer using the same add-on contracts (a definite benefit to consumers), it can fairly be said that the company was not making much of an effort to disclose the terms of the contract to the buyer. Not only was it physically hidden on the contract, but the true nature of the agreement was obscured in convoluted language and complicated calculations. Although the court did not decide the case based on the unconscionability doctrine, its decision reveals that the doctrine of unconscionability certainly did not play much upon the minds of the furniture company's attorneys when they drafted this contract to extend credit to buyers. This contract was used in all sales that extended credit and the transaction in this case is representative of the way that the company continued to do business. It cannot be said, as some of the doctrine's supporters predicted, that the doctrine of unconscionability acted as a "mandate for disclosure." Any benefit to the buyer in terms of less surprise in the agreement, or influence on the company's contract drafting process, appears to be a result of consumer protection legislation and not the common law.

The supporters of the doctrine and the *Williams* decision also argued that both the doctrine and the decision would have a deterrent effect on businesses seeking to use form contracts to take advantage of buyers that either had to purchase subject to the contracts or not purchase at all—that it would level the playing field of modern commerce which was, after all, going to be dominated by form contracts. Again, this appears not to have happened. The contract the furniture company was using in 1977, that was at issue in the *Blackmond* case, demonstrates the failure of the doctrine in this regard because it was, in a sense, a schizophrenic document. On one hand, the company made an obvious effort to comply with the letter of the law, which is embodied by the truth in lending requirement that the security interest be clearly disclosed on the document. On the other hand, the company also made a determined effort to subvert the spirit of the law, which is embodied by the unconscionability requirement that the buyer be fully aware of the terms of the contract to which he or she is agreeing. In the aftermath of the *Williams* decision, an author noted that the doctrine would give indigents needed protection from unethical business practices that were not prohibited by statute. In other words, unconscionability would be a tool for enforcing practices that might not violate the letter of the law, but that violated the spirit of the law. However, the unconsionability doctrine does not seem to have deterred the Walker–Thomas Furniture Company from violating the spirit of statutory disclosure requirements when drafting its form contract. * * *

* * *

In the ten years prior to the *Williams* case, perhaps as many as *one thousand* people found themselves facing writs of replevin from the Walker–Thomas Furniture Company. After the *Williams* decision, the furniture company continued to pursue customers in default with equal or greater vigor—the only change being that the furniture company stopped using writs of replevin, and instead sued customers for the balance of the contract instead. While the doctrine of unconscionability may have helped protect customers from the specific form of add-on contracts that the company used, it did not appear to substantially advance justice and fair play for the customers of the company.

Moving on to the arguments of the doctrine's detractors: (a) that most of the heavy-lifting in consumer protection would be done by specific consumer protection legislation and not a general common law doctrine; and (b) that unconscionability would either hurt the poor by contracting credit or have no effect because it was a middle-class solution to a lower-class problem. These appear to have been accurate arguments.

Of the four cases with recorded decisions that were litigated by the furniture company since *Williams*, three have been decided based on their compliance with Truth in Lending Act requirements, and only one was decided as a question of unconscionability. This might not be comprehensive of all the litigation that the company was involved in, but the issues that made it to appeal are likely to be substantially similar to the issues raised by attorneys representing buyers at trial. More importantly, the cases that are appealed represent business practices that the furniture company was forced to change—they were the pressure points where the judicial system influenced how the company did business. Of the three cases decided on substantive issues, the two Truth in Lending Act claims caused the furniture company to change its contract to be more clear in its terms, a direct benefit to consumers. The unconscionability case, *Patterson*, led the court only to conclude that price could be considered a "term" of the contract that, when examined in its commercial context and considering the existence of meaningful choice, could be the basis for a claim of unconscionability. Also, as discussed above, it is clear from the truth in lending cases, *Blackmond* and *Lewis*, that it was the consumer protection legislation that loomed in the minds of those who drafted the furniture company's contracts, not the doctrine of unconscionability. The company made every effort to comply with the technical requirements of consumer protection legislation but clearly made little effort to make its contracts fundamentally more fair.

[handwritten margin note: importance of legislation b/c covers everyone, as opposed to individual judicial remedies]

While the *Williams* decision may not have had a profound or lasting effect on the furniture company, its apparent significance and the accompanying amount of attention paid to the company did have its effects. One account of the business practices of the furniture company indicates that the decision made the furniture company wary of running afoul of the courts at least until it became clear that consumer protection legislation would be of more immediate concern. However, to the detriment of its customers, the furniture company "certainly tightened up" the amount of credit that it made available to customers after the *Williams* decision, further reducing the credit available to Washington's poor. Although this is one of the most difficult effects of the decision to evaluate, the critics of the decision seemed to have been accurate in their prediction that unconscionability would contract the credit extended, at least by Walker–Thomas.

Second, the unconscionability naysayers may have been correct in declaring that, whatever its virtues, the doctrine of unconscionability was a middle-class solution to a lower-class problem. Substantial harm to the indigent in Washington, D.C. was illustrated by the fact that the Walker–Thomas Furniture Company had filed as many as one thousand writs of replevin in the decade before *Williams* and successfully executed almost all of them, most by default. Once unconscionability failed to act as a mandate for disclosure, and once it failed to cause more equitable form contracts, the company continued its aggressive pursuit of customers in default.

In 1969, Judge J. Skelly Wright, author of the *Williams* decision, wrote an article for the *New York Times Magazine* entitled *The Courts Have Failed the Poor*. He explains fully what the critics of unrescionability hinted at, that most of the people that purchased goods subject to unfair and unreasonable contracts do not avail themselves of the benefits of the court system. There were several reasons for this, including intentionally poor notice and service of process, lack of legal representation, and an inherent fear of the legal system. The year after *Williams*, a study by the Federal Trade Commission examined the small claims court where the furniture company and other similar retailers filed their actions. It discovered that eleven "ghetto" retailers reported 2690 court judgments, one for every $2200 in sales. The report also found that retailers that catered to the poor depended on the recovery actions as a normal order of business. The study even found that often the sales were pursuant to installment contracts with the "expectation and hope" that the goods would be repossessed and resold. In Harlem, for example, ninety-seven percent of merchant-initiated recovery suits never went to trial.

The merchants were not unwitting beneficiaries of this apparent hesitancy to seek judicial relief. In one action for recovery by Walker–Thomas, the defendant testified that the company's representative "advised her that it would do her no good to go to court." Then, after the company seized the furniture, but before her time for filing a defense had expired, a representative of the company told her that "the matter could be resolved by direct communications between the parties, and that he would 'send someone around to straighten out the account.'"

Against this background, it is no surprise that unconscionability did not appear to have much of an effect on the Walker–Thomas Furniture Company. In order for it to set meaningful precedent and influence the way that merchants drafted contracts and disclosed the terms of those contracts, it would have to have been repeatedly enforced against the company by the courts. Since the people who bought goods from the company rarely litigated claims of unconscionability, it never had that chance. For the same reason, the doctrine of unconscionability also did not have the effects that its critics warned it might. It did not appear to result in an increase in litigation even though the furniture company appeared to be "pushing the envelope" of legal contracts, repeatedly making slight changes to their contracts so as to stay one step ahead of the courts. Finally, if buyers were not willing and able to avail themselves of the unconscionability defense in court, it is unreasonable that it was really an incentive for them to breach their contracts with the furniture company.

* * *

Notes and Questions

1. Do you think a reasonable inference could be drawn that Ora Lee Williams knew what would happen if she failed to make a payment?

2. Do you think the decision made a difference in the lives of future customers of Williams–Walker Thomas Furniture Co.? If not, who bears the blame?

3. The opinion does not mention Ora Lee Williams' race and many commentators state that she is African–American without a reference. Professor Blake Morant, however, documents that she is African–American. *See* Blake D. Morant, *The Relevance of Race and Disparity in Discussions of Contract Law*, 31 New Eng. L. Rev. 889, 926 fn. 208 (1997) (While it is unclear as to how other scholars have discovered this fact, I received verification through more familiar, yet personal means. Professor Rhoda Berkowitz, a colleague, worked in the Legal Services Office of Washington, D.C., during the middle to late 1960s. She was exceedingly familiar with the case, including the characteristics of both litigants. She confirmed the fact that Ms. Williams was African American, and that Walker–Thomas Furniture Company comprised a large and, at that time, successful furniture merchant in the Washington area.) Professor Morant discusses the absence of race from the Court's opinion and suggests that Ms. Williams' racial identity and her socioeconomic status caused the furniture company to draft the onerous agreement. The furniture company and their employees may have held negative stereotypes and prejudices about African–Americans that caused it to draft the agreement. This possibility should have been considered by the court. *Id.* at 929–939.

4. Professor Morant has argued that courts which rely on contractual formalism ignore the reality of beliefs, prejudices, and stereotypes held by those entering into contracts. *See* Blake D. Morant, *The Relevance of Race and Disparity in Discussions of Contract Law*, 31 New Eng. L. Rev. 889 (1997); Blake D. Morant, *Law, Literature, and Contract: An Essay in Realism*, 4 Mich. J. of Race & L. 1 (1998) (argues that those who enter into contracts have inherent beliefs about others which influence their behavior); Blake D. Morant, *The Teaching of Martin Luther King, Jr. and Contract Theory: An Intriguing Comparison*, 50 Ala. L. Rev. 63 (1998) (emphasizes the importance of considering context, such as racial considerations, when courts analyze contractual disputes). *See also* Julian S. Lim, *Tongue-Tied in the Market: The Relevance of Contract Law to Racial–Language Minorities*, 91 Cal. L. Rev. 579 (2003) (author criticizes the court for ignoring that race may have been a factor in the contractual behavior of the parties. By ignoring race, the court reinforces the disconnect between contract law and race and implies that race is irrelevant to discussions of fairness.)

5. What if Ora Lee Williams was White and received a different type of governmental assistance? Would your views of Ms. Williams change? Would the court's analysis change? Consider the following hypothetical.

MURIEL MORISEY SPENCE
Teaching Williams v. Walker–Thomas Furniture Co.
3 Temp. Pol. & Civ. Rts. L. Rev. 89, 89, 92, 93–98, 102–104 (1993/1994).

* * * Even as I participate in and applaud these efforts, I worry that as we enrich the law school curriculum and dialogue we may perpetuate assumptions and stereotypes about the people whose perspectives we seek to incorporate.

* * *

In addition to being useful for teaching about the doctrine of unconscionability, Williams presents an opportunity to explore with students issues of race, gender and class. My concerns about how we teach Williams center on the intersection of these two potential uses of the case. Pursuing these issues requires a close look at the facts in Williams and how they are reported and discussed by the court and in law classrooms.

Comparing two versions of the facts in Williams helps us examine the relationship between pertinent facts, assumptions and stereotypes. The actual facts are presented here, [*see* p. 142] followed by a fictionalized account.

* * *

Williams v. Walker-Thomas Furniture Co.: A Fictionalized Account © 1993 Muriel Morisey Spence

Mary Williams and her seven children lived on her social security disability payments and a modest pension she received as a widow. Her husband, Harvey, had died from injuries sustained in a car accident while Mary was pregnant with their seventh child.

Harvey and Mary had often discussed the importance of family and education. Left to raise the children on her own, Mary knew she must make their home life enjoyable, for they could not afford vacation trips or even regular outings to the movies. The Veterans' Administration hospital where her husband died provided a social worker to give Mary and her family periodic assistance coping with their many pressures. With the social worker's support Mary reasoned that a color television would allow the children to watch many interesting and educational programs on PBS. With a stereo set they could enjoy all kinds of music on second-hand tapes and compact discs. Mary also decided she should have the biggest refrigerator she could afford so that she could buy food in money-saving, bulk quantities. She bought all of the children's clothes at second-hand stores in order to be able to afford the television, the stereo and the refrigerator.

Mary managed to take care of her family for five years, paying 10% of her income each month on installment purchases for the television and refrigerator. During the fifth year, she decided she could finally afford the stereo. She purchased it at the Walker–Thomas Furniture Company, the same store where she had bought the television, the refrigerator, a bed and a sofa.

Mary didn't understand the significance of a provision in the contract she signed each time she acquired the items from Walker–Thomas. It provided that title would remain in Walker–Thomas until the total of all the monthly payments made equaled the stated value of the item. The contract also provided that if Mary missed any payments on the items she bought at the store, it could repossess any of them until she had finished paying for all of them completely.

Soon after she bought the stereo, a burglar stole the $400 in cash Mary had on hand to purchase a money order for her rent. Two days later her youngest child was admitted to the hospital for a stay that lasted six weeks. In the wake of these two events, Mary missed two monthly payments to Walker–Thomas. The store sought to retrieve all of the items Mary had purchased over the last five years.

In each of these accounts the essential facts about Williams' financial circumstances, her credit history and her family size are the same, but the fictionalized account embellishes the story to provide a fuller and deliberately sympathetic portrait of Williams. Armed with both the actual facts and the invented ones, we can explore the interplay of facts, assumptions and stereotypes.

Typically, readers of the case assume that Williams is on welfare. This assumption is understandable, for the dissent implicitly tells us that. It asks whether, as a matter of policy, we should require public oversight of "expenditures of relief funds." The dissenting judge also notes that "many relief clients may well need credit, and certain business establishments will take long chances on the sale of items, expecting their pricing policies will afford a degree of protection commensurate with the risk." So, having read the dissent, we are on fairly solid ground in believing Williams to be on welfare. Nevertheless, as the fictional story of Mary Williams illustrates, there are other reasons that people live on government stipends.

The rest of our assumptions require more scrutiny. My own experience and the comments of other Contracts professors with whom I have discussed the case is that we and our students assume that Williams is black. Why? Perhaps it is because the events take place in Washington, D.C., a city that has had an African–American majority in its population for decades.

But even with that explanation, we are in dangerous territory. Most people on welfare in the United States are not black, yet the case reinforces the stereotype that equates welfare recipients with African–Americans. A classroom anecdote supports this point: A white male student once commented that the store's position was understandable when dealing with people who "looked like her." It is significant that no physical description of Williams appears in the decision.

A particularly disturbing assumption is that, as the mother of seven children, Williams was fiscally irresponsible in buying a stereo that cost more than twice her monthly income. Another anecdote from my own teaching illustrates the force of this assumption: Several students argued in class that the store was justified in using contracts providing for the repossession of expensive items sold to people who "could not afford them." Among those making this argument was an African–American woman. This fact reminded me that the impact of stereotypes is felt both across and within racial and gender lines.

Perhaps the most troubling aspect of the assumption about Williams' ability to handle money responsibly is how readily students ignore the reported facts on her payment history. For five years Williams managed to pay approximately 10% of her monthly income in uninterrupted installments to Walker–Thomas. It was the interruption in this pattern of payment that led to the store's repossession of her belongings and then to the lawsuit. Although she paid more than two month's income for the stereo, one must consider this fact within the context of her payment history, a record which suggests significant money handling skills.

We, and the court also, seem quite ready to assume that Williams' lack of education accounts for her failure to understand the legal and practical significance of the offending clause. This assumption is troubling on at least three grounds.

First, it is arguably paternalistic. Why should the court assume that Williams is uneducated to the point that she, particularly, is unable to comprehend the clause's meaning? Another perspective might be that her long experience with such stores leaves her acutely "street wise" about how such stores work. She might even know people who have had their belongings repossessed by the same store. This alternative view credits Williams with having the resources and the capacity to operate knowingly in the commercial world.

Second, even if one views the assumption as paternalistic and troubling, it may nevertheless be that the assumption is essential to the holding. Without the notion that Williams is relatively uneducated, the court may be reluctant to conclude that the disputed clause involved the "oppression and unfair surprise" that the U.C.C. suggests is a pivotal element of unconscionability. Do courts help or hinder low-income consumers when their decisions depend upon the view that such consumers are weak, uninformed participants in the retail marketplace?

A third implication of the assumption involves the manner in which we teach unconscionability. If we regard Williams' education level as a key factor in her ability to understand the provision, we obscure the possibility that a provision may be incomprehensible (and, indeed, unconscionable) without regard to the education level of the person reading it. * * *

Concern about the impact of these assumptions led me to decide that students' first contact with the disputed contract clause should precede their exposure to the particular facts of Williams. Therefore, in a class session held before we were to discuss the case, I distributed to students the text of the contract's pertinent provision. I gave them a full two minutes to read it and then asked someone to state its legal and practical significance. After about ten minutes of awkward attempts at explanation by several students, someone finally stated with reasonable accuracy how the provision would work.

This experience with students and my strong doubt that anyone would have given Williams two minutes to read the pertinent clause, reinforced to me that the doctrinal point about unconscionability is, to some degree, separable from Williams' status as a welfare recipient and her level of educational attainment. At the same time, we should not overlook or ignore those facts about her, for they are pertinent to important themes about race, gender and class in the law. In short, we must reflect deeply upon how we teach this case. * * *

During a workshop on teaching Contracts, an African–American law professor described what may be a common reaction to the opportunity the Williams case presents. He told how his students, particularly his minority students, welcome the case as a chance to reinforce the fact that people of color and people who are not middle-class help shape the law and experience many of its effects. His positive experiences teaching the case support my sanguine reactions to its use. Williams has the relatively rare feature of a plaintiff in a civil suit who is not middle-class. Ora Williams was a single parent struggling to raise a large family in a major city. These facts make her situation appealing as an opportunity to explore with students issues of gender and class. They permit students and teacher alike to confront and examine some of their own perceptions and assumptions. The facts and the way they inform the decision invite us to consider how the law may be used as a tool to protect the unprotected.

Taking all of this into account, my conclusion is that Williams is well worth teaching. But the case raises troubling possibilities that require examination. For example, why do many African–American professors and students welcome into Contracts discussions a case that reinforces some of the most pervasive stereotypes of African–American women? I fear that in our longing to see people of color in the law school curriculum we grasp rather desperately at any opportunity to discuss them, overlooking or ignoring the potential for reinforcing stereotypes.

Perhaps these fears are misplaced. One might argue that students in many law school classrooms are in little danger of reinforcing stereotypes of African–American women, particularly if the faculty and student body include black women. Yet the power of stereotypes is that they defy and survive contrary factual evidence. The students or faculty of color whose accomplishments challenge the stereotypes may be dismissed as anomalies, proving nothing except that every rule has exceptions.

Alternatively, these concerns may reflect little more than a middle-class law professor's wish to be distinguished at all times from welfare mothers. Either of these perspectives might suggest that worrying about stereotypes is not time well spent. Yet discrimination based on race, gender, disability and sexual orientation remains a pervasive feature of American life. Discriminatory behavior is grounded in biased and prejudicial attitudes reinforced by stereotypes. The compelling reason for legal educators to teach in ways that confront and challenge stereotypes is that it is our duty to educate law students who can help eradicate discriminatory behavior. This is a difficult and time-consuming goal, but we must make the effort.

Notes and Questions

1. Do you agree with Professor Morissey? If the only way students see African–Americans in their casebooks are helpless, in need of protection, unable to understand commercial transactions, isn't that perpetuating negative stereotypes about African–Americans?

2. Do you think the decision in Williams would have been different if Professor Morissey's hypothetical were the facts of the case? NO.

3. As you read the following quote from Professor Anthony Chase, what are your thoughts? Have you ever thought about the ways in which casebooks are constructed and the unconscious messages the authors send—and you've received? Professor Chase performed an analysis of the four principle first-year contracts casebooks. "They are authored by Knapp and Crystal, Dawson, Harvey, and Henderson, Farnsworth and Young, and Murphy and Speidel." Anthony R. Chase, *Race, Culture, and Contract Law: From the Cottonfield to the Courtroom*, 28 Conn. L. Rev. 1, 60 (1995). He observes "[t]here are very few explicit instances of mention of African–Americans as characters in the cases. . . . Williams v. Walker–Thomas Furniture Co. is just such a case. . . . Appellant, Williams á welfare recipient, defaulted on her monthly payments to the Walker Furniture Co. The court held that the contract was unconscionable by reason of the one-sided bargain. While unstated, there is an unspoken presumption that Mrs. Williams is a black woman, a welfare recipient, with a large family to support. One professor even comments that Mrs. Williams is a black woman though no distinction of race is given in the opinion. Such editorial comment mirrors and reinforces negative stereotypes without providing any balancing commentary to mitigate its impact." *Id.* at 63. Professor Chase continues to document the absence in any of the casebooks of either law review articles included in the casebooks that were written by authors of color or judicial opinions written by jurists of color. *Id.*

4. As discussed earlier, Professor Williams argues that the doctrine of unconscionability can be a useful tool to combat race discrimination. Using the *Williams* decision as a case study, do you agree?

Can unconscicrability be as a tool to fight racial discrimination?

5. Professor Williams also argues that the duty of good faith can be effective in eliminating race discrimination. We turn to that doctrine next.

SECTION 3. THE DUTY OF GOOD FAITH

NEIL G. WILLIAMS

Offer, Acceptance, and Improper Considerations: A Common–Law Model For
the Prohibition of Racial Discrimination in the Contracting Process
62 Geo. Wash. L. Rev. 183, 206–207, 218–220 (1994).

* * *

Section 205 of the Second Restatement explicitly subjects the behavior of parties to community standards once they have entered into a contract:

Every contract imposes upon each party a duty of good faith and fair dealing in its performance and its enforcement.

The comments to section 205 state that the gravamen of the duty of good faith and fair dealing is "faithfulness to an agreed common purpose and consistency with the justified expectations of the other party." The drafters of section 205 stopped short of providing an all-encompassing definition of "good faith" in either section 205 or its comments, however. They avoided doing so out of a belief that such an effort would circumscribe the doctrine needlessly; they were convinced that the general requirement of good faith is best conceptualized as "excluding a variety of types of conduct characterized as involving 'bad faith' because they violate community standards of decency, fairness or reasonableness." Although the comments to section 205 contain several illustrations of conduct constituting bad faith, it is conceded that "a complete catalogue of types of bad faith is impossible."

The manner in which section 205 conceptualizes good faith derives largely from a seminal article written by Professor Robert Summers in 1968. Professor Summers demonstrated in painstaking detail that, although then not widely realized, the recognition of a general duty of good faith and fair dealing was supported extensively by the case law and statutes of numerous American jurisdictions. Shortly after the finalization of the Second Restatement in 1981, Professor Summers wrote a follow-up article on this topic that praised section 205's adoption of his formulation of the good-faith performance obligation. A central tenet of both articles is that the duty of good faith and fair dealing represents an attempt to impose upon parties a requirement of "contractual morality," a characterization that is implicit in the Second Restatement's tying the scope of the duty to community norms of decency, fairness, and reasonableness. For present purposes, the good-faith performance doctrine is important because it represents another instance in which modern contract law explicitly subjects the conduct of parties to community standards. I argue below that racial discrimination should be considered bad-faith behavior proscribed by the duty of good faith and fair dealing.

* * *

An extensive review of the case law revealed no decision finding unequivocally that discrimination on the basis of race in the performance, enforcement, or termination of a contract violates the duty of good faith and fair dealing. Just as important, though, no decision that openly staked a contrary position was found. The absence of case law directly on point is not surprising, because litigants in contractual racial discrimination cases tend to focus on theories of well-established recovery (such as the antidiscrimination statutes). Two 1987 federal cases from Maine, however, provide strong inferential support for the proposition that race discrimination is inconsistent with requirements of good faith and fair dealing.

In *Reid v. Key Bank*, Mr. Reid, an African American who operated a painting business, was extended a $25,000 commercial line of credit by a bank that had granted him several prior loans. Less than three months after the extension of credit, without discussing the matter with Mr.

*[handwritten margin note: * it seems that much racial discrimination would happen prior to contracting, thus preventing contracting altogether, in addition a standard applied to the K, post-K.]*

Reid, the bank refused to make any further advances to him under the line and began seizing assets that collateralized Mr. Reid's obligations, including his personal automobile and a sizeable check for work he had done on a large housing project. Eventually, after his business collapsed and he lost his home, Mr. Reid and his wife filed for bankruptcy and brought a suit against the bank alleging, inter alia, that the bank's actions were racially motivated (in violation of federal law) and violated its duty of good faith and fair dealing. At trial, a jury entered a verdict for the bank on the claim of racial discrimination but found for the Reids on the claim that the bank had not acted in good faith.

On appeal, the bank argued that, because the transaction was governed by the Uniform Commercial Code instead of the common law, the good-faith standard applicable to the bank's termination of the line of credit was a rather minimal one: honesty in fact, a subjective formulation. Accordingly, the bank reasoned, the district judge erred in instructing the jury by tying good faith to objective commercial norms of reasonableness and fairness. Although it seriously questioned whether a Maine court would limit a party's contractual obligation to act in good faith in this context to mere honesty in fact, the court felt no need to resolve the issue because it felt that, when read in their entirety, the instructions given by the district court clearly directed the jury to apply the narrow, subjective formulation of good faith argued for by the bank.

The bank further argued, however, that there was no basis for the jury to conclude that it had failed to act honestly in fact given the jury's finding that the bank had not discriminated against the Reids on the basis of their race. In making this argument, the bank effectively conceded that, if the jury had found the termination of Mr. Reid's line of credit to have been racially motivated, there would have been ample grounds for it to have concluded that the termination violated even a narrow, subjective requirement of good faith. Moreover, the manner in which the court addressed this argument demonstrates its implicit acceptance of such a proposition. Upon examining the evidence, the court concluded that there was an ample factual basis for the jury to find "that in restricting Mr. Reid's credit when and as it did the bank was motivated by ulterior considerations, not a good faith concern for its financial security." Indeed, the jury could have made such a finding, the court continued, "even if it did not believe that racial prejudice was the effective factor that motivated the bank's bad faith." Thus, the court appeared willing to accept a conclusion, by the jury, that the bank had acted in bad faith, if the jury believed that the bank's actions were motivated by ulterior considerations grounded in racial prejudice. In essence, the court acknowledged that the universe of ulterior considerations that constitutes bad faith includes, but is not limited to, racial prejudice. If the bank had been racially motivated in deciding to terminate Mr. Reid's credit, it necessarily would not have acted out of an honest, good-faith concern about his financial situation.

In the light of its implicit acknowledgment that racial discrimination is inimical to the duty of good faith and fair dealing even when narrowly defined in terms of honesty in fact, the Reid court, if called upon to apply an objective formulation, could logically find that racial discrimination in the performance, enforcement, or termination of a contract violates community norms of decency, fairness, and reasonableness.

In *Ricci v. Key Bancshares*, a case decided less than two months after Reid, a federal district court sustained a jury verdict in favor of Joseph Ricci, an Italian American who, like Mr. Reid, was financially damaged when the defendant banks terminated a line of credit extended to his companies. One of the counts sustained by the court claimed that the bank had discriminated against Mr. Ricci and his companies, because of Mr. Ricci's national origin, in violation of a provision of the Equal Credit Opportunity Act; and another alleged that the banks had conducted themselves in a manner that violated the duty of good faith and fair dealing. In finding for Mr. Ricci on both of these counts, the jury implicitly found the same conduct to constitute both unlawful discrimination and bad faith, thereby apparently agreeing with the basic point of this Article: One who discriminates against another in performing or enforcing a contract does not deal with that party fairly or in good faith. The time has come for the common law of contracts to recognize this truth explicitly.

* * *

REID v. KEY BANK OF SOUTHERN MAINE, INC.

821 F.2d 9 (1st Cir. 1987).

BOWNES, CIRCUIT JUDGE.

Plaintiffs Paul and Mary J. Reid brought a seventeen-count action in United States District Court for the District of Maine against Key Bank of Southern Maine, Inc., defendant. Plaintiffs alleged various federal and state claims resulting from the actions of Depositors Trust Co. of Southern Maine (Depositors), Key Bank's predecessor in interest. The suit grew out of the circumstances surrounding the termination by Depositors of plaintiffs' credit arrangement with it. A jury trial resulted in a verdict for plaintiffs on one of the counts and an award of damages. Both parties have appealed.

I. SUMMARY OF THE FACTS

In mid–1975, Paul Reid approached Depositors to obtain financing for the establishment of a painting business. From 1976 through 1979, Depositors granted Reid a series of loans which Reid used for the operation of his business, Pro Paint and Decorating. During this period, Peter H. Traill was the loan officer responsible for Reid's accounts, Marco F. DeSalle was the president of the bank, and Henry Lawson was, for a time, an assistant vice-president.

On March 2, 1979, Reid and Depositors entered into a $25,000 commercial credit agreement. The agreement was variously explained at trial as a "line of credit" and an "incomplete loan." However defined, it was the largest amount of credit Depositors had yet extended to Reid. Reid sought the credit primarily to finance work he was performing at the Bucksport Housing Project for Nickerson & O'Day, Inc., a general contractor.

In mid-May, 1979, Traill telephoned Reid and informed him that Depositors would not grant him any further advances under the March agreement. Reid had thought at the time that this halt of further advances might only be temporary. Defendant claimed that Traill sent Reid a follow-up letter on May 18, 1979, stating that Depositors would no longer honor overdrafts on Reid's accounts and suggesting that Reid restructure his debts with another lender. Reid denied receiving the letter and alleged that it was never, in fact, sent to him.

On May 29, 1979, Nickerson & O'Day sent a check to Depositors as payment for Reid's work at the Bucksport Housing Project. The check was for $6,507.90. It was made out to Depositors and to Pro Paint pursuant to an agreement between Depositors and Reid whereby Reid assigned his accounts receivable to Depositors as security for the March loan. Depositors credited $2,500 to the account of Pro Paint and applied the remaining $4,007.90 to offset part of the outstanding balance on Reid's March loan. Reid claimed that Depositors undertook this action without his authorization.

Reid claimed that another check was also inappropriately handled by Depositors. He testified that on June 8, 1979, he gave Traill a check for an amount somewhere between eleven and fifteen thousand dollars. Reid contended that this check represented the proceeds for work he performed at Brunswick Naval Air Station. He alleged that Depositors converted the check and used it to offset part of the balance on the March loan. Defendant strongly contested this claim and implied at trial that the check in question existed only in Reid's imagination.

On September 20, 1979, Reid received a past-due notice on the March loan. The notice requested payment of $694.84 in interest and stated that the payment had been due on September 5, 1979. Reid testified that this was the first notice he had received concerning the March loan.

On November 5, 1979, Depositors repossessed Reid's personal automobile and one of his vans. Reid discovered one of the vehicles in a lot and attempted to drive it away. He testified that he did not know it had been repossessed and thought it had been stolen. On a complaint by Lawson, Reid was arrested in connection with this incident and was placed for a time in jail.

Reid's business collapsed and he lost his four vehicles and his home. On November 7, 1979, Reid filed a Chapter 13 bankruptcy proceeding which was converted to a Chapter 11 proceeding in January, 1980. Mrs. Reid suffered emotional problems and drug dependency. The couple separated for a period of a year and a half. The Reids, who are black, claimed that Depositors acted in bad faith to limit and then terminate their credit. They also claimed that Depositors' actions were motivated by racial prejudice. Defendant claimed that Depositors acted in good faith to secure its financial interests when it learned of Reid's personal difficulties and mismanagement of his business; it denied that its actions were racially motivated.

At trial, the district court directed a verdict for defendant on plaintiffs' claims for violations of the Fair Credit Reporting Act and for breach of fiduciary duties. Plaintiffs withdrew their claims for interference with contractual relations and wrongful dishonoring of checks. The jury found for defendant on plaintiffs' claims for violation of the express terms of the credit agreement, racial discrimination, two counts for infliction of emotional distress, and failure to comply with Article 9 of the Uniform Commercial Code. The jury found for plaintiffs on their pendent state claim for breach of the March loan agreement based on violation of an implied covenant of good faith and fair dealing. It awarded plaintiffs $100,000 in compensatory and $500,000 in exemplary damages; the exemplary damages award was struck by the court. Both parties have appealed. In Part II, we address defendant's arguments on appeal; in Parts III–VI we address those of plaintiffs.

II. Implied Covenant of Good Faith and Fair Dealing

* * *[The court begins by analyzing Maine case law to find that the implied covenant of good faith and fair dealing is a cause of action in Maine.] * * *

B. The "Demand" Provision

Defendant argues that the "demand" provision of the note establishing the credit agreement precludes a good faith requirement in this case, even if such a requirement is recognized in general. Defendant contends that this exception to the general good faith requirement is mandated by section 1–208 of the U.C.C., as interpreted by the U.C.C. Comment to the section. Section 1–208 states:

> § 1–208. Option to accelerate at will
>
> A term providing that one party or his successor in interest may accelerate payment or performance or require collateral or additional collateral "at will" or "when he deems himself insecure" or in words of similar import shall be construed to mean that he shall have power to do so only if he in good faith believes that the prospect of payment or performance is impaired. . . .

The U.C.C. Comment observes:

> Obviously this section has no application to demand instruments or obligations whose very nature permits call at any time with or without reason.

We turn, therefore, to the documents establishing the loan to see whether they clearly gave Depositors the right to demand payment or terminate the relationship on demand and without cause. The "Secured Interest Note," dated March 2, 1979, states in its opening paragraph:

On Demand, after date, for value received, [Paul Reid d/b/a Pro Paint & Decorating] . . . promise[s] to pay to the order of [Depositors] . . . Twenty-five Thousand and no/100 DOLLARS with interest at 13.75 per cent per annum payable quarterly.

This provision appears, at first glance, to be an unambiguous demand clause. It cannot, however, possibly be read literally in the context of the kind of agreement entered into here. Although the note seems to grant Depositors the right to immediate repayment of $25,000 "on demand," Reid had not yet received that sum of money from the bank. Indeed, he was never to receive the full amount. The "demand" provision thus cannot represent the beginning and end of the inquiry into the time term of the contract.

DeSalle, president of Depositors, testified to similar effect at trial, based on his knowledge of banking practices. He said that the "demand" provision in such an agreement is to be interpreted in light of the other conditions in the note and that a bank could not simply terminate the agreement capriciously. He also thought that the absence of a time term in such a note indicated the likelihood that the schedule for repayment of the principal was governed by a verbal agreement between the loan officer and the debtor. In view both of our reading of the document and of DeSalle's testimony about banking practices, we find that the "demand" provision in the note should not be understood as a completely integrated agreement on the time term of the contract. *See Astor v. Boulos Co.,* 451 A.2d 903, 905 (Me.1982); Restatement (Second) of Contracts § 209 (1979).

Furthermore, the documents establishing the loan place conditions on the acceleration of payment or termination of the agreement. The "Secured Interest Note" provides for various conditions which would "render" the obligation "payable on demand." The "Security Agreement," also signed March 2, 1979, lists a series of events whose occurrence would signify that Reid would be in "default." The presence of such conditions in both documents indicates that the agreement could not simply be terminated at the whim of the parties; rather, the right of termination or acceleration was subjected to various limitations. The detailed enumeration of events that would "*render*" the note "payable on demand," or which would put Reid in "default," shows the qualified and relative nature of any "demand" provision. It would be illogical to construe an agreement, providing for repayment or default in the event of certain contingencies, as permitting the creditor, in the absence of the occurrence of those contingencies, to terminate the agreement without any cause whatsoever. Under such a construction, the enumerated conditions would be rendered meaningless. We find, therefore, that the documents establishing the loan defeat neither the legal obligation nor the justifiable expectation of the parties that the contract be performed in good faith.

* * *[The court then finds that the lower court judge properly instructed the jury to decide the issue of good faith under a subjective standard.] * * *

D. Sufficiency of Evidence

Finally, defendant contends that there was insufficient evidence to support a finding of an absence of good faith, particularly in view of the jury's failure to find that racial discrimination had been an "effective factor" in the termination of Reid's credit at Depositors. We disagree. We affirm the district court's holding that evidence concerning the manner in which Depositors conducted their dealings with Reid was sufficient to support a jury verdict of bad faith and was not based on mere speculation. The standard for defendant's motion for a judgment notwithstanding the verdict was whether the evidence, viewed in the light most favorable to plaintiffs, would lead to the conclusion that no reasonable jury could have found for plaintiffs on the good faith issue. This heavy burden was not met by defendant.

We think the jury could have reasonably inferred that Depositors' actions were not taken in good faith. The March, 1979, credit agreement represented the largest amount of credit extended to Reid by the bank, and could be seen as the culmination of an ongoing and mutually beneficial relationship. The jury could have found that by mid-May, when Reid's line of credit was abruptly shut off, he was not in default and his overall position had not changed that significantly, especially as the bank did not first register complaints to him or ask him to alter his conduct in some manner. The bank's president testified that it was customary before cutting off a customer's line of credit to send notices in advance and call the customer to the bank for discussion. This was not done as to Reid, nor was any convincing reason advanced by the bank for not doing so. (The bank, indeed, did not even call as a witness the officer who had dealt directly with Reid and could have best explained why the bank acted as it did.) The jury could have found that in restricting Reid's credit when and as it did the bank was motivated by ulterior considerations, not a good faith concern for its financial security. The jury could have found that the bank decided in bad faith and without notice to terminate the credit relationship as a whole. The jury might have viewed the bank's actions to restrict and terminate Reid's credit to be in bad faith in part because they were taken only a short time after the bank had shown confidence in Reid and had given him grounds to rely on the continuation of the relationship. The jury might have inferred bad faith from these actions of the bank, even if it did not believe that racial prejudice was the effective factor that motivated the bank's bad faith. In sum, the jury could have reasonably found that the bank acted in bad faith in precipitously and without warning halting further advances on which it knew Reid's business depended, in failing to make a sufficient effort to negotiate alternative solutions to any problems it perceived in its relationship with Reid, and in failing to give notice that it intended to terminate the relationship entirely. The evidence concerning these and other aspects of Depositors' actions provided a sufficient basis for a jury finding that the bank's actions were not taken in good faith.

* * * [The balance of the decision upholds the district judge in striking the exemplary damage award because they cannot be awarded

on a contract claim in Maine; in directing a verdict for defendant on plaintiffs' claim for breach of fiduciary duties; and finding harmless error on jury instructions.]* * *

Notes and Questions

1.   Did the jury verdict support Professor Lawrence's thesis that people are uncomfortable acknowledging race-based discrimination? Why do you think Mr. Reid lost the racial discrimination part of his lawsuit?   *nexus?*

2.   What other explanation could there be for the bank not treating Mr. Reid like other customers? Is it incompetence or racism? Does it matter as far as Mr. Reid is concerned?

3.   How far can this doctrine be stretched? Can this doctrine be stretched to assist Whites?

RICCI v. KEY BANCSHARES OF MAINE, INC.

662 F.Supp. 1132 (D.Me.1987).

MEMORANDUM OPINION AND ORDER

WATSON, JUDGE, Sitting by Designation.

* * *

This case proceeded to trial on nine separate counts, arising from the decision of the defendant banks to terminate their lending relationship with the plaintiffs. The plaintiffs were Joseph J. Ricci, Gerald E. Davidson and their various wholly-owned corporations * * *. The defendants were Key Bank of Southern Maine, Inc. f/k/a Depositors Trust Company of Southern Maine, Inc. ("Depositors–Southern"); Key Bank of Central Maine, Inc. f/k/a Depositors Trust Company of Augusta, Inc.; and Key Bancshares of Maine, Inc. ("Key Bancshares") f/k/a Depositors Corporation, the holding company of the other two defendant banks. Five counts alleged violations of federal statutory provisions, and four counts alleged pendent claims under the common law of the State of Maine.

* * *

After careful consideration, the Court concludes the plaintiff failed to produce sufficient evidence from which a jury could reasonably find it highly probable that the defendant acted with malice. Viewed in the light most favorable to the plaintiff, the evidence showed that defendant Depositors Corporation responded recklessly, callously and discriminatorily upon hearing allegations from state and federal law enforcement officials connecting plaintiff Ricci to organized crime. That response included the immediate and permanent cancellation of further credit to plaintiff; the concealment from plaintiff of the specific actual reasons for the cancellation; the refusal to even discuss the allegations with the plaintiff or with the officers of Depositors–Southern most familiar with plaintiff's businesses; and the subsequent failure to take adequate remedial steps to cure the devastating injuries its actions caused to plaintiff's business operations and personal reputation. The evidence supported a finding that, by those actions, the defendant recklessly inflicted severe emotional distress upon the plaintiff, or was certain or substantially certain that such distress would result from its conduct. However, there was no showing—and certainly no showing to a "high probability"—that the defendant acted with the sort of malice towards the plaintiff which the law requires to support a claim for exemplary damages, i.e., deliberate conduct motivated by ill-will or specifically intended to injure the plaintiff. Viewed in the light most favorable to the plaintiff, the evidence reasonably shows only that the defendant was motivated by self-centered, business interests (such as its ambitions to merge with other banks) and placed those interests above any concern for the impact its actions had or might have upon the plaintiff. Such motives do not, in the Court's view, rise to the level of "malice" required under *Tuttle* to support a claim for exemplary damages.

not "with malice;" no exemplary damages

Accordingly, the Court will grant the defendant's motion for directed verdict on the issue of exemplary damages and will set aside the jury's award of 12.5 million dollars.

* * *

The Court emphasizes, however, that it finds sufficient evidence was presented to support the jury's finding of liability for compensatory damages against defendant Key Bancshares under Count 10. The plaintiff's burden with respect to that finding, in contrast with the finding of liability for punitive damages, is merely proof by a "preponderance of the evidence." Most importantly, the jury's verdict that the defendant *intentionally* inflicted severe emotional distress did not necessarily entail a determination that the defendant acted with malice. Under Maine law, the jury could find the requisite intent upon a showing that the defendant acted "intentionally or recklessly," or that the defendant was "certain or substantially certain" that severe emotional distress would result. *Vicnire v. Ford Motor Credit Co.,* 401 A.2d 148, 154 (Me.1979). "Intentional" infliction, as so defined, is not necessarily equivalent to malice (either actual or implied), because intent can be found based upon a showing of reckless or callous indifference. However, as *Tuttle* makes clear, conduct which is reckless or grossly negligent is not sufficient to justify an award of exemplary damages. 494 A.2d at 1361.

evidence sufficient to prove by a preponderance liability for compensatory damages.

The Court next turns to plaintiffs' claims for statutory punitive damages under Counts 1 and 2. As previously discussed, under the Equal Credit Opportunity Act a plaintiff may seek, in addition to actual damages, an award of punitive damages limited to $10,000. The statute provides that, among other factors, the Court must consider the "extent to which the creditor's failure of compliance was intentional" when determining the amount of such damages. 15 U.S.C. § 1691e(b). Numerous courts have reasoned that, by including this language, Congress intended to limit awards of punitive damages to cases where the defendant's violation was "wanton, malicious, or opressive [sic]" or was at least committed with "reckless disregard of the requirements of law." *See Fischl v. General Motors Acceptance Corp., supra; Anderson v. United Finance Corp., supra; Sayers v. General Motors Acceptance Corp., supra; Schuman v. Standard Oil Corp., supra.* Accordingly, the Court asked the jury, under Counts 1 and 2, to determine whether the plaintiffs demonstrated by a preponderance of the evidence that any defendant whose conduct it found to violate the requirements of the Equal Credit Opportunity Act, acted maliciously, wantonly, oppressively or with reckless disregard for the law in committing the violation. Under Count 1, the jury answered affirmatively as to defendant Key Bancshares, in favor of plaintiffs Ricci, Davidson and Golden Ark Enterprises. Under Count 2, the jury answered affirmatively as to defendant Key Bank of Southern Maine, in favor of plaintiffs Ricci, Davidson and Golden Ark Enterprises. The evidence presented at trial reasonably supports those findings. They are therefore binding upon this Court in determining the amount of punitive damages to be imposed under Counts 1 and 2.

[margin annotation: adequate findings to uphold punitive damage award]

Having considered all of the factors listed in 15 U.S.C. § 1691e(b) and other relevant factors, the Court concludes that defendant Key Bancshares should be held liable under Count 1 for an amount of punitive damages totalling $10,000, to be divided equally between plaintiffs Joseph Ricci and Gerald E. Davidson; and that defendant Key Bank of Southern Maine should be held liable under Count 2 for an amount of punitive damages totalling $10,000, also to be divided equally between plaintiffs Ricci and Davidson.[12] Particularly in view of the serious consequences of the violations that the respective defendants were found to have committed under Counts 1 and 2, which is reflected in the jury's substantial overall awards of actual damages, the Court finds it appropriate to impose a full $10,000 award of punitive damages under each count. Liability of either defendant for a total amount greater than that, however, is not warranted. Even though the jury found the respective defendants liable to all three plaintiffs—Ricci, Davidson and Golden Ark Enterprises—the evidence only supports a finding of one violation by each defendant which affected all three plaintiffs. Finally, the Court finds that the considerations supporting an award of punitive damages under Count 2 warrant that the award should be divided equally between plaintiffs Ricci and Davidson even though the jury only found actual damages in favor of the latter. It is clear from the structure and purpose of the Act that proof of actual damages is not a prerequisite to entitlement to punitive damages. *Anderson United Finance Corp., supra; Cherry v. Amoco Oil Co.,* 490 F.Supp. 1026, 1029 (N.D.Ga.1980); *Smith v. Lakeside Foods Inc.,* 449 F.Supp. 171, 172 (N.D.Ill.1978).

* * *

OPINION AND ORDER ON POST-JUDGMENT MOTIONS

* * * Specifically, as to the verdict on Count I there was a reasonable basis in law and sufficient evidence for the jury to conclude first,

---

12. The Court has not specified that the respective award should be split *three* ways because a two-way split between Ricci and Davidson is easier and achieves the same result, since Ricci and Davidson are each half-owners of Golden Ark Enterprises.

that Key Bancshares was involved in the extension of credit to plaintiffs to the point of being a "creditor" within the meaning of 15 U.S.C. § 1691e, and second, that plaintiff Ricci's national origin was a factor causing Key Bancshares to treat Ricci and his associates less favorably than it treated or would have treated customers who were not of that national origin. Evidence from which the jury could reasonably have found or inferred discrimination included plaintiff Ricci's testimony that Leo Amato, a bank officer who, like Ricci, is an American of Italian descent, suggested that the bank was discriminating against Ricci because of his national origin and evidence that Amato, the bank officer most familiar with Ricci's account, was not allowed to participate nor was he consulted on the decisions made with respect to the events that led to this lawsuit.

the other way it was gone may have if was Italian-American

* * *

* * * The Court instructed the jury, that an implied covenant of good faith and fair dealing applied to this contract under Maine law. The Court notes that the opinion of the First Circuit Court of Appeals in *Reid v. Key Bank of Southern Maine, Inc.*, 821 F.2d 9 (1st Cir.1987) issued subsequent to the Court's instruction of the jury in this case holds that a covenant of good faith and fair dealing is implied in every contract under Maine law.

* * *

Notes and Questions

1. Why do you think the Bank treated Mr. Ricci the way it did?

2. Notice that Mr. Ricci was successful in the discriminatory aspect of his lawsuit. Under the Equal Credit Opportunity Act and Mr. Reid was not. Why? What evidence was Mr. Ricci able to present that Mr. Reid was unable to present? *Specific allegations/conversations; Leo @ the bank.*

3. Do you think Mr. Ricci's race played a role in his victory? *YES*

NEIL G. WILLIAMS

Offer, Acceptance, and Improper Considerations: A Common–Law Model For
the Prohibition of Racial Discrimination in the Contracting Process
62 Geo. Wash. L. Rev. 183, 228–229 (1993).

* * *

As shown in the discussion of the *Reid* and *Ricci* cases, however, a contract-based antidiscrimination norm can be more flexible than an intentional-discrimination approach. In *Reid*, the plaintiffs were able to establish that the defendant bank violated its duty of good faith and fair dealing even though they could not prove that it acted with a conscious racist motive. It often will be easier to convince a jury that a plaintiff was treated indecently, unfairly, or unreasonably (regardless of the motivation for doing so) than to prove the motivation giving rise to the mistreatment. Accordingly, an approach grounded in the duty of good faith and fair dealing has the potential to reach a broader range of discriminatory acts than can be reached by the antidiscrimination statutes.

* * *

In order to facilitate the acceptance of the common-law reforms advocated in this Article, I propose that the following new section be included in the Third Restatement of Contracts, whenever it is adopted:

> No one may discriminate on the basis of race while entering into, performing, enforcing, or terminating a contract.

It is important to keep in mind that a common-law rule need not necessarily be adopted broadly before qualifying for inclusion in a Restatement of Contracts. The Second Restatement, for instance, has been described as being both "descriptive" and "prescriptive"; that is, in addition to simply presenting the rules of contract law actually adopted in a majority of American jurisdictions, the Restatements have sought in some instances to present an ideal vision of American contract law, and to point the direction in which the common law ought to head. As shown in this Article, that direction is towards the recognition of a norm prohibiting racial discrimination at all stages of the contracting process.

Notes and Questions

1.   What do you think of Professor Williams' suggestion that the good faith standard specifically include a prohibition against race-based discrimination?

2.   Is Professor Williams correct when he states that "a contract-based antidiscrimination norm can be more flexible than an intentional-discrimination approach?" Is that good or bad?

3.   Professor Anne–Marie Harris describes the risks faced by African–American consumers as "shopping while black." *See* Anne–Marie G. Harris, *Shopping While Black: Applying 42 U.S.C. § 1981 to Cases of Consumer Racial Profiling*, 23 B.C. Third World L. J. 1 (2003). She is less optimistic than Professor Williams about the success of convincing courts to impute an anti-discrimination principle into the duty of good faith and fair dealing. ("[I]t is unclear that the law will evolve to incorporate a proscription against racial discrimination into the duty of good faith and fair dealing." *Id*. at 18–19.)

Chapter 5

CRITICAL RACE THEORY AND CRIMINAL PROCEDURE

This chapter and the next chapter deal with issues of race and criminal procedure, law, and sentencing. The challenge was to decide how to limit the materials to only two chapters. Unlike many of the areas that we have studied so far, making the connection between race and crime is a familiar one. In 1993 Rev. Jesse Jackson stated "[t]here is nothing more painful to me at this stage in my life than to walk down the street and hear footsteps and start thinking about robbery, then look around and see somebody white and feel relieved." Lynne Duke, *Confronting Violence; African American Conferees Look Inward*, Jan. 8, 1994, THE WASHINGTON POST, A01. "Driving while black" and "racial profiling" are common phrases we hear on the news or read in the newspaper. Who can forget how the O.J. Simpson trial crystallized in the minds of many the different views of Whites and people of color towards the judicial system?

This chapter begins with an overview of the decision to prosecute. It then discusses the phenomenon of "driving while black" and the Supreme Court's decision in *Whren v. U.S.* in which the Supreme Court finds traffic violations constitute probable cause for a stop of the car. The Chapter continues with an article excerpt that places *Whren* in context by examining the targeting of African–Americans by the police throughout American history. This chapter concludes by examining *U.S. v. Jones*, in which the Fourth Circuit vacated a conviction of an African–American male driver who was stopped by police for no reason other than he was African–American.

SECTION 1. THE DECISION TO PROSECUTE: LET THE BIAS BEGIN

Prosecutors (with the assistance of the police) decide whether an arrest should be made, what charges should be filed, whether to accept a plea or go to trial. Could unconscious racism play a role in any of those decisions? Consider the following article.

ANGELA J. DAVIS

Prosecution and Race: The Power and Privilege of Discretion
67 Fordham L. Rev. 13, 13–38, 54–67 (1998).

For everyone to whom much is given, from him much will be required; and to whom much has been committed, of him they will ask the more.

It was the happiest day of David McKnight's life. That evening, he went to a bar in Washington, D.C., to celebrate. Mr. McKnight bought a bottle of Dom Perignon and popped it open ceremoniously. "Drinks for everybody—my treat!," he announced. "What are we celebrating?," someone asked. "I killed someone and got away with it!," replied Mr. McKnight. He had just learned that a District of Columbia grand jury had voted not to indict him for the murder of John Nguyen.

The year was 1987. I was a staff attorney at the Public Defender Service for the District of Columbia ("PDS"). The court had appointed Michele Roberts, the chief of our trial division, to represent Mr. McKnight. The case was one of the most peculiar I observed in my dozen years as a public defender in the nation's capital. Two factors were noteworthy. First, someone had been brutally killed, and the grand jury, with a silent and consenting prosecuting attorney, decided that the killer should go free. Second, the accused killer was white. The way the case was handled convinced me that the two factors were related.

David McKnight was a twenty-five year old white male who worked as a bartender in a restaurant in Washington, D.C. He lived in a small, one bedroom apartment that he shared with John Nguyen, a fifty-five year old Vietnamese immigrant who worked as a cook in the restaurant. Mr. Nguyen paid Mr. McKnight rent to sleep in the walk-in closet of the apartment, a space barely large enough for a small bed.

One Saturday evening, McKnight invited a woman friend to the apartment. Nguyen was in the apartment at the time, resting in his "bedroom" closet. McKnight tried to persuade the woman to spend the night with him, but she declined. After she left, Nguyen came out of the closet and teased McKnight about his failed romance. Already upset about the turn of the evening's events, McKnight became even more enraged. He attacked Nguyen with a large machete. McKnight was much taller and heavier than Nguyen, who was just over five feet tall. Nguyen was able to escape into the bathroom, but McKnight hacked the bathroom door open with the machete. He then "almost sliced [Mr. Nguyen] in half." Nguyen managed to stagger out of the apartment and into the street. Both men were covered with Nguyen's blood. Ironically, the first ambulance on the scene picked up McKnight, leaving Nguyen dying in the street. A second ambulance came for Nguyen and took him to the hospital. He died later that night.

Michele Roberts was appointed to represent McKnight on the following Monday morning. The United States Attorney's office charged

McKnight with assault with a dangerous weapon, not murder, despite the fact that Nguyen had died the previous Saturday night. The magistrate released McKnight pending the trial of his case.

The case never went to trial. The prosecutor, who was white, called Ms. Roberts within a day or two and invited her to identify witnesses who might testify before the grand jury on behalf of McKnight. The prosecutor suggested that McKnight might have a good claim of self-defense and thought there might be witnesses who could testify about Nguyen's reputation for violence and McKnight's peaceful reputation. Ms. Roberts was stunned. She had been a trial lawyer at PDS for seven years and had probably tried more homicide cases than any other lawyer in the office. As the trial chief of the office, she had supervised most of the homicide cases handled by PDS. Ms. Roberts had never before received or heard of such an offer by a prosecutor to assist a criminal defendant, especially one who may have been guilty of murder.

Ms. Roberts identified witnesses willing to testify on behalf of McKnight. Although defense attorneys are not allowed to be present during grand jury hearings, the witnesses informed her that they would testify about McKnight's good character. **Several weeks later, the prosecutor informed Ms. Roberts that the grand jury voted not to indict McKnight.** All charges were dismissed. Ms. Roberts was never told about the testimony before the grand jury or whether the prosecutor advocated for McKnight.

Did race have anything to do with the outcome of McKnight's case? My colleagues and I were convinced that it did. It seemed obvious to us that the fact that McKnight was white and his victim was a Vietnamese immigrant had everything to do with the prosecutor's unusual attitude about prosecuting the case. **Most of my colleagues and I had handled cases with much stronger evidence of self defense, but never had the prosecutor offered to present this exculpatory evidence to the grand jury.** These cases generally proceeded to trial.

Mr. McKnight's case is just one example of many cases I handled or observed during my dozen years as a public defender in Washington, D.C., in which it appeared that the defendant or victim was treated differently based on his race. **Almost always, this disparate treatment was the result of action taken by the prosecutor at the charging, plea bargaining, trial, or sentencing stage of the case.** This phenomenon was so common that the attorneys in my office assumed that if the victim in a particular case was white, the defendant would surely be treated more harshly by the prosecutor. The plea bargain would be either unattractive or nonexistent and the prosecutor would devote more attention to the case. The converse was true for the few white clients represented by the office during my twelve-year stint. They would receive favorable treatment or, like Mr. McKnight, even have their cases dismissed.

At every step of the criminal process, there is evidence that African Americans are not treated as well as whites—both as victims of crime and as criminal defendants. And because prosecutors play such a dominant and commanding role in the criminal justice system through the exercise of broad, unchecked discretion, their role in the complexities of racial inequality in the criminal process is inextricable and profound.

In this article, I examine prosecutorial discretion—a major cause of racial inequality in the criminal justice system. I argue that prosecutorial discretion may instead be used to construct effective solutions to racial injustice. Prosecutors, more than any other officials in the system, have the power, discretion, and responsibility to remedy the discriminatory treatment of African Americans in the criminal justice process. Through the exercise of prosecutorial discretion, prosecutors make decisions that not only often predetermine the outcome of criminal cases, but also contribute to the discriminatory treatment of African Americans as both criminal defendants and victims of crime. I suggest that this discretion, which is almost always exercised in private, gives prosecutors more power than any other criminal justice officials, with practically no corresponding accountability to the public they serve. Thus, I maintain that prosecutors, through their overall duty to pursue justice, have the responsibility to use their discretion to help eradicate the discriminatory treatment of African Americans in the criminal justice system.

Courts have consistently upheld and sanctioned prosecutorial discretion, and make it increasingly difficult to mount legal challenges to discretionary decisions that have a discriminatory effect on African American criminal defendants and crime victims. These challenges are usually brought as selective prosecution claims under the Equal Protection Clause, requiring a nearly impossible showing that the prosecutor intentionally discriminated against the defendant or the victim. One reason this standard is so difficult to meet is that much of the discriminatory treatment of defendants and victims may be based on unconscious racism and institutional bias rather than on discriminatory intent. Another reason is the exacting legal standard for obtaining discovery of information that would help to prove discriminatory intent when it does exist.

In this article, I suggest a solution that would promote equal protection of the laws through the electoral process and help address the difficult legal challenges to discriminatory treatment. I propose the use of racial impact studies in prosecution offices to advance the responsible, nondiscriminatory exercise of prosecutorial discretion. The crux of the racial impact studies is the collection and publication of data on the race of the defendant and the victim in each case for each category of offense, and the action taken at each step of the criminal process. This data would then be analyzed to determine if race had a statistically significant correlation with various prosecutorial decisions. The studies would serve a number of purposes. First, they would reveal whether there is disparate treatment of African American defendants or victims. Second, they may reveal the discriminatory impact of race-neutral discretionary decisions and policies. Third, they would help prosecutors make informed decisions about the formulation of policies and establish standards to guide the exercise of discretion in specific cases. Finally, the publication of these studies would inform criminal defendants, crime victims, and the general public about the exercise of prosecutorial discretion and force prosecutors to be accountable for their decisions. Publication of the information would help inform the general public about prosecutorial practices so they may more effectively hold prosecutors accountable through the electoral process. Publication may also help criminal defendants alleging race-based selective prosecution to overcome the strict discovery standard set by the Supreme Court in *United States v. Armstrong.*

Racial impact studies may reveal illegitimate differential treatment based on unconscious racism or class bias, or legitimately different outcomes based on disproportionate offending and uninterested or uncooperative victims. The studies may also reveal that there is no differential treatment, thereby invalidating misperceptions of unfairness. In any case, the availability of the information would be invaluable in improving the overall administration of criminal justice. As Justice Brandeis said, "Sunlight is said to be the best of disinfectants."

* * *

Like the decisions of many officials in the criminal justice system, prosecutorial decisions often have a discriminatory effect on African Americans. The decisions and actions of prosecutors—and thus the discriminatory effect of these decisions—have greater impact and more serious consequences than those of any other criminal justice official. This great influence and its consequences stem from the extraordinary, almost unreviewable, discretion and power of prosecutors.

The Supreme Court has consistently advanced a number of reasons for deferring to the exercise of prosecutorial discretion. These reasons include: "(1) promoting prosecutorial and judicial economy and avoiding delay; (2) preventing the chilling of law enforcement; (3) avoiding the undermining of prosecutorial effectiveness; and (4) adhering to the constitutional principle of separation of powers" and deferring to the expertise of prosecutors. The Court has expressed concern that allowing inquiries into a prosecutor's motives might have a chilling effect on the performance of her law enforcement duties and may undermine her effectiveness by disclosing law enforcement policies. Although these concerns may have some merit, they cannot be used to justify the abuse of prosecutorial power.

Despite its potential abuse, however, prosecutorial discretion is necessary. It is difficult to imagine a fair and workable system that does not include some level of measured discretion in the prosecutorial process. One easily thinks of the prototypical case of a poor man who steals a loaf of bread to feed his starving family. Few would question the propriety or fairness of a prosecutorial decision to dismiss criminal charges against this criminal defendant. Such a decision could not be made in the absence of some level of discretion.

→ I'd like to hear more critique of its existence...

The deficiency of prosecutorial discretion lies not in its existence, but in the randomness and arbitrariness of its application. Even in prosecution offices that promulgate general policies for the prosecution of criminal cases, there is no effective mechanism for enforcement or public accountability. Self-regulation by prosecution offices is largely nonexistent or ineffective, and Supreme Court jurisprudence has protected prosecutors from both public and judicial scrutiny.

The arbitrary use of prosecutorial discretion greatly exacerbates racial disparities in the criminal process. The collection and publication of data in the form of racial impact studies would educate prosecutors and the public about the racial effects of discretionary prosecutorial decisions. Before exploring these effects, though, it is important to understand the function and significance of prosecutorial decisions in the criminal process. The remainder of this part explores the prosecutor's role in charging and plea bargaining decisions.

The first and "most important function exercised by a prosecutor" is the charging decision. Although police officers decide whether to arrest a suspect, the prosecutor decides whether he should be formally charged with a crime and what the charge should be. This decision is entirely discretionary. Even if there is probable cause to believe the suspect has committed a crime, the prosecutor may decide to dismiss the case and release the suspect. She may also file a charge that is either more or less serious than that recommended by the police officer, as long as there is probable cause to believe the suspect committed the crime. Other than a constitutional challenge by a criminal defendant, there is very little process for review of these decisions.

Some states require that felony charges be formally instituted by a grand jury, but the grand jury process is controlled entirely by the prosecutor. The grand jury can be as small as five members and as large as about two dozen. Grand jurors hear the testimony of witnesses, ask questions, and decide whether and with what offenses the suspect should be charged. The prosecutor, however, usually decides which witnesses will be called, directs the questioning of those witnesses, interprets the law, and makes a recommendation to the grand jury. Neither the target of the investigation nor his counsel may be present during the grand jury proceedings, nor may they or any member of the general public be informed of the substance of the witnesses' testimony or any other details of these proceedings.

The charging decision is one of the most important decisions a prosecutor makes. In conjunction with the plea bargaining process, the charging decision almost predetermines the outcome of a criminal case, because the vast majority of criminal cases result in guilty pleas or guilty verdicts. The charge also often determines the sentence that the defendant will receive, particularly in federal court, where criminal sentences are governed by the federal sentencing guidelines, and in state cases involving mandatory sentences. Because the sentencing guidelines and mandatory sentencing laws virtually eliminate judicial discretion, the prosecutor often effectively determines the defendant's sentence at the charging stage of the process, if the defendant is eventually found guilty. The charging decision's effect on the outcome of a case is felt to a lesser degree in state court. Although some state courts have some form of sentencing guidelines, most states give judges more discretion in determining the sentence for a convicted defendant. Nonetheless, the range of penalties is set by the initial charging decision.

The gravity of the charging decision is epitomized by a prosecutor's decision to seek the death penalty. No state's laws require that the death penalty be sought in any particular case, and all thirty-eight states that currently provide for the death penalty leave the decision to the discretion of the prosecutor. Most state death penalty laws allow the prosecutor to seek the death penalty in cases involving specific aggravating factors. The decision to seek the death penalty, like all charging decisions, can only be challenged on constitutional grounds, and these challenges are extremely difficult to sustain.

Most criminal cases end in a guilty plea. The typical plea bargain arrangement involves an agreement by the prosecutor to dismiss the most serious charge or charges in exchange for the defendant's guilty plea to a less serious offense. The defendant gives up his right to a trial and avoids the possibility of being convicted of a more serious offense and being imprisoned for a longer period of time. Sometimes, the plea bargain offers the possibility of avoiding imprisonment entirely. Although the judge must approve plea bargains in most jurisdictions, judges routinely approve these agreements because they expedite the process by disposing of criminal cases without the time and expense of a trial.

Like the charging decision, the plea bargaining process is controlled entirely by the prosecutor and decisions are entirely within her discretion. A criminal defendant cannot plead guilty to a less serious offense unless the prosecutor decides to make a plea offer. While the defense attorney may attempt to negotiate the best possible offer, the decision is ultimately left to the prosecutor's discretion.

Although prosecutors make important, influential decisions at other stages of the criminal process, the charging and plea bargaining stages provide the most independent power and control and allow the least opportunity for counterbalancing input from the defense. Prosecutors do not control the trial stage of the process and defense attorneys are theoretically on equal footing at this stage, as judges control the pace and content of the trial through their rulings. The sentencing hearing also provides for participation by the defense attorney and is controlled by the judge, unless mandatory sentencing laws are involved. In mandatory sentencing cases, which are increasingly common, the prior charging and plea bargaining decisions of the prosecutor often determine the sentence the defendant will receive, making the input of the defense attorney and the judge almost irrelevant.

Because prosecutors are arguably the most powerful decisionmakers in the process, their decisions potentially have the greatest discriminatory impact. No discussion of the impact of prosecutorial discretion on racial disparities in the criminal justice system would be complete, however, without a discussion of the discretionary decisions of police officers. Prosecutors typically do not become involved in a criminal case unless and until a police officer makes an arrest. If race is a factor in the decision to arrest a suspect, the police officer has infused the process with a layer of racial discrimination even before the prosecutor has an opportunity to exercise her discretion.

Racial impact studies in prosecutor offices may reveal racial disparaties [sic] in law enforcement. These studies may demonstrate that police are arresting African Americans and presenting them for prosecution at disproportionately higher rates than their similarly situated white counterparts. If such evidence is revealed, police should be compelled to explain or remedy the disparities. The available literature suggests that such racial disparities frequently exist in the arrest stage of the criminal process.

Police officers often act in a discriminatory manner in the performance of their official duties when they disproportionately stop, detain, and arrest African American men, with or without probable cause, and with or without articulable suspicion. In fact, courts have upheld race as a legitimate factor in the decision to stop and detain a suspect.

One factor that contributes to discrimination at the arrest stage is the discretion afforded police officers in deciding who to stop and whether to make an arrest. Despite the requirement that a police officer's decision to stop a suspect must be based on an articulable suspicion, the Supreme Court has shown increasing deference to the judgment of police officers in its interpretation of this requirement. The practical effect of this deference is the assimilation of police officers' subjective beliefs, biases, hunches, and prejudices into law. Because police officers are not required to make an arrest when they observe conduct creating probable cause, their discretion may result in the failure to detain or arrest whites who commit acts for which their African American counterparts would often be detained or arrested.

Police officers engage in discriminatory conduct in numerous forums. Traffic stops provide a particularly egregious example. Police officers use alleged traffic violations as an excuse for stopping and detaining motorists they suspect of other criminal conduct. Once the driver is stopped, the police officer will use the opportunity to observe the interior of the car for any items that might be in "plain view." The officer may also obtain the consent of an intimidated driver to conduct a full search of the car. Even if the driver refuses to give the officer consent to search the car, the police officer often may arrest the driver, rather than simply issue a citation, as long as there is probable cause to believe that a traffic violation has been committed. Once an arrest is made, the officer is justified in conducting a full-fledged search of the person and the surrounding area. Police officers may use minor traffic violations as an excuse to stop individuals they would otherwise have no legitimate reason to detain. These so-called "pretextual stops" allow police officers to use any traffic violation, no matter how minor, as a justification for a stop and possible arrest. Because police officers do not stop motorists every time they observe a traffic violation, the stops can be used in a discriminatory manner. The Supreme Court has unanimously upheld the constitutionality of pretextual stops, despite studies showing that they are disproportionately used to stop and detain African Americans and Latinos.

The racial impact of discretionary arrest decisions is particularly significant for drug offenses. Although whites use drugs in far greater numbers than African Americans, African Americans comprise a disproportionate percentage of drug arrests, convictions, and imprisonments. Law enforcement agents concede that drugs are used and sold in middle and upper class neighborhoods and business districts, but they have focused their law enforcement efforts in urban and inner-city areas which are populated primarily by African Americans and other people of color. These decisions have obvious racial effects.

Although some prosecutors are involved in the investigatory stage of the criminal process, most prosecutors enter the process after an arrest is made. A prosecutor may not know about racial considerations in the arrest process, and in most instances, does not have jurisdiction or control over the police department or other law enforcement agencies. If a prosecutor is aware of the inappropriate or illegal consideration of race at the arrest stage of the process, she may legitimately decide to exercise her discretion to decline prosecution. The consideration of race in the arrest process is usually not obvious, however, and unless a prosecutor were intentionally attempting to ferret out such decisions, she may not discover them. Additionally, because prosecutors must rely on police officers to prosecute their cases successfully, they are not motivated to confront them with accusations of racism and discrimination.

Prosecutors should bear the brunt of the remedial responsibility to eliminate racism in the criminal process, even though inappropriate or illegal considerations of race may occur at the arrest stage, often before prosecutorial participation in the process. The Supreme Court's decision in *Whren v. United States* has created the same kind of constitutional hurdles in cases involving police officers as *Armstrong v. United States* has created in selective prosecution cases—namely, the virtual impossibility of proving intentional discrimination based on race. Police officers, however, have less power and opportunity than prosecutors to move beyond constitutional limitations. Although police officers may and should take steps to discover and eliminate the inappropriate consideration of race, their power to affect and influence the criminal process begins and ends at the arrest stage. Prosecutorial power affects every stage of the process, including the arrest stage.

Like police officers, prosecutors often make decisions that discriminate against African American victims and defendants. These decisions may or may not be intentional or conscious. Although it may be difficult to prove intentional discrimination when it exists, unintentional discrimination poses even greater challenges. Prosecutors may not be aware that the seemingly harmless, reasonable, race-neutral decisions they make every day may have a racially discriminatory impact. This discriminatory impact may occur because of unconscious racism—a phenomenon that plays a powerful role in so many discretionary decisions in the criminal process—and because the lack of power and disadvantaged circumstances of so many African American defendants and victims make it more likely that prosecutors will treat them less well than whites.

If one acknowledges that African Americans experience both disparate and discriminatory treatment in the criminal justice system, the discussion ultimately turns to the issue of blame. Whose fault is it? Who has committed the invidious act or acts that have caused African Americans to experience this discriminatory treatment? It is this intent-focused analysis, sanctioned by the Supreme Court in its equal protection analysis, that has stymied legal challenges to discrimination in the criminal context. Instead of focusing on the harm experienced by African Americans as a result of actions by state actors, the Court has focused on whether the act itself is inherently invidious and whether the actor intended to cause the harm. In addition, the Court has placed the burden of proving intent on the shoulders of the victim. If the victim is unable to prove the actor's bad intent or, in certain contexts, if the actor can establish a nondiscriminatory explanation for his behavior, the Court offers no remedy for the harm experienced by the victim.

The main problem with this intent-focused analysis is that it is backward-looking. Although perhaps adequate in combating straightforward and explicit discrimination as it existed in the past, it is totally deficient as a remedy for the more complex and systemic discrimination that African Americans currently experience. When state actors openly expressed their racist views, it was easy to identify and label the invidious nature of their actions. But today, with some notable exceptions, most racist behavior is not openly expressed. More significantly, some racist behavior is committed unconsciously, and many who engage in this behavior are well-intentioned people who would be appalled by the notion that they would be seen as behaving in a racist or discriminatory manner.

Unconscious racism, although arguably less offensive than purposeful discrimination, is no less harmful. In fact, in many ways it is more perilous because it is often unrecognizable to the victim as well as the perpetrator. And the Court, by focusing on intent rather than harm, has refused to recognize, much less provide a remedy for, this most common and widespread form of racism. By focusing on blame rather than injury, the Court serves to satisfy the psychological needs of the uninjured party while leaving the victim without relief.

Professor Charles Lawrence defines unconscious racism as the ideas, attitudes, and beliefs developed in American historical and cultural heritage that cause Americans unconsciously to "attach significance to an individual's race and [which] induce negative feelings and opinions about nonwhites." He argues that, although America's historical experience has made racism an integral part of our culture, most people exclude it from their conscious minds because it is rejected as immoral. Professor Lawrence's definition of unconscious racism provides a useful framework in which to examine the discriminatory impact of prosecutorial decisionmaking.

Most prosecutors today would vehemently deny that they have ever discriminated against African American defendants or victims or that they take race into account in any way in the exercise of their prosecutorial duties. Prosecutors exercise a tremendous amount of discretion without governing rules and regulations and are not legally required to exercise their discretion in any particular way. Nonetheless, many prosecutors informally consider nonracial factors in making charging and plea bargaining decisions. Factors that prosecutors frequently cite as reasons for making certain charging and plea bargaining decisions are: the seriousness of the offense, the defendant's prior criminal record, the victim's interest in prosecution, the strength of the evidence, the likelihood of conviction, and the availability of alternative dispositions. These otherwise legitimate, race-neutral factors may be permeated with unconscious racism.

The seriousness of the offense is certainly a legitimate factor in making a charging decision. A prosecutor may decide to dismiss a case involving the possession of a single marijuana cigarette while charging and vigorously prosecuting a case involving distribution of a large amount of cocaine. Few would question this decision regardless of the race of the defendants. The more difficult issue arises when two cases involving the same offense but defendants or victims of different races are charged differently. If two murder cases involving similar facts with victims of different races are charged differently, the issue of unconscious racism becomes relevant. If a defendant in a case involving a white victim is charged with capital murder while a defendant in a similar case involving a black victim is charged with second-degree murder, questions arise about the value the prosecutors unconsciously placed on the lives of the respective victims. A prosecutor may unconsciously consider a case involving a white victim as more serious than a case involving a black victim. This unconscious view may influence not only the charging decision, but related decisions as well.

For example, if a prosecutor deems a particular case to be more serious than others, she will tend to invest more time and resources in that case, both investigating and preparing for trial. Such an increased investment would consequently yield more evidence and stiffen prosecutorial resolve. The likelihood of conviction is also obviously increased by the additional investment in investigation. Thus, although the strength of the evidence and the likelihood of conviction are facially race-neutral factors, they may be influenced by an unconsciously racist valuation of a case involving a white victim.

The victim's interest in prosecution is another legitimate factor that prosecutors consider in making charging and plea bargaining decisions. If the victim of a crime informs the prosecutor that he has no interest in the prosecution of his case and no desire to see the defendant punished, the prosecutor may legitimately dismiss the case based on the victim's feelings, especially if she believes that the defendant does not pose a danger to society and there are no other legitimate reasons for pursuing the prosecution. Few would question this decision, especially if the victim of the crime considered the prosecution process too onerous and difficult.

On the other hand, should a prosecutor pursue a prosecution in a case that she would otherwise dismiss for legitimate reasons simply because the victim wants to see the defendant punished? Or should a prosecutor assume that a victim is not interested in prosecution when the victim does not appear for witness conferences or respond to a subpoena? These questions demonstrate the significance of the intersection of class and race in the criminal process. They also raise fundamental questions about the duty and responsibility of the prosecutor to seek justice for all parties—defendants as well as victims—and to assure that all parties receive equal protection under the law.

The prior record of the defendant is another legitimate, seemingly race-neutral factor considered by prosecutors in the charging/plea bargaining process. Defendants with prior records are more likely to be charged and less likely to receive a favorable plea offer. Prosecutors consider both arrest and conviction records; defendants with recidivist tendencies are arguably more deserving of prosecution. Race, however, may affect the existence of a prior criminal record even in the absence of recidivist tendencies on the part of the suspect.

As previously noted, race plays a role in the decision to detain and/or arrest a suspect. Some courts have even legitimized this practice. In addition, policy decisions about where police officers should be deployed and what offenses they should investigate have racial ramifications. The fact that a white defendant has no criminal arrest or conviction record may not be a reflection of a lack of criminality on his part. If he lives in a neighborhood or attends a school that resolves certain criminal offenses (drug use, assault, etc.) without police intervention, he may be a recidivist without a record. Likewise, a black defendant who lives in a designated "high crime" area may have been detained and arrested on numerous occasions with or without probable cause. Thus, the existence or nonexistence of an arrest or conviction record may or may not reflect relative criminality in black and white defendants. A prosecutor without knowledge of or sensitivity to this issue may give prior arrests undue consideration in making charging and plea bargaining decisions.

Another factor that prosecutors sometimes consider is the availability of alternative dispositions. For some less serious offenses, prosecutors may be willing to consider dismissing a case based on the existence of alternative resolutions that serve the overall interest of justice. For example, if a defendant who has stolen is able to make restitution and the victim is satisfied with this resolution and would be burdened by numerous court appearances, dismissal of the case may be the best disposition for all parties. The dismissal would also have the added benefit of eliminating the time and expense of trying another case for the prosecutor, the defense attorney, and the court. As with all of the otherwise legitimate considerations, however, this issue also has class and racial ramifications.

The murder case discussed in the introduction to this article demonstrates the complexity of these issues. There is no way of determining whether the prosecutor in Mr. McKnight's case considered any of the traditional nonracial factors in deciding not to vigorously prosecute this murder case, or if he did, which factors he considered. Even if he did consider these factors, his decisions unconsciously may have been influenced by race.

The seriousness of the alleged offense—murder—would urge prosecution. The defendant had no prior record. In a murder case this factor would, at best, suggest leniency in sentencing or a favorable plea bargain, not total dismissal of the case. As far as the victim's interest was concerned, Mr. Nguyen had no relatives in the District of Columbia willing or able to lobby the prosecutor to vigorously prosecute the case, nor did the prosecutor seek to locate interested family members. Although the strength of the government's case was unclear, the prosecutor's failure to actively investigate the case certainly would have contributed to any weaknesses in the government's evidence and, consequently, the likelihood of conviction.

The prosecutor would probably deny that race or class had anything to do with the decisions made in McKnight's case. His unconscious racial biases, however, may have played a significant role in the process. It is doubtful that the white male prosecutor empathized with the middle-aged Vietnamese immigrant; it is likely that he would identify with the defendant who was a white male college student. In the absence of family members or others to advocate on his behalf, Mr. Nguyen was almost invisible—a foreign person of color whose life had little or no value.

Mr. McKnight's case illustrates how the discretionary decisions of prosecutors affect both offenders and victims in the criminal process. Although the prosecutor may not act invidiously, the discriminatory effects of his unconscious, race-neutral decisions may harm both victims and offenders. Current legal remedies are totally inadequate to address this harm.

* * *

Not every disparity is evidence of discrimination. Since many legitimate factors affect prosecutorial decisions, it may be appropriate to treat victims and defendants differently, even in similar cases. A prerequisite to eliminating race discrimination in the criminal process is the determination of whether the dissimilar treatment of similarly situated people is based on race rather than some legitimate reason. Whether the treatment is intentional or purposeful should not matter—the goal should be elimination of harm. Thus, the first step is the implementation of racial · impact studies designed to reveal racially discriminatory treatment. The second step is the publication of these studies so victims of discrimination and the general public may act to eradicate undesired policies and practices.

Racial impact studies would involve the collection of data on the race of the defendant and victim for each category of offense and the status of the case at each step of the prosecutorial process. For example, in each case involving an arrest for possession of cocaine, the prosecutor would document the race of the defendant, the defendant's criminal history, the initial charging decision, each plea offer made, accepted, or rejected, and the sentence advocated by the prosecutor. If relevant, the prosecutor should also document whether and how a decision was made to charge in federal versus state court and whether a departure from the sentencing guidelines was sought.

The statistics would be collected for each type of offense so that an appropriate statistical analysis comparing the disposition of the cases of white and African American defendants and victims could be done. These studies would not only be helpful in determining whether defendants of color receive harsher treatment for the same criminal behavior, but in cases involving victims, they would also demonstrate whether cases involving white victims were prosecuted more vigorously than cases involving African American victims. The data would also indicate whether similarly situated defendants and victims of different races are treated the same at each step of the process. Are defendants in cases involving white victims initially charged with the same offense as similarly situated defendants in cases involving black victims? Do they receive the same plea offers? Are the same sentences advocated at the sentencing hearing?

The data may help to reveal the extent to which whites are being arrested and presented for prosecution by law enforcement officers. If the majority of the cases in any particular category of offense involve African American defendants, the prosecutor should investigate further to determine whether African Americans comprise a majority of the population in that jurisdiction. If they do, the data would not necessarily indicate the selective detention and prosecution of African Americans. If African Americans do not comprise a majority of the population, further investigation would certainly be warranted, particularly if there is a considerable difference between the arrest rates and the African American population. The further investigation should attempt to determine whether African Americans commit the crime in question at greater rates than whites. In the absence of credible evidence that they do, the prosecutor should presume that no one particular race is inherently more likely to commit certain types of crimes.

Significant conclusions could not be reached from the simple collection of data without the appropriate statistical analysis. The Baldus study used in *McCleskey v. Kemp* exemplifies the model statistical analysis of this type of data. Widely acclaimed as one of the most thorough and statistically sound analyses of sentencing, the Baldus study examined thousands of murder cases over a seven-year period and took into account thirty-nine nonracial variables most likely to influence sentencing patterns in Georgia before reaching the conclusion that the race of the victim had a statistically significant correlation with the imposition of the death penalty.

Similar studies in prosecutors' offices would determine whether racial disparities exist in the prosecution of all types of cases and whether the disparities are statistically significant. A Baldus-type study which takes those factors into account would be essential to the credibility of the evaluation because there are so many legitimate, nonracial factors that may be considered in prosecutorial decisions. This type of evaluation would determine whether race is the determinative factor.

The racial impact studies will indicate whether, and to what extent, disparate treatment of similarly situated victims and defendants is based on race. How, then, might these studies be used to help eradicate race-based disparities? How these studies are used depends, to a large degree, on whether they are made public. If the results of the studies are revealed only to the prosecutor, she would have no legal obligation to take any action. The difficult discovery standard established in Armstrong would rarely require a prosecutor to turn over a racial impact study in a selective prosecution case. Similarly, difficult standing requirements in civil selective prosecution cases make it unlikely that such cases will be brought, much less reach the discovery stage.

If the studies are revealed only to the prosecutor, she would be free either to do nothing or to take some action to eliminate the disparities. The Rules of Professional Responsibility suggest that the prosecutor would have an ethical obligation to take steps to remedy the disparities. Prosecutors willing to voluntarily fulfill this obligation would face the difficult task of establishing and implementing some workable remedy. Prosecutors who do not view the elimination of racial disparities as a priority would do nothing.

Publication of the studies to the general public would be an important first step that might serve as a catalyst for developing workable remedies. The public could hold the prosecutor accountable through the electoral process by requiring that the disparities either be explained or remedied. In addition, litigants in selective prosecution actions could attempt to force similar action.

Forty-three states hold popular elections for Attorney General. At the county and municipal level, more than ninety-five percent of the chief prosecutors are elected. These positions are highly political, and candidates usually campaign on general crime themes, not on specific proposals about how they plan to exercise their prosecutorial power. Prosecutors are usually elected in the same general elections as other public officials. The state and county prosecutors hire assistant district attorneys to handle the caseloads of their offices.

Federal prosecutors are appointed, but their selection is also political. The President of the United States appoints the Attorney General who oversees the entire Justice Department. The President also appoints a United States Attorney for each of the federal judicial districts. The Attorney General may appoint additional Assistant United States Attorneys for any of the districts. The Attorney General and each United States Attorney must be confirmed by the United States Senate. Thus, the selection and confirmation of the Attorney General and the United States Attorneys are greatly influenced by the political party of the President and a majority of the Senate. Theoretically, the confirmation hearings provide an opportunity to inform the public of the practices and policies of a particular prosecutor since the hearings are open to members of the public, who may express their views by writing or calling their senators.

Ironically, the current system of choosing state and local prosecutors through the electoral process was established for the purpose of holding prosecutors accountable to the people they serve. The elected prosecutor emerged during the rise of Jeffersonian democracy in the 1820s, when the system of popularly elected officials was adopted. No longer beholden to the governor or the court, the prosecutor was deemed accountable to this amorphous body called "the people," specifically his constituents. Of course, the actions and decisions of the prosecutor were not generally a matter of public record, so the people's ability to hold the prosecutor accountable was quite limited. Nonetheless, the ballot box was seen as the most democratic and effective mechanism for achieving this goal.

The public's access to information about prosecutorial decisions has not expanded since the 1820s. The electorate has very little information about a prosecutor's specific charging and plea bargaining practices or how he plans to exercise his discretion before electing him to office, or, in the case of appointed prosecutors, before commenting on his appointment. Elected prosecutors typically run on very general "tough on crime" themes with no information about specific office policies. Certainly issues concerning race, such as strategies for preventing selective prosecution or other types of discriminatory treatment, are rarely discussed. Because of the paucity of such relevant information, the Jeffersonian democratic ideals that inspired the first elected prosecutors in the 1820s have never been achieved. Although the electorate can and does vote prosecutors out of office, it is not making these decisions in a fully informed manner.

The publication of racial impact studies would inform the public about the possible discriminatory effects of prosecution policies and practices. Such studies would force a public debate about racial disparities and compel prosecutors to be truly accountable to their constituents. Prosecutors could do this by either establishing policies and practices to help eliminate the disparities or by explaining that there are legitimate, race-neutral reasons for such disparities. If the public was not satisfied with the results of the study, the efforts to eliminate the disparities, or the prosecutor's explanation for disparities, it could then remove the prosecutor from office through the electoral process. The public debate would also help the prosecutor to establish workable remedial policies and practices. Thus, public access to the studies would motivate prosecutors to correct inequities and help to make the electoral process a more meaningful check on unacceptable prosecutorial practices.

Publication of racial impact studies would also allow for their use in selective prosecution claims brought by either defendants or crime victims. To the extent that such studies reveal that a prosecutor used his dismissal power in cases involving white defendants rather than black defendants, a black defendant claiming selective prosecution would be able to prove that similarly situated white defendants could have been prosecuted, but were not. Conversely, if a prosecutor dismisses cases involving black victims more than those with white victims, black victims claiming selective prosecution in civil cases would be able to prove that the cases of similarly situated white victims were prosecuted when cases of black victims were not prosecuted. In other words, the racial impact studies would obviate the need for discovery, thereby making it unnecessary to meet the impossible standard for discovery established in the Armstrong case.

The racial impact studies would not provide sufficient evidence to meet the standard of proof for prevailing on the merits in selective prosecution cases. Presumably, the studies would be sufficient to prove disparate impact if they reveal disparate dismissal rates based on race. They undoubtedly would be insufficient to prove the necessary discriminatory intent, however, in light of the Court's rejection of the Baldus study in McCleskey.

At least one scholar has suggested that the legal process achieved through selective prosecution hearings serves a useful purpose despite the improbability of success on the merits. Professor Anne Bowen Poulin argues that courts should continue to consider claims of selective prosecution despite the restrictions imposed since Armstrong because "even if the court ultimately denied relief, the exposure of disparate treatment through legal process may effect some reduction in improper selective prosecution as the government and the public respond to reduce or eliminate improper disparity." The use of racial impact studies in selective prosecution hearings would certainly help to achieve this goal.

National and state legislation should be enacted to require the use of racial impact reports in prosecution offices because reliance on voluntary efforts may not produce significant results. Few elected prosecutors are motivated to campaign on themes involving the promotion of racial equality. Like most politicians, prosecutors view "tough on crime" themes as the most effective tools to assure re-election. Legislation requiring the production and publication of racial impact studies would give prosecutors the necessary political cover. If the studies were required by law, no prosecutor could be accused of being "soft on crime" for focusing her attention on these issues. Furthermore, since the legislation would not require that prosecutors take any particular action, but would require only the collection and publication of information, it would not be subject to the criticisms raised by the Supreme Court in *Wayte v. United States*.

The publication of racial impact studies should have a significant impact on prosecutors, police, and the general public. Although it is difficult to determine what that impact would be, the goal would be to deter policies and practices that have a discriminatory impact on African Americans and other people of color, and encourage the development of policies and practices that would further the equitable treatment of defendants and victims of crime, regardless of race. This section will explore possible responses to the proposal.

Prosecutors might object to racial impact studies and/or the publication of the studies as a significant interference with their law enforcement duties. Criticisms would undoubtedly include the Supreme Court's reasons for deferring to prosecutorial discretion in *Wayte v. United States*: "Examining the basis of a prosecution delays the criminal proceeding, threatens to chill law enforcement by subjecting the prosecutor's motives and decisionmaking to outside inquiry, and may undermine prosecutorial effectiveness by revealing the Government's enforcement policy."

Prosecutors understandably would be concerned about the time and resources necessary to implement racial impact studies. The prosecutor's primary function is law enforcement; any undertaking which substantially interferes with that responsibility would be subject to legitimate criticism. If the collection of data were a tedious process that substantially interfered with the performance of important prosecutorial duties, most prosecutors would object to the studies. Prosecutors, however, could collect the relevant information in an efficient, non-intrusive manner. Prosecutorial offices could create forms with checklists on which the prosecutors could quickly and easily note the relevant information. Most prosecutors routinely make written entries in case files whenever an action is taken in a particular case. These forms or checklists could be kept in the same case file and would involve no more time than the routine case file entries. The only difference would be the type of information and the format for its collection.

Time is not the only relevant factor. Few prosecutor offices would have the expertise or resources to perform the necessary statistical analysis of the collected data. Social scientists or other researchers with expertise in this field would have to be hired, and few prosecutor offices have the financial resources for such an investment. Although prosecutor offices tend to have more financial resources than defender offices,

Couldn't it just also reinforce negative stereotypes?

many prosecutor offices lack the resources to adequately perform their basic prosecutorial responsibilities efficiently and effectively.

One possible solution to the resource problem may be the volunteer efforts of local colleges and universities. Criminology and criminal justice departments may be willing to conduct such research and would provide a wealth of resources through the use of graduate students from various departments. The studies would provide a great public service as well as a rich academic experience for professors, scholars, and students. Use of university resources would also give the project the necessary objectivity that would be lacking if the project were conducted by the prosecutors themselves.

Prosecutors may claim that the publication of the studies may chill law enforcement by subjecting the prosecutor's motives to outside inquiry. This argument suggests that prosecutors may be hesitant to prosecute certain cases if they believe that members of the public, criminal defendants, or victims will question their decisions. Thus, some criminal activity will not be prosecuted.

The goal of the publication of the studies is not to chill appropriate and fair law enforcement, but to totally eliminate unfair, discriminatory law enforcement. To the extent that law enforcement tactics or prosecutorial policies discriminate based on race, they should not merely be chilled—they should be entirely eliminated and replaced with tactics that enforce the law fairly and impartially. The studies, and the knowledge that they will be published, should cause prosecutors to be more careful and meticulous in making decisions. They should motivate prosecutors to assure that similarly situated victims and defendants are treated equitably.

The Supreme Court's concern that judicial interference with prosecutorial discretion would undermine prosecutorial effectiveness by revealing the government's enforcement policy cannot apply to the publication of racial impact studies. That argument suggests that if the public is aware of how and under what circumstances cases are prosecuted, they will adjust their behavior to avoid prosecution. For example, if the public is aware that a prosecutor has a policy of only prosecuting cases involving more than five grams of cocaine, dealers and users will only distribute or possess quantities less than five grams. The publication of racial impact studies should not raise this concern because the studies would not reveal specific law enforcement policies. The information would be limited to racial and other demographic data.

The studies may reveal that police or other law enforcement officers are disproportionately arresting African American criminal defendants. Such information may prompt an inquiry of the police chief or federal law enforcement agent and subject him to the same accountability as the prosecutor. The police would be compelled to explain racially disparate arrest patterns. If the public were not satisfied with the explanation, the chief may be required to develop policies designed to eliminate the unacceptable practices.

If the studies implicate police in discriminatory behavior, they may cause tension between prosecutors and police. Prosecutors must rely on the cooperation of police officers and other law enforcement officers long after they complete the arrest process. Police officers continue to investigate cases during the grand jury process and help prosecutors prepare for trials and other hearings. The testimony of arresting officers and other law enforcement personnel is almost always needed in grand jury and trial proceedings. Preparation for trial and other proceedings would certainly be more difficult for prosecutors with hostile, uncooperative law enforcement officers.

By declining to prosecute cases where they suspect police misconduct, prosecutors may deter discriminatory law enforcement. Such action would compel police to develop policies to ferret out discriminatory practices and promote the fair and equitable enforcement of the law. Ideally, prosecutors and police would work together to establish these policies in their respective offices. Such collaborative efforts would have to be voluntary, as police and prosecutors are generally governed by different political entities.

One of the primary goals of the publication of racial impact studies is to inspire the electorate to hold prosecutors accountable for their actions. The public would require prosecutors to explain statistics which suggest discriminatory practices and would compel them to remedy the disparities if they found the explanations to be unsatisfactory. Prosecutors who failed to remedy unacceptable disparities would be voted out of office.

One possible criticism of this proposal is its possible ineffectiveness in communities in which African Americans are a small minority of the population. One might argue that such minority communities may not be able to effectively influence prosecutorial decisions because of their lack of political power. Such criticisms assume that white voters do not care about issues of racial disparity and discrimination which harm African Americans. If such a view proved to be true in certain communities, the widespread publication of such information might serve to stigmatize those communities and indirectly force a change in policies or practices.

Even if the studies were published in communities with a politically powerful African American community, the proposal assumes that these communities would view the racial disparities as harmful. Professor Randall Kennedy, however, has a different view. He is a proponent of laws and practices which provide more law enforcement resources to African American communities, even those laws or practices may have a racially discriminatory impact on African American criminal defendants. He argues that such law enforcement only harms African Americans who violate the law while benefiting law-abiding African American citizens.

There is much evidence suggesting that Professor Kennedy's view is not the prevailing sentiment in most African American communities. African Americans led the fight to change federal cocaine sentencing laws which discriminate against them. Numerous civil rights organizations, including the National Association for the Advancement of Colored People, the National Rainbow Coalition, the National Council of Negro Women, the Southern Christian Leadership Conference, and the National Political Congress of Black Women fought to eliminate the sentencing disparities which discriminate against African Americans. The National Black Police Organization, the Progressive Baptist Convention, and the National Black Caucus of State Legislators—African American organizations which represent vastly different constituencies—also lobbied to eliminate the discriminatory aspects of the law.

Despite the efforts of these groups, the recommendation of the United States Sentencing Commission, and the opposition of Congressional Black Caucus, Congress passed legislation maintaining the disparity in sentencing between crack and powder cocaine offenses. President Clinton refused to veto Congress's action.

The response of widely divergent segments of the African American community to the discriminatory federal cocaine laws suggests that African Americans will be troubled by studies revealing that law enforcement and prosecutorial practices have a racially discriminatory impact. That experience also suggests that the African American community will take action to assure that discriminatory policies and practices are eliminated. Although the efforts in opposition to the cocaine laws were not totally successful, they did prompt some action. In 1997, Attorney General Janet Reno recommended that the federal cocaine laws be amended to reduce the disparity from 100:1 to 10:1. Although this compromise did not achieve the stated goal, it demonstrates how political action can hold elected officials accountable.

The biblical quote cited at the beginning of this article has a simple meaning: From whom much is given, much is expected. Prosecutors have been given more power and discretion than any other criminal justice official, so they have a greater ability to affect change where it is needed. The Supreme Court has not required much of prosecutors, but the Court's standards should serve as a floor rather than a ceiling, as a base rather than a goal. Prosecutors can, and should, seek to eliminate racial disparities regardless of blame and intent. They can, and should, set a higher standard of performance for themselves than the requirements set by the Supreme Court. They have both the power and privilege to do so. The publication of racial impact studies will help to assure that they do.

Notes and Questions

1. Describe the prosecutorial discretion that is involved in convicting someone of a crime. How can unconscious racism impact that discretion?

2. Do you think Professor Davis' racial impact study recommendation is a feasible solution?

3. What alternative suggestions do you have?

SECTION 2. DRIVING WHILE BLACK AND THE FOURTH AMENDMENT

WHREN v. U.S.

517 U.S. 806, 116 S.Ct. 1769, 135 L.Ed.2d 89 (1996).

JUSTICE SCALIA delivered the opinion of the Court.

In this case we decide whether the temporary detention of a motorist who the police have probable cause to believe has committed a civil traffic violation is inconsistent with the Fourth Amendment's prohibition against unreasonable seizures unless a reasonable officer would have been motivated to stop the car by a desire to enforce the traffic laws.

I

On the evening of June 10, 1993, plainclothes vice-squad officers of the District of Columbia Metropolitan Police Department were patrolling a "high drug area" of the city in an unmarked car. Their suspicions were aroused when they passed a dark Pathfinder truck with temporary license plates and youthful occupants waiting at a stop sign, the driver looking down into the lap of the passenger at his right. The truck remained stopped at the intersection for what seemed an unusually long time—more than 20 seconds. When the police car executed a U-turn in order to head back toward the truck, the Pathfinder turned suddenly to its right, without signaling, and sped off at an "unreasonable" speed. The policemen followed, and in a short while overtook the Pathfinder when it stopped behind other traffic at a red light. They pulled up alongside, and Officer Ephraim Soto stepped out and approached the driver's door, identifying himself as a police officer and directing the driver, petitioner Brown, to put the vehicle in park. When Soto drew up to the driver's window, he immediately observed two large plastic bags of what appeared to be crack cocaine in petitioner Whren's hands. Petitioners were arrested, and quantities of several types of illegal drugs were retrieved from the vehicle.

Petitioners were charged in a four-count indictment with violating various federal drug laws, including 21 U.S.C. §§ 844(a) and 860(a). At a pretrial suppression hearing, they challenged the legality of the stop and the resulting seizure of the drugs. They argued that the stop had not been justified by probable cause to believe, or even reasonable suspicion, that petitioners were engaged in illegal drug-dealing activity; and that Officer Soto's asserted ground for approaching the vehicle—to give the driver a warning concerning traffic violations—was pretextual. The District Court denied the suppression motion, concluding that "the facts of the stop were not controverted," and "there was nothing to really demonstrate that the actions of the officers were contrary to a normal traffic stop." App. 5.

Petitioners were convicted of the counts at issue here. The Court of Appeals affirmed the convictions, holding with respect to the suppression issue that, "regardless of whether a police officer subjectively believes that the occupants of an automobile may be engaging in some other illegal behavior, a traffic stop is permissible as long as a reasonable officer in the same circumstances could have stopped the car for the suspected traffic violation." 311 U.S.App.D.C. 300, 53 F.3d 371, 374–375 (CADC 1995). We granted certiorari. 516 U.S. 1036, 133 L.Ed.2d 595, 116 S.Ct. 690 (1996).

II

The Fourth Amendment guarantees "the right of the people to be secure in their persons, houses, papers, and effects, against unreasonable searches and seizures." Temporary detention of individuals during the stop of an automobile by the police, even if only for a brief period and for a limited purpose, constitutes a "seizure" of "persons" within the meaning of this provision. *See Delaware v. Prouse*, 440 U.S. 648, 653, 59 L.Ed.2d 660, 99 S.Ct. 1391 (1979); *United States v. Martinez–Fuerte*, 428 U.S. 543, 556, 49 L. Ed. 2d 1116, 96 S. Ct. 3074 (1976); *United States v. Brignoni–Ponce*, 422 U.S. 873, 878, 45 L.Ed.2d 607, 95 S.Ct. 2574 (1975). An automobile stop is thus subject to the constitutional imperative that it not be "unreasonable" under the circumstances. As a general matter, the decision to stop an automobile is reasonable where the police have probable cause to believe that a <u>traffic violation</u> has occurred. *See Prouse, supra,* at 659, 99 S.Ct. at 1399; *Pennsylvania v. Mimms*, 434 U.S. 106, 109, 54 L.Ed.2d 331, 98 S.Ct. 330 (1977) (per curiam).

Petitioners accept that Officer Soto had probable cause to believe that various provisions of the District of Columbia traffic code had been violated. See 18 D. C. Mun. Regs. §§ 2213.4 (1995) ("An operator shall . . . give full time and attention to the operation of the vehicle"); 2204.3 ("No person shall turn any vehicle . . . without giving an appropriate signal"); 2200.3 ("No person shall drive a vehicle . . . at a speed greater than is reasonable and prudent under the conditions"). They argue, however, that "in the unique context of civil traffic regulations" probable cause is not enough. Since, they contend, the use of automobiles is so heavily and minutely regulated that total compliance with traffic and safety rules is nearly impossible, a police officer will almost invariably be able to catch any given motorist in a technical violation. This creates the temptation to use traffic stops as a means of investigating other law violations, as to which no probable cause or even articulable suspicion exists. Petitioners, who are both black, further contend that police officers might decide which motorists to stop based on decidedly impermissible factors, such as the race of the car's occupants. To avoid this danger, they say, the Fourth Amendment test for traffic stops should be, not the normal one (applied by the Court of Appeals) of whether probable cause existed to justify the stop; but rather, whether a police officer, acting reasonably, would have made the stop for the reason given.

Petitioners contend that the standard they propose is consistent with our past cases' disapproval of police attempts to use valid bases of action against citizens as pretexts for pursuing other investigatory agendas. We are reminded that in *Florida v. Wells*, 495 U.S. 1, 4, 109 L.Ed.2d 1, 110 S.Ct. 1632 (1990), we stated that "an inventory search[1] must not be a ruse for a general rummaging in order to discover incriminating evidence"; that in *Colorado v. Bertine*, 479 U.S. 367, 372, 93 L.Ed.2d 739, 107 S.Ct. 738 (1987), in approving an inventory search, we apparently thought it significant that there had been "no showing that the police, who were following standardized procedures, acted in bad faith or for the sole purpose of investigation"; and that in *New York v. Burger*, 482 U.S. 691, 716–717, n. 27, 96 L.Ed.2d 601, 107 S.Ct. 2636 (1987), we observed, in upholding the constitutionality of a warrantless administrative inspection,[2] that the search did not appear to be "a 'pretext' for obtaining evidence of ... violation of ... penal laws." But only an undiscerning reader would regard these cases as endorsing the principle that ulterior motives can invalidate police conduct that is justifiable on the basis of probable cause to believe that a violation of law has occurred. In each case we were addressing the validity of a search conducted in the absence of probable cause. Our quoted statements simply explain that the exemption from the need for probable cause (and warrant), which is accorded to searches made for the purpose of inventory or administrative regulation, is not accorded to searches that are not made for those purposes. *See Bertine, supra*, at 371–372, 107 S.Ct., at 740–741; *Burger, supra*, at 702–703, 107 S.Ct., at 2643–2644.

Petitioners also rely upon *Colorado v. Bannister*, 449 U.S. 1, 66 L.Ed.2d 1, 101 S.Ct. 42 (1980) (per curiam), a case which, like this one, involved a traffic stop as the prelude to a plain-view sighting and arrest on charges wholly unrelated to the basis for the stop. Petitioners point to our statement that "there was no evidence whatsoever that the officer's presence to issue a traffic citation was a pretext to confirm any other previous suspicion about the occupants" of the car. *Id.*, at 4, n. 4, 101 S.Ct., at 44 n. 4. That dictum at most demonstrates that the Court in *Bannister* found no need to inquire into the question now under discussion; not that it was certain of the answer. And it may demonstrate even less than that: If by "pretext" the Court meant that the officer really had not seen the car speeding, the statement would mean only that there was no reason to doubt probable cause for the traffic stop.

It would, moreover, be anomalous, to say the least, to treat a statement in a footnote in the per curiam *Bannister* opinion as indicating a reversal of our prior law. Petitioners' difficulty is not simply a lack of

---

1. An inventory search is the search of property lawfully seized and detained, in order to ensure that it is harmless, to secure valuable items (such as might be kept in a towed car), and to protect against false claims of loss or damage. *See South Dakota v. Opperman*, 428 U.S. 364, 369, 49 L.Ed.2d 1000, 96 S.Ct. 3092 (1976).

2. An administrative inspection is the inspection of business premises conducted by authorities responsible for enforcing a pervasive regulatory scheme—for example, unannounced inspection of a mine for compliance with health and safety standards. *See Donovan v. Dewey*, 452 U.S. 594, 599–605, 69 L.Ed.2d 262, 101 S.Ct. 2534 (1981).

affirmative support for their position. Not only have we never held, outside the context of inventory search or administrative inspection (discussed above), that an officer's motive invalidates objectively justifiable behavior under the Fourth Amendment; but we have repeatedly held and asserted the contrary. In *United States v. Villamonte–Marquez,* 462 U.S. 579, 584, n. 3, 77 L.Ed.2d 22, 103 S.Ct. 2573 (1983), we held that **an otherwise valid warrantless boarding of a vessel by customs officials was not rendered invalid** "because the customs officers were accompanied by a Louisiana state policeman, and were following an informant's tip that a vessel in the ship channel was thought to be carrying marihuana." We flatly dismissed the idea that an ulterior motive might serve to strip the agents of their legal justification. In *United States v. Robinson,* 414 U.S. 218, 38 L.Ed.2d 427, 94 S.Ct. 467 (1973), we held that a traffic-violation arrest (of the sort here) would not be rendered invalid by the fact that it was "a mere pretext for a narcotics search," *id.,* at 221, n. 1, 94 S.Ct., at 470, n. 1; and that a lawful postarrest search of the person would not be rendered invalid by the fact that it was not motivated by the officer-safety concern that justifies such searches, *see id.,* at 236, 94 S.Ct., at 477. *See also Gustafson v. Florida,* 414 U.S. 260, 266, 38 L.Ed.2d 456, 94 S.Ct. 488 (1973). And in *Scott v. United States,* 436 U.S. 128, 138, 56 L.Ed.2d 168, 98 S.Ct. 1717 (1978), in rejecting the contention that wiretap evidence was subject to exclusion because the agents conducting the tap had failed to make any effort to comply with the statutory requirement that unauthorized acquisitions be minimized, we said that "subjective intent alone . . . does not make otherwise lawful conduct illegal or unconstitutional." We described *Robinson* as having established that "the fact that the officer does not have the state of mind which is hypothecated by the reasons which provide the legal justification for the officer's action does not invalidate the action taken as long as the circumstances, viewed objectively, justify that action." 436 U.S. at 136, 138, 98 S.Ct., at 1723.

We think these cases foreclose any argument that the constitutional reasonableness of traffic stops depends on the actual motivations of the individual officers involved. We of course agree with petitioners that the Constitution prohibits selective enforcement of the law based on considerations such as race. But the constitutional basis for objecting to intentionally discriminatory application of laws is the Equal Protection Clause, not the Fourth Amendment. Subjective intentions play no role in ordinary, probable-cause Fourth Amendment analysis.

B

Recognizing that we have been unwilling to entertain Fourth Amendment challenges based on the actual motivations of individual officers, petitioners disavow any intention to make the individual officer's subjective good faith the touchstone of "reasonableness." They insist that the standard they have put forward—whether the officer's conduct deviated materially from usual police practices, so that a reasonable officer in the same circumstances would not have made the stop for the reasons given—is an "objective" one.

But although framed in empirical terms, this approach is plainly and indisputably driven by subjective considerations. Its whole purpose is to prevent the police from doing under the guise of enforcing the traffic code what they would like to do for different reasons. Petitioners' proposed standard may not use the word "pretext," but it is designed to combat nothing other than the perceived "danger" of the pretextual stop, albeit only indirectly and over the run of cases. Instead of asking whether the individual officer had the proper state of mind, the petitioners would have us ask, in effect, whether (based on general police practices) it is plausible to believe that the officer had the proper state of mind.

[margin note: ISN'T EVERYTHING?]

Why one would frame a test designed to combat pretext in such fashion that the court cannot take into account actual and admitted pretext is a curiosity that can only be explained by the fact that our cases have foreclosed the more sensible option. If those cases were based only upon the evidentiary difficulty of establishing subjective intent, petitioners' attempt to root out subjective vices through objective means might make sense. But they were not based only upon that, or indeed even principally upon that. Their principal basis—which applies equally to attempts to reach subjective intent through ostensibly objective means—is simply that the Fourth Amendment's concern with "reasonableness" allows certain actions to be taken in certain circumstances, whatever the subjective intent. *See, e.g., Robinson, supra*, at 236, 94 S.Ct., at 477 ("Since it is the fact of custodial arrest which gives rise to the authority to search, it is of no moment that [the officer] did not indicate any subjective fear of the [arrestee] or that he did not himself suspect that [the arrestee] was armed") (footnotes omitted); *Gustafson, supra*, at 266, 94 S.Ct., at 492 (same). But even if our concern had been only an evidentiary one, petitioners' proposal would by no means assuage it. Indeed, it seems to us somewhat easier to figure out the intent of an individual officer than to plumb the collective consciousness of law enforcement in order to determine whether a "reasonable officer" would have been moved to act upon the traffic violation. While police manuals and standard procedures may sometimes provide objective assistance, ordinarily one would be reduced to speculating about the hypothetical reaction of a hypothetical constable—an exercise that might be called virtual subjectivity.

[margin note: except that you could rely on factors, rather than intent]

Moreover, police enforcement practices, even if they could be practicably assessed by a judge, vary from place to place and from time to time. We cannot accept that the search and seizure protections of the Fourth Amendment are so variable, cf. *Gustafson, supra*, at 265, 94 S.Ct., at 491; *United States v. Caceres*, 440 U.S. 741, 755–756, 59 L.Ed.2d 733, 99 S.Ct. 1465 (1979), and can be made to turn upon such trivialities. The difficulty is illustrated by petitioners' arguments in this case. Their claim that a reasonable officer would not have made this stop is based largely on District of Columbia police regulations which permit plainclothes officers in unmarked vehicles to enforce traffic laws "only in the case of a violation that is so grave as to pose an immediate threat to the safety of others." Metropolitan Police Department, Washington, D.C., General Order 303.1, pt. 1, Objectives and Policies (A)(2)(4) (Apr. 30, 1992), reprinted as Addendum to Brief for Petitioners. This basis of invalidation would not apply in jurisdictions that had a different practice. And it would not have applied even in the District of Columbia, if Officer Soto had been wearing a uniform or patrolling in a marked police cruiser.

Petitioners argue that our cases support insistence upon police adherence to standard practices as an objective means of rooting out pretext. They cite no holding to that effect, and dicta in only two cases. In *Abel v. United States*, 362 U.S. 217, 4 L.Ed.2d 668, 80 S.Ct. 683 (1960), the petitioner had been arrested by the Immigration and Naturalization Service (INS), on the basis of an administrative warrant that, he claimed, had been issued on pretextual grounds in order to enable the Federal Bureau of Investigation (FBI) to search his room after his arrest. We regarded this as an allegation of "serious misconduct," but rejected Abel's claims on the ground that "[a] finding of bad faith is . . . not open to us on th[e] record" in light of the findings below, including the finding that " 'the proceedings taken by the [INS] differed in no respect from what would have been done in the case of an individual concerning whom [there was no pending FBI investigation],' " *id.*, at 226–227, 80 S.Ct., at 690–691. But it is a long leap from the proposition that following regular procedures is some evidence of lack of pretext to the proposition that failure to follow regular procedures proves (or is an operational substitute for) pretext. *Abel*, moreover, did not involve the assertion that pretext could invalidate a search or seizure for which there was probable cause—and even what it said about pretext in other contexts is plainly inconsistent with the views we later stated in *Robinson*, *Gustafson*, *Scott*, and *Villamonte–Marquez*. In the other case claimed to contain supportive dicta, *United States v. Robinson*, 414 U.S. 218, 38 L.Ed.2d 427, 94 S.Ct. 467(1973), in approving a search incident to an arrest for driving without a license, we noted that the arrest was "not a departure from established police department practice." *Id.*, at 221, n. 1, 94 S.Ct., at 470, n. 1. That was followed, however, by the statement that "we leave for another day questions which would arise on facts different from these." *Ibid.* This is not even a dictum that purports to provide an answer, but merely one that leaves the question open.

III

In what would appear to be an elaboration on the "reasonable officer" test, petitioners argue that the balancing inherent in any Fourth Amendment inquiry requires us to weigh the governmental and individual interests implicated in a traffic stop such as we have here. That balancing, petitioners claim, does not support investigation of minor traffic infractions by plainclothes police in unmarked vehicles; such investigation only minimally advances the government's interest in traffic safety, and may indeed retard it by producing motorist confusion and alarm—a view said to be supported by the Metropolitan Police Department's own regulations generally prohibiting this practice. And as for the Fourth Amendment interests of the individuals concerned, petitioners point out that our cases acknowledge that even ordinary traffic stops entail "a possibly unsettling show of authority"; that they at best "interfere with freedom of movement, are inconvenient, and consume time" and at worst "may create substantial anxiety," *Prouse*, 440 U.S. at 657, 99 S.Ct., at 1398. That anxiety is likely to be even more pronounced when the stop is conducted by plainclothes officers in unmarked cars.

It is of course true that in principle every Fourth Amendment case, since it turns upon a "reasonableness" determination, involves a balancing of all relevant factors. With rare exceptions not applicable here, however, the result of that balancing is not in doubt where the search or seizure is based upon probable cause. That is why petitioners must rely upon cases like *Prouse* to provide examples of actual "balancing" analysis. There, the police action in question was a random traffic stop for the purpose of checking a motorist's license and vehicle registration, a practice that—like the practices at issue in the inventory search and administrative inspection cases upon which petitioners rely in making their "pretext" claim—involves police intrusion without the probable cause that is its traditional justification. Our opinion in *Prouse* expressly distinguished the case from a stop based on precisely what is at issue here: "probable cause to believe that a driver is violating any one of the multitude of applicable traffic and equipment regulations." *Id.*, at 661, 99 S.Ct. at 1400. It noted approvingly that "the foremost method of enforcing traffic and vehicle safety regulations . . . is acting upon observed violations," *id.*, at 659, 99 S.Ct., at 1399, which afford the " 'quantum of individualized suspicion' " necessary to ensure that police discretion is sufficiently constrained, *id.*, at 654–655, 99 S.Ct., at 1396 (quoting *United States v. Martinez–Fuerte*, 428 U.S. at 560, 96 S.Ct., at 3084). What is true of *Prouse* is also true of other cases that engaged in detailed "balancing" to decide the constitutionality of automobile stops, such as *Martinez–Fuerte*, which upheld checkpoint stops, *see* 428 U.S., at 556–562, 96 S.Ct., at 3082-3085, and *Brignoni–Ponce*, which disallowed so-called "roving patrol" stops, *see* 422 U.S. at 882–884, 95 S.Ct., at 2580-2582: The detailed "balancing" analysis was necessary because they involved seizures without probable cause.

Where probable cause has existed, the only cases in which we have found it necessary actually to perform the "balancing" analysis involved searches or seizures conducted in an extraordinary manner, unusually harmful to an individual's privacy or even physical interests—such as, for example, seizure by means of deadly force, *see Tennessee v. Garner*, 471 U.S. 1, 85 L.Ed.2d 1, 105 S.Ct. 1694 (1985), unannounced entry into a home, *see Wilson v. Arkansas*, 514 U.S. 927, 131 L.Ed.2d 976, 115 S.Ct. 1914 (1995), entry into a home without a warrant, *see Welsh v. Wisconsin*, 466 U.S. 740, 80 L.Ed.2d 732, 104 S.Ct. 2091 (1984), or physical penetration of the body, *see Winston v. Lee*, 470 U.S. 753, 84 L.Ed.2d

662, 105 S.Ct. 1611 (1985). The making of a traffic stop out of uniform does not remotely qualify as such an extreme practice, and so is governed by the usual rule that probable cause to believe the law has been broken "outbalances" private interest in avoiding police contact.

Petitioners urge as an extraordinary factor in this case that the "multitude of applicable traffic and equipment regulations" is so large and so difficult to obey perfectly that virtually everyone is guilty of violation, permitting the police to single out almost whomever they wish for a stop. But we are aware of no principle that would allow us to decide at what point a code of law becomes so expansive and so commonly violated that infraction itself can no longer be the ordinary measure of the lawfulness of enforcement. And even if we could identify such exorbitant codes, we do not know by what standard (or what right) we would decide, as petitioners would have us do, which particular provisions are sufficiently important to merit enforcement.

For the run-of-the-mill case, which this surely is, we think there is no realistic alternative to the traditional common-law rule that probable cause justifies a search and seizure.

* * *

Here the District Court found that the officers had probable cause to believe that petitioners had violated the traffic code. That rendered the stop reasonable under the Fourth Amendment, the evidence thereby discovered admissible, and the upholding of the convictions by the Court of Appeals for the District of Columbia Circuit correct. The judgment is

Affirmed .

Notes and Questions

1. Why were the motorists in *Whren* stopped?

2. What does the rule of *Whren* do for African–American motorists and other motorists of color?

3. Should only the guilty worry about this decision?

4. For some historical perspective, read the following excerpt.

TRACEY MACLIN
Race and the Fourth Amendment
51 Vand. L. Rev. 333, 333–341, 342–362, 375–393 (1998).

In America, police targeting of black people for excessive and disproportionate search and seizure is a practice older than the Republic itself. Thus, it was not startling to learn that a special squad of the North Carolina Highway Patrol that uses traffic stops to interdict illegal narcotics charged black male drivers with traffic offenses at nearly twice the rate of other troopers patrolling the same roads. The commander of the drug team issued more than sixty percent of his traffic citations to black men. When confronted with this evidence, he could not explain why he disproportionately stopped black men: "I can't say I'm surprised, and I can't say I'm not surprised. It doesn't bother me either way, to be honest with you."

The commander's conduct comes from an ancient pedigree. In 1693, court officials in Philadelphia responded to complaints about the congregating and traveling of blacks without their masters by authorizing the constables and citizens of the city to "take up" any black person seen "gadding abroad" without a pass from his or her master. Of course, the order to stop and detain any Negro found on the street did not distinguish between free and enslaved blacks.

Three years later, colonial South Carolina initiated a series of measures that subjected blacks to frequent and arbitrary searches and seizures. One such measure required state slave patrols to search the homes of slaves for concealed weapons on a weekly basis. These searches became biweekly in 1712 and extended to contraband as well as weapons. In 1722, South Carolina authorized its slave patrols to forcibly enter any home where the concealed weapons of blacks might be found, and to detain suspicious blacks they encountered. By 1737, slave patrols had power to search taverns and homes suspected of serving blacks or housing stolen goods. Three years later, South Carolina authorized its justices of the peace to conduct warrantless searches for weapons and stolen goods and to seize any slave suspected of any crime "whatsoever."

To inhibit seditious meetings, Virginia, in 1726, permitted its slave patrols to arrest slaves on bare suspicion. By 1738, Virginia's patrols conducted mandatory searches of the homes of all blacks. The patrols also possessed power to arrest blacks whose presence excited suspicion and to detain any slave found off his master's property without a pass. In Virginia, as in its sister colonies, judges did not supervise the activities of state slave patrols. Throughout the southern colonies, "no neutral and detached magistrate intervened between a patrolman's suspicions and his power to arrest or search, for that power was ex officio."

By the mid–1700s, oppressive British search and seizure practices that affected white colonists became a potent political issue throughout the colonies. But resistance to high-handed British intrusions did not inspire colonial officials to check the search and seizure powers of southern slave patrols. In the mid–1760s, Virginia, South Carolina, and Georgia reaffirmed their laws on slave patrols enacted earlier in the century. A black resident of Savannah recalled that in 1767, the slave patrol of that city would "enter the house of any black person who kept his lights on after 9 P.M. and fine, flog, and extort food from him."

While many white colonists experienced arbitrary and suspicionless intrusions of their homes and businesses, these practices paled in comparison to the indignities and invasions suffered by blacks at the hands of colonial officials. White colonists rightfully protested that certain British search and seizure practices conferred "a power that places the liberty of every man in the hands of every petty officer," but at the same time, colonial officials denied blacks the privacy and personal security that white colonists claimed as a birthright. Blacks, both slave and free, were targeted for searches and seizures solely because of their race—a phenomenon never experienced by white colonists.

Today, police departments across the nation, like the special narcotics unit of the North Carolina Highway Patrol, continue to target blacks in a manner reminiscent of the slave patrols of colonial America. Using minor, generally under-enforced, traffic violations as a pretext, officers target and stop black and Hispanic motorists because they hope to discover illegal narcotics or other criminal evidence. Despite criticism of this practice, a unanimous Supreme Court recently stated that pretextual stops of black motorists do not implicate the Fourth Amendment's guarantee against unreasonable searches and seizures. In *Whren v. United States*, the Court acknowledged that race-based enforcement of traffic laws violates the Constitution, but it explained that "the constitutional basis for objecting to intentionally discriminatory application of laws is the Equal Protection Clause, not the Fourth Amendment." According to the Court, the subjective intentions of the police, including police motives based on racial stereotypes or bias, are irrelevant to ordinary Fourth Amendment analysis.

The Court's conclusion that the Fourth Amendment has nothing to say about pretextual stops of black motorists is not surprising. The reasonableness analysis of recent Fourth Amendment cases emphasizes objective standards. The Court disfavors criteria and standards that require judges to ascertain the motivations and expectations of police officers and citizens enmeshed in confrontations that rarely have neutral observers. Moreover, the Whren Court's unwillingness to consider the impact that pretextual traffic stops have on black and Hispanic motorists is consistent with the modern Court's trend of ignoring evidence of racial impact as a factor in the reasonableness analysis mandated by the Fourth Amendment.

For example, in two earlier decisions, the Court refused to consider or discuss evidence of racial impact. In *Florida v. Bostick*, narcotic officers boarded an interstate bus, randomly and without suspicion, approached seated passengers, requested to see their identification and tickets, and asked for permission to search their luggage. Despite being informed that drug interdiction raids on inter state buses have a disparate impact on minority citizens, the Court, without commenting on the racial impact of this confrontation, held that a bus raid did not automatically trigger Fourth Amendment protection because this tactic was not a per se seizure under the amendment.

Likewise, in *Tennessee v. Garner*, the Court ignored evidence of racial impact. Garner concerned the validity of police using deadly force to prevent the escape of an unarmed, fleeing felon. As in Bostick, the Garner Court had evidence before it indicating that unrestricted deadly force had a disproportionate impact on blacks. But neither the majority nor dissenting opinions discussed the fact that unregulated deadly force policies result in the police shooting, or shooting at, a disproportionate number of blacks. The majority opinion did not even acknowledge that Edward Garner, who was shot in the back of the head by a Memphis officer as he fled the scene of a burglary, was a skinny, unarmed black teenager.

Considering the Court's prior rulings, the decision in Whren to ignore racial impact when marking the protective boundaries of the Fourth Amendment was predictable. But predictability is not equivalent to correctness. In Whren, the Court repeats its earlier mistakes in Garner and Bostick by neglecting racial concerns when constructing Fourth Amendment rules that govern police-citizen interactions.

Although the casual reader of the Court's Fourth Amendment opinions would never know it, race matters when measuring the dynamics and legitimacy of certain police-citizen encounters. Indeed, in light of past and present tensions between the police and minority groups, it is startling that the Court would ignore racial concerns when formulating constitutional rules that control police discretion to search and seize persons on the street. The Court currently focuses solely on whether probable cause of a traffic offense exists when judging the legality of pretextual seizures. Curiously, this analysis, taken from the Fourth Amendment's mandate of "reasonable" searches and seizures, fails to consider a factor that often stands at the core of pretextual traffic stops and makes those encounters particularly unreasonable—race. In this Article, I argue that the Court should make racial concerns a part of its Fourth Amendment analysis. In particular, where evidence indicates racial targeting by the police, the state should be required to provide a race neutral explanation for the seizure other than probable cause of a traffic violation.

Part II of this Article offers objective evidence that police officers seize black and Hispanic motorists for arbitrary traffic stops. Much of this evidence consists of empirical data indicating that black motorists are stopped for traffic offenses at a rate highly disproportionate to the percentage of black motorists eligible for lawful traffic detentions. Whren concluded that the subjective intentions of the police are irrelevant in Fourth Amendment cases, but the evidence of racial targeting discussed here does not measure the subjective motivations of officers. Rather, this evidence describes the racial population of motorists actually stopped by officers. Ironically, this evidence is more objective and reliable than other evidence the Court has sanctioned in determining the reasonableness of investigative detentions.

* * *

Part IV contends that when police target a black or Hispanic motorist for a pretextual traffic stop, this stop violates the Fourth Amendment. Currently, the Amendment protects a black motorist only when there is no probable cause that he has committed a traffic offense; if probable cause exists, police are free to conduct a traffic stop at their whim. The procedural right established under this regime does not stop arbitrary seizures because it fails to consider that police discretion, police perjury, and the mutual distrust between blacks and the police are issues intertwined with the enforcement of traffic stops.

In Whren, the two black defendants argued that plain clothes vice-squad officers of the District of Columbia Metropolitan Police Department conducted a pretextual stop of their car in violation of the Fourth Amendment. That is, the officers used the existence of a traffic violation as an excuse to stop the defendants' car when the officers lacked evidence of other criminal conduct. The officers did not intend to enforce the District's traffic code, but suspected the defendants of narcotics violations. As happens so often, the officers observed, in plain view, drugs in the lap of one of the defendants before the investigation could unfold.

In addition to their argument that the Court's precedents disfavored pretextual seizures as a general matter, the defendants also pointed to evidence that officers often target black and Hispanic motorists for pretextual traffic stops to launch unwarranted criminal investigations. According to the defendants, this evidence indicated that police discretion and bias, rather than a bona fide interest in enforcing the traffic code, motivated the traffic stops. Without questioning the validity of the defendants' evidence, the Court rejected the argument and dismissed the notion that the Fourth Amendment is concerned about the racial motives of police officers when making traffic stops. The Court concluded that if there is objective probable cause of a traffic violation, a stop is always reasonable under the Fourth Amendment regardless of the subjective reasons that may have actually motivated the challenged stop.

The reasoning of Whren begs the obvious question of why the Court considers police reliance on race when making a traffic stop reasonable conduct under the Fourth Amendment. Although the Court reaffirmed its unwillingness to consider subjective motives in Fourth Amendment analysis, it mistakenly suggests that the evidence of racial impact connected with pretextual traffic stops falls into a category of "subjective" evidence. On the contrary, evidence of racial decisionmaking by officers often rests on solid empirical data and indicates much more than the subjective bias of a few rogue officers. Not only does evidence of racial impact linked to pretextual traffic stops indicate arbitrary and discriminatory seizures, but much of the evidence produced to date is far more objective than other types of evidence the Court has sanctioned when upholding police detentions of persons and effects.

Those familiar with law enforcement methods know that police target black and Hispanic motorists for pretextual traffic stops. The police in Avon, Connecticut, a predominately white suburb near the City of Hartford, for example, have been conducting pretextual stops for years. They even have a name for the practice: the "Barkhamsted Express." They use the expression "to refer to carloads of black and Puerto Rican people traveling through town in the summer from Hartford to the Barkhamsted reservoir." The town's attorney wrote in a report that the supervising sergeant of the Avon Police Department instructed his officers to find a reason to stop black and Hispanic motorists driving through Avon. The sergeant thought it proper to scrutinize and run license plate checks on motorists who "do not appear to have business in Avon." He also believed that "the presence of a large number of blacks or Hispanics in a vehicle would fall within the category of people 'not appearing to have business in Avon.' "

After public disclosure of the sergeant's instructions, other officers and former officers in the department admitted that "top Avon police officials have long tolerated a practice of targeting blacks and Hispanics" who drive through Avon. It was alleged that nearly one-third of the department's officers targeted minority drivers, although no formal policy ordered the practice. A subsequent internal police investigation also showed that the department accepted the practice of pretextual traffic stops of minority drivers. This later report stated that higher-ranking officers told patrol officers to stop vehicles containing minorities to " 'see what they are up to out here.' "

The practice of targeting black and Hispanic motorists is not confined to police departments that patrol white suburbs surrounding America's urban centers. Police also employ the tactic on the interstate highways. Two recent court cases, from New Jersey and Maryland, indicate that state troopers target black motorists for pretextual traffic stops on America's busiest highway, Interstate 95.

In the late 1980s, New Jersey criminal defense lawyers and civil rights advocates often complained that state troopers targeted black motorists on the New Jersey Turnpike for pretextual traffic stops to launch unwarranted narcotics investigations. State officials denied the charges and critics of the state police could not produce a "smoking gun" to substantiate their charges. But in 1990, the newly appointed State Police Superintendent made an astonishing statement: He conceded that " 'a very small number' " of troopers engaged in racially discriminatory stops. Then, in April 1993, a Superior Court judge found that twenty troopers may have arrested motorists based on racial considerations. A few months later, after urging the dismissal of 618 narcotics cases, the Middlesex County Prosecutor stated: "Twenty particular state troopers may have enforced the law in a racially selective way on their own initiative."

Complaints of race-based traffic enforcement continued, but no empirical evidence supported the allegations until *New Jersey v. Pedro Soto*. In Pedro Soto, decided three months before Whren, the black defendants were stopped by troopers on the southern portion of the Turnpike. The trial court judge ruled that the defendants proved that state troopers seized black motorists for traffic stops because of their race. The trial judge found that the defendants had established a prima facie case of selective enforcement which the State failed to rebut. The trial judge required the suppression of all contraband and evidence seized by troopers patrolling the exits in question for a three-year period.

The trial judge based his conclusion on a voluminous record. The prosecution and defense agreed upon a database of 3,060 traffic stops, which were broken down according to the race of the occupants of the vehicles. Relying on testimony and statistical surveys provided by experts for the defense, the trial judge noted the following statistical data for traffic patterns on the Turnpike between exits 1 and 7A: A count of the traffic indicated that 13.5% of the automobiles carried a black occupant. A count of the traffic surveyed for speeding indicated that 98.1% of the vehicles on the road exceeded the speed limit. Fifteen percent of the speeding vehicles had a black occupant. Fifteen percent of the automobiles that both violated the speed limit and committed some other moving violation also had a black occupant.

Comparing these percentages with the data on racially identified stops, the trial judge found that while automobiles with black occupants represented only 15% of the motorists who violated the speeding laws, 46.2% of the race identified stops between exits 1 and 3 were of black motorists. Using the data for the entire portion of the Turnpike patrolled by the troopers of the Moorestown Station, the trial judge concluded that 35.6% of the race identified stops between exits 1 and 7A involved vehicles with black occupants. The trial judge did not dispute the defense expert's opinion that "it is highly unlikely such statistics could have occurred randomly or by chance."

The trial judge also took note of another defense survey designed to measure the discretion of troopers when issuing traffic tickets. The database for this survey contained 533 racially identified tickets issued by three different trooper units. The "Radar Unit" concentrated on speeding vehicles "using a radar van and chase cars and exercised limited discretion regarding which vehicles to stop." The "Tactical Patrol Unit" focused on "traffic problems at specific locations and exercised somewhat more discretion as regards which vehicles to stop." Troopers of the "Patrol Unit" were responsible for providing general law enforcement and exercised "by far the most discretion among the three units."

The statistical study of race identified traffic tickets indicated the following:

> 18% of the tickets issued by the Radar Unit were to blacks, 23.8% of the tickets issued by the [Tactical Unit] were to blacks while 34.2% of the tickets issued by the Patrol Unit were to blacks. South of exit 3, [the defense expert] computed that 19.4% of the tickets issued by the Radar Unit were to blacks, 0.0% of the tickets issued by the [Tactical Unit] were to blacks while 43.8% of the tickets issued by the Patrol Unit were to blacks.

Based on all of this statistical evidence, the trial judge concluded that the defendants established a "de facto policy" by Moorestown Station troopers of "targeting blacks for investigation and arrest between April 1988 and May 1991 both south of exit 3 and between exits 1 and 7A of the Turnpike." According to the trial judge the "statistical disparities and standard deviations revealed are indeed stark."

In the second case demonstrating racial targeting of black motorists for pretextual traffic stops on Interstate 95, *Wilkins v. Maryland State Police*, a state trooper stopped an automobile with four black occupants for speeding in April 1992 in Allegheny County. One of the occupants was Robert Wilkins, a Washington, D.C., criminal defense lawyer, who with his family, was returning to Washington after attending a funeral in Chicago.

The officer requested permission for a consent search, but Wilkins told the trooper that he was an attorney who had a court appearance later in the morning, and that the officer had no right to search the car without arresting the driver. After the request to search was denied, the officer ordered the occupants out of the car and detained them while a drug-sniffing dog was brought to the scene. The canine sniff revealed no narcotics. The officer then permitted Wilkins and his family to leave after more than a half-hour detention. The driver was given a $105 speeding ticket.

Wilkins subsequently filed a class action lawsuit alleging Maryland troopers were illegally stopping black motorists because of their race. During the initial stages of the litigation, a state police intelligence report was discovered which warned troopers in Allegheny County to be alert for "dealers and couriers (traffickers) who are predominately black males and black females ... utilizing Interstate 68." As part of the final settlement, the Maryland State Police were required to provide the federal district court and plaintiffs' counsel with data on state police searches of motorists conducted from January 1995 through September 1996.

In addition to the police data, the plaintiffs' expert designed a statistical plan to determine whether Maryland troopers stop and search black motorists at a rate disproportionate to their numbers on the roads. Part of this plan included a "rolling survey" which determined, inter alia, the racial composition of motorists on Interstate 95 in the counties north of Baltimore, and the racial composition of those motorists on Interstate 95 in the counties north of Baltimore who were violating traffic laws.

The rolling survey indicated that 93.3% of the drivers on Interstate 95 "were violating traffic laws and thus were eligible to be stopped by State Police. Of the violators, 17.5% were black, and 74.7% were white." Data from the Maryland State Police measured the number of motorists stopped and searched by troopers on Interstate 95, north of Baltimore between January 1995 and September 1996. The police data indicated the following: 72.9% of the motorists stopped and searched were black; 80.3% of the motorists searched were black, Hispanic or some other racial minority group; 19.7% of those searched were white.

The police data also measured the number of searches conducted by individual troopers on Interstate 95 north of Baltimore. This data indicated that thirteen troopers conducted 85.4% of the searches. With the exception of one trooper, all of these troopers searched black and other minority motorists at much higher rates than these motorists travel on the highway. The trooper (omitting the trooper who searched black motorists at a rate close to their presence on the roads) with the lowest percentage of black motorist searches still searched black motorists at nearly twice the rate they were found to travel on the highway. The trooper with the highest percentage of black motorist searches searched only black motorists. Ten of the thirteen troopers searched minority motorists at least 80% of the time.

The police data also included information on motorists searched by the police who traveled on roads outside of the northern portion of Interstate 95. This data contrasted significantly with the searches conducted on Interstate 95. For example, while troopers searched white motorists 19.7% of the time on Interstate 95, troopers patrolling outside of Interstate 95 searched white motorists 63.7% of the time. Troopers searched 72.9% of the black motorists on Interstate 95, but only 32% on other state roads. According to the plaintiffs' expert, black motorists "traveling I–95 are searched by state police more than twice as often as are black motorists traveling other Maryland roadways."

Finally, the police data included information on the number of searches that revealed contraband. Troopers found contraband in 28.1% of the cars they searched. The success rate of troopers on Interstate 95 was approximately the same as for searches on other state roads: Troopers found contraband in 29.9% of the cars on Interstate 95 and in 27.1% of the cars on roads outside of Interstate 95. According to the plaintiffs' expert, the police data reported no statewide differences in the success rate of troopers when searching black and white motorists: Troopers recovered contraband from 28.4% of the black motorists searched and from 28.8% of the white motorists searched. Thus, seventy percent of the searches uncovered no contraband. Finally, of all the searches conducted on Interstate 95, troopers arrested the driver in 29.9% of the searches.

According to the plaintiffs' expert, the sum of this information "reveals dramatic and highly statistically significant disparities between the percentage of black Interstate 95 motorists legitimately subject to stop by Maryland State Police and the percentage of black motorists detained and searched by [Maryland State Police] troopers on this roadway." Particularly noteworthy is the difference between the percentage of blacks subject to lawful stops (17.5%) and the percentage of blacks actually stopped and searched (72.9%). The percentage of blacks stopped and searched on Interstate 95 (72.9%) also contrasts significantly with the percentage of blacks stopped and searched on other state roads (32%). Put in simpler terms, "the probability that black Interstate 95 drivers are subjected to searches at so high a rate by chance is less than one in one quintillion. It is wildly significant by statistical measures."

The statistics from Pedro Soto and Wilkins demonstrate that some state troopers in New Jersey and Maryland are seizing black motorists for traffic violations at a rate highly disproportionate to the percentage of black motorists eligible for lawful stops. The evidence in these cases is distinctive only because the statistics were generated in actual court cases. The phenomenon that produced the data is hardly unique, nor has it dissipated. In a report published a year after Whren was decided, the Orlando Sentinel newspaper found that the Criminal Patrol Unit of the Orange County Sheriff's Office is six-and-a-half times more likely to search black motorists on the Florida Turnpike than white motorists.

The Criminal Patrol Unit is a special patrol squad that uses routine traffic stops to search for narcotics. Reviewing records of more than 3,800 stops by the Unit, the Sentinel report noted that black drivers represented 16.3% of the drivers stopped, but constituted more than 50% of the searches and more than 70% of the canine searches. The Sentinel report also found that troopers search black motorists after traffic detentions at a rate substantially higher than white motorists. For example, a traffic count of more than 10,000 vehicles in April and May 1997 found that blacks constituted less than 5% of the motorists on the Florida Turnpike. But receipts from traffic tickets and warning notices for stops from January 1996 through April 1997 reveal that "39.6% of black motorists were searched, compared with 6.2% of white motorists. Motorists listed as Asian, Hispanic or other ethnicities were searched 17.9% of the time." Eighty percent of all the searches uncovered no contraband.

The data on the searches conducted by the supervising sergeant of the Criminal Patrol Unit is particularly revealing. The sergeant "led by example, stopping as many cars as possible [for traffic violations] to increase the odds of finding drugs." He searched only 2% of the white drivers he stopped, but searched 35.5% of the black drivers he stopped. Asked about the disparity, the sergeant stated: "I run through the same thing every time, whether they're black, white or Hispanic. I just don't know." While the sergeant and other officers denied that race influences their decisions to search motorists, the sergeant could not explain why black motorists were six-and-a-half times more likely to be searched than white motorists.

Faced with similar evidence of racial targeting, the supervising sergeant of a special drug patrol squad in western North Carolina expressed indifference to the fact that his drug squad stopped black motorists for traffic violations more frequently than other troopers patrolling the same roads, and that his squad searched black motorists at a higher rate than white motorists after routine traffic stops. The News & Observer newspaper of Raleigh, North Carolina, conducted a study of 1995 patrol records of the Special Emphasis Team of the North Carolina Highway Patrol, whose goal was to interdict narcotics through traffic stops on Interstates 85 and 95. The study found that the Team "charged black male drivers [with traffic offenses] at nearly twice the rate of other troopers working the same roads."

According to the News & Observer report, black male drivers received almost 45% of the traffic citations issued by the Special Emphasis Team, while black male drivers received only 24.2% of the traffic citations issued by other North Carolina troopers patrolling the same highways. The report explained that statistical experts believed that it was " 'wildly improbable' " that two groups of troopers patrolling the same highways would produce such disparate results by chance. The supervising sergeant for the Special Emphasis Team, like other government officials, refused to disclose what criteria troopers use in determining which cars to search. But the News & Observer report determined that in 1995, the "Special Emphasis Team searched about 3,501 vehicles and found drugs in 210—about one in every 17 vehicles searched." According to the sergeant, his squad was doing a good job and the success rate was good enough: " 'You may have had 17 cars searched where drugs are only found one time,' he said. 'But that's not to say that that person who didn't have it wasn't involved.' "

While reasonable minds may differ over whether contraband found in only one of every seventeen vehicles searched (a five percent payoff) is worth the cost in constitutional liberty and privacy that is imposed by these intrusions, the above statistics on traffic stops in New Jersey, Maryland, Florida, and North Carolina should raise judicial eyebrows and trigger Fourth Amendment questions concerning the enforcement practices of officers in these jurisdictions. As the official who trained the Orange County drug squad noted, police statistics on traffic stops "should reflect the ratio of people who are passing through or reside in the area, neighborhood or on the highway."

In the constitutional context of equal protection, similar statistical evidence has failed to prove that a particular state actor or group of actors acted with a specific intent to discriminate. The same might be said about these statistics: While they indicate substantial racial disparities in the percentage of black motorists that troopers stop and search, the statistics do not prove that any particular officer discriminated against any particular black motorist. Like other provisions of the Bill of Rights that have been interpreted to incorporate equality norms as part of the substantive right accorded by the provision, the Fourth Amendment right against unreasonable searches and seizures is sufficiently important and spacious enough to include a concern with equality. Further, the history and purpose of the Fourth Amendment provide ample justification for embracing equality norms when deciding the reasonableness of an intrusion. At its core, the Amendment is aimed at discretionary police power. Traffic enforcement obviously affords police officers "a good deal of low visibility discretion. In addition they are likely in such situations to be sensitive to social station and other factors that should not bear on the decision." Therefore, where unequal or arbitrary enforcement exists, the protection afforded by the Fourth Amendment is properly directed at such intrusions and "can be seen as another harbinger of the Equal Protection Clause, concerned with avoiding indefensible inequities in treatment." Moreover, because these statistics do not show actual racial discrimination in a particular case does not render them constitutionally worthless. On the contrary, the statistics, considered as a whole, provide concrete evidence that state police officers are targeting black motorists for unwarranted narcotics investigations under the guise of traffic enforcement. The statistics indicate large-scale, arbitrary, and biased police seizures that implicate essential Fourth Amendment protections.

The statistical disparities discussed above cannot be explained away by claiming that blacks are worse drivers than whites, simply because there is no evidence that blacks as a group drive differently from whites. When statistical surveys indicate the type and degree of racial disparities shown above, courts should, at the very least, require state officials to provide race-neutral explanations for the statistics. When officials cannot explain the disparities, then the statistics offer conclusive evidence that race matters in predicting which types of motorists are more likely to be stopped for traffic offenses, and which vehicles will probably be searched during such stops. Under this model, if the State is unable to rebut the statistical proof that race matters in making traffic stops, the defense has established a Fourth Amendment violation notwithstanding probable cause for a particular traffic stop.

Nor should this statistical evidence be dismissed because the Whren Court stated that the subjective motives of an officer will not undermine "objectively justifiable behavior under the Fourth Amendment." The statistical data proffered in Pedro Soto and Wilkins, and uncovered in Orange County, Florida, and North Carolina does not purport to measure the subjective motives of officers. On the contrary, this evidence depicts the racial composition of motorists eligible for traffic stops, and describes which motorists are actually stopped and searched by the police, regardless of the subjective bias or motives of individual officers. This empirical data provides the type of specific and articulable evidence that the Court traditionally looks for in Fourth Amendment cases. Moreover, the statistical evidence developed in these cases and obtained from police records is more probative than other evidence the Court has sanctioned when judging the reasonableness of investigative detentions and searches. * * *

Ultimately, the Whren Court casually sanctioned the "costs" imposed on black motorists by pretextual stops because of its unwillingness to perform a balancing analysis for an "exceedingly important issue regarding a pervasive law enforcement practice" which has caused consternation among large segments of the minority community. Perhaps, if such a balancing analysis had been performed, the Court might have still ruled in favor of the government, albeit under a different rationale. Alternatively, a balancing analysis that actually weighed the costs and benefits associated with race-based pretextual traffic stops might have prompted the Court to conclude that such seizures are "unreasonable," despite the existence of probable cause for a traffic stop. The Whren Court, however, found the burden of pretextual stops on black motorists so insignificant that it saw no reason to perform any balancing analysis. The Court's performance and judgment on this point is a perfect illustration of why many blacks feel like second-class citizens in America's judicial system.

* * *

Putting aside the Court's prior cases acknowledging that race matters in the adjudication of search and seizure law, Whren was wrong to segregate racial concerns and Fourth Amendment values for other reasons. The model of the Fourth Amendment envisioned by the Whren Court provides only procedural protection for the individual. Under Whren, the Amendment protects a motorist from unwarranted discretionary seizures provided there is no probable cause to believe that he has committed a traffic offense. Once probable cause exists, Fourth Amendment protection terminates and the police are free to conduct a seizure at their whim.

This constitutional interpretation is wrong because it overlooks that the Fourth Amendment provides substantive, as well as procedural, protection. In the context of traffic stops, the substantive protection afforded by the Amendment requires the judiciary to consider the real world of law enforcement and to reconcile that reality with a meaningful right to be free from unreasonable seizures. When viewed this way, the analysis of Whren is more than "quite disappointing." The opinion is spurious because it disregards, or at best is indifferent to, police discretion, police perjury, and the mutual distrust between blacks and the police—issues intertwined with the enforcement of traffic stops.

The constitutional liberty of motorists to drive the nation's highways cannot be confined to the procedural right announced in Whren. Under Whren, if the police have probable cause that any motorist has committed a traffic offense, a routine traffic stop is per se permissible under the Fourth Amendment. This interpretation, one could argue, is not only consistent with constitutional text and history, but highly pragmatic because it eases the burden of judges faced with claims of pretextual behavior. This reasoning, however, ignores the substantial discretion officers possess in deciding which vehicles to stop for the myriad of traffic offenses they observe daily.

The Court, however, responds that probable cause of a traffic violation sufficiently checks police discretion. This answer is illusory. Probable cause of a traffic offense not only fails to diminish the discretion possessed by officers, but may actually facilitate arbitrary seizures. If 98.1% of the drivers on a section of the New Jersey Turnpike are committing a traffic offense, and 15% percent of those violators are black motorists, but 46% of the stops by state troopers on that section of the Turnpike are of black motorists and there is not a race-neutral explanation for the disparity, then probable cause is not acting as a check on police discretion.

If 93.3% of the drivers on a portion of Interstate 95 in Maryland are violating the traffic laws, and only 17.5% of those violators are black motorists, but 72.9% of the vehicles stopped and searched by state troopers are driven by black motorists and the head of the state police defends this disparity by noting that traffic stops are made on a case-by-case judgment based on "intelligence information" that he will not reveal to the public, then probable cause is not acting as a check on police discretion. Similarly, if black men account for 45% of the traffic citations issued by a special drug patrol in western North Carolina that uses traffic stops as a means to interdict narcotics, but black men received only 24.2% of the traffic citations issued by other officers patrolling the same highways, and the commander of the special drug patrol cannot provide a race-neutral explanation for the disparity of black men stopped by the special patrol, then probable cause is not acting as a check on police discretion. Faced with this evidence, it is easy to see that when police target minority motorists for pretextual traffic stops, probable cause is an insufficient check against unreasonable seizures. Rather than protect motorists, in this context, probable cause acts as a lever to initiate an arbitrary seizure, and then insulates the decision from judicial review.

Wren's "procedural" model of the Fourth Amendment does not curtail the enormous discretion officers possess in deciding which motorists to stop. And the Court's sarcastic response to this logic only adds insult to the constitutional injury suffered by black and Hispanic motorists:

We are aware of no principle that would allow us to decide at what point a code of law becomes so expansive and so commonly violated that infraction itself can no longer be the ordinary measure of the lawfulness of enforcement. And even if we could identify such exorbitant codes, we do not know by what standard (or what right) we would decide ... which particular provisions are sufficiently important to merit enforcement.

As the Court well knows, the complaint of black motorists is not the expansiveness of the traffic code itself, but the arbitrary and discriminatory seizures effectuated under the code by police. Nor is there an absence of legal "principle" to handle this symptom of discretionary and arbitrary power. The principle of preventing discretionary enforcement of the law has been asserted in other constitutional contexts and fits nicely with the purpose of the Fourth Amendment to check police power. Justice Robert Jackson explained why the judiciary must remain alert to official abuses under the guise of discretionary authority:

Nothing opens the door to arbitrary action so effectively as to allow government officials to pick and choose only a few to whom they will apply legislation and thus to escape the political retribution that might be visited upon them if larger numbers were affected. Courts can take no better measure to assure that laws will be just than to require that laws be equal in operation.

Justice Jackson's logic also extends to the power of police officers who enforce the traffic laws. The problem in Wren and other pretextual stop cases is not deciding "at what point a code of law becomes so expansive and so commonly violated that infraction itself can no longer be the ordinary measure of the lawfulness of enforcement." Rather, the problem is deciding whether officers jeopardize Fourth Amendment norms when they conduct seizures under a traffic code in a manner that brazenly deviates from normal procedures or wildly defies statistical expectations. As Professor Davis has already noted, the police can execute arbitrary seizures even under an otherwise reasonable and neutral law: "If the police enforce a statute against one out of a hundred known violators, and no one can know in advance which one will be selected or why, does not the system of enforcement encourage arbitrariness and discrimination, and is it not therefore unconstitutional?" Finally, the Court will not have to search in vain to determine which provisions of the traffic code are "sufficiently important to merit enforcement." Where police discretion produces arbitrary seizures under a facially valid provision, the solution is not to invalidate the particular provision of the code, but to nullify the police conduct itself.

The discretionary power of officers to effectuate arbitrary seizures under the traffic laws is just one tool available to police to deny black and Hispanic motorists their substantive rights under the Fourth Amendment. Police often commit perjury to achieve the same end. While the practice of police perjury may not be as old as police targeting of blacks for disproportionate search and seizure, it often works hand in glove with police intrusions that have a disparate impact on minority persons.

The Mollen Commission, impaneled to study police corruption in New York City, has documented the linkage between police perjury and police misconduct. The Commission did not mince words in describing the extent of police perjury it found:

As with other forms of corruption, it is impossible to gauge the full extent of police falsifications. Our investigation indicated, however, that this is probably the most common form of police corruption facing the criminal justice system, particularly in connection with arrests for possession of narcotics and guns. Several officers also told us that the practice of police falsification in connection with such arrests is so common in certain precincts that it has spawned its own word: "testilying."

The Commission described the typical forms of perjury, the motivations for it, and the failure to stop it by supervisory and prosecutorial officials in blunt terms:

When the stop or search [of a vehicle] was unlawful, officers falsified their statements about the arrest to cover for the unlawful acts. Fabricating a traffic violation or claiming to see contraband in plain view was a commonly used pretext—which was virtually never questioned by supervisory officers. In one score from a car, for example, the records indicate that the officers fabricated a story for the District Attorney's Office about a car running a red light, and that they then observed the butt of a gun in plain view.

The Commission continued:

What breeds this tolerance is a deep-rooted perception among many officers of all ranks within the Department that nothing is really wrong with compromising facts to fight crime in the real world. . . . As one dedicated officer put it, police officers often view falsification as, to use his words, "doing God's work"—doing whatever it takes to get a suspected criminal off the streets. This attitude is so entrenched, especially in high-crime precincts, that when investigators confronted one recently arrested officer with evidence of perjury, he asked in disbelief, "What's wrong with that? They're guilty." . . .

Several former and current prosecutors acknowledged—"off the record"—that perjury and falsifications are serious problems in law enforcement that, though not condoned, are ignored. The form this tolerance takes, however, is subtle which makes accountability in this area especially difficult. . . . A story that sounds suspicious to the trained ear; patterns of coincidences that are possible, but highly unlikely; inconsistencies that could be explained, but sound doubtful. In short, the tolerance the criminal justice system exhibits takes the form of a lesser level of scrutiny when it comes to police officers' testimony. Fewer questions are asked; weaker explanations are accepted.

One need not accept that perjury is a pervasive problem in every police department to recognize that perjury (or the potential for perjury) may play a central role in how pretextual traffic stops are carried out. When narcotics officers and their supervisors admit to stopping as many cars as possible under the guise of traffic stops to investigate drug trafficking, the possibilities and temptation to lie about a motorist's driving skills are manifest. When patrol officers know that higher-ranking officers tolerate and sometimes encourage targeting minority motorists, but frown upon the practice when publicly disclosed, the incentive for the police to falsely claim that a black motorist was not wearing his seatbelt or failed to signal a turn is substantial. When subjective traffic violations—like driving unreasonably slowly or not paying full attention to driving—can be falsely lodged against a motorist and the officer knows that his testimony is unlikely to be contradicted by a neutral source, the chances for perjury increase. Finally, when actual police perjury is captured on film, showing a Louisiana officer stopping a motorist for "improper lane change," and research shows that this officer has issued hundreds of other traffic tickets for the same violation and minority drivers are the overwhelming targets of these traffic stops, then police perjury is no longer an isolated phenomenon, but part and parcel of the process used to deny black motorists their substantive rights under the Fourth Amendment.

Despite these realities, the Court rarely, if ever, considers police perjury when resolving Fourth Amendment cases. Evidently, the Court believes that police perjury (or the potential for perjury) is not a problem and has no bearing on the meaning of the Fourth Amendment.

This type of thinking is misplaced for several reasons. To begin with, officers do routinely lie about searches and seizures. The Court's refusal to acknowledge police perjury (or the potential for perjury) in a case like Whren is particularly unfortunate since "motivations to falsify are often present in narcotics enforcement units, especially to justify unlawful searches or arrests." Second, successful police perjury "can defeat any constitutional rule." By deciding Fourth Amendment cases without accounting for the potential for police perjury, judges appear naive and Fourth Amendment rules take on a "make-believe" quality to the police and the public. In the end, because police can lie without fear of the consequences and the public is aware of this fact, nobody will take the Fourth Amendment seriously.

Furthermore, police perjury is often difficult to detect at first glance. Trial judges must "decide cases one at a time, so the police almost always win the swearing contest" between officer and defendant. Police perjury becomes evident when "one stands back from the particular case and looks at a series of cases. It then becomes apparent that policemen are committing perjury at least in some of them, and perhaps in nearly all of them." When the difficulty of proving police falsehoods in a particular case is combined with the strong incentives influencing a trial judge to accept the police version of the facts, the chances of a trial judge dismissing a case or suppressing evidence because of police perjury are remote. Because of these problems and incentives confronting trial judges, appellate courts are more likely to discern police perjury and are better positioned to construct Fourth Amendment standards that account for the possibility or likelihood of police perjury in the future. Nevertheless, appellate courts rarely discuss police perjury when adjudicating Fourth Amendment cases.

These realities suggest that police perjury is a legitimate (but neglected) concern of judges in the adjudication of Fourth Amendment cases. But there is an additional reason why police perjury should be a factor in a case like Whren. When officers target minority motorists for traffic stops to initiate unwarrated [sic] narcotics investigations, falsification is more easily committed by the police and accepted by judges. When the discovery of narcotics is the goal, the catalysts for police perjury increase.

[F]alsifications are most prevalent in high-crime precincts [in New York City] where opportunities for narcotics and gun arrests abound. In such precincts, the prevalence of open criminal activity is high and the utility of an illegal search or arrest is perceived as great. Officers-often correctly-believe that if they search a particular person, or enter an apartment without a warrant, they will find drugs or guns. Frustrated by what they perceive to be unrealistic rules of law and by their own inability to stem the crime in their precincts through legal means, officers take the law into their own hands. And police falsification is the result.

New York City is not the only place where police perjury and falsehoods facilitated illegal searches and seizures. In Philadelphia, operating under the pretense of a war on drugs, individual police officers flagrantly violated the rights of black residents and lied about their actions without fear of retribution. "A handful of officers conducted a virtual reign of terror in poor black neighborhoods for years, stopping suspects at will, stealing money, searching homes with phony warrants, and sometimes even planting drugs" on innocent persons. As one elderly resident of North Philadelphia put it:

"Man, this stuff has been going on for years in North Philadelphia. . . . I can remember it all the way into the Sixties. Cops stop anybody they want, do whatever they want, whenever they want. They beat people up and lock people up. It [sic] they don't have evidence, they make up evidence. And when you go to court, who the judge and jury going to believe? Some nigger or the policeman?"

The same police perspectives and law enforcement interests that induce police perjury in the high-crime neighborhoods of New York and Philadelphia also exist on the highways patrolled by officers responsible for interdicting illegal drugs. Many officers see nothing wrong with targeting innocent minority drivers for traffic stops to intercept narcotics because they believe (or are told) that blacks and Hispanics dominate narcotics trafficking and other criminal conduct. Officers also believe that if they stop and search enough cars they will eventually find drugs. Finally, from a police perspective, the benefit of catching a guilty person justifies the perjury. An officer may falsely assert that she saw drugs in plain view, or add a fact to create probable cause or to validate a consent search—particularly where she perceives that the judiciary has imposed unrealistic barriers to the efforts to snare drug traffickers.

All of this suggests that perjury (or the potential for perjury) is a real problem with pretextual traffic stops, particularly when minority motorists are involved. At a minimum, judges should incorporate the likelihood of perjury into their deliberations when adjudicating Fourth Amendment claims in this context. Otherwise, pretextual traffic stops will continue, immunized by an "objective" analysis that leaves unnoticed and unaccountable the realities of the street. This state of affairs is unfortunate because the "Fourth Amendment operates most of the time not in the rarefied world of legal theory, but in the gritty reality of the thousands of encounters each day between citizens and the armed representatives of government."

A final aspect of police targeting minority motorists for pretextual traffic stops merits judicial attention: the distrust and loathing of the police engendered among some blacks by this practice. Blacks correctly see pretextual traffic stops as another sign that police officers view blacks, particularly black males, as criminals who deserve singular scrutiny and treatment as second-class citizens.

Selecting minority motorists for pretextual traffic stops is a predictable phenomenon in American culture. When police officers either believe or are taught that black and Hispanic motorists are the "mules" who transport illegal narcotics across the nation's highways, one naturally expects disproportionate stops of minority motorists. This anticipation, however, does not remove the resulting insult and harm. Indeed, these seizures provoke an attitude of distrust of the police that was prevalent among blacks thirty years ago when the Court sanctioned the practice of stop and frisk notwithstanding the ill effects that the intrusion engendered among blacks.

In Terry, the amicus brief of the NAACP Legal Defense and Educational Fund provided the Court with an argument which depicted the realities that blacks confront during police encounters and expressed a different perspective on stop and frisk tactics. Emphasizing that the Court should not determine the issue of stop and frisk in a manner oblivious to race, the brief pointed to "the obvious, unhappy fact that the policeman today is the object of widespread and intense hatred in our inner cities" because of aggressive patrol practices used against blacks. The brief also called attention to the different ways that blacks and the police perceive each other. Blacks, more so than whites, had negative opinions about police courtesy, performance, and honesty. Inner city black males viewed officers as brutal and sadistic individuals. Similarly, according to the brief:

Police attitudes toward working class Negro youths and young adults are often based on the concept of the Negro as a savage, or animal, or some being outside of the human species. Therefore, the police expect behavior from Negroes in accordance with this concept.... Because of the police officer's conception of the Negro male, he frequently feels that most Negroes are dangerous and need to be dealt with as an enemy even in the absence of visible criminal behavior.

These "complementary attitudes result in a vicious circle of behavior which serves to confirm the image which Negro males and police officers hold of each other." Finally, the brief cautioned the Court not to be swayed by "the familiar inflated claims for stop and frisk as tools of law and order," without also considering the consequences engendered by the intrusion:

Whatever its conveniences and benefits to a narrow view of law-enforcement, stop and frisk carries with it an intense danger of inciting destructive community conflict. To arm the police with an inherently vague and standardless power to detain and search, especially where that power cannot effectively be regulated, contributes to the belief which many Negroes undeniably have that police suspicion is mainly suspicion of them, and police oppression their main lot in life.

Today, there are troubling parallels to the atmosphere that existed when Terry was decided. Despite impressive reductions in the crime rate in many urban areas, "many blacks have come to see the police as just another gang." From Los Angeles to Philadelphia, blue ribbon commissions, the press, and scholars continue to document the immense distrust that minority groups feel towards the police. In many places, minorities have good reason for their misgivings. For example, New York City officials like to brag that they have the nation's most professional and well-trained police force. The force has been run by two black police commissioners in the last fifteen years, but deadly force, brutality, and abuse of power by officers remains a problem in minority communities. The human rights group Amnesty International recently released a report noting that:

> the most serious complaints [of police misconduct and brutality in New York City] tended to be concentrated in high crime precincts and in precincts with large minority populations. More than two-thirds of the victims in the cases examined were African–American or Latino and most, though not all, of the officers involved were white. Nearly all of the victims in the cases of deaths in custody (including shootings) reviewed by Amnesty International were members of racial minorities.

Police contempt for minority citizens and its nexus to police abuse, although hard to quantify empirically, remains a problem. Six years ago, the Christopher Commission found, in the wake of the Rodney King beating, significant evidence of police bias against minority citizens. This conclusion was bolstered, in part, by a Los Angeles Police Department survey of 960 officers noting "that approximately one-quarter (24.5%) of 650 officers responding agreed that 'racial bias (prejudice) on the part of officers toward minority citizens currently exists and contributes to a negative interaction between police and the community.'" More recently, criminologist Robert E. Worden, after surveying the scholarship on the causes of police brutality, noted that a suspect's race "has significant effects on the use of force" by police officers. According to Worden, the fact that "officers are more likely to use even reasonable force against blacks might suggest that officers are, on average, more likely to adopt a punitive or coercive approach to black suspects than they are to white suspects."

Adopting a more cautious stance than Professor Worden, Dean Hubert G. Locke finds that many empirical studies are ambiguous on the connection between race and police misconduct. "Researchers do not know or cannot assert much, with empirical reliability, about whether there are racial reasons for police behavior because other possible explanations cannot be ruled out." Dean Locke concedes, however, that the "evidence is indisputable that, compared to general population distributions, persons of color are disproportionately represented among those subjected to police use of force where the discharge of a firearm is involved." These findings confirm the anecdotal testimony that has filled the nation's newspapers and radio and television news programs for the last decade. Blacks from all walks of society perceive the police as their antagonist.

To this list of grievances, blacks can now add pretextual traffic stops which, according to the Court, raise no Fourth Amendment concerns. Of course, some may doubt the legitimacy of blacks' protest against pretextual stops. After all, if a black motorist commits a traffic offense, what's wrong with a police stop? And if the police can use the stop to piggyback a drug investigation, all the better.

This type of thinking is wrong. Police do not target minority motorists for traffic stops because they are poor drivers. Nor does police scrutiny occur by chance. Police target blacks and Hispanics because the officers believe that blacks and Hispanics are involved with narcotics. Large percentages of blacks and Hispanics are stopped, interrogated, and searched because the police do not respect their Fourth Amendment rights. Put simply, the police are encouraged to do all of this because minority persons, particularly black men, are deemed second-class citizens in the eyes of law enforcement.

Three hundred years ago colonial officials ordered the arbitrary seizure of both slave and free blacks for "gadding abroad" the streets. Before the Constitution recognized blacks as citizens of the United States, protest against arbitrary intrusions was futile because blacks "had no rights which the white man was bound to respect." For black motorists, things have not changed significantly. Police are free to target blacks for traffic seizures and use those intrusions to initiate unwarranted criminal investigations.

If the Supreme Court is serious about protecting the Fourth Amendment interests of minority motorists, it should reverse *Whren v. United States* forthwith. Realistically, of course, this will not happen. State judges, however, need not tolerate the status quo on the nation's highways and roads. Ideally, state judges should rule that pretextual stops violate the search and seizure provisions of their state constitutions.

At a minimum, state courts should allow a criminal defendant the opportunity to show that the facts surrounding his traffic stop raise an inference of a race-based seizure. This would then require the prosecution to provide a race-neutral explanation other than the fact that a traffic offense was observed.

Until this is done, it will be "reasonable," according to the Supreme Court, for the police to target minority motorists for pretextual stops. *Whren* assures that black and Hispanic motorists will continue to be treated as second-class citizens on the nation's roads—subject to seizure, interrogation, and search at the whim of a police officer. If *Whren* is a positive result for some because it adds another weapon to the police arsenal in the war on drugs, it only confirms what blacks have always known about police power. "With reason, African–Americans tend to grow up believing that the law is the enemy, because those who are sworn to uphold the law so often enforce it in a biased way."

Notes and Questions

1. What do you make of Professor Maclin's statistical data? Does it impact your analysis of *Whren*? Should it? How does that data impact the argument that "if you haven't done anything wrong, you don't have anything to worry about?"

2. Professor Maclin is talking about police discretion, as compared with prosecutorial discretion. Is there any reason to believe that unconscious racism may play a role here as well? See Devon W. Carbado,(E) Racing the Fourth Amendment, 100 Mich. L. Rev. 946, 1018–20 (2002) (describing strategies to be used when people of color interact with the police in a racial profiling context.)

3. How does the historical context of the relationship between African–Americans and the police impact your analysis? *See also* Tracey Maclin, *Terry and Race: Terry v. Ohio's Fourth Amendment Legacy: Black Men and Police Discretion*, 72 St. John's L. Rev. 1271, 1279–1287 (1998). Law enforcement agencies typically treat race as the principal component in suspect descriptions. *See* R. Richard Banks, *Race-Based Suspect Selection and Colorblind Equal Protection Doctrine and Discourse*, 48 UCLA L. Rev. 1075 (2001).

4. Professor Frank Cooper argues that "law enforcement's call for a drug war has influenced the United States Supreme Court to accept racial profiling and limit appellate review of police activity." Frank Rudy Cooper, *The Un–Balanced Fourth Amendment: A Cultural Study of the Drug War, Racial Profiling and Arvizu*, 47 Vill. L. Rev. 851, 852 (2002). *See also* Kenneth B. Nunn, *Race, Crime and the Pool of Surplus Criminality: Or Why the "War on Drugs" was a "War on Blacks,"* 6 J. Gender Race & Just. 381 (2002).

5. Professor Katheryn K. Russell states "[I]n recent years, there has been mounting evidence that Blackness has become an acceptable 'risk factor' for criminal behavior." Katheryn K. Russell, *"Driving While Black": Corollary Phenomena and Collateral Consequences*, 40 B.C. L. Rev. 717, 721 (1999). Professor Russell also describes the phenomenon of "walking while black" "idling while black" and "standing while black." *Id.* at 721–722.

6. Numerous articles have been written about the phenomenon of "driving while black." *See e.g.* Angela J. Davis, *Race, Cops, and Traffic Stops*, 51 U. Miami L. Rev. 425 (1997); David A. Harris, *"Driving While Black" and All Other Traffic Offenses: The Supreme Court and Pretextual Traffic Stops*, 87 J. Crim. L. & Criminology 544 (1997).

7. For additional critiques of *Whren*, *see* David O. Markus, *Whren v. United States: A Pretext to Subvert the Fourth Amendment*, 14 Harv. Blackletter J. 91 (1998); Alberto B. Lopez; *Racial Profiling and Whren: Searching for Objective Evidence of the Fourth Amendment on the Nation's Roads*, 90 Ky. L. J. 75 (2001/2002); Peter A. Lyle, Note: *Racial Profiling and the Fourth Amendment: Applying the Minority Victim Perspective to Ensure Equal Protection Under the Law*, 21 B.C. Third World L. J. 243 (2001).

8. Several authors argue that the drug war is targeted against racial minorities. "Jim Crow is alive and well on American's highways.... Around

the nation Jim Crow exists as a by-product in the 'War on Drugs' spun out of control." William H. Buckman & John Lamberth, *U.S. Drug Laws: The New Jim Crow on the Interstate*, 10 Temp. Pol. & Civ. Rts. L. Rev. 387 (2001).

9. For a poignant account of a "walking while black" encounter with the police, *see* Paul Butler, "Walking While Black" Encounters with the Police on my Street, Legal Times, Nov. 10, 1997. Paul Butler ironically is an African–American Professor of Law whose scholarly work is in the area of criminal law and procedure. He has argued in support of jury nullification for non-violent crime. *See* Paul Butler, *Racially Based Jury Nullification: Black Power in the Criminal Justice System*, 105 Yale L. J. 677 (1995). Jury nullification occurs when a jury decides to acquit an individual even though the prosecution has proven its case. As Professor Butler states "[m]y thesis is that, for pragmatic and political reasons, the black community is better off when some nonviolent lawbreakers remain in the community rather than go to prison. The decision as to what kind of conduct by African–Americans ought to be punished is better made by African–Americans themselves, based on the costs and benefits to their community, than by the traditional criminal justice process, which is controlled by white lawmakers and white law enforcers." *Id*. at 679.

10. Is "walking while white" a crime? A Roanoke, Virginia judge dismissed a cocaine charge where a man was stopped and searched by police because he was a "suspicious white male" walking in a predominantly black neighborhood late at night. Laurence Hammack, *Drug Charge Dismissed; Judge Rules Search Illegal*, The Roanoke Times, PA1 (October 2, 1998).

11. Judge Damon Keith, an African–American judge, in a dissenting opinion described the state of affairs even before *Whren* as a "system where one set of traffic regulations exist for African–Americans, like myself, and a more lenient set exists for white Americans. For the same minor traffic infraction, a white motorist remains an unimpeded violator, whereas an African–American motorist automatically becomes a suspected felon and menace to society." *U.S. v. Harvey*, 16 F.3d 109, 114 (6th Cir.1994). Do you agree? Have you ever been stopped by the police? Has anyone you've known been stopped by the police?

12. Black women have also been targeted by the criminal justice system. *See* Dorothy E. Roberts, *Punishing Drug Addicts Who Have Babies: Women of Color, Equality, and the Right of Privacy*, 104 Harv. L. Rev. 1419 (1991) ("A growing number of women across the country have been charged with criminal offenses after giving birth to babies who test positive for drugs. The majority of these women ... are poor and Black.... Such government intrusion is particularly harsh for poor women of color. They are the least likely to obtain adequate prenatal care, the most vulnerable to government monitoring, and the least able to conform to the white, middle-class standard of motherhood." *Id*. at 1420–1422). If these women were alcoholics instead of drug addicts, what would the outcome be?

SECTION 3. DRIVING WHILE BLACK ... PERFECTLY

U.S. v. JONES

242 F.3d 215 (4th Cir. 2001).

MICHAEL, CIRCUIT JUDGE:

Rodney Jones appeals his conviction for possessing with intent to distribute cocaine base (crack cocaine) in violation of 21 U.S.C. § 841. Jones moved to suppress the crack on the ground that it was discovered by the police during the illegal stop of an automobile occupied by Jones and three other African American men. The race of the occupants prompted a city police officer to make the stop shortly after police had been unable to corroborate an anonymous tip that "several black males" were causing a disturbance at a certain intersection. The district court denied the suppression motion and admitted the crack cocaine into evidence. Because the tip proved to be unreliable and the driver of the car was obeying the rules of the road, the stop violated the Fourth Amendment, and the crack should have been excluded from Jones's trial. We therefore vacate his conviction.

I.

Union, South Carolina, is a city of about 10,000 people, nearly forty percent of whom are African American. Sometime before 1:13 a.m. on March 17, 1998, the police dispatcher in Union received an anonymous 911 call. The caller complained that "several black males" were drinking beer and causing a disturbance in the roadway at the intersection of Lybrand and Pond Streets. Aside from mentioning their race, the caller did not provide any physical description of the men and did not say whether they were in or near a vehicle. The dispatcher did not intrude upon the caller's anonymity or press the caller for any details. At 1:13 a.m., acting on this anonymous tip, the dispatcher radioed City Officer Rickey Mallet, asking that Mallet investigate the reported disturbance. Officer Claude Hart, who happened to be near the intersection in a separate police car, also responded to the dispatcher's call. Each officer approached the intersection from a different direction. When they arrived at the scene, the officers did not find anyone or see any signs of a disturbance. After scouting the neighborhood in and around the intersection, the officers confirmed that the area was clear.

The officers then departed, and after Officer Hart had traveled about two-tenths of a mile, he met a white Chevrolet coming into the area. The driver of the car was not committing any traffic infractions, and there were no signs of any other violations. Officer Hart noticed, however, that there were four African American men in the Chevrolet. Solely because the earlier call to the dispatcher had mentioned several black males, Hart decided to stop the car. Hart quickly made a U-turn, switched on his blue lights, and the driver of the Chevrolet pulled over and stopped. Officer Mallet arrived moments later to assist Hart. Hart went to the driver's window and asked the driver for his license, registration, and insurance information. While Officer Hart was waiting for the documents, he noticed an open bottle of beer at the feet of the passenger in the front seat. After the driver, Jamel Good, produced his documents, Officer Hart asked Good to step out of the car, and he complied. Hart then mentioned the open bottle of beer and obtained Good's consent to search the car. Hart ordered the passengers, including the front-seat passenger, Rodney Jones, to get out of the vehicle. Hart then searched the front passenger area and found two open beer bottles. After he recovered the bottles, Hart placed Jones under arrest for violating South Carolina's open container law. *See* S.C. Code Ann. § 61–4–110. While Hart was handcuffing Jones, Officer Mallet patted him down. As he felt the front of Jones's jacket, Mallet heard a "crinkling" sound. Mallet checked the front jacket pocket and found a plastic bag that contained 23.92 grams of crack cocaine, according to subsequent laboratory analysis.

Jones was indicted in April 1998 and charged with possession with intent to distribute crack cocaine. *See* 21 U.S.C. § 841. Jones's first trial ended in a hung jury. At his second trial he moved to suppress the crack cocaine that Officer Mallet discovered on the ground that it was the fruit of an unlawful stop. The district court denied the motion, and the jury returned a guilty verdict. Jones appeals his conviction, challenging only the denial of his suppression motion.

II.

The Fourth Amendment protects "persons" from "unreasonable searches and seizures." U.S. Const. amend. IV. A discretionary automobile stop by the police is a seizure of the person and therefore "must be justified by ... a reasonable suspicion, based on specific and articulable facts, of unlawful conduct." *United States v. Wilson*, 205 F.3d 720, 722–23 (4th Cir. 2000) (quoting *United States v. Hassan El*, 5 F.3d 726, 729 (4th Cir. 1993)). Reasonable suspicion, of course, is "more than an 'inchoate' and unparticularized suspicion or 'hunch' of criminal activity." *Illinois v. Wardlow*, 528 U.S. 119, 120 S.Ct. 673, 676, 145 L.Ed.2d 570 (2000) (quoting *Terry v. Ohio*, 392 U.S. 1, 27, 20 L.Ed.2d 889, 88 S.Ct. 1868 (1968)). In this case, we must determine whether the anonymous tip to 911 together with Officer Hart's observations of the white Chevrolet provided reasonable suspicion to justify his investigative stop of the car.

Recently, in *Florida v. J.L.*, 529 U.S. 266, 146 L.Ed.2d 254, 120 S.Ct. 1375 (2000), the Supreme Court revisited the issue of when an anonymous tip may provide reasonable suspicion for an investigative stop.[1] In J.L. the Court suppressed a handgun that the Miami–Dade Police had

---

1. The district court in this case did not have the benefit of J.L. when it denied   Jones's motion to suppress.

seized from an African American juvenile who was stopped and frisked on the basis of an anonymous tip. The police had received an anonymous telephone tip that a young African American male in a plaid shirt standing at a certain bus stop was carrying a gun. The police went to the bus stop and found three African American males, one of whom was wearing a plaid shirt. Aside from the tip, the police did not have any reason to suspect any of the three men of unlawful activity. The officers did not see a firearm, and the men did not make any moves that were threatening or unusual. One of the officers stepped up to the young man with the plaid shirt, frisked him, and recovered a gun from his pocket. *See id.* at 270, 120 S.Ct. 1375.

The Court held unanimously that the stop and frisk violated the juvenile's Fourth Amendment rights. The Court acknowledged that "there are situations in which an anonymous tip, suitably corroborated, exhibits 'sufficient indicia of reliability to provide reasonable suspicion to make the investigatory stop.' " *Id.* (quoting *Alabama v. White*, 496 U.S. 325, 327, 110 L.Ed.2d 301, 110 S.Ct. 2412 (1990)). The Court nevertheless concluded that this tip lacked the necessary indicia of reliability. According to the Court, the tip "provided no predictive information and therefore left the police without means to test the informant's credibility or knowledge." 529 U.S. at 271, 120 S.Ct. 1375. The police improperly relied on "the bare report of an unknown, unaccountable informant who neither explained how he knew about the gun nor supplied any basis for believing he had inside information about [the juvenile]." *Id.* Although the tip was reliable in the limited sense that it accurately described the juvenile's clothing and location, the Court held that the tip was insufficient to establish reasonable suspicion. The Court noted that reasonable suspicion "requires that a tip be reliable in its assertion of illegality, not just in its tendency to identify a determinate person." *Id.* at 272, 120 S.Ct. 1375. Thus, because the police could not verify the informant's credibility and they had no reason to suspect the juvenile of unlawful behavior apart from the tip, the Court held that the stop was unjustified and that the gun was the fruit of an unlawful search. *See id.* at 274, 120 S.Ct. 1375.[2]

The anonymous tip in this case, like the one in J.L., lacks sufficient indicia of reliability. In fact, the tip here was so barren of detail about the alleged culprits' physical descriptions that it was even less reliable than the deficient tip in J.L. The 911 caller told the Union police dispatcher that several black males were drinking and causing a disturbance at a certain intersection. The caller said nothing else. Specifically, he did not identify himself, did not give his location or vantage point, and did not explain how he knew about the disturbance. The tipster did not say exactly how many men were present, and apart from mentioning their race, gave no information about their appearance. The caller did

---

2. The Court in J.L. was careful to note that the facts of the case did "not require [it] to speculate about the circumstances under which the danger alleged in an anon-ymous tip might be so great as to justify a search even without a showing of reliability." J.L., 529 U.S. at 274, 120 S.Ct. 1375.

not mention whether the men were residents of the neighborhood or outsiders. Finally, he did not say whether the men were in an automobile or whether they had access to one. Union police went to the intersection and saw no one. They undertook an inspection of the immediate area and still found no one and saw no signs that there had been a disturbance. At that point, the anonymous tip was totally uncorroborated. Cf. *United States v. Thompson*, 234 F.3d 725, 729–30 (D.C.Cir. 2000) (holding that stop and frisk was supported by reasonable suspicion because anonymous tip was corroborated when "the police themselves observed [the defendant] engaging in suspicious conduct"); *United States v. Perrin*, 45 F.3d 869, 872 (4th Cir. 1995) (recognizing that an informant's tip can provide the justification for an investigative stop if the information in the tip is sufficiently corroborated).

In this case, the anonymous tip became essentially useless once the police found no one and no illegal activity at the intersection. If the police wished to investigate any further, they were relegated to looking for several African American men, who had not been described or otherwise identified. Indeed, as Officer Hart admitted, when he met the white Chevrolet two-tenths of a mile from the empty intersection, he "saw four black guys ... and stopped them for that." Officer Hart saw no traffic or equipment violations or any suspicious activity. He stopped the car simply because the earlier, uncorroborated tip mentioned several black men. Because Officer Hart had not been able to confirm the 911 "informant's knowledge or credibility," J.L., 529 U.S. at 271, 120 S.Ct. 1375, the tip was not a reliable accusation against the men in the white Chevrolet. In short, the uncorroborated tip and Officer Hart's sighting of four African American men in a car were insufficient to establish reasonable suspicion for a stop. The stop was therefore illegal, and the crack cocaine that Officer Mallet discovered during his search of Jones should have been excluded at trial. Jones's judgment of conviction is therefore vacated, and the case is remanded for any further proceedings that would be consistent with this opinion.

Notes and Questions

1.   What do you think would have been the outcome if the driver had not been obeying the traffic laws? Have you broken any traffic laws lately? What is the likelihood that you could be pulled over by the police?

2.   Does the race of the police officers matter? Would you like to have this information?

3.   Would you expect the arresting officers in the future to be less truthful? What would it take for the officer to find "suspicious activity?" Recall Professor Maclin's description of "testilying," *supra* at 216.

Chapter 6

CRITICAL RACE THEORY AND CRIMINAL LAW AND SENTENCING

This Chapter addresses issues of criminal law and sentencing. As Professor Mari Matsuda writes "[i]deas about crime: what is a crime, who is a criminal, and how we choose to punish and prevent crime–none of our ideas in this regard are developed free from the intellectual poisons of racism, sexism, homophobia, and class oppression." Mari J. Matsuda, *Crime and Affirmative Action*, 1 J. Gender Race & Just. 309, 312 (1998). This Chapter seeks to uncover some of those ideas in the criminal law and sentencing context.

We begin by analyzing the doctrine of self-defense and how the race of the victim often determines its success. We then turn to sentencing issues and examine two cases where courts used different approaches to address the racial bias currently existing in how our traffic and drug laws are written and enforced. (*See* discussion in Chapter 5 *supra*.)

SECTION 1.   CRIMINAL LAW: WHAT CONSTITUTES SELF–DEFENSE?

CYNTHIA KWEI YUNG LEE

Race and Self–Defense: Toward a Normative Conception of Reasonableness,
81 Minn. L. Rev. 367, 369–374, 398–452, 495–499 (1996).

* * *

This Article examines the topic of race and self-defense through the lens of socially constructed stereotypes about Blacks, Asian Americans, and Latinos. Crimes of violence involving claims of self-defense and victims of color represent a microcosm of broader questions concerning race and the criminal justice system. The term "race" is utilized broadly in this Article to include race, ethnicity, and culture, recognizing that race is a shifting concept which means different things to different people. Even though stereotypes based on a person's perceived race may be described more accurately as cultural or ethnic stereotypes, this paper purposely describes these stereotypes, using a race rather than an ethnicity model, as a means of linking the common experiences of African Americans, Asian Americans, and Latinos. The commonality of such experiences may be obscured when certain people of color are treated as a race and others are treated as an ethnicity.

To a large extent, legal scholarship about race and the criminal justice system has focused on how legal decisionmaking by police officers, prosecutors, jurors, judges, and others involved in the criminal justice system might be unduly influenced by the race of the defendant. The discussion has centered around Black and White defendants; other non-White defendants have received little attention. The influence of racial stereotypes about the victim on legal decisionmaking has also received less attention than the influence of racial stereotypes about the defendant.

Racial stereotypes about members of the victim's racial group may influence jurors and other legal decisionmakers in two ways. First, many tend to view individuals who belong to particular racial groups in certain ways because of deeply ingrained racial stereotypes. If the victim belongs to a racial group whose members are stereotyped as dangerous or violent criminals or gang members, jurors may be more likely to perceive actions of the victim as hostile or violent than if the victim belonged to another racial group. Second, members of society tend to value people who are similar to themselves more than those who are different from them. This phenomenon has been described as in-group favoritism and out-group antagonism. If the victim belongs to a racial group whose members have been socially constructed as foreigners or illegal immigrants, such as Asian Americans and Latinos, jurors may subconsciously minimize the harm suffered by the victim and may be more willing to view the defendant's use of force as reasonable than if the victim were perceived to be an "average" American.

Whether racial stereotypes about the victim actually influence verdicts in self-defense cases is difficult to prove empirically. The universe of self-defense cases resulting in acquittals is elusive because the Double Jeopardy Clause of the Fifth Amendment prevents reversal of an acquittal. Acquittals in self-defense cases, like acquittals in other cases, generally are not appealed, and consequently are not reported in the case reporters. Only acquittals in high-publicity cases end up on the printed pages of newspapers and magazines.

Because reasonableness is the touchstone of self-defense jurisprudence, this paper examines the impact of racial stereotypes on the reasonableness requirement in self-defense doctrine in an effort to confront the larger question of how to minimize the influence of racial stereotypes leading to bias in criminal justice decisionmaking. This Article adds to the legal landscape in three ways. First, in examining self-defense doctrine, this Article focuses on substantive criminal law, as opposed to criminal procedure. Most race-based legal scholarship focuses on race and criminal procedure, rather than on race and substantive criminal law. Second, this Article looks at how racial stereotypes about the victim might influence legal decisionmaking, in contrast to the more common focus on the defendant. Finally, discussions about race are often binary, centering on the Black–White dichotomy, while ignoring other non-Whites (i.e., non-Black racial minorities) who also face stigma and racial discrimination in the United States. This Article abandons the Black–White paradigm in favor of a multi-layered examination of how racial stereotyping of African Americans, Asian Americans, and Latinos may influence legal decisionmaking about self-defense. This is neither an exclusively White problem (i.e., Whites are not the only people who are influenced by racial stereotypes about Blacks, Asian Americans, and Latinos) nor an exclusively interracial problem. It includes intraracial crimes, such as Black-on-Black crimes, as well as other color-on-color crimes, such as Asian-on-Black crimes.

* * *

This Part examines ways in which racial stereotypes about the defendant or victim may influence legal decisionmaking. Traditionally, scholars and people in general equated the terms "stereotypes" and "prejudice." Recently, scholars have begun to distinguish the two concepts. Under the current view, "stereotypes" constitute well-learned sets of associations among groups that result in automatic, gut-level responses. Stereotypes are correlational constructs, reflected in statements such as "Blacks are athletic," "Hawaiians are friendly," "Women are emotional." Stereotypes correlate membership in a particular group (e.g., Blacks, Hawaiians, women) with particular traits (e.g., athleticism, friendliness, emotionalism).

"Prejudice," in contrast, is defined as one's set of personal beliefs which may or may not be congruent with the stereotypes one has learned. A person may be either a "high-prejudiced" or a "low-prejudiced" individual. These terms of art regarding degrees of prejudice are defined in relation to stereotypes. If one's personal beliefs about a particular group of people are congruent with the stereotypes about that group, one is considered "high-prejudiced." If one's personal beliefs about a particular group of people are not necessarily congruent with the stereotypes about that group, one is considered "low-prejudiced."

Recognizing the distinction between stereotypes and prejudice is useful because doing so reveals the possibility of disassociating one's automatic stereotype-congruent responses from one's controlled personal beliefs. Making racial stereotypes salient in criminal trials through limiting jury instructions may encourage low-prejudiced jurors (i.e., jurors whose personal beliefs are inconsistent with the stereotype at issue) to decide cases in accordance with their egalitarian-congruent personal beliefs rather than their stereotype-congruent responses.

In self-defense cases, racial stereotypes about either the defendant or the victim can influence the reasonableness determination in different ways. For example, we all tend to associate certain characteristics with particular racial groups. If the defendant or victim belongs to a racial group whose members are perceived as dangerous or violent criminals, jurors may perceive ambiguous actions of the actor to be more hostile or violent than they actually are. Additionally, we tend to emphasize the positive attributes of others who are perceived to be more like ourselves while focusing on the negative traits in people we perceive to be different from us. In general, people tend to value those who are like them, or perceived to be like them, more than others who are perceived to be different. For instance, if the victim belongs to a racial group whose members are associated with foreignness or immigrant status, jurors may subconsciously minimize the harm suffered by the victim and may be more willing to view the defendant's use of force as reasonable than they would otherwise.

Fact finding is a difficult task, even when race is not an issue. First-hand observation is no guarantee that people will reach the same conclusion about the observed events. In criminal cases, jurors do not observe the alleged criminal conduct first hand. Instead, they learn the facts through eye-witness testimony and other circumstantial evidence. Factual disagreement results from the different lenses through which we view the world. One's interpretation of the facts is influenced by one's background and experience. Recent research on cognitive theory suggests that "decision-makers actively construct representations of the trial evidence based on their prior expectations about what constitutes an adequate explanation of the litigated event.... These representations, rather than the original 'raw' evidence, form the basis of the jurors' final decision."

When race is a consideration, fact finding can be even more difficult. Race, to a large extent, is a product of social construction. Our thoughts and beliefs about race are shaped by social influences and personal experiences. To say that race is socially constructed, though, is "not to say that race is a useless idea in talking about American society or responding to social needs." In self-defense cases involving defendants or victims of color, race or, to be more precise, racial stereotypes, may influence our assessment of whether the defendant's use of force against the victim was reasonable. This Part selectively examines only a few of the numerous stereotypes about Blacks, Asian Americans, and Latinos, those which might directly or indirectly influence juror determinations of reasonableness in self-defense cases.

The existence of the Black-as-criminal stereotype, discussed * * *[infra], is supported by social science studies showing that people tend to view the behavior of Blacks as more hostile or aggressive than the same behavior conducted by Whites. Actual cases also illustrate the pervasiveness of this stereotype. The Bernhard Goetz case is used to illustrate how the Black-as-criminal stereotype may have influenced one jury to return a verdict of acquittal in a racially charged case involving a White defendant who claimed he shot at four Black victims in self-defense.

With respect to stereotypes about Asian Americans and Latino/as, there is a striking paucity of social science research on the existence of such stereotypes and the influence such stereotypes might have on jurors. Just as race-based legal scholarship focuses on the Black–White paradigm to the exclusion of other non-Black minorities, the social science research also largely ignores Asian American and Latino/a interests. To fill the void, * * * [I] draw upon actual cases to illustrate how stereotypes about Asian Americans and Latino/as might influence juror perceptions of reasonableness in self-defense cases.

Despite the abolition of slavery, passage of the Civil Rights Act, and other positive changes in the law following the Civil Rights Movement, many African Americans today still suffer from discrimination based on race. Over time, as society has publicly denounced racism, overt racial prejudice appears to have declined. Negative stereotypes of African Americans, however, still persist. One of the stereotypes most often applied to African American males is that they are more dangerous, more prone to violence, and more likely to be criminals or gang members than other members of society. Adeno Addis has aptly observed that crime has "become a metaphor to describe young black men." Although the Black-as-criminal stereotype is mostly a gendered concept that applies to Black men, Black women have also suffered from the perception that they are untrustworthy, criminal, or dangerous.

The Black-as-criminal stereotype may cause people to perceive ambiguously hostile acts (i.e., acts that can be perceived as either violent or nonviolent) as violent when a Black person engages in these acts and non-violent when a non-Black person engages in the same acts. Birt Duncan tested this hypothesis on 104 White undergraduate students at the University of California at Irvine. Subjects observed two people involved in a heated argument which resulted in one shoving the other. Just after the shove, the subjects were asked to rate the behavior of the person who shoved the other person. The subjects were randomly assigned to one of four experimental conditions: Black shover/White victim, White shover/Black victim, Black shover/Black victim, and White shover/White victim.

Duncan found that when the person shoving was a Black person and the person being shoved was White, 75% of the subjects thought the shove constituted "violent" behavior, while only 6% characterized the shove as "playing around." When subjects observed the same events with a White person as the shover and a Black person as the victim, only 17% characterized the White person's shove as "violent," while 42% described the White person's shove as "playing around." Duncan concluded that the threshold for labeling an act as violent was significantly lower when subjects viewed a Black person committing the act than when subjects viewed a White person committing the same act.

In 1980, H. Andrew Sagar and Janet Ward Schofield conducted a similar study, testing whether Black as well as White children perceive ambiguously aggressive behavior by Blacks as more violent or aggressive than similar behavior by Whites. Sagar and Schofield, expanding on Duncan's study which only tested reactions to ambiguously hostile behavior, also examined whether clearly non-aggressive behavior by Blacks also triggered the Black-as-violent stereotype. They found that both Black and White children tended to rate relatively innocuous behavior by Blacks as more threatening than similar behavior by Whites.

These studies suggest that stereotypes about Blacks as violent or dangerous people influence perception and judgment. As Birt Duncan observed,

> If this finding is so readily available for college subjects, its generalizability to other subject populations can be expected to be even more dramatic. One may be tempted to ask, in the real world where violence is a fact of life, have Blacks been the victims of mislabeling or errors in cases where there was a "reasonable doubt" (i.e., low perceptual threshold acts)?

* * *

The Black-as-criminal stereotype is so deeply entrenched in American culture that false claims of Black criminality are made and, in many cases, readily believed. In 1989, Carol Stuart, who was seven months pregnant at the time, was shot and killed in an inner-city neighborhood of Boston, Massachusetts. Carol's husband, Charles Stuart, told police that a Black man had abducted them at gunpoint, robbed the couple, and then shot Carol in the head and Charles in the abdomen. Police arrested William Bennett, a Black man who had spent most of his life in trouble with the law and had served two terms in prison for threatening and shooting police officers. Later, Charles Stuart admitted to a family member that he killed his wife for the insurance money; Stuart then committed suicide.

Charles Stuart's false claim that a Black man murdered his wife is not the only case of its kind. In 1992, Jesse Anderson claimed two Black men attacked his wife by stabbing her in the face and neck. Anderson was later convicted of first-degree murder. In 1994, Susan Smith told police that a Black man took her car at gunpoint and kidnapped her two young boys. Smith later confessed to pushing her car into a lake and watching it sink with her two young children strapped inside, and was convicted of first-degree murder.

Social cognition theorists would explain the willingness of many Americans to accept Charles Stuart's, Jesse Anderson's, and Susan Smith's claims that a Black man committed the violent criminal acts they themselves committed as a natural function of the human need to categorize in order to make sense of experience. Stuart, Anderson, and Smith, consciously or subconsciously, relied on the Black-as-criminal stereotype when they falsely accused Black men of committing these crimes. At some level, Stuart, Anderson, and Smith knew that others would be most likely to believe their false claims if they attributed their crimes to Black men.

To justify the fear of Blacks as criminals, many people point to statistics which show that Blacks are arrested and convicted of crime far more often than Whites. In 1990, the Sentencing Project published a report entitled Young Black Men and the Criminal Justice System: A Growing National Problem. The report found that on any given day in 1989, 23% of Black men between the ages of twenty to twenty-nine were in prison, on probation or parole, or in some way connected with the criminal justice system. Five years later, the Sentencing Project updated its study, reporting that "as of 1994, 30.2% of African American males in the age group 20–29 were under criminal justice control—prison, jail, probation, or parole—on any given day."

While these statistics appear at first glance to provide support for some people's conclusion that it is reasonable to fear all Black men because there is a one-in-three chance that any given Black man is a criminal, and thus violent and dangerous, an accurate reading of the report casts doubt on such a proposition. According to the Sentencing Project, "The typical African American male in the criminal justice system is not a violent offender." The large number of African American males connected with the criminal justice system is largely due to the "War on Drugs" and increased law enforcement of drug crimes. Moreover, the statistics only show that 30% of Black men in their 20s are connected with the criminal justice system, presumably a much smaller population than 30% of all Black men.

The Sentencing Project also reports that contrary to common expectations, "the majority of arrestees for violent offenses are white." The Federal Bureau of Investigation's Uniform Crime Reports (UCR) for 1993 confirms this. According to the 1993 UCR, 52.6% of arrestees for violent crime were White, while only 45.7% were Black. In 1994, the percentage of White arrestees for violent crime went up to 53.4% and the percentage of Black arrestees for violent crime declined to 44.7%. Given that Whites constitute 82.9% of the population in the United States, it is not surprising that Whites would constitute a majority of those arrested for violent crimes. The fact that Blacks constitute approximately 12% of the population, but almost half of those arrested for violent crimes (44.7%), is disturbingly disproportionate. Some people might interpret such statistics as supporting the view that it is reasonable to fear Blacks because they constitute a disproportionate number of violent crime arrestees. This view, however, attributes the criminality of some Blacks to the entire Black population. When the total number of Blacks arrested for violent offenses is compared to the total number of Blacks in America, only a small percentage of the Black population are arrested for violent crimes. In 1991, for example, Blacks arrested for violent crimes comprised less than 1% of the total Black population and less than 1.7% of the Black male population. In 1994, Blacks arrested for violent crime still comprised less than 1% of the total Black population and only 1.86% of the total Black male population.

It is not reasonable to attribute the criminality of a few Blacks to the entire Black population or even the entire Black male population.

The illogic of the statistical argument in support of the Black-as-criminal stereotype becomes apparent if one considers using a similar argument to support an all-men-are-criminal stereotype:

> According to the FBI Uniform Crime Report, in 1990, men, regardless of age, were arrested for violent crimes at levels that dwarfed the numbers for women. Men twenty-five to thirty-four years old were seven times as likely as women in the same age bracket to be arrested for murder, forcible rape, robbery, and aggravated assault. Those from thirty-five to forty-four were seven to eight times as likely to land in jail, and those over sixty-five were nearly fifteen times as likely.

> If one applies [the argument that it is reasonable to fear Blacks over Whites because Blacks are arrested for violent crimes at rates greater than Whites] to those statistics, one would expect discrimination against men to be much more prevalent than discrimination against women. One would expect that until such time as the male crime rate is made to equal the female crime rate, society would treat men as objects of fear and horror.

* * *

To state the argument in these terms is to suggest exactly how ridiculous it is. Yet it is the kind of absurd argument that extremely intelligent people make with perfectly straight faces when discussing the treatment of blacks. And it feeds on the oft-unstated assumption that blacks are still on probation—that unlike white men, who are demonstrably more dangerous than white women (and even more dangerous than black women), blacks are not necessarily granted a presumption of innocence, competence, or even complete humanity.

Ultimately, the use of statistics is problematic because statistics can be manipulated either to support or refute the claim that it is reasonable to fear Blacks. While it is more common to hear the statistical argument in support of the claim that it is reasonable to fear a Black person, a statistical argument can also be made that it is unreasonable to fear a Black person. Which statistical argument is more persuasive may depend more on the reader's own biases than on the actual validity of the statistical argument. This is because individuals often "credit only those statistics and images which confirm their preexisting biases."

According to government statistics, a White person is more than four times as likely to be killed by another White person than by a Black person. These statistics might be interpreted to support the argument that it is more reasonable for a White person to fear being killed by another White person than to fear being killed by a Black person. The "more than four times as likely" statistic, however, does not separate out homicides between people who know one another, arising out of domestic violence, love triangles, business deals gone bad, and other unfortunate situations, from stranger-on-stranger homicides. Such separation may be necessary before one can draw any inferences either for or against the argument. Additionally, the use of statistics to support or refute claims of reasonableness in self-defense cases involving Black male victims is of little help because people in situations of perceived danger often do not act in reliance on statistics, but instead respond to deeply ingrained racial stereotypes.

The fear of Black-on-White violence is reinforced by incidents such as the Reginald Denny beating in which several Black men pulled a White truck driver from his truck and brutally beat him during the 1992 Los Angeles riots. It is important, however, to keep in mind that hate crimes are not just Black-on-White incidents. Ellis Cose reminds us that when hate crimes occur, it is more often Whites who attack Blacks (and other minorities) than Blacks who attack Whites:

> In 1992, the FBI published its first tabulation ever of "hate crime offenses," covering cases of murder, forcible rape, robbery, aggravated assault, burglary, larceny-theft, motor vehicle theft, arson, simple assault, intimidation, and vandalism, as reported by local law enforcement agencies for 1991. In instances where the perpetrator's race was recorded, 65 percent of assailants were believed to be white, 29 percent to be black, and less than 3 percent to belong to "multiracial" groups. Conversely, of those thought to be targeted because of race, 57 percent were black and 30 percent were white. In other words (calculating from statistics that are admittedly flawed since many localities did not keep good records, and adjusting for the fact that the white population is almost seven times the size of the black population), any particular black person is thirteen times more likely to be the victim of a so-called bias crime than any particular white person.

Despite these statistics, the fear of Black criminality is so pervasive that many well-intentioned people empathize with the White woman who crosses the street when she sees a Black man coming her way even if she were to continue walking on the same side of the street if the man were White, and the taxi driver who passes up the Black man waiting for a ride and picks up the White man on the next block. Having concern for one's physical safety does not mean one is a bad person. What drives many to empathize with the woman who crosses the street and the taxi driver who refuses to pick up Black passengers may be bias in perception resulting from racial stereotypes such as the Black-as-criminal stereotype. Similar racial filtering might cause some individuals to use deadly force on non-culpable Black persons when they would not react similarly to non-Black persons.

Without trivializing the stigma that comes from being repeatedly snubbed, it is important to recognize the difference between attempting to avoid perceived danger by crossing the street and using deadly force to kill someone. The rationality or accuracy of the factual judgment may be the same in both situations, but the social consequences or costs of error in the two situations are strikingly different. This difference suggests the importance of examining whether racial stereotypes influence jurors to find reasonableness in self-defense cases. The Bernhard Goetz case is a useful vehicle to explore this question.

On December 22, 1984, at about 1:00 p.m., Troy Canty, Darryl Cabey, James Ramseur, and Barry Allen, four Black youths, boarded an express subway train in the Bronx. The four youths rode together in the rear portion of one of the cars of the train. Bernhard Goetz, a White man, boarded the same car a little later and sat down on a bench near the rear section. Goetz was carrying an unlicensed .38 caliber pistol loaded with five rounds of ammunition and concealed in a waistband holster.

Canty, accompanied by Allen, approached Goetz and said, "Give me five dollars." Neither Canty nor any of the other youths displayed a weapon. Goetz responded by standing up, pulling out his handgun, and firing it rapidly at the four youths. Noticing that Cabey seemed to be unhurt, Goetz walked up to him and said, "You seem to be all right, here's another," then fired his last bullet at Cabey. This last bullet severed Cabey's spinal cord, paralyzing him permanently. Later, Goetz would admit, "If I had had more [bullets], I would have shot them again, and again, and again."

After the shooting, Goetz fled. Interestingly, while flight is usually considered evidence of guilt, Goetz's flight did not seem to affect his popularity with a large segment of the American people. Complete strangers called Goetz a subway hero, an average man-on-the-street citizen who had courageously stood up to the bad guys. Goetz was reconstructed as the true victim while the four Black youths were constructed as menacing criminals who had threatened Goetz.

On December 31, 1984, Goetz surrendered himself to the police. Goetz admitted that when he shot at the youths, he was certain none of them had a gun, but claimed he could tell from the smile on one of the youth's faces that the youths wanted to "play with me." Goetz admitted that he intended to kill the youths, telling police:

> When I saw what they intended for me, my intention was worse than shooting. My intention was to do anything I could do to hurt them. My intention ... I know this sounds horrible, but my intention was to murder them, to hurt them, to make them suffer as much as possible.

At his trial for assault, attempted murder, reckless endangerment and illegal possession of a weapon, Goetz claimed he acted in self-defense. The jury found Goetz not guilty on all of the charges except illegal possession of a weapon.

As a textbook criminal law hypothetical, Goetz's self-defense claim should have been rejected for several reasons. First, under New York law, a defendant is justified in using defensive physical force only if he honestly and reasonably believed two things: (1) that his assailant was attacking or was about to attack him (i.e., an attack was imminent), and (2) that the use of physical force was necessary to defend himself. Even though Goetz may have subjectively feared an attack, and even if his fear seemed reasonable to him, a strong argument can be made that it was not objectively reasonable for Goetz to believe that he was under threat of imminent death or great bodily harm. Neither of the two youths who approached Goetz displayed a weapon, and neither made any menacing movement suggesting an imminent physical attack. An even stronger argument can be made that it was not necessary for Goetz to shoot at the youths to defend himself. Goetz could have chosen less violent means of resolving the conflict. He could have said "No" to the youths' demand for money. He also could have moved to another section of the subway car—perhaps even another car altogether. Goetz might have given the youths something less than the five dollars they requested. Or, Goetz could have warned the youths not to bother him by showing them his gun (not shooting it), and then he could have walked away. Instead, Goetz's immediate response was to fire upon the youths, endangering the lives of the youths and everyone else in that subway car.

Second, Goetz's use of a loaded gun was not proportionate to the threatened harm. Goetz admitted that he was certain that none of the youths had a gun, yet he chose to shoot them. Under New York law, deadly force is not an appropriate response unless the defendant reasonably believes that such deadly force is necessary to defend himself from the imminent use of deadly physical force against him and that he cannot retreat. Here, Goetz's use of deadly force was inappropriate because Goetz was responding to a verbal request for five dollars, a request unaccompanied by any show of force, movement, or other indication of an imminent unlawful deadly attack. Goetz admitted that he knew none of the youths had a gun. Therefore, he could not have reasonably believed it was necessary to use deadly force to protect against deadly force.

Third, one who does not reasonably believe that he is being attacked, but strikes first anyway, is the initial aggressor and loses all right to avail himself of the self-defense doctrine unless he withdraws from the encounter and effectively communicates his withdrawal to the other person. If Goetz did not reasonably believe he was being attacked, his use of a loaded gun in response to a request for five dollars made him the initial aggressor. As an aggressor, Goetz did not have the right to use deadly force in self-defense.

Finally, Goetz admitted his intent was to murder the youths, to hurt them, and make them suffer as much as possible. Far from constituting self-defense, Goetz's act of shooting the youths with the intent to kill them fits the textbook definition of attempted murder.

Some who commented on the Goetz case believed race was not a significant factor leading to the verdict. Yet, whether the jurors were conscious of it or not, race probably influenced the jury's perception of whether Goetz acted reasonably.

The interesting thing about the Goetz case is that race was never explicitly mentioned during the trial. Perhaps if the racial nature of the case had been made salient during the trial, the jury might have come to a different conclusion. Instead, Barry Slotnick, Goetz's attorney, appealed to the Black-as-criminal stereotype in a subtle, almost covert, manner. In his opening statement, Slotnick referred to the victims as "savages," "predators," "vultures," and the "gang of four," conjuring up images of gang members preying on society. Additionally, Slotnick cleverly played the race card when he re-created the subway shooting using four young Black men from the Guardian Angels to play the victims.

The covert appeal to racial bias came out most dramatically in the re-creation of the shooting, played out while Joseph Quirk was testifying. The defendant called in four props to stand in for the four victims Canty, Allen, Ramseur, and Cabey. The nominal purpose of the demonstration was to show the way in which each bullet entered the body of each victim. The defense's real purpose, however, was to re-create for the jury, as dramatically as possible, the scene that Goetz encountered when four young black passengers began to surround him. For that reason Barry Slotnick asked the Guardian Angels to send him the four young black men to act as the props in the demonstration. In came the four young black Guardian Angels, fit and muscular, dressed in T-shirts, to play the parts of the four victims in a courtroom minidrama.

In the Goetz case, the jury instructions, which did not mention race or racial stereotypes, did not reduce the chances that the race of the victims might prejudice the jurors in Goetz's favor. If the jurors were inclined to perceive the actions of the four Black youths as hostile or violent, at least in part because the youths were Black, they were allowed to rely on these stereotype-driven feelings. If the jurors were inclined to empathize more with Goetz than his victims because of racial affinity, the jury instructions did nothing to discourage such racially selective empathy.

Additionally, the jury instructions did not clearly distinguish between beliefs that are reasonable and conduct that is reasonable. The jurors may have imagined themselves in Goetz's situation and felt that they too would have been afraid of four Black youths asking them for five dollars. Apprehension of some speculative future bodily harm, however, is not sufficient to acquit a defendant on self-defense grounds. Both the defendant's beliefs and actions must have been reasonable.

Most discussions on the subject of race and the American criminal justice system have focused on the Black–White paradigm. Such focus may be justified because of the history of slavery and the current discrimination practiced against Blacks in this country. Nonetheless, because of this focus, issues concerning other non-Whites tend to be overlooked. This is unfortunate because other non-Whites are also subject to socially constructed notions about race.

The ways in which Asian Americans have been socially constructed in American society are contradictory. While racial representations of Blacks are largely negative, Asian Americans have been racially represented in conflicting ways. For example, Asian Americans appear to benefit from the model minority stereotype that seems to have become the predominant image in the 1990s. Under the Asian-as-model-minority stereotype, Asian Americans are perceived as smart, hard-working, law-abiding, and respectful of authority. This stereotype may have operated to benefit a Korean American woman store owner who shot and killed a fifteen-year-old African American girl, claimed she acted in self-defense, and was placed on probation, serving no jail time.

On March 16, 1991, Soon Ja Du, a Korean American woman who owned and operated a liquor store in Los Angeles with her husband, shot and killed Latasha Harlins, a fifteen-year-old African American girl, after a dispute over a bottle of orange juice. Harlins had entered the store, gone to the section where the orange juice was shelved, selected a bottle of orange juice, and placed it in her backpack. Harlins then approached the counter with two dollars visible in her hand. The bottle of orange juice, which cost only $1.79, was also partially visible from the backpack. Du confronted Harlins and accused her of trying to steal the orange juice. After a verbal (Du called Harlins a "bitch") and physical (Du pulled on Harlins sweater and Harlins hit Du in the eye twice with her fist) altercation, Harlins put the orange juice on the counter. As Harlins turned to leave, Du reached under the counter and pulled out a .38 caliber revolver. Du then shot Harlins in the back of the head from a distance of about three feet, killing Harlins instantly. At trial, Du claimed she shot Harlins in self-defense.

Although Du was found guilty of voluntary manslaughter, which indicates that the jury rejected her claim of self-defense, the sentencing judge imposed an extraordinarily lenient sentence. By using a firearm in the commission of a crime, Du was presumptively ineligible for probation under California Penal Code section 1203(e)(2). Nonetheless, Judge Joyce Karlin suspended execution of Du's prison sentence and placed Du on probation for five years without imposing any jail time as a condition of probation. Professor Neil Gotanda has aptly observed that Judge Karlin's sentencing colloquy suggests Karlin relied on positive stereo-types about Korean Americans and negative stereotypes about Blacks in deciding Du's sentence. Judge Karlin described Du as a dutiful mother who was tending the store that day "to shield her son from repeated robberies." In contrast, Judge Karlin portrayed Latasha Harlins, the victim, as a criminal associated with gangs and gang theft. Notably, Judge Karlin ignored several positive facts about Harlins. As the Court of Appeals noted:

> The probation report also reveals that Latasha had suffered many painful experiences during her life, including the violent death of her mother. Latasha lived with her extended family (her grandmother, younger brother and sister, aunt, uncle and niece) in what the probation officer described as "a clean, attractively furnished three-bedroom apartment" in South Central Los Angeles. Latasha had been an honor student at Bret Hart Junior High School, from which she had graduated the previous spring. Although she was making only average grades in high school, she had promised that she would

bring her grades up to her former standard. Latasha was involved in activities at a youth center as an assistant cheerleader, a member of the drill team and a summer junior camp counselor. She was a good athlete and an active church member.

The Soon Ja Du case illustrates how the model minority stereotype can benefit some Asian Americans. What is often overlooked, however, is the fact that the positive attributes of the model minority stereotype (e.g., intelligent, hard-working, law-abiding) are linked with corresponding negative attributes (e.g., lacking personality, unfairly competitive, clannish, unwilling to assimilate, rigidly rule-bound). Frank Wu observes:

> In the [model minority] stereotype, every positive element is matched to a negative counterpart. To be intelligent is to lack personality. To be hard-working is to be unfairly competitive. To be family-oriented is to be clannish, "too ethnic," and unwilling to assimilate. To be law-abiding is to be rigidly rule-bound, tied to traditions in the homeland, unappreciative of democracy and free expression.

In times of economic uncertainty, resentment against Asian Americans seems to increase, perhaps because of the perception that "model" Asian Americans take away valuable job opportunities from other Americans. Reactions to the Los Angeles riots of 1992 following the Simi Valley jury's acquittal of the four White police officers who brutally beat African American Rodney King reflected conflicting sentiments of sympathy for and resentment against the Korean Americans caught up in the destruction. On the one hand, Korean American store owners were constructed oppositionally to African American and Latino looters as unfortunate victims of the riots and looting. On the other hand, Korean Americans were portrayed as property-loving, gun-toting store owners who valued material possessions over human life.

> Fear of the foreign is sometimes a black streak that runs through America's political culture. We see instances of [this] when it involves hate crimes, not necessarily directed at black Americans, but at foreign Americans.

— Mike McCurry

White House Press Secretary

It is almost oxymoronic to speak of foreign Americans, yet the term "foreign American" conveys meaning—Asian Americans and Latinos. Many Americans associate Asian Americans with foreignness. The person who asks an Asian American "Where are you from?" usually expects a response like "Japan" (or China or Korea)—not "Texas" (or Ohio or Northern California). This focus on the Asian in Asian American is deep-rooted. During World War II, when the United States was at war with Japan, hostility toward Japan was extended to all persons of Japanese ancestry. From 1942 to 1945, Japanese Americans were incarcerated in internment camps because of their Japanese heritage. The internment took place even though there was no evidence that Americans of Japanese descent were disloyal to the United States. Even though the United States was at war with Germany and Italy, as well as with Japan, persons of German and Italian ancestry were not similarly incarcerated.

The Asian-as-foreigner stereotype is evident today, though it has taken on more subtle forms. During the O.J. Simpson trial, much of the racial joking in the case was directed at two Asian Americans associated with the case. The Honorable Lance Ito, the judge who presided over the trial, and criminalist Dennis Fung, two Asian Americans who speak articulately and without a noticeable accent, were portrayed as bumbling, heavily-accented Asians who could barely speak English by radio station disc jockeys, publishing houses, and even a United States senator. During the Simpson trial, the historical impulse to mock others on the basis of racial difference was fulfilled by poking fun at the Asian Americans associated with the trial, constructing them as Asians with heavy accents characteristic of the Asian-as-foreigner stereotype.

Sometimes the Asian-as-foreigner stereotype takes on more ominous manifestations. In 1982, Vincent Chin, a Chinese American, was beaten to death with a baseball bat by Ronald Ebens and Michael Nitz, two White Detroit autoworkers. Before killing Chin, Ebens and Nitz, illustrating the all-too-common confusion between Chinese Americans and Japanese Americans and between Asian Americans and Asian nationals, called Chin a "Nip." They also accused Chin of contributing to the loss of jobs in the automobile industry, yelling "It's because of you little mother fuckers that we're out of work." They pled guilty to manslaughter and were each sentenced to three years of probation and fined $3,780. When discussing the no jail time sentence that he imposed on the two men, the judge explained, "Had it been a brutal murder, those fellows would be in jail now." It is unclear what led the judge to think the baseball bat beating was not a brutal murder, yet the judge was not alone in his sentiments. Friends of Ebens and Nitz claimed the beating was just an accident, despite the fact that witnesses reported that Ebens swung the baseball bat at Chin's head as if he were hitting a home run, Chin's skull was fractured in several places, and police officers who arrived on the scene said pieces of Chin's brain were splattered all over the sidewalk.

Because of the confusion between Asian Americans and Asian nationals, symptomatic of the Asian-as-foreigner stereotype, the killing of Yoshihiro Hattori, a Japanese foreign exchange student, by Rodney Peairs, a Louisiana homeowner who claimed he acted in self-defense and was acquitted, has special significance for both Asian nationals and Asian Americans. On October 17, 1992, two sixteen-year-old high school students, Yoshihiro Hattori and Webb Haymaker were looking for a Halloween party in the suburbs of Baton Rouge, Louisiana when they came to the home of Rodney and Bonnie Peairs and rang the doorbell. The Peairs's home was decorated for Halloween and was only a few doors away from the correct house. Hattori was dressed as the character played by John Travolta in "Saturday Night Fever," wearing a white tuxedo jacket and carrying a small camera. No one answered the front door, but the boys heard the clinking of window blinds coming from the rear of the carport area. The boys walked around the house in that direction. A moment later, Bonnie Peairs opened the door. Webb Haymaker started to say, "We're here for the party." When Yoshi came around the corner to join Webb, Mrs. Peairs slammed the door and screamed for her husband to get the gun. Without asking any questions, Rodney Peairs went to the bedroom and grabbed a laser-scoped .44 magnum Smith and Wesson, one of a number of guns Peairs owned.

The two boys had walked away from the house and were on the sidewalk about ten yards from the house when Peairs rushed out of the house and into the carport area. The carport light was on and a street light was located in front of the house, illuminating the carport and sidewalk area. Hattori, the Japanese exchange student, turned and approached Peairs, smiling apologetically and explaining, "We're here for the party," in heavily accented English. Rather than explaining to Hattori that he had the wrong house, Peairs pointed his gun at Hattori and shouted the word "freeze." Hattori, who did not understand the English word "freeze," continued to approach Peairs. Peairs fired one shot at Hattori's chest. Hattori collapsed and died on the spot. The entire incident—from the time Peairs opened the door to the time he fired his gun at Hattori—took place in approximately three seconds.

Peairs was charged with manslaughter. At trial, Peairs's attorney argued that Peairs shot Hattori because he honestly and reasonably believed the unarmed Hattori was about to kill or seriously harm him. The judge instructed the jury that in order to acquit Peairs on the ground of self-defense, the jury needed to find that Peairs reasonably believed he was in imminent danger of losing his life or receiving great bodily harm and that the killing was necessary to save himself from that danger. After little more than three hours of deliberating, the jury returned a verdict of not guilty. Spectators in the courtroom responded to the verdict with applause. In contrast to the public's outrage at the perceived shortness of the deliberation process in the O.J. Simpson case when jurors in that case reached a verdict in less than four hours, there was little if any public outrage at the three hours of deliberation and resulting acquittal in the Peairs case.

The not guilty verdict is legally defensible in a narrow context. Peairs claimed he believed Hattori was armed, and it is conceivable that Peairs mistook the camera in Hattori's hand for a gun. When Hattori failed to stop after Peairs yelled "Freeze!" it might have been reasonable for Peairs to have believed Hattori was about to attack him—especially if one believes Peairs's testimony at trial that he said "Stop" several times before firing (a claim disputed by Webb Haymaker). One has the right to use deadly force to protect oneself against what one reasonably believes to be deadly force. As Justice Oliver Wendell Holmes once stated, "Detached reflection cannot be demanded in the presence of an uplifted knife."

On the other hand, a guilty verdict would have been legally defensible as well. On the issue of whether Peairs acted with the intent to kill or seriously injure Hattori, several facts suggest that Peairs acted with such purpose. On the issue of whether Peairs acted reasonably in self-defense, several facts suggest Peairs acted hastily and unreasonably. Rather than calling the police, looking outside the window to see what was outside, or even asking his wife why she was screaming, Peairs immediately went to his bedroom closet, grabbed a loaded gun, and went to the carport area to confront the boys outside. At that time, the boys were in the process of leaving the premises. Peairs easily could have avoided any confrontation by permitting them to leave. Additionally, Peairs might have chosen a less fatal course of action. Peairs could have fired a warning shot or aimed for a less vital portion of Hattori's body. Instead, Peairs, whose familiarity with guns might be assumed since he had several other firearms in his house that night, shot Hattori directly in the chest with his laser-scoped .44 magnum.

The Peairs case is complicated by the fact that the racial nature of the case was less obvious than that of the Goetz case. While many Asian American groups felt the verdict was unjust and racist, non-Asian Americans explained the verdict as merely a tragic misunderstanding or an unfortunate incident. Most people have overlooked the degree to which racial stereotypes about Japanese people might have affected the jury's interpretation of the facts and their determination that Peairs acted reasonably.

Just as the attorney representing Bernhard Goetz covertly and effectively played the race card, Peairs's attorney subtly and effectively appealed to prejudice against the Japanese "enemy." Playing on the Asian-as-foreigner stereotype, which was all the more readily believed in this case involving a true Asian foreigner, Peairs's attorney told the jury that Hattori was acting in a menacing, aggressive fashion, "like a stranger invading someone's home turf." The use of language suggesting an invasion of home turf is striking in light of the way Japanese people have been viewed in this country. Historically, Japanese nationals and Japanese Americans have been viewed as the enemy. In more recent times, the Japanese have also been viewed as the enemy—the economic yellow peril responsible for the loss of American jobs. Indicative of this tendency to view Japan as the enemy, one writer, commenting on Japanese outrage at the not guilty verdict in the Peairs case, wrote: "America excels at overreaction to a singular occurrence; it's gratifying to witness our economic arch rival suffer the same weakness. They've bloodied our nose enough in the business markets of the world.... At least Americans can see hysteria is no less common in 'perfect Japan.'" "The notion of foreignness embedded in this 'invasion of home turf' language was so subtle that this indirect reference to national origin went unnoticed by the prosecution."

Bonnie Peairs's trial testimony is also significant. When asked to describe Hattori, Mrs. Peairs responded, "I guess he appeared Oriental. He could have been Mexican or whatever." Mrs. Peairs was unable to tell whether Hattori was "Oriental" or "Mexican" or neither. All she knew was that Hattori looked different, foreign. Her comment highlights the way minorities are often lumped together as a homogeneous group outside the American community.

If Webb Haymaker had been the victim, it is unlikely that the spectators in the courtroom would have responded with applause to the not guilty verdict. If Haymaker, the boy from the neighborhood, rather than Hattori, a foreigner from Japan, had been the victim in this case, the defense would have had a more difficult time portraying the victim as "a crazy man," "frightening," or "scary," terms used to describe Hattori. If Haymaker had been the victim, the presence of Haymaker's parents in the courtroom and in the community would have made it much more difficult for the defense to paint a credible picture of the victim as the bad guy. But Haymaker was not the victim; Hattori, a Japanese foreigner, was the one shot and killed.

Another common belief about Asians and Asian Americans is encompassed in the Asian-as-martial artist stereotype. Many people assume that young Asian men know martial arts. In *State v. Simon*, the Asian-as-martial artist stereotype helped secure an acquittal for a man who shot his Chinese neighbor and then claimed self-defense. Anthony Simon, an elderly homeowner, shot his neighbor, Steffen Wong, a Chinese man, as Wong was entering his own duplex. Simon was charged with two counts of aggravated assault.

At trial, Simon argued that he assumed, by virtue of Wong's racial heritage, that Wong was an expert in the martial arts. Simon claimed he was afraid of Wong and that heated words had been exchanged between the two neighbors. Simon also said he was fearful because more Orientals were moving into the neighborhood and one had even expressed interest in purchasing Simon's home. In addition to Simon's testimony, the defense called a clinical psychologist who testified Simon was a psychological invalid who suffered from anxiety neurosis. Defense counsel argued to the jury that the evidence showed Simon reasonably believed Wong was an imminent threat to him.

The jury acquitted Simon on all counts. Although the instruction on self-defense given to the jury utilized a subjective standard of reasonableness, the fact that the jury could find Simon's fear to be reasonable when it was quite clear that his fear of Wong was based almost solely on a racial stereotype is quite astounding. The Asian-as-martial artist stereotype may have influenced jurors to sympathize with Simon's misplaced belief that because of Wong's Asian heritage, Wong must have been a dangerous martial arts expert.

Racial representations of Asian Americans, like the Asian-as-foreigner and Asian-as-martial artist stereotypes, can have a subtle, but far-reaching impact. Such racial representations might influence legal decisionmakers to discount injuries suffered by Asians and Asian Americans. The judge who sentenced the men who killed Vincent Chin by beating him with a baseball bat felt that what happened to Chin was not a brutal murder even though Chin's brains were splattered all over the sidewalk and his skull fractured in several places. Likewise, the juries which acquitted Rodney Peairs and Anthony Simon believed each defendant's claim of self-defense even though it is difficult in hindsight to understand how the jurors could find these defendants' beliefs and actions objectively reasonable. Racial stereotypes about Asians as foreigners, economic rivals, "gooks" we fought in Vietnam, "Japs" responsible for Pearl Harbor, "chinks" who take our jobs, not only deindividualize, they also dehumanize Asian Americans. Racial representations might also influence legal decisionmakers to accept more readily claims of self-defense by defendants who kill Asian Americans, not necessarily because Asian Americans are thought to be more violent or more dangerous than others (although this may occur under the Asian-as-martial artist stereotype), but because Asian and Asian American lives, seen as foreign or outside the American community, are not valued to the same extent as other lives.

The stereotyping of Latinos and Latinas in American culture has received relatively little attention in legal scholarship. Notwithstanding the paucity of legal attention to Latino stereotypes, it is clear that Latino stereotypes are varied and complex. Not all Latinos suffer from the same stereotypes because some Latinos look like their White but non-Latino counterparts, while other Latinos do not. The fair-skinned Cuban in Florida who can pass as White may receive different treatment than the dark-skinned Mexican American in the Southwest.

Unfortunately, Latinos suffer from an aggregation of negative stereotypes experienced by both African Americans and Asian Americans. Perhaps most commonly, Latinos, like Asian Americans, are perceived as foreigners, outsiders, or immigrants. Kevin Johnson discusses how the Latino-as-foreigner stereotype may have influenced a Capitol police security aide to accuse Congressman Luis Gutierrez, a Puerto Rican American who was born in Chicago and is a United States citizen, of presenting false congressional credentials. Leaping to the conclusion that the Congressman was a foreigner after seeing his daughter and niece with two small Puerto Rican flags, the security aide told Gutierrez that he should go back to where he came from.

The Latino-as-foreigner stereotype is particularly troublesome when it slides into the Latino-as-illegal immigrant stereotype. In certain parts of the country, people commonly associate brown-skinned persons who speak English with a Spanish accent with illegal immigration, particularly if those persons are unskilled or employed as domestic or menial laborers. Even if the person speaks English without an accent, he or she may be subject to the illegal immigrant stereotype.

Like African Americans, Latinos suffer from a Latino-as-criminal stereotype. The Latino-as-criminal stereotype often affects young male Latinos who are assumed to be gang members, particularly if they live in a low-income high-crime neighborhood and wear baggy pants and T-shirts. The Latino-as-criminal stereotype is linked to the Latino-as-illegal immigrant stereotype because the undocumented are often characterized as lawbreakers. Another stereotype, the Latino-as-macho stereotype, casts Latinos as hot-tempered and prone to violence. When a Latino loses his temper, his outburst is often characterized as a cultural manifestation of "machismo." The Latino-as-macho stereotype is gendered; "macho" and "machismo" are terms used to describe males from Latin American countries, not females.

The perception that young Latinos who dress a certain way are dangerous criminal gang members who pose a threat of serious bodily injury to those who confront them, coupled with the notion that Latinos tend to be hot-blooded and prone to violence, may contribute to the frequency with which homicide and assault cases involving Latino victims are not prosecuted. In numerous instances, Latinos have been shot, beaten, and/or killed by citizens or police officers claiming justifiable use of deadly force under circumstances calling into question whether the use of deadly force was truly warranted. In many of these cases, despite the fact that the Latino victim was unarmed or shot in the back, criminal charges were not brought against the person claiming justifiable homicide. In recent history, the most widely publicized incident of this type occurred in January 1995.

On January 31, 1995, eighteen-year-old Cesar Rene Arce and twenty-year-old David Hillo, two young Mexican Americans, were spray-painting columns supporting the Hollywood Freeway in Los Angeles at about 1:00 a.m. William Masters II, a White man carrying a loaded gun without a permit in his fanny pack, was out for a late-night walk and saw the two boys spray-painting the columns. Masters picked up a piece of paper from the ground and wrote down the license plate number of the young men's car. Masters claims that when Arce saw him writing, Arce blocked the sidewalk and demanded that he hand over the paper. A scuffle ensued in which Arce tried to rip the paper from Masters's hand and Masters tried to jam the rest of the paper into his pocket. According to Masters, when Hillo held up a screwdriver in a threatening manner, Masters handed over the piece of paper and began walking away. Masters claims he thought the boys were behind him, so he swung around, and fired at Arce. Masters then shot Hillo in the buttocks. Arce died from the shot which entered him from his back.

Masters told the first police officers at the scene, "I shot him because he was spray-painting." Later, Masters claimed he shot the boys in self-defense. In yet another explanation, Masters claimed that he shot the boys because they tried to rob him. Masters was arrested and jailed on suspicion of murder. When he was released from custody, Masters called the two youths he shot "skinhead Mexicans," blamed Arce's mother for his death because she failed to raise Arce well, and said that as a former Marine, he was trained to take down as many of the enemy as he could.

The Los Angeles County District Attorney's Office declined to prosecute Masters on the ground that Masters acted in self-defense when he shot Arce. The determination that Masters reasonably believed he was about to be attacked by Arce is surprising given the fact that the shot that killed Arce entered him from his back. In contrast, the Los Angeles County District Attorney's Office filed murder and manslaughter charges against two Black men (one of whom was the rap singer known as Snoop Doggy Dogg) who claimed they shot another Black man in self-defense, disbelieving their self-defense claim largely because the victim was shot in the back and buttocks.

The decision not to file criminal homicide charges against Masters was also based on the prediction that the government would have had a difficult time convincing a jury to return a conviction against Masters. The government's case would have rested primarily on testimony by Hillo, the young man who survived the shooting. Hillo would have been a problematic witness since he gave conflicting versions of the facts in interviews with the police. Moreover, judging from public reaction to the event, the community was extremely supportive of Masters. Telephone calls reportedly flooded into the police station where Masters was held, offering money and legal assistance. Sandi Webb, a Simi Valley Council-woman, declared her support for Masters by stating, "Kudos to William Masters for his vigilant anti-graffiti efforts and for his foresight in carrying a gun for self protection. If [Los Angeles] refuses to honor Masters as a crime-fighting hero, then I invite him to relocate to our town."

While the Masters case is about the exercise of prosecutorial, not jury, discretion, it is nevertheless relevant to the discussion of the effect of racial stereotypes on legal decisionmaking. Racial stereotypes affect all people, including prosecutors, judges, and jurors. The Masters case is difficult because fear of crime and increasing gang violence are legitimate fears held by many people, particularly in Southern California. Graffiti on freeway overpasses, public buildings, and private property is a reminder that the threat of violent crime is not far off. Supporters of Masters were likely reacting to this fear of crime and gang violence. As one supporter explained, "Whatever he did doesn't bother me. I'm not saying shooting people is the way to do it.... But [the graffiti] is just disgusting. It doesn't seem like anyone's doing anything about it."

However legitimate the fear of crime and the threat of gang violence that graffiti symbolizes, such fear of crime in general does not satisfy the more specific requirement in self-defense doctrine that one have a reasonable belief in an imminent threat of death or serious bodily injury by a particular individual. In this country, defacing property with graffiti is not a capital offense. If the state is not permitted to execute graffiti offenders after a trial and conviction, surely private citizens have no greater right to kill such offenders.

One finds this modern conception in Blackstone, who argued that if we do not execute petty thieves for their crimes, neither should we permit the use of deadly force in resisting petty theft. The property

owner should not be able to react more severely on the street than does
the sentencing authority in the courtroom.

* * *

Jurisdictions utilizing an objective or hybrid subjectivized-objective
standard of reasonableness currently employ what I call a positivist
model of reasonableness. By positivist, I mean that the model is descriptive rather than normative. Applying a positivist model of reasonableness, legal decisionmakers evaluate the reasonableness of the defendant's beliefs and actions by trying to determine whether the ordinary
reasonable person would have believed and acted the way the defendant
did. The reasonable person is a fictional character who is supposed to
represent the average American. If most Americans would have had the
same fears as the defendant and acted similarly, then the defendant's
use of force is considered reasonable and the defendant will be acquitted
on the ground of self-defense or may not even be prosecuted.

The reasonable person, when defined by reference to the ordinary or
average person, suggests a need to consider how most people would have
felt or reacted. If the defendant's beliefs and actions are typical of the
beliefs and actions of the average American in the mind of the decisionmaker, the defendant will be acquitted on the ground of self-defense.
Reasonableness under a positivist model means typical or common.

A typical or common belief, however, is not necessarily a reasonable
belief. At one time, most Americans believed there was nothing wrong
with slavery. The fact that slavery was not only accepted but approved of
by most people did not mean that such a belief was reasonable. Reliance
on a conception of reasonableness that focuses on what the average
American thinks may be problematic in self-defense cases because socially constructed racial images of Blacks and other non-Whites may influence what the average American thinks. The average American might
fear a Black man simply because of the Black man's race when it is not
normatively justified to assume that another person is violent or dangerous based on race.

Interpreting reasonableness as a function of typicality is problematic
because it permits racial stereotypes to have too great an influence on
juror determinations in self-defense cases. The objective standard of
reasonableness as currently constructed is insufficient to guard against
such influence. In assessing reasonableness, perhaps something more
than typicality ought to be required. To find that a defendant acted
reasonably in self-defense, perhaps the jury should find not only that the
defendant's beliefs and actions were those of the average person, but
that the defendant's beliefs and actions were also normatively justified.
Use of a normative standard seems particularly appropriate given the
fact that self-defense is generally considered a justification defense
rather than an excuse. A finding that the defendant acted in self-defense
represents a normative conclusion that the defendant's conduct was the
correct thing to do. This is not to suggest that the reasonableness
standard currently lacks a normative content. When a jury in a self-

defense case finds that a defendant acted unreasonably or held unreason-able beliefs, it is also sending a message that the defendant acted culpably. Use of a normative conception of reasonableness in self-defense cases would merely help make explicit the normative content of the reasonableness inquiry.

Use of a normative conception of reasonableness may be novel in the self-defense context, but it is not a radical concept. Courts have used a normative conception of reasonableness in other legal contexts. For example, under Fourth Amendment jurisprudence, a search has taken place if: "first [the defendant] exhibited an actual (or subjective) expec-tation of privacy, and, second, . . . the expectation [is] one that society is prepared to recognize as reasonable." In his concurring opinion, Justice Harlan used the term "reasonable" to describe what was required for a search under his two-prong test; Justice Stewart, writing for the majori-ty, used the word "justifiable" to describe the privacy Katz expected in the public telephone booth at issue. Subsequent Fourth Amendment opinions have used the terms "reasonable," "legitimate," and "justifi-able" interchangeably. Joshua Dressler explains why the choice of terms is significant: "To say that a person's belief is 'reasonable' ordinarily means that it is one that a reasonable person in D's situation would hold. In the privacy context, this would mean that an expectation of privacy is 'reasonable' when a reasonable person would not expect her privacy to be invaded." In other words, under a positivist model of reasonableness, the term "reasonable" is usually a referent for what the reasonable person would expect or believe. Dressler continues:

> In contrast, to say that D has a "legitimate" or "justifiable" expectation of privacy is to draw a normative conclusion that she has a right to that expectation. Or, as one court has put it, the privacy protected by the Fourth Amendment under this view "is not the privacy that one reasonably expects but the privacy to which one has a right."

Use of the terms "legitimate" and "justifiable" to describe the reasonableness of a defendant's expectation of privacy exemplifies reli-ance on a normative conception of reasonableness. *Dressler* explains how the two conceptions of reasonableness (positivist vs. normative) are different in the following hypothetical:

> For example, suppose that D commits a crime in a secluded spot in a park during the middle of the night after carefully ascertaining that the area is virtually never frequented at that hour. Based on this informa-tion, D expects that her actions will not be observed. That expectation might be "reasonable" in the sense that a reasonable person would expect to be free from observation.

> Nonetheless, if a police officer happens by and observes the criminal conduct, most commentators agree that D's subjective privacy expecta-tion will not be protected. If this is so, it is because D's expectation, although perhaps "reasonable," was "unjustifiable" or "illegitimate." That is, as a normative matter, people have no right to expect privacy if

they conduct crime in the open, no matter how unlikely it is that they will be discovered.

When we say that the police officer's observation of D's criminal conduct did not constitute a search within the meaning of the Fourth Amendment, we are resting this legal conclusion upon a normative conception of reasonableness. Even though D may have had an actual (or subjective) expectation of privacy, and even though D's expectation of privacy may have been one that other reasonable people might have had, D's expectation is not one that society is prepared to accept as reasonable because it is not a justifiable or legitimate expectation of privacy.

In the self-defense context, a positivist model of reasonableness might lead to the conclusion that a defendant's belief that a Black man posed an imminent threat is reasonable if the average American in the same circumstances would have also believed the Black man posed an imminent threat. If, however, the inquiry were shifted from the question whether most Americans would have believed and acted as the defendant did to the question should the defendant's beliefs and actions be regarded as reasonable, meaning legitimate or justifiable (i.e., from a positivist to a normative model of reasonableness), jurors might conclude that the defendant did not act reasonably in self-defense.

One problem with replacing or supplementing the positivist model of reasonableness with a normative model is the potential conflation of the positive and normative standards. If jurors feel that the defendant acted as a typical person would have acted, they may also conclude that the defendant acted as she should have acted. While conflation is a troubling possibility, it highlights why perhaps a normative model of reasonableness should be employed. Unless jurors are explicitly instructed that they should consider whether the defendant's beliefs and actions were normatively justified, they may continue to equate reasonableness with typicality.

Another difficulty with a normative conception of reasonableness is that the scope of the normative standard is almost by definition amorphous. It is difficult to define ex ante what constitutes reasonableness from a normative perspective. Whether a defendant's actions are normatively reasonable will depend in part on where the crime occurred, who is deciding the question, and the facts of the specific case.

These problems suggest that while it is important to recognize the normative nature of the reasonableness inquiry, doing so by supplementing the positivist model of reasonableness with a normative model may not be advisable at this time. A full discussion of this idea is beyond the scope of this Article but provides fertile ground for future inquiry.

* * *

Notes and Questions

1. How does Professor Lee's race and self-defense thesis explain the prosecutorial decisions described by Professor Davis concerning David McKnight and John Nguyen? *See supra* at 175–176. What stereotype regarding Asian–Americans was operating against Mr. Nguyen?

2. Consider the "black as criminal stereotype." Studies show that Blacks are arrested and convicted far more often than Whites. Is it reasonable therefore to fear Blacks? What's the solution? How does popular culture reinforce this stereotype? Should Black actors refuse to accept such roles?

3. What do you think of Professor Lee's theory of self-defense that jury's be required to find that the defendant's beliefs and actions were those of the average person and the defendant's beliefs and actions were also normatively justified? When should the defendant's actions be regarded as reasonable or justifiable? How does changing the analysis minimize the impact of racial stereotyping? How would it change the results in the cases that she described in her article?

4. Professor Jody Armour argues against the use of race-based self-defense claims because of concerns that Whites will be able to use the doctrine and escape punishment. *See* Jody D. Armour, *Race Ipsa Loquitor: Of Reasonable Racists, Intelligent Bayesians, and Involuntary Negrophobes*, 46 Stan. L. Rev. 781 (1994). For example, Professor Armour states "[t]he Reasonable Racist asserts that, even if his belief that blacks are 'prone to violence' stems from pure prejudice, he should be excused for considering the victim's race before using force because most similarly situated Americans would have done so as well." *Id.* at 787. How would Professor Lee respond to that concern?

SECTION 2.   CRITICAL RACE THEORY AND SENTENCING

As you read this case, see if you can find the Critical Race Theory influence on the Court's decision.

A.   JUDICIAL RESPONSE TO "DRIVING WHILE BLACK"

U.S. v. LEVINER

31 F.Supp.2d 23 (D.Mass.1998).

GERTNER, DISTRICT JUDGE.

* * *

I. FACTS[1]

A. *Offense*

The car in which Leviner was a passenger was observed by police officers as traveling at a high rate of speed, without headlights, from an area in which shots had reportedly been fired. The officers followed the car and stopped it. The officers reported that the occupants of the car (the driver—Denise Cummings, the front seat passenger—Derrick Johnson, and Leviner, who was seated in the rear) were cooperative, that they produced the requested documentation (license and registration for the driver, identification for the passengers), answered all questions posed to them, and even agreed to be searched. But for the fact that Cumming's registration did not match the car she was driving, the officers were prepared to allow them to leave. As a result of the registration disparity, Leviner and the others were asked to step out of the car. At some point the officers found a holster on Leviner, and he fled. The officers apprehended him almost immediately and found the gun in question on the car floor near where Leviner had been sitting.

The Government has also represented that tests indicate that shots had been fired from Leviner's gun and a shell casing was found on the car floor. There was, however, no indication that the gun was fired at anyone in particular, or even that anyone was threatened by its use. The Government does not even make such an accusation.

The offense is unquestionably a serious one. The Assistant United States Attorney quite appropriately points out that this was not the mere possession of the firearm, but its firing. While the gun was not used to threaten anyone, it was nevertheless used.[2]

B. *Offender*

Leviner has had a consistent employment record. He is a trained asbestos removal worker, regularly employed over the past ten years. Moreover, he was raised in a stable family situation, and has maintained close ties with his extended family and his children. Impressively, the courtroom was filed [sic] with family and friends for each hearing.

Additionally, while Leviner has a relatively long record, it consists almost entirely of motor vehicle offenses, and minor drug possession charges. Except for a conviction for assault when he was seventeen (Leviner is now thirty-three), his record is overwhelmingly non-violent.

If I were to apply the Sentencing Guidelines to this case uncritically, none of these facts would make much of a difference. Instead, what would matter most in determining Leviner's sentence would be two numbers on a grid—the fact that this offender has a relatively high criminal history score—a Category V, without regard to its nature, and

---

1. These facts derive from two sources: The Presentence Report and my Memorandum on Defendants' Motion To Suppress (dated June 29, 1998).

2. In his Sentencing Memorandum, Leviner suggests that he was drunk, and on a sort of a "joyride." "Joyride" or not, the community had a right to its tranquility without gunshots piercing the night's calm.

the fact this Felon in Possession of a Firearm offense is graded more severely because Leviner has two felony convictions, without regard to the fact that one conviction took place two weeks after Leviner possessed the gun.

While the Sentencing Guidelines were designed to eliminate unwarranted disparities in sentencing, and constrain a judge's discretion, they are not to be applied mechanistically, wholly ignoring fairness, logic, and the underlying statutory scheme.

II.   GUIDELINE CALCULATIONS

The Guideline calculations reflected in the Presentence Report, and endorsed by the Government, are the following:

A.   The base offense level: Based on Probation's conclusion that Leviner has two prior convictions for controlled substance offenses, under USSG § 2K2.1(a)(2) the offense level is 24.

I reject this interpretation for the reasons described in Section III. Consequently, considering only the one felony conviction within the meaning of the Guidelines—the one that actually occurred prior to the firearm possession—the base offense level is 20.

B.   Adjustment for Acceptance of Responsibility: All parties agree that Leviner is entitled to a 3 point reduction for acceptance of responsibility.

C.   Total offense level: The offense level is 17.

D.   Criminal History: Leviner's criminal history score, according to the Presentence Report, is a Category V, based on a score of 11.

I reject this calculation for the reasons described *infra* in Section IV. Instead, I conclude that Leviner's criminal history vastly overstates his true culpability and his likelihood of recidivism on this offense. Accordingly, I base my calculations on a criminal history score of 4.

Based on the Sentencing Table, the Guideline imprisonment range is 30 to 37 months. I will sentence this defendant to a term of 30 months.[3]

* * *

IV.   WHETHER LEVINER'S CRIMINAL HISTORY OVERSTATES HIS CULPABILITY

Leviner's criminal history category score is 11. It is the second highest category that an offender can receive under the Sentencing

---

3.   Leviner mounts a number of challenges to the Government's calculations, in addition to those described above. Leviner objects to assessing one criminal history point for a drug conviction arising out of a 1985 arrest. He argues that the Guidelines place a cap at 4 criminal history points for all convictions for which he received less than sixty days in jail. Leviner contends that Probation is obliged to begin "counting" criminal history convictions with the most recent one first and then stop when the score 4 is reached. Since Leviner has offenses which are more recent than the 1985 offense, he contends that these offenses should be counted first and that the 1985 offense (for possession with intent to distribute marijuana) should not have been considered at all. Nothing in the Guidelines supports this approach. Rather, Probation appropriately scored all offenses, and then "capped" the criminal history total score for them at 4.

Guidelines; a Category V out of a possible VI.[17] If the numerical scores accurately reflect Leviner's likelihood of recidivism, I would be deeply concerned, but they do not. Indeed, Leviner's case acutely demonstrates the limitations of the criminal history rankings under the Guidelines.

Leviner receives seven criminal history points as a result of motor vehicle offenses, all but one of which was operating a motor vehicle after suspension of his license:

1. On January 20, 1994, Leviner used a motor vehicle without authority and illegally possessed marijuana. Charges were brought in the Boston Municipal Court, Leviner was sentenced to three months in the House of Correction, suspended. For this, he received one criminal history point under the Guidelines.

2. On September 21, 1994, he was charged in the Waltham District Court with operating a motor vehicle after his license had been suspended (2d offense). On May 31, 1995, he received a six months House of Correction sentence, suspended. One criminal history point was assigned.

3. On March 2, 1995, he was arrested by the Brookline Police and charged with operating after his license was suspended and operating an uninsured motor vehicle. On November 5, 1997, he received sixty days in the House of Correction. As a result of the sentence, two criminal history points were assigned.

4. On April 21, 1995, he was arrested by the Milton Police Department, and charged with operating a motor vehicle after his license was suspended, and, on the same day, pled guilty to the charge. He was sentenced to ten days in a House of Correction. One criminal history point was assigned.

When the instant offense was committed on September 14, 1997, Leviner was on probation for the motor vehicle convictions in Quincy and Waltham, and the Boston Municipal Court use without authority/marijuana possession case. As a result, two more points were added to his score pursuant to USSG § 4A1.1(d), for a total of seven points.

The remaining four criminal history points were for possession of a class B substance (crack cocaine), over nine years ago, when Leviner was twenty-three years old, and for the conviction which followed the instant felon in possession case, on September 30, 1997, for possession with intent to distribute a class D substance, marijuana.[18]

The Commission made certain compromises when it promulgated the criminal history guidelines.[19] Recognizing that those compromises

17. There are six criminal history categories (I–VI). Scores 10, 11, and 12 are in Category V.

18. The Boston Municipal Court's conviction was for possession of marijuana, a class D substance as well as for use of a motor vehicle without authority. If I were to count that offense as a drug offense, rather than a motor vehicle related charge, five points would be attributable to minor drug charges.

19. Stephen G. Breyer, The Federal Sentencing Guidelines and the Key Compromises Upon Which They Rest, 17 Hofstra L. Rev. 1, 19–20 (1988).

necessarily diluted the validity of the criminal history measure, USSG § 4A1.3 authorizes a downward departure when the criminal history category over-represents the "seriousness of the defendant's criminal history or the likelihood that the defendant will commit further crimes." USSG § 4A1.3 (1997).

Obviously, trial courts should not make this determination out of thin air. Rather, it is appropriate to analyze the purpose of the criminal history system, its structure and its limitations, and then to determine where this defendant's record fits: Does the record suggest the likelihood of recidivism for a felon in possession charge, as opposed to minor drug possession or motor vehicle offenses? How does the defendant's record compare with other Category V offenders? What does the record teach the Court about the nature of this offender, relative to other information available to the Court?

A. Purpose of the Criminal History System

Criminal history has been described by one commentator as an "anomaly" in the guidelines system.[20] Like traditional offender characteristics, such as employment history and family background which the Commission rejected for the most part in the determination of the sentence, criminal history has no direct relationship to the offender's current offense of conviction. Employment history and family background factors arguably point in opposite directions.[21] Criminal history, so the Commission thought, did not. Instead, criminal history was found to be a strong predictor of recidivism and a good measure of culpability.[22] But while that may be so in general, in particular cases, as with Leviner, the relationship breaks down.

B. The Significance of Measuring Criminal History Points by the Length of Sentence the Prior Conviction Received

The current system scores convictions based on the length of the sentence imposed for the offense. Prior sentences of more than thirteen months receive three points, sentences between six and thirteen months receive two points, and those of less than six months receive one point. See § 4A1.1. The system has three problems, all of which resonate in this case:

1. The criminal history score does not accurately reflect the relatively minor nature of Leviner's record.

The criminal history system of the Guidelines does not accurately account for differences in the seriousness of the defendant's prior

---

20. Aaron J. Rappaport, Criminal History and the Purposes of Sentencing, 9 FSR 184 (February 1997).

21. Breyer, *supra* at 19–20. An abusive family background on the one hand might suggest a higher likelihood of recidivism; it may also suggest that the criminal activities are more "understandable" and thus less culpable. Rappaport, *supra* at 184.

22. United States Sentencing Commission, Supplementary Report on the Initial Sentencing Guidelines and Policy Statements 42 (1987) (quoting American Bar Association, Standards for Criminal Justice: Sentencing § 18–2.2, commentary at 68).

convictions. In the case of Leviner's record, for example, his eighteen month term for possession with intent to distribute drugs (the May 13, 1997, charge) would receive the same score as would an eighteen year sentence for murder.[23] Furthermore, the cumulative effect of all the minor convictions and their interrelationships is to put Leviner in the same class as would be a far more serious offender.

2. *The criminal history score does not accurately reflect the non-violent nature of Leviner's record.*

Since the criminal history system is focused entirely on the sentences received for the prior convictions, it does not make distinctions concerning the kind of offense: Motor vehicle versus fraud, violent versus non-violent. Indeed, the violent/non-violent line, for example, may well be more meaningful in terms of predicting recidivism and evaluating the offender's culpability.[24]

Again, in Leviner's case, except for one offense, at age seventeen, none of the convictions reflect a crime of violence, or indeed, even the use of a gun. The instant charge is the first.

To treat this man as if he were only a point on a grid, the intersection of an offense score of seventeen and a criminal history of Category V, would do violence to the purposes of the Sentencing Guidelines. It would treat someone convicted of Felon in Possession of a Firearm with a minor record, solely because he had a few sentences in the criminal history (1), (2), and, (3) range, the same as someone with multiple, violent crimes, and multiple ten to fifteen year sentences. It would create a new form of disparity, treating offenders that are completely different in a like way.

3. *The criminal history score mirrors disparities in state sentencing, and in particular, racial disparities.*

By counting the imprisonment that the defendant has received for the prior offenses, the system effectively replicates disparities in sentencing in the state system.[25] This would include not only the ordinary disparities between similarly situated defendants, but racial disparities.

Motor vehicle offenses, in particular, raise deep concerns about racial disparity. Studies from a number of scholars, and articles in the popular literature have focused on the fact that African American motorists are stopped and prosecuted for traffic stops, more than any other citizens.[26] And if that is so, then it is not unreasonable to believe

23. *See* Michael Gelacak, Ilene Nagel, Barry Johnson, Departures Under the Federal Sentencing Guidelines: An Empirical and Jurisprudential Analysis, 81 Minn. L.Rev. 299, 355 (1996).

24. *See* Tom Hillier, Chapter Four: Time for an Overhaul, Or a Tuneup, 9 Fed. Sent. R. 201, 202.

25. *See Id.* at 201.

26. Tracey Maclin, Race and the Fourth Amendment, 51 Vand. L. Rev. 333, 341–352 (1998); Sean Hecker, Race and Pretextual Traffic Stops: An Expanded Role for Civilian Review Board, 28 Colum. Hum. Rts. L. Rev. 551, 554–569 (1997); Jennifer A. Larrabee, "DWB (Driving While Black)" and Equal Protection: The Realities of an Unconstitutional Police Practice, 6 J.L. & Pl'y 291, 296 (1997); David Harris, Driving While Black and All Other Traffic Offenses:

that African Americans would also be imprisoned at a higher rate for these offenses, as well.

Leviner's motor vehicle offenses were mainly for driving while his license was suspended (except for one use without authority)—not one charge involved driving erratically, or violating a traffic law. The distinction is important. While I can make no judgment about what happened specifically with Leviner's motor vehicle charges, surely, the studies described above raise questions about what drew the officer's attention to Leviner in the first place.

Moreover, these stops evolved into "countable" offenses under the Guidelines only because they were offenses for which Leviner received more than thirty days' imprisonment. Again, without knowing the specific facts surrounding each sentence, this record raises concerns at the very least. Would others have received the same sentence who were similarly situated, no matter how often they had been apprehended driving after their license had been suspended?

C.   The Defendant's Overall Record Relative to Other Offender Information

Leviner's record shows a man who, until 1997, worked consistently and took care of his family. He had an eleven year period with nothing but operating after suspended license offenses, with two exceptions—a possession with intent conviction arising from a 1985 arrest in which he was found in possession of five $10 bags of marijuana and a 1994 use without authority and possession of marijuana charge.

In 1997 circumstances changed. Leviner believed he was passed over for more responsible work at his place of employment because of his race. More serious offenses followed—possession with intent to distribute marijuana and this Felon in Possession offense. While age and employment records have been rejected by the Commission as not ordinarily relevant, *see e.g.*, USSG §§ 5H1.1 (age); 5H1.5 (employment record); 5H1.6 (family ties and responsibilities), in this case they help to illuminate the relationship between this record and Leviner's likely recidivism and culpability. A succession of non-violent offenses, and minor drug possession charges, mixed in with consistent employment and family obligations suggest someone whose drug problems had never been addressed in the past and thus he continued to re-offend. If the purpose of criminal history computations is to predict recidivism and reflect culpability, this record at the most suggests the likelihood that

The Supreme Court and Pretextual Traffic Stops, 87 J. Crim. L. & Criminology, 544, 560–69; Christopher Hall, Challenging Selective Enforcement of Traffic Regulations After the Disharmonic Convergence: *Whren v. United States, United States v. Armstrong*, and the Evolution of Police Discretion, 76 Tex. L. Rev. 1083, 1088 (1998); Matthew Dolan, Summit Addresses Biased Police Stops Officials, Citizens Discuss Solutions in the Shadow of Hampton Incident, The Virginian—Pilot and The Ledger—Star, Norfolk, Va., November 22, 1998, Al; Rick Sarlat, Racial Profiling on Interstates is Under Attack: Pa. Legislation drafted, The Philadelphia Tribune, May 26, 1998, 1A.

without help, Leviner will repeat his minor drug and motor vehicle crimes—not gun offenses or crimes of violence.

As noted above, to treat this defendant the same as an offender with a Category V criminal history of violent offenses, no employment history to speak of, or family life, would be to create a new, and even more grotesque disparity than in the past. I will consider Leviner as having a criminal history of four, taking out the seven points attributable to the motor vehicle offenses.

V.   The Relationship Between This Federal Sentence and a Pending State Sentence

The defendant is currently serving an eighteen month House of Correction sentence for the drug offense for which he was convicted two weeks after the instant offense. He will be released from the state sentence in February of 1999. The defendant argues that I should make the instant sentence concurrent with the state sentence he is currently serving and indeed, should credit time already served under the state sentence. Had the defendant been arrested for the two offenses at the same time, the defendant argues, he would have received a concurrent sentence even under the Guideline grouping rules.

Although the argument is interesting, the defendant was not arrested for the two offenses at the same time. While it is not significant for the Felon in Possession calculation that two weeks after his arrest for gun possession Leviner was convicted for the drug offense, it surely bears on the ultimate sentence. Leviner, for whatever reasons, had obviously begun to hurtle out of control, in a way that was distinctly different from anything he had done in the past.

Accordingly, I will make this sentence concurrent, but only to the extent that two months of the state sentence overlap the beginning of the federal sentence. However, I will not deduct the remaining months already served under state auspices.

VI.   Sentence

In order to deal with Leviner's obvious drug problem and mental issues, I have ordered thirty months' incarceration, at a facility to address those problems. F.C.I. Raybrook has been recommended in order for Leviner to participate in the 500 hour Bureau of Prisons ("BOP") Drug Treatment Program and BOP mental health program. BOP will report the results of this placement to me, on a regular basis, should the Bureau agree.

Supervised release of three years will follow, during which time Leviner will be subject to specific conditions, including mental health and drug counseling.

Notes and Questions

1. The Court observes that "Leviner's motor vehicle offenses were mainly for driving while his license was suspended (except for one use without authority)—not one charge involved driving erratically, or violating a traffic law." What made the police pull Mr. Leviner over?

2. How does Critical Race Theory lead Judge Gertner to reduce Leviner's sentence because the majority of his criminal history points were a result of motor vehicle offenses? Does Critical Race Theory suggest that whenever persons of color violate the traffic laws they should receive a "free pass?"

3. For a further discussion of the case *see* Katheryn Russell, *"Driving While Black": Corollary Phenomena and Collateral Consequences*, 40 B.C. L. Rev. 717, 728–729 (1999). The author observes that although she hasn't found any other decisions of judges taking a similar approach to Judge Gertner, other judges have been willing to use their discretion in other contexts, such as in crack cocaine cases. *Id*.

B. Constitutional Limits on Sentencing: Disparate Impact Analysis

The next case analyzes whether the Minnesota statutory classification scheme that permits different sentencing for powder and crack cocaine possession is unconstitutional under the state constitution. Professor Butler explains that "[c]rack cocaine is created by 'cooking' powder cocaine and baking soda," and acknowledges that the experts disagree over whether one is more dangerous and addictive than the other. Paul Butler, *By Any Means Necessary: Using Violence and Subversion to Change Unjust Law*, 50 UCLA L. Rev. 721,733 (2003). Do you agree with the Court's decision?

STATE v. RUSSELL

477 N.W.2d 886 (Minn.1991).

WAHL, JUSTICE.

We are asked, in this pretrial appeal, to consider the following certified question:

Does Minnesota Statute 152.023, Subd. 2(1) (1989), as it is applied, violate the equal protection clauses of the Fourteenth Amendment of the United States Constitution and the Minnesota Constitution, Article 1, Section 2?

Under Minn. Stat. § 152.023, subd. 2, a person is guilty of a third degree offense if he or she possesses three or more grams of cocaine base [hereinafter "crack cocaine"]. Under the same statute, a person must possess ten or more grams of cocaine powder to be guilty of the same offense. A person who possesses less than 10 grams of cocaine powder is guilty of a fifth degree offense. Minn. Stat. § 152.025 (1990).

Pursuant to these statutes, possession of three grams of crack cocaine carries a penalty of up to 20 years in prison while possession of an equal amount of cocaine powder carries a penalty of up to five years in prison. Under the sentencing guidelines, the presumptive sentence for possession of three grams of crack cocaine is an executed 48 months imprisonment. The presumptive sentence for possession of an equal amount of cocaine powder is a stayed 12 months of imprisonment and probation.

Defendants, five African–American men who were charged with violating Minn. Stat. § 152.023, subd. 2, jointly moved the trial court to dismiss the charges on the ground that the statute has a discriminatory impact on black persons and violates the equal protection guarantees of the federal and state constitutions.

The trial court found that crack cocaine is used predominantly by blacks and that cocaine powder is used predominantly by whites.[1] As a result, a far greater percentage of blacks than whites are sentenced for possession of three or more grams of crack cocaine under Minn.Stat. § 152.023 with more severe consequences than their white counterparts who possess three or more grams of cocaine powder. The trial court concluded that the law has a discriminatory impact on black persons.

The trial court then determined that no rational basis supported the distinction between crack-cocaine and cocaine powder and that the law therefore violated constitutional guarantees of equal protection. The trial court granted the defendants' joint motion to dismiss and certified the question of the statute's constitutionality to the court of appeals pursuant to Minn.R.Crim P. 28.03. We granted a joint petition for accelerated review filed by both the state and the defendants pursuant to Minn. R.Civ. App. P. 118 and Minn.R.Crim. P. 29.02, subd. 1. We affirm.

Review of an equal protection challenge under the federal rational basis test requires (1) a legitimate purpose for the challenged legislation, and (2) that it was reasonable for the lawmakers to believe that use of the challenged classification would promote that purpose. *Western & S. Life Ins. Co. v. State Bd. of Equalization*, 451 U.S. 648, 668, 68 L.Ed.2d 514 , 101 S.Ct. 2070, 2083 (1981).[2]

---

1. Among the many statistics provided to the trial court were those showing that of all persons charged with possession of cocaine base in 1988, 96.6% were black. Of all persons charged with possession of powder cocaine, 79.6% were white.

2. To invoke strict scrutiny of a statute that has a racially discriminatory impact, under current federal equal protection analysis, requires a showing that the legislature enacted the particular statute " 'because of' not merely "in spite of" an anticipated racially discriminatory effect.' " *McCleskey v. Kemp*, 481 U.S. 279, 298, 95 L.Ed.2d 262 , 107 S.Ct. 1756, 1770 (1987). This standard not only places a virtually insurmountable burden on the challenger, who has the least access to the information necessary to es-

tablish a possible invidious purpose, but it also defies the fundamental tenets of equal protection. In the words of Professor Tribe, Government officials cannot be held accountable to the constitutional norm of equality unless they "selected or reaffirmed a particular course of action at least in part 'because of,' not merely 'in spite of,' its adverse effects upon an identifiable group." This overlooks the fact that minorities can also be injured when the government is "only" indifferent to their suffering or "merely" blind to how prior official discrimination contributed to it and how current acts will perpetuate it.

* * *

If government is barred from enacting laws with an eye to invidious discrimination

The state argues that the challenged statute passes muster under that test. It contends that the legislature has a permissible and legitimate interest in regulating the possession and sale of crack cocaine and cocaine powder and that it was reasonable for lawmakers to believe that the three grams of crack—ten grams of powder classification would regulate the possession of those drugs by the "street level" dealers at whom the statute was primarily aimed.

Even if we were to agree with the state's argument as to the analysis under the federal test, we strike the statute as unconstitutional under the rationale basis test as articulated under Minnesota law. Since the early eighties, this court has, in equal protection cases, articulated a rational basis test that differs from the federal standard, requiring:

> (1) The distinctions which separate those included within the classification from those excluded must not be manifestly arbitrary or fanciful but must be genuine and substantial, thereby providing a natural and reasonable basis to justify legislation adapted to peculiar conditions and needs; (2) the classification must be genuine or relevant to the purpose of the law; that is there must be an evident connection between the distinctive needs peculiar to the class and the prescribed remedy; and (3) the purpose of the statute must be one that the state can legitimately attempt to achieve.

Wegan v. Village of Lexington, 309 N.W.2d 273, 280 (Minn.1981) (quoting *Guilliams v. Commissioner of Revenue*, 299 N.W.2d 138, 142 (1980)).

This court has not been consistent in explaining whether the rational basis standard under Minnesota law, although articulated differently, is identical to the federal standard or represents a less deferential

against a particular group, it should not be free to visit the same wrong whenever it happens to be looking the other way. If a state may not club minorities with its fist, surely it may not indifferently inflict the same wound with the back of its hand. L. Tribe, American Constitutional Law, § 16–21, at 1518–19 (2nd ed. 1988).

There comes a time when we cannot and must not close our eyes when presented with evidence that certain laws, regardless of the purpose for which they were enacted, discriminate unfairly, on the basis of race, e.g., that for the murder of a white person in Georgia, a black person is more than twice as likely as a white person to be sentenced to death (*See McCleskey v. Kemp*, 481 U.S. at 286, 107 S.Ct. at 1763); that, in Minnesota, the predominantly black possessors of three grams of crack cocaine face a long term of imprisonment with presumptive execution of sentence while the predominantly white possessors of three grams of powder cocaine face a lesser term of imprisonment with presumptive probation and stay of sentence.

We have our state constitution and in interpreting our state equal protection clause, "we are not bound by federal court interpretation of the federal equal protection clause." *AFSCME Councils 6, 14, 65 & 96 v. Sundquist*, 338 N.W.2d 560, 580 (Minn.1983) (Yetka, J., dissenting). While we are ordinarily loathe to intrude or even inquire into the legislative process on matters of criminal punishment, the correlation between race and the use of cocaine base or powder and the gross disparity in resulting punishment cries out for closer scrutiny of the challenged laws. Under Article 1, Section 2 of the Minnesota Constitution, the statistics showing the effect of the statute in operation combined with relevant factors that appear in the statute's history could be held to create an inference of invidious discrimination which would trigger the need for satisfaction of a compelling state interest not shown on the record before us. This issue need not be decided today, however, because we find the statute unconstitutional under the Minnesota rational basis test.

standard under the Minnesota Constitution.[3] What has been consistent, however, is that in the cases where we have applied what may be characterized as the Minnesota rational basis analysis, we have been unwilling to hypothesize a rational basis to justify a classification, as the more deferential federal standard requires. Instead, we have required a reasonable connection between the actual, and not just the theoretical, effect of the challenged classification and the statutory goals. *See* McKnight, Minnesota Rational Relation Test: The Lochner Monster in the 10,000 Lakes, 10 Wm. Mitchell L. Rev. 709, 726 (1984) (analyzing the cases of *Wegan v. Village of Lexington*, 309 N.W.2d 273 (Minn.1981); *Nelson v. Peterson*, 313 N.W.2d 580 (Minn. 1981); and *Thompson v. Estate of Petroff*, 319 N.W.2d 400 (Minn.1982)).

Nothing prevents this court from applying a more stringent standard of review as a matter of state law under our state constitutional equivalent to the equal protection clause. *Minnesota v. Clover Leaf Creamery Co.*, 449 U.S. 456, 461, 66 L.Ed.2d 659, 101 S.Ct. 715, 723 n.6 (1981). Moreover, there is every reason for us to continue to articulate and apply an independent Minnesota constitutional standard of rational basis review. *See In Re Estate of Turner*, 391 N.W.2d 767, 771–73 (Minn.1986) (Wahl, J., concurring specially). To harness interpretation of our state constitutional guarantees of equal protection to federal standards and shift the meaning of Minnesota's constitution every time federal case law changes would undermine the integrity and independence of our state constitution and degrade the special role of this court, as the highest court of a sovereign state, to respond to the needs of Minnesota citizens. *Id.* at 773. It is particularly appropriate that we apply our stricter standard of rational basis review in a case such as this where the challenged classification appears to impose a substantially disproportionate burden on the very class of persons whose history inspired the principles of equal protection.

We therefore hold that under our state constitutional standard of rational basis review the challenged statute cannot stand. First, the statute fails for lack of a genuine and substantial distinction between those inside and outside the class. In order to meet this standard, the state must provide more than anecdotal support for classifying users of crack cocaine differently from users of cocaine powder. The primary justification advanced by the state in support of the crack/cocaine classification is that it serves to facilitate prosecution of "street level" drug dealers.[4] The three grams of crack—ten grams of powder formula was adopted because it was thought those amounts indicated a level at which dealing, not merely using, took place.

3. This court has recognized that our state constitution embodies principles of equal protection synonymous to the equal protection clause of the Fourteenth Amendment to the United States Constitution. *See State v. Forge*, 262 N.W.2d 341, 347 n.23 (Minn.1977).

4. In fact the state argues to this court that this purpose was the sole basis of the legislation and that any pharmacological difference between the substances is irrelevant to the constitutional analysis.

The primary testimony before the legislature on the distinction between crack cocaine and cocaine powder in terms of the respective amounts of the drugs that indicate street-level dealing came from Mr. James Kamin of the Hennepin County Attorney's Office. He stated at legislative hearings that his knowledge of the quantities possessed by drug dealers did not come from study but "simply from talking with people like Sergeant Strauss and informants, people who have been convicted or are being prosecuted for drug offenses. My knowledge of these numbers come from the streets." Minnesota Senate Criminal Law Subcommittee, 76th Minn. Leg., March 16, 1989.

This purely anecdotal testimony does not establish a substantial and genuine distinction. A statutory distinction that provides the basis for prescribing widely disparate criminal penalties is not sufficiently justified when based on the anecdotal observations of one expert witness. This is especially true in light of evidence presented that undermines the conclusion reached by the legislature. For instance, respondents point to a recent report by the Minnesota Department of Public Safety Office of Drug Policy[5] that states that police and prosecutors contacted by researchers are not persuaded by the "street dealer" distinction because they believe that most cocaine powder users are dealers as well. Minnesota Department of Public Safety Office of Drug Policy, Minnesota Drug Strategy 1991, p. 14. Without more factual support, the three grams of crack—ten grams of powder distinction appears to be based upon an arbitrary rather than a genuine and substantial distinction.

The second proffered basis for the disparate treatment of crack versus cocaine powder users is that crack is more addictive and dangerous than cocaine powder. The evidence on this point similarly fails to establish a genuine and substantial distinction between those inside and outside the class. The primary legislative testimony on this point was presented by Michael Strauss, an officer from the Minneapolis Narcotics Division, who testified from his experience and training in the Narcotics Division but who did not profess to be a trained scientist.

Further evidence on the chemical properties and physiological effects of crack and cocaine powder was presented to the trial court through the testimony of Dawn Speier, a chemist for the City of Minneapolis. She testified that there is a difference between crack and cocaine powder in the severity of the attack on the central nervous system and respiratory function, and, based on what she had read or heard, that a smaller amount of crack will produce the same effect as cocaine powder. She also testified, however, that the mood altering ingredient in both powder and base was the same—cocaine. Further, she testified that the difference in effect between the two was based on the way the drug was ingested (cocaine powder being generally sniffed through the nostrils, crack cocaine being smoked). In fact, Speier con-

---

5.   Cited by the trial court in her Supplemental Findings of Fact and Conclusions of Law.

firmed that if cocaine powder is dissolved in water and injected intravenously, the effect on the body is similar to the effect of smoking crack cocaine. Thus, as respondents argue, evidence as to the degree of dangerousness between crack and cocaine powder is based on testimony as to effects resulting from different methods of ingestion, rather than on an inherent difference between the forms of the drug. Disparate treatment of crack and powder cocaine users is not justified on the basis of crack's greater dangerousness when there is evidence that powder cocaine could readily produce the effects purported to justify a harsher penalty for possession of crack.

There is also evidence in the legislative record that there is more violence associated with the use of crack than with the use of cocaine powder. This evidence is not only anecdotal, but pales in light of official observation that if there is more violence associated with crack use, "that difference could be caused more by factors such as gang warfare and certain group behaviors than by the pharmacological effects of crack." Minnesota Department of Public Safety Office of Drug Policy, Minnesota Drug Strategy 1991, p. 14. Although under the more deferential rational basis test, we may not second guess the scientific accuracy of legislative determinations of fact absent overwhelming contrary evidence, *Moes v. City of St. Paul*, 402 N.W.2d 520, 525 (1987), the rational basis test under the Minnesota Constitution requires more factual support than is present here to establish a genuine and substantial distinction between the two substances.[6]

The crack-cocaine distinction also fails because the classification is not relevant to the statutory purpose. Without more evidence to support the asserted dealership levels of drug possession, the three grams of crack—ten grams of cocaine distinction does not further its statutory purpose of penalizing street level drug dealers. Without more evidence, it is as easily assumed that individuals jailed for possession of three grams of crack are mere personal users who were arbitrarily penalized as dealers. Furthermore, a statute which permits a person possessing less than ten grams of powder cocaine, which can be easily converted into more than three grams of crack,[7] to be punished only for 5th degree possession of cocaine, is not only irrelevant to its purpose of penalizing drug dealers, it is also arbitrary and unreasonable.

6. The legislature has recently recognized that there is cause for further study of the distinction between crack and cocaine as it relates to sentencing. In a recent bill the legislature has directed the sentencing guidelines commission to study sentencing practices under Minn. Stat. § 152.023, subd. 2(1) including review of the proportionality of the penalties for and severity level ranking of crack possession, the characteristics of offenders sentenced for crack use relative to other controlled substance offenders and harm to the community resulting from crack possession relative to other controlled substance crimes. 1991 Minn. Laws ch. 279 sec. 37.

7. The trial court found, based on the testimony of Dawn Speier, that powder cocaine can be converted into crack cocaine by removing the hydrochloride from the powder cocaine with baking soda and water. Speier stated that nine grams of powder cocaine that is pure will convert into a little over eight grams of crack cocaine.

Lastly, the crack-cocaine classification, while perhaps aimed at the legitimate purpose of eradicating street level drug dealers, employs an illegitimate means to achieve that purpose. The legislature determined that three grams of crack and ten grams of powder indicate a level at which dealing, not merely using, takes place. Once possession of the indicated amounts is proved, intent to sell is presumed, justifying a harsher penalty than that for mere possession. In effect, the statute punishes a person for possession with intent to sell without requiring the prosecution to prove, as an element of the crime, that an actual sale was intended, thus creating an irrebuttable presumption of fact. Leavenworth, Note, Illegal Drugs and New Laws, 16 Wm. Mitchell L. Rev. 499, 526 (1990). This court has recognized that statutes creating conclusive presumptions of law or fact have been almost uniformly declared unconstitutional as denying due process of law. *State v. Kelly*, 218 Minn. 247, 250, 15 N.W.2d 554, 557 (1944). Because the statute creates an irrebuttable presumption of intent to sell without affording the defendant an affirmative defense of lack of intent to sell, and on the basis of that presumption automatically metes out a harsher punishment, the means chosen to affect its purposes are constitutionally suspect.

We answer the certified question in the affirmative and affirm the decision of the trial court. Minn. Stat. § 152.023, subd. 2(1) (1989), violates the Minnesota Constitution, Article 1, Section 2.

Affirmed.

* * *

Notes and Questions

1. Did Minnesota lose the case because the legislature didn't have good experts? Should the Minnesota legislature have been deferred to by the State Supreme Court? Should the court substitute it's judgment for the State legislature's?

2. If you are the chief legal advisor to a member of the Minnesota Legislature who wanted to re-enact the bill providing for harsher sentences for crack cocaine, what advice would you give in light of *State v. Russell*? Could you enact the same law with different expert testimony? Would you change the statute to allow for a rebuttal of whether defendant intended to distribute? Would you change the statute to allow for identical sentencing/punishment for crack and powder cocaine? The Minnesota legislature responded to the *State v. Russell* decision by enacting Minn. Stat. §§ 152.021–.023 (Supp. 1993), which increased the punishment for powdered cocaine offenses to make the punishment of such offenses the same as for crack cocaine offenses. *See e.g.* Debra L. Dailey, *Prison and Race in Minnesota*, 64 U. Colo. L. Rev. 761, 776–7 (1993); Ann L. Iijima, *Minnesota Equal Protection in the Third Millennium, "Old Formulations" or "New Articulations,"* 20 Wm. Mitchell L. Rev. 338, 351–352 (1994); Randall Kennedy, *The State, Criminal Law, and Racial Discrimination: A Comment*, 107 Harv. L. Rev. 1255, 1270 (1994).

3. *State v. Russell* is the exception rather than the rule in this area of the law. Consider the following comments of Professor David Sklansky. "Indeed, since 1986 federal crack defendants have received by law the same sentences imposed on defendants convicted of trafficking in one hundred times as much cocaine powder. Almost without exception, constitutional claims of unequal treatment raised by the crack defendants have been rejected out of hand.... What [this] tells us, I argue, is that there are certain important dimensions of racial injustice our law does not see." David A. Sklansky, *Cocaine, Race, and Equal Protection*, 47 Stan. L. Rev. 1283, 1283–1284 (1995). In *U.S. v. Clary*, 846 F.Supp. 768 (E.D.Mo.1994), the District Judge held a statute that carried a ten year mandatory minimum for possession and distribution of either 50 grams of crack cocaine or 5000 grams of powder cocaine violated the equal protection rights of blacks. The Court cited to Professor Charles Lawrence's article *The Id, The Ego, and Equal Protection: Reckoning with Unconscious Racism*, *supra* at 12, numerous times. The Court acknowledged that "[t]he influence of 'unconscious racism' on legislative decisions has never been presented to any court in this context. Constitutional redress to racial discrimination has resulted primarily from judicial vigilance directed toward correcting overt and facially discriminatory legislation forged first by slavery and followed by continuing racial animosity toward blacks and other ethnic minorities. Remaining still is a more pernicious, albeit intangible, form of race discrimination in the individual's unconscious thoughts that influences the decision making process. As a result, 'individuals ... ubiquitously attach a significance to race that is irrational and often used outside their awareness.'" The case was overturned on appeal. *U.S. v. Clary*, 34 F.3d 709 (1994). The Eighth Circuit was not persuaded by the District Court's reliance on unconscious racism to find discrimination. *Id.* at 713–714. Would you imagine that after the powder cocaine penalty was increased, that more whites would be imprisoned? At the time of *State v. Russell*, African-Americans were incarcerated at a rate 19 times greater than that of whites. Ten years later, the incarceration rate of African-Americans is 27 times greater than that of whites. *See* DJ Silton, *U.S. Prisons and Racial Profiling: A Covertly Racist Nation Rides A Vicious Cycle*, 20 Law & Ineq. 53, 64 (2002). One potential explanation is that the majority of those arrested for powder cocaine offenses were black.

4. "According to U.S. Sentencing Commission statistics, most people accused of crack cocaine offenses are black, and most powder cocaine defendants are nonblack." Paul Butler, *By Any Means Necessary: Using Violence and Subversion to Change Unjust Law*, 50 UCLA L. Rev. 721,734 (2003). Professor Butler continues "[t]he federal penalty includes mandatory prison sentences for distributing either form of cocaine, but only for possession of crack." *Id.* Can you think of a non-racially motivated basis for treating the two substances differently?

5. For a critique of *State v. Russell*, see Randall Kennedy, *The State, Criminal Law, and Racial Discrimination: A Comment*, 107 Harv. L. Rev. 1255, 1264–1265 (1994). Consider the following quote from Professor Kennedy: "Given the complexity of 'the black community,' conflicting desires among its various sectors, differential effects upon these sectors by facially race neutral laws, and hence, the difficulty of confidently identifying racial

subordination in the absence of discriminatory purpose, the federal constitutional standard for determining what counts as impermissible state action is attractively prudent. In contrast to the approach typified by Russell, it does not force legislatures to erase what appear to be 'racial' disparities either by leveling down (for example, lowering to the powdered cocaine standard the punishment for possessors of crack) or leveling up (for example, raising to the crack cocaine standard the punishment for possessors of powder). To be sure, appearances are important. Indeed, the strength of that concern, measured against competing considerations, might well counsel in favor of pursuing one policy over another. The conclusion reached here is simply that, in the absence of findings of discriminatory purpose (or some such other violation of constitutional norms) legislatures are more fitting fora than courts for such calculations." *Id*. at 1277–1278. Do you agree with the Court or Professor Kennedy—who has the better argument here? *See also* Jeffery A. Kruse, *Substantive Equal Protection Analysis Under State v. Russell, and the Potential Impact on the Criminal Justice Center*, 50 Wash. & Lee L. Rev. 1791 (1993). (where author states that "legislatures, and not the judiciary should become the leaders in preserving equal protection guarantees from policies that disproportionately burden minorities." *Id*. at 1831). How long should people of color wait for legislatures to pass laws eliminating the disparity?

6. For favorable commentary on *State v. Russell, see* Knoll D. Lowney, *Smoked Not Snorted: Is Racism Inherent in Our Crack Cocaine Laws?*, 45 Wash. U. J. Urb. & Contemp. L. 121 (1994).

7. How would the statute have been viewed under Professor Lawrence's cultural meaning test?

8. Professor Dorothy Roberts states "[n]ot only is race used to identify criminals, it is embedded in the very foundation of our criminal law. Race helps to determine who the criminals are, what conduct constitutes a crime, and which crimes society treats most seriously." Dorothy E. Roberts, *Crime, Race, and Reproduction*, 67 Tul. L. Rev. 1945 (1993). Does this explain why the penalties for crack cocaine are so much more severe than for powdered cocaine?

9. The death penalty is another example of a sentence with a racially discriminatory impact. The United States Supreme Court in *McCleskey v. Kemp*, 481 U.S. 279, 107 S.Ct. 1756, 95 L.Ed.2d 262 (1987), found that a racially disparate impact in the implementation of the death penalty was insufficient to find a constitutional violation. Proof of discriminatory intent was required. *Id*. For a comprehensive empirical analysis *see* David C. Baldus et al., Equal Justice and the Death Penalty: A Legal and Empirical Analysis (1990); David C. Baldus et al., *Racial Discrimination and the Death Penalty in the Post-Furman Era: An Empirical and Legal Overview, with Recent Findings from Philadelphia*, 83 Cornell L. Rev. 1638 (1998). *See also* Sheri Lynn Johnson, *Unconscious Racism and the Criminal Law*, 73 Cornell L. Rev.1016, 1017–1021 (1988).

10. Professor Dorothy Roberts makes a compelling argument that racial disparity in the implementation of our criminal justice system has a significant impact on the African–American community in ways not often discussed. First, African–Americans who are incarcerated are often disen-

franchised. "Nearly one in seven Black males of voting age have been disenfranchised as a result of incarceration." Dorothy E. Roberts, *Criminal Justice and Black Families: The Collateral Damage of Over-enforcement*, 34 U.C. Davis L. Rev. 1005, 1008 (2001). Second, spending time in prison negatively impacts the participation of African–Americans in the paid labor market. "When inmates return from prison they typically lack the education and skills needed to compete in the labor market. Imprisonment not only reduces the opportunities inmates have for legal work, it also strengthens their connections to criminal networks." *Id*. at 1008–1009. Third, the significant percentage of African–American men and juveniles in the criminal justice system has a "devastating impact on Black family life." *Id*.

C.   CAN LOOKING BLACK IMPACT YOUR SENTENCE?

WILLIAM T. PIZZI AND IRENE V. BLAIR AND CHARLES M. JUDD

Discrimination in Sentencing on the Basis of Afrocentric Features
10 Mich. J. Race & L. 327, 327–329, 330–332, 350–352.(2005).

INTRODUCTION: SENTENCING AND RACE

With a huge population of approximately two million prisoners, the United States has a particularly disturbing problem—the disproportional racial makeup of that population. Although African Americans constitute only 12% of this country's population, approximately 44% of those incarcerated are African American. This composition is discouraging and troubling. Not surprisingly, practically a cottage industry has emerged to examine our prison population from many different angles in an attempt to explain why African Americans are incarcerated at a rate six or seven times greater than Whites. Judicial sentencing discretion, in particular, has come under scrutiny. The discrepancies are so troubling that it is natural to wonder if some of the disparity might be due to racial discrimination by judges in their sentencing decisions.

However, empirical studies fail to show strong evidence of racial discrimination by judges in sentencing. Probably the most well-known of these studies was conducted by Alfred Blumstein; it examined arrest statistics and prison population statistics both by offense and by race. The Blumstein study concluded that 80% of the racial disparity in incarceration statistics was attributable to disparate racial arrest patterns, meaning that the great bulk of the disparity was not the result of post-arrest discrimination. While the study did not account for all of the disproportionality (Blumstein was careful to point out that his study did not show that sentencing was devoid of racial discrimination), it found the amount of disproportionality left unexplained differed with the seriousness of the crime. For example, the differential arrest rate explained almost all the disproportion in the incarceration rate of African Americans for serious crimes, such as murder and aggravated assault. However, less serious offenses exhibited larger unexplained variations.

The Blumstein study seemed to allow judges to breathe a sigh of relief because it suggested that racial discrimination in sentencing was not a major factor in the disproportionate percentage of African Americans in United States prisons.

* * *

Our overall assessment of the available research suggests that factors other than racial discrimination in the sentencing process account for most of the disproportionate representation of Black males in [United States] prisons, although discrimination in sentencing may play a more important role in some regions, jurisdictions, crime types, or the decisions of individual participants.

Despite what the studies seem to show, not everyone is convinced that race is not a factor in sentencing disparities. Some suggest that racial discrimination may be hidden in some way that makes it difficult to detect in these studies. For example, special circumstances, such as the race of the victim, might trigger racial discrimination in a way that the studies miss. Others suggest that data might show racial discrimination if studies examined more discrete aspects of sentencing, such as particular crimes or particular jurisdictions; these results may be missed when large amounts of data are analyzed. Finally, some insist that the researchers used outdated econometric tools in these studies.

This Article does not challenge the prior research on sentencing discrimination between racial categories that found no significant difference in sentences given to similarly-situated African Americans and Whites. In fact, in the jurisdiction we investigated—Florida—we found no discrimination between African Americans and Whites in the sentences imposed on defendants, looking only at racial category differences. Rather, our research suggests that in focusing exclusively on discrimination between racial groups, the research has missed a type of discrimination related to race that is taking place within racial categories: namely, discrimination on the basis of a person's Afrocentric features. By Afrocentric features, we mean those features that are perceived as typical of African Americans, e.g., darker skin, fuller lips, or a broader nose. Our research found that when one examines sentencing from this perspective, those defendants who have more pronounced Afrocentric features tend to receive longer sentences than others within their racial category who have less pronounced Afrocentric features.

It may seem puzzling that there may be no discrimination in sentencing between African Americans and Whites, yet there is definite discrimination against those with more pronounced Afrocentric features within each of these racial groups. However, it is our thesis that judges have learned to be more careful to impose similar sentences between racial groups, but they have not been similarly sensitized to the possibility of discrimination based on Afrocentric features within racial categories. This Article intends to begin the process of making the legal community aware of the potency that a person's Afrocentric features may have in biasing judgment within racial categories.

The research that forms the basis of this Article relates to research on an idea referred to as "colorism," which deals with prejudice and discrimination directed against African Americans with darker skin when, for example, benefits are more likely to be given to those with lighter skin. But important differences separate the research on colorism from our research. For one thing, colorism focuses primarily on skin color, while our research is broader and includes any facial features associated with African Americans, including, for example, hair texture, nose width, and lip fullness. But even more importantly, our research is not limited to examining bias toward African Americans. Our research finds a biasing effect of Afrocentric features among Whites that mirrors the biasing effect of Afrocentric features among African Americans. The bottom line is the same for the two racial categories: African American and White defendants who have stronger Afrocentric features within their racial category receive longer sentences than those with less pronounced Afrocentric features.

* * *

4.   Evaluating the Results

The results when we compared the sentences of African American and White inmates by racial category were consistent with the earlier findings reached by the state of Florida. We observed no adverse effect on sentencing when we looked only at the race of the inmate: African American and White offenders in the state of Florida, given equivalent criminal records, receive roughly equivalent sentences. This result seems to suggest that Florida has been able to meet the objective in its statute that sentences be "neutral with respect to race."

But when one looks more closely at features associated with race, the sentencing inmates receive is not unbiased—offenders with equivalent criminal records within the same racial category (African American or White) receive longer sentences if they have stronger Afrocentric features.

That Afrocentric features might distort criminal sentences when judges have the most relevant information about offenders at their disposal may seem surprising as well as disheartening. Before accusations of unbridled bias begin to fly, we remind readers that this result is consistent with our laboratory studies that show the difficulty of eliminating the influence of Afrocentric features on judgment. Even when subjects were given very clear and diagnostic information upon which to base their judgments, and even when they were told explicitly about the influence of Afrocentric features and told to avoid it, such features continued to influence their judgments. Although one might argue that judges have the most pertinent information, they must still rely on their subjective perceptions to some extent. As a consequence, stereotypes may lead to the conclusion that some individuals (e.g., those with stronger Afrocentric features) are more threatening, more dangerous, less remorseful, and more culpable, and thus more deserving of longer sentences.

We must acknowledge, of course, that the effects we have shown may be attributable to a series of stages or decisions during the criminal sentencing process. For instance, the inmate records to which we had access contained no indication of whether plea-bargaining had taken place, either to determine the primary offense or the resulting sentence length. It may well be the case that the biases due to Afrocentric facial features that we have shown are attributable not only to judges but also to district attorneys and many others involved in the plea bargaining and sentencing process. Thus, throughout our discussion we have referred to judges being influenced by Afrocentric features, but the more appropriate characterization is that there may be biases in the whole process of which sentencing is the final outcome.

Taking the results as a whole, some might be tempted to say that the picture is fairly positive. Race is not being used in sentencing decisions, and if anything, African Americans are coming out ahead of Whites when Afrocentric features are equated. But such a conclusion is a serious misinterpretation of the study's results. Racial stereotyping in sentencing decisions still persists. But it is not a function of the racial category of the individual; instead, there seems to be an equally pernicious and less controllable process at work. Racial stereotyping in sentencing still occurs based on the facial appearance of the offender. Be they White or African American, those offenders who possess stronger Afrocentric features receive harsher sentences for the same crimes.

How large are the impacts of Afrocentric features on sentences? One way to calibrate them is to derive predicted sentence lengths (for the mean levels of the criminal history variables) for individuals within each race who are one standard deviation above and below the mean level of Afrocentric features for their racial group. When we did this and compared the length of sentences, we found that individuals one standard deviation above their group mean on Afrocentric features are receiving sentences about 7–8 months longer than individuals one standard deviation below their group mean with the same criminal record. This difference is clearly meaningful.

CONCLUSION

Our laboratory research described in Part I of this Article shows that people use Afrocentric features to infer traits that are stereotypic of African Americans, and importantly, this form of stereotyping appears to occur without people's awareness and outside of their immediate control. Given the laboratory findings, it is not surprising that we found similar results, as described in Part II, when we looked at the influence of Afrocentric features on sentencing decisions. Judges appear to behave like the laboratory participants in the studies, and this suggests that they were unaware of the fact that Afrocentric features were influencing their decisions.

What causes this bias based on Afrocentric features is unclear, but we theorize that a person's facial features lead to stereotyping in two ways. Of course, one can use a person's facial features to infer that a person is a member of a racial category, and racial stereotyping can then ensue on that basis. But we believe that something else is going on at this point in time, and that a person's Afrocentric features can trigger stereotypic inferences about that person even within a racial category. In short, Afrocentric features have potency on their own to influence judgment and trigger stereotypic inferences.

Obviously, race-based stereotypes have the potential to lead judges to perceive African American offenders more negatively than White offenders, and for that reason our criminal justice system continues to monitor sentencing from that perspective. But judges have been well-sensitized to this form of possible bias and it seems that they are able to avoid it for that reason. However, judges have not been sensitized to the discrimination that has been described in this Article, namely discrimination on the basis of a person's Afrocentric features. The perception that a particular offender appears more dangerous or culpable than other offenders within the same racial group is unlikely to raise the red flag of racial bias as it is customarily understood, and thus no steps are taken to ensure that sentencing is not biased by the mere fact that the offender has more pronounced Afrocentric features. It is the purpose of this Article to call attention to this form of bias and to start sensitizing those in the criminal justice system to the unfairness, irrationality, and injustice that can result from this form of bias.

Notes and Questions

1. How can this form of bias be eliminated or minimized, when their study shows even when you point out to people that the potential for bias exists, their behavior doesn't change?

2. For an excellent article discussing the phenomenon of colorism *see* Trina Jones, *Shades of Brown: The Law of Skin Color*, 49 Duke L. J. 1487 (2000).

3. There have been several articles written describing the impact on sentencing of the defendant's physical appearance. *See e.g.*, Jennifer L. Eberhardt et al., Looking Deathworthy: Perceived Stereotypicality of Black Defendants Predicts Capital–Sentencing Outcomes, 17 Psychol. Sci. 383 (2006).

Chapter 7

CRITICAL RACE THEORY AND PROPERTY

This Chapter looks at Critical Race Theory and property rights. It begins with Professor Cheryl Harris' article that requires us to look at property in a different way. She encourages us to examine the question whether our property laws are based upon "neutral" and "objective" rules or are another mechanism for racial subordination. She compares the treatment of African–Americans under the law with the treatment of Native Americans under the law. The Chapter then considers two cases that deal with the property rights of Native Americans and Professor Joseph Singer's analysis who argues that viewing property law through the lens of our treatment of Native Americans will teach us much about property rights. The Chapter closes with a consideration of a modern day take on the issue.

SECTION 1.   WHAT IS PROPERTY?

CHERYL I. HARRIS

Whiteness as Property
106 Harv. L. Rev. 1707, 1714–1720, 1721–1724,
1725–1731, 1758–1761, 1763 (1993).

* * *

My Article investigates the relationships between concepts of race and property and reflects on how rights in property are contingent on, intertwined with, and conflated with race. Through this entangled relationship between race and property, historical forms of domination have evolved to reproduce subordination in the present. * * * I examine the emergence of whiteness as property and trace the evolution of whiteness from color to race to status to property as a progression historically rooted in white supremacy and economic hegemony over Black and Native American peoples. The origins of whiteness as property lie in the parallel systems of domination of Black and Native American peoples out of which were created racially contingent forms of property and property rights. I further argue that whiteness shares the critical characteristics of property even as the meaning of property has changed over time. In particular, whiteness and property share a common premise—a conceptual nucleus—of a right to exclude. This conceptual nucleus has proven to be a powerful center around which whiteness as property has taken shape. Following the period of slavery and conquest, white identity became the basis of racialized privilege that was ratified and legitimated in law as a type of status property. After legalized segregation was overturned, whiteness as property evolved into a more modern form through the law's ratification of the settled expectations of relative white privilege as a legitimate and natural baseline.

* * *

[The Article] considers the persistence of whiteness as property. I first examine how subordination is reinstituted through modern conceptions of race and identity embraced in law. Whiteness as property has taken on more subtle forms, but retains its core characteristic—the legal legitimation of expectations of power and control that enshrine the status quo as a neutral baseline, while masking the maintenance of white privilege and domination.

* * *

The racialization of identity and the racial subordination of Blacks and Native Americans provided the ideological basis for slavery and conquest. Although the systems of oppression of Blacks and Native Americans differed in form—the former involving the seizure and appropriation of labor, the latter entailing the seizure and appropriation of land—undergirding both was a racialized conception of property implemented by force and ratified by law.

The origins of property rights in the United States are rooted in racial domination. Even in the early years of the country, it was not the concept of race alone that operated to oppress Blacks and Indians; rather, it was the interaction between conceptions of race and property that played a critical role in establishing and maintaining racial and economic subordination.

The hyper-exploitation of Black labor was accomplished by treating Black people themselves as objects of property. Race and property were thus conflated by establishing a form of property contingent on race—only Blacks were subjugated as slaves and treated as property. Similarly, the conquest, removal, and extermination of Native American life and culture were ratified by conferring and acknowledging the property rights of whites in Native American land. Only white possession and occupation of land was validated and therefore privileged as a basis for property rights. These distinct forms of exploitation each contributed in varying ways to the construction of whiteness as property.

Although the early colonists were cognizant of race, racial lines were neither consistently nor sharply delineated among or within all social groups. Captured Africans sold in the Americas were distinguished from the population of indentured or bond servants—"unfree" white labor—

but it was not an irrebuttable presumption that all Africans were "slaves" or that slavery was the only appropriate status for them. The distinction between African and white indentured labor grew, however, as decreasing terms of service were introduced for white bond servants. Simultaneously, the demand for labor intensified, resulting in a greater reliance on African labor and a rapid increase in the number of Africans imported into the colonies.

The construction of white identity and the ideology of racial hierarchy also were intimately tied to the evolution and expansion of the system of chattel slavery. The further entrenchment of plantation slavery was in part an answer to a social crisis produced by the eroding capacity of the landed class to control the white labor population. The dominant paradigm of social relations, however, was that, although not all Africans were slaves, virtually all slaves were not white. It was their racial otherness that came to justify the subordinated status of Blacks. The result was a classification system that "key[ed] official rules of descent to national origin" so that "[m]embership in the new social category of 'Negro' became itself sufficient justification for enslaveability." Although the cause of the increasing gap between the status of African and white labor is contested by historians, it is clear that "[t]he economic and political interests defending Black slavery were far more powerful than those defending indentured servitude."

By the 1660s, the especially degraded status of Blacks as chattel slaves was recognized by law. Between 1680 and 1682, the first slave codes appeared, codifying the extreme deprivations of liberty already existing in social practice. Many laws parceled out differential treatment based on racial categories: Blacks were not permitted to travel without permits, to own property, to assemble publicly, or to own weapons; nor were they to be educated. Racial identity was further merged with stratified social and legal status: "Black" racial identity marked who was subject to enslavement; "white" racial identity marked who was "free" or, at minimum, not a slave. The ideological and rhetorical move from "slave" and "free" to "Black" and "white" as polar constructs marked an important step in the social construction of race.

The social relations that produced racial identity as a justification for slavery also had implications for the conceptualization of property. This result was predictable, as the institution of slavery, lying at the very core of economic relations, was bound up with the idea of property. Through slavery, race and economic domination were fused.

Slavery produced a peculiar, mixed category of property and humanity—a hybrid possessing inherent instabilities that were reflected in its treatment and ratification by the law. The dual and contradictory character of slaves as property and persons was exemplified in the Representation Clause of the Constitution. Representation in the House of Representatives was apportioned on the basis of population computed by counting all persons and "three-fifths of all other persons"—slaves. Gouveneur Morris's remarks before the Constitutional Convention posed the essential question: "Upon what principle is it that slaves shall be computed in the representation? Are they men? Then make them Citizens & let them vote? Are they property? Why then is no other property included?"

The cruel tension between property and humanity was also reflected in the law's legitimation of the use of Blackwomen's bodies as a means of increasing property. In 1662, the Virginia colonial assembly provided that "[c]hildren got by an Englishman upon a Negro woman shall be bond or free according to the condition of the mother...." In reversing the usual common law presumption that the status of the child was determined by the father, the rule facilitated the reproduction of one's own labor force. Because the children of Blackwomen assumed the status of their mother, slaves were bred through Blackwomen's bodies. The economic significance of this form of exploitation of female slaves should not be underestimated. Despite Thomas Jefferson's belief that slavery should be abolished, like other slaveholders, he viewed slaves as economic assets, noting that their value could be realized more efficiently from breeding than from labor. A letter he wrote in 1805 stated: "I consider the labor of a breeding woman as no object, and that a child raised every 2 years is of more profit than the crop of the best laboring man."

* * *

Slavery as a system of property facilitated the merger of white identity and property. Because the system of slavery was contingent on and conflated with racial identity, it became crucial to be "white," to be identified as white, to have the property of being white. Whiteness was the characteristic, the attribute, the property of free human beings.

Slavery linked the privilege of whites to the subordination of Blacks through a legal regime that attempted the conversion of Blacks into objects of property. Similarly, the settlement and seizure of Native American land supported white privilege through a system of property rights in land in which the "race" of the Native Americans rendered their first possession rights invisible and justified conquest. This racist formulation embedded the fact of white privilege into the very definition of property, marking another stage in the evolution of the property interest in whiteness. Possession—the act necessary to lay the basis for rights in property—was defined to include only the cultural practices of whites. This definition laid the foundation for the idea that whiteness— that which whites alone possess—is valuable and is property.

Although the Indians were the first occupants and possessors of the land of the New World, their racial and cultural otherness allowed this fact to be reinterpreted and ultimately erased as a basis for asserting rights in land. Because the land had been left in its natural state, untilled and unmarked by human hands, it was "waste" and, therefore, the appropriate object of settlement and appropriation. Thus, the possession maintained by the Indians was not "true" possession and could safely be ignored. This interpretation of the rule of first possession effectively rendered the rights of first possessors contingent on the race of the possessor. Only particular forms of possession—those that were characteristic of white settlement—would be recognized and legitimated. Indian forms of possession were perceived to be too ambiguous and unclear.

The conquest and occupation of Indian land was wrapped in the rule of law. The law provided not only a defense of conquest and colonization, but also a naturalized regime of rights and disabilities, power and disadvantage that flowed from it, so that no further justifications or rationalizations were required. A key decision defending the right of conquest was *Johnson and Graham's Lessee v. M'Intosh*, in which both parties to the action claimed the same land through title descendant from different Indian tribes. The issue specifically presented was not merely whether Indians had the power to convey title, but to whom the conveyance could be made—to individuals or to the government that "discovered" land. In holding that Indians could only convey to the latter, the Court reasoned that Indian title was subordinate to the absolute title of the sovereign that was achieved by conquest because "[c]onquest gives a title which the Courts of the conqueror cannot deny. . . ." If property is understood as a delegation of sovereign power— the product of the power of the state—then a fair reading of history reveals the racial oppression of Indians inherent in the American regime of property.

In Johnson and similar cases, courts established whiteness as a prerequisite to the exercise of enforceable property rights. Not all first possession or labor gave rise to property rights; rather, the rules of first possession and labor as a basis for property rights were qualified by race. This fact infused whiteness with significance and value because it was solely through being white that property could be acquired and secured under law. Only whites possessed whiteness, a highly valued and exclusive form of property.

* * *

Whiteness fits the broad historical concept of property described by classical theorists. In James Madison's view, for example, property "embraces every thing to which a man may attach a value and have a right," referring to all of a person's legal rights. Property as conceived in the founding era

> included not only external objects and people's relationships to them, but also all of those human rights, liberties, powers, and immunities that are important for human well-being, including: freedom of expression, freedom of conscience, freedom from bodily harm, and free and equal opportunities to use personal faculties.

Whiteness defined the legal status of a person as slave or free. White identity conferred tangible and economically valuable benefits and was jealously guarded as a valued possession, allowed only to those who met a strict standard of proof. Whiteness—the right to white identity as embraced by the law—is property if by property one means all of a person's legal rights.

Other traditional theories of property emphasize that the "natural" character of property is derivative of custom, contrary to the notion that property is the product of a delegation of sovereign power. This "bottom up" theory holds that the law of property merely codifies existing customs and social relations. Under that view, government-created rights such as social welfare payments cannot constitute legitimate property interests because they are positivistic in nature. Other theorists have challenged this conception, and argued that even the most basic of "customary" property rights—the rule of first possession, for example—is dependent on its acceptance or rejection in particular instances by the government. Citing custom as a source of property law begs the central question: whose custom?

Rather than remaining within the bipolar confines of custom or command, it is crucial to recognize the dynamic and multifaceted relationship among custom, command, and law, as well as the extent to which positionality determines how each may be experienced and understood. Indian custom was obliterated by force and replaced with the regimes of common law that embodied the customs of the conquerors. The assumption of American law as it related to Native Americans was that conquest did give rise to sovereignty. Indians experienced the property laws of the colonizers and the emergent American nation as acts of violence perpetuated by the exercise of power and ratified through the rule of law. At the same time, these laws were perceived as custom and "common sense" by the colonizers. The Founders, for instance, so thoroughly embraced Lockean labor theory as the basis for a right of acquisition because it affirmed the right of the New World settlers to settle on and acquire the frontier. It confirmed and ratified their experience.

Selective literalism

The law's interpretation of those encounters between whites and Native Americans not only inflicted vastly different results on them, but also established a pattern—a custom—of valorizing whiteness. As the forms of racialized property were perfected, the value and protection extended to whiteness increased. Regardless of which theory of property one adopts, the concept of whiteness—established by centuries of custom (illegitimate custom, but custom nonetheless) and codified by law—may be understood as a property interest.

Although property in the classical sense refers to everything that is valued and to which a person has a right, the modern concept of property focuses on its function and the social relations reflected therein. In this sense, modern property doctrine emphasizes the more contingent nature of property and has been the basis for the argument that property rights should be expanded.

Modern theories of property reject the assumption that property is "objectively definable or identifiable, apart from social context." Charles Reich's ground-breaking work, The New Property, was an early effort to focus on the function of property and note the changing social relations reflected and constructed by new forms of property derived from the government. Property in this broader sense encompassed jobs, entitlements, occupational licenses, contracts, subsidies, and indeed a whole host of intangibles that are the product of labor, time, and creativity, such as intellectual property, business goodwill, and enhanced earning potential from graduate degrees. Notwithstanding the dilution of new property since *Goldberg v. Kelly* and its progeny as well as continued attacks on the concept, the legacy of new property infuses the concept of property with questions of power, selection, and allocation. Reich's argument that property is not a natural right but a construction by society resonates in current theories of property that describe the allocation of property rights as a series of choices. This construction directs attention toward issues of relative power and social relations inherent in any definition of property.

[margin note: BJU]

[margin note: property— education]

"Property is nothing but the basis of expectation," according to Bentham, "consist[ing] in an established expectation, in the persuasion of being able to draw such and such advantage from the thing possessed." The relationship between expectations and property remains highly significant, as the law "has recognized and protected even the expectation of rights as actual legal property." This theory does not suggest that all value or all expectations give rise to property, but those expectations in tangible or intangible things that are valued and protected by the law are property.

[margin note: in this way, the court was taking away BJU's property]

[margin note: BJU]

[margin note: right of BJU / Right to return / regain structuring of social relations]

In fact, the difficulty lies not in identifying expectations as a part of property, but in distinguishing which expectations are reasonable and therefore merit the protection of the law as property. Although the existence of certain property rights may seem self-evident and the protection of certain expectations may seem essential for social stability, property is a legal construct by which selected private interests are protected and upheld. In creating property "rights," the law draws boundaries and enforces or reorders existing regimes of power. The inequalities that are produced and reproduced are not givens or inevitabilities, but rather are conscious selections regarding the structuring of social relations. In this sense, it is contended that property rights and interests are not "natural," but are "creation[s] of law."

In a society structured on racial subordination, white privilege became an expectation and, to apply Margaret Radin's concept, whiteness became the quintessential property for personhood. The law constructed "whiteness" as an objective fact, although in reality it is an ideological proposition imposed through subordination. This move is the central feature of "reification": "Its basis is that a relation between people takes on the character of a thing and thus acquires a 'phantom objectivity,' an autonomy that seems so strictly rational and all-embracing as to conceal every trace of its fundamental nature: the relation between people." Whiteness was an "object" over which continued control was—and is—expected. The protection of these expectations is central because, as Radin notes: "If an object you now control is bound up in your future plans or in your anticipation of your future self, and it is partly these plans for your own continuity that make you a person, then your personhood depends on the realization of these expectations.''

Because the law recognized and protected expectations grounded in white privilege (albeit not explicitly in all instances), these expectations became tantamount to property that could not permissibly be intruded upon without consent. As the law explicitly ratified those expectations in continued privilege or extended ongoing protection to those illegitimate expectations by failing to expose or to radically disturb them, the dominant and subordinate positions within the racial hierarchy were reified in law. When the law recognizes, either implicitly or explicitly, the settled expectations of whites built on the privileges and benefits produced by white supremacy, it acknowledges and reinforces a property interest in whiteness that reproduces Black subordination.

didn't want to have to share priv., redistribute educational privilege / property

* * *

Even as the capacity of whiteness to deliver is arguably diminished by the elimination of rigid racial stratifications, whiteness continues to be perceived as materially significant. Because real power and wealth never have been accessible to more than a narrowly defined ruling elite, for many whites the benefits of whiteness as property, in the absence of legislated privilege, may have been reduced to a claim of relative privilege only in comparison to people of color. Nevertheless, whiteness retains its value as a "consolation prize": it does not mean that all whites will win, but simply that they will not lose, if losing is defined as being on the bottom of the social and economic hierarchy—the position to which Blacks have been consigned.

Andrew Hacker, in his 1992 book Two Nations, recounts the results of a recent exercise that probed the value of whiteness according to the perceptions of whites. The study asked a group of white students how much money they would seek if they were changed from white to Black. "Most seemed to feel that it would not be out of place to ask for $50 million, or $1 million for each coming black year." Whether this figure represents an accurate amortization of the societal cost of being Black in the United States, it is clear that whiteness is still perceived to be valuable. The wages of whiteness are available to all whites regardless of class position, even to those whites who are without power, money, or influence. Whiteness, the characteristic that distinguishes them from Blacks, serves as compensation even to those who lack material wealth. It is the relative political advantages extended to whites, rather than actual economic gains, that are crucial to white workers. Thus, as Kimberle' Crenshaw points out, whites have an actual stake in racism. Because Blacks are held to be inferior, although no longer on the basis of science as antecedent determinant, but by virtue of their position at the bottom, it allows whites—all whites—to "include themselves in the dominant circle. [Although most whites] hold no real power, [all can claim] their privileged racial identity.''

White workers often identify primarily as white rather than as workers because it is through their whiteness that they are afforded access to a host of public, private, and psychological benefits. It is through the concept of whiteness that class consciousness among white workers is subordinated and attention is diverted from class oppression.

Although dominant societal norms have embraced the idea of fairness and nondiscrimination, removal of privilege and antisubordination principles are actively rejected or at best ambiguously received because expectations of white privilege are bound up with what is considered essential for self-realization. Among whites, the idea persists that their whiteness is meaningful. Whiteness is an aspect of racial identity surely, but it is much more; it remains a concept based on relations of power, a social construct predicated on white dominance and Black subordination.

legacy admissions a good example

* * * The questions pertaining to definitions of race then are not principally biological or genetic, but social and political: what must be addressed is who is defining, how is the definition constructed, and why is the definition being propounded. Because definition is so often a central part of domination, critical thinking about these issues must precede and adjoin any definition. The law has not attended to these questions. Instead, identity of "the other" is still objectified, the complex, negotiated quality of identity is ignored, and the impact of inequitable power on identity is masked.

instead of seeking a change in interpretation, seek to change those who interpret

* * *

Notes and Questions

1. Why is history relevant here? How would you respond to the argument that slavery was abolished over 100 years ago and isn't really relevant to legal analysis today?

2. What characteristics do you find in property? How many of the following characteristics does "whiteness" have? The incidents of ownership have been described as "1. right to possess; 2. right to use; 3. right to manage; 4. right to income; 5. right to the capital; 6. right to security; 7. the incident of transmissibility; 8. the incident of absence of term; 9. the prohibition of harmful use; 10. liability for execution [for debts]...." Anthony M. Honoré, *Ownership* in A. Guest ed., OXFORD ESSAYS IN JURISPRUDENCE 107, 108–124.

3. The law for years constructed blacks as property and owned as slaves. Should the law remedy that? How? Similarly, the law has been constructed to strip land away from Native Americans. Should the law remedy that? How?

4. For an interesting article examining how the courts handled claims arising from White men who sought to leave property to formerly enslaved women and their children, *see* Adrienne D. Davis, *The Private Law of Race and Sex: An Antebellum Perspective*, 51 Stan. L. Rev. 221 (1999).

SECTION 2.   WHOSE PROPERTY RIGHTS
WILL THE LAW RECOGNIZE?

JOHNSON v. McINTOSH

21 U.S. (8 Wheat.) 543, 5 L.Ed. 681 (1823).

* * *

MR. CHIEF JUSTICE MARSHALL delivered the opinion of the Court.

The plaintiffs in this cause claim the land, in their declaration mentioned, under two grants, purporting to be made, the first in 1773, and the last in 1775, by the chiefs of certain Indian tribes, constituting the Illinois and the Piankeshaw nations; and the question is, whether this title can be recognised in the Courts of the United States?

The facts, as stated in the case agreed, show the authority of the chiefs who executed this conveyance, so far as it could be given by their own people; and likewis [sic] show, that the particular tribes for whom these chiefs acted were in rightful possession of the land they sold. The inquiry, therefore, is, in a great measure, confined to the power of Indians to give, and of private individuals to receive, a title which can be sustained in the Courts of this country.

As the right of society, to prescribe those rules by which property may be acquired and preserved is not, and cannot be drawn into question; as the title to lands, especially, is and must be admitted to depend entirely on the law of the nation in which they lie; it will be necessary, in pursuing this inquiry, to examine, not singly those principles of abstract justice, which the Creator of all things has impressed on the mind of his creature man, and which are admitted to regulate, in a great degree, the rights of civilized nations, whose perfect independence is acknowledged; but those principles also which our own government has adopted in the particular case, and given us as the rule for our decision.

On the discovery of this immense continent, the great nations of Europe were eager to appropriate to themselves so much of it as they could respectively acquire. Its vast extent offered and [sic] ample field to the ambition and enterprise of all; and the character and religion of its inhabitants afforded an apology for considering them as a people over whom the superior genius of Europe might claim an ascendency. The potentates of the old world found no difficulty in convincing themselves that they made ample compensation to the inhabitants of the new, by bestowing on them civilization and Christianity, in exchange for unlimited independence. But, as they were all in pursuit of nearly the same object, it was necessary, in order to avoid conflicting settlements, and consequent war with each other, to establish a principle, which all should acknowledge as the law by which the right of acquisition, which they all asserted, should be regulated as between themselves. This principle was, that discovery gave title to the government by whose subjects, or by whose authority, it was made, against all other European governments, which title might be consummated by possession.

The exclusion of all other Europeans, necessarily gave to the nation making the discovery the sole right of acquiring the soil from the natives, and establishing settlements upon it. It was a right with which no Europeans could interfere. It was a right which all asserted for themselves, and to the assertion of which, by others, all assented.

Those relations which were to exist between the discoverer and the natives, were to be regulated by themselves. The rights thus acquired being exclusive, no other power could interpose between them.

In the establishment of these relations, the rights of the original inhabitants were, in no instance, entirely disregarded; but were necessarily, to a considerable extent, impaired. They were admitted to be the rightful occupants of the soil, with a legal as well as just claim to retain possession of it, and to use it according to their own discretion; but their rights to complete sovereignty, as independent nations, were necessarily diminished, and their power to dispose of the soil at their own will, to whomsoever they pleased, was denied by the original fundamental principle, that discovery gave exclusive title to those who made it.

While the different nations of Europe respected the right of the natives, as occupants, they asserted the ultimate dominion to be in themselves; and claimed and exercised, as a consequence of this ultimate dominion, a power to grant the soil, while yet in possession of the natives. These grants have been understood by all, to convey a title to the grantees, subject only to the Indian right of occupancy.

The history of America, from its discovery to the present day, proves, we think, the universal recognition of these principles.

* * *

The ceded territory was occupied by numerous and warlike tribes of Indians; but the exclusive right of the United States to extinguish their title, and to grant the soil, has never, we believe, been doubted.

After these States became independent, a controversy subsisted between them and Spain respecting boundary. By the treaty of 1795, this controversy was adjusted, and Spain ceded to the United States the territory in question. This territory, though claimed by both nations, was chiefly in the actual occupation of Indians.

The magnificent purchase of Louisiana, was the purchase from France of a country almost entirely occupied by numerous tribes of Indians, who are in fact independent. Yet, any attempt of others to intrude into that country, would be considered as an aggression which would justify war.

* * *

The title by conquest is acquired and maintained by force. The conqueror prescribes the limits. Humanity, however, acting on public opinion, has established as a general rule, that the conquered shall not be wantonly oppressed, and that their condition shall remain as eligible as is compatible with the objects of the conquest. Most usually, they are incorporated with the victorious nation, and become subjects or citizens of the government with which they are connected. The new and old members of the society mingle with each other; the distinction between them is gradually lost, and they make one people. Where this incorporation is practicable, humanity demands, and a wise policy requires, that the rights of the conquered to property should remain unimpaired; that the new subjects should be governed as equitably as the old, and that confidence in their security should gradually banish the painful sense of being separated from their ancient connexions, and united by force to strangers.

When the conquest is complete, and the conquered inhabitants can be blended with the conquerors, or safely governed as a distinct people, public opinion, which not even the conqueror can disregard, imposes these restraints upon him; and he cannot neglect them without injury to his fame, and hazard to his power.

But the tribes of Indians inhabiting this country were fierce savages, whose occupation was war, and whose subsistence was drawn chiefly from the forest. To leave them in possession of their country, was to leave the country a wilderness; to govern them as a distinct people, was impossible, because they were as brave and high spirited as they were fierce, and were ready to repel by arms every attempt on their independence.

What was the inevitable consequence of this state of things? The Europeans were under the necessity either of abandoning the country, and relinquishing their pompous claims to it, or of enforcing those claims by the sword, and by the adoption of principles adapted to the condition of a people with whom it was impossible to mix, and who could not be governed as a distinct society, or of remaining in their neighbourhood, and exposing themselves and their families to the perpetual hazard of being massacred.

* * *

However extravagant the pretension of converting the discovery of an inhabited country into conquest may appear; if the principle has been asserted in the first instance, and afterwards sustained; if a country has been acquired and held under it; if the property of the great mass of the community originates in it, it becomes the law of the land, and cannot be questioned. So, too, with respect to the concomitant principle, that the Indian inhabitants are to be considered merely as occupants, to be protected, indeed, while in peace, in the possession of their lands, but to be deemed incapable of transferring the absolute title to others. However this restriction may be opposed to natural right, and to the usages of civilized nations, yet, if it be indispensable to that system under which the country has been settled, and be adapted to the actual condition of the two people, it may, perhaps, be supported by reason, and certainly cannot be rejected by Courts of justice.

* * *

It is supposed to be a principle of universal law, that, if an uninhabited country be discovered by a number of individuals, who acknowledge no connexion with, and owe no allegiance to, any government whatever, the country becomes the property of the discoverers, so far at least as they can use it. They acquire a title in common. The title of the whole land is in the whole society. It is to be divided and parcelled out according to the will of the society, expressed by the whole body, or by that organ which is authorized by the whole to express it.

* * *

After bestowing on this subject a degree of attention which was more required by the magnitude of the interest in litigation, and the able and elaborate arguments of the bar, than by its intrinsic difficulty, the Court is decidedly of opinion, that the plaintiffs do not exhibit a title which can be sustained in the Courts of the United States; and that there is no error in the judgment which was rendered against them in the District Court of Illinois.

Judgment affirmed, with costs.

Notes and Questions

1. The irony of *Johnson v. McIntosh* is that neither of the parties in *Johnson v. McIntosh* were Native Americans. The case was a dispute between non-Native American claimants, all of whom traced their title to two purchases from the Illinois and Piankeshaw Indians. The plaintiffs traced their title to two land speculation syndicates which had each purchased the land directly from the Illinois and Piankeshaw Indians in 1773 and 1775 for $54,000. The defendant, McIntosh, traced his title to his purchase of the land from the United States in 1818. The United States had received the lands by treaties of cession from the Illinois and Piankeshaw Indians and other Indians, after the grants to the two land speculation syndicates. *See* Kenneth H. Bobroff, *Indian Law in Property: Johnson v. M'Intosh and Beyond*, 37 Tulsa L. Rev. 521 (2001); Sally Ackerman, *The White Supremacist Status Quo: How the American Legal System Perpetuates Racism as Seen Through the Lens of Property Law*, 21 Hamline J. Publ. L. & Pol'y 137 (1999). It didn't matter that the defendant purchased the land after the plaintiffs, because the plaintiffs purchased their land from the Native Americans—who the court determined could not pass title.

2. Describe the Court's legal analysis which led to the holding that the Native Americans only had possessory rights and not title.

3. How could the United States pass good title to the defendant, when it originally acquired title from the Native Americans? The Supreme Court in 1810 in *Fletcher v. Peck*, 10 U.S. (6 Cranch) 87, 3 L.Ed. 162 (1810) held that the state did have the power to convey that which it did not own entirely. Chief Justice Marshall asserted that "Indian title" vested possesso-

ry rights in the native inhabitants, while also leaving ultimate ownership in the state. *Id.* at 142–143. *See also* John P. Lowndes, *When History Outweighs Law: Extinguishment of Abenaki Aboriginal Title*, 42 Buffalo L. Rev. 77 (1994).

4. In *Johnson v. McIntosh*, the Court based its holding on the doctrine of discovery which provided that absolute title was granted to the nation of the discoverers. Absolute title was not achieved until the lands were actually possessed by the discovering nation. As a result, the Supreme Court established a doctrine which provided an incentive for discoverers to physically drive out Native Americans from the land they lived on. How much influence do you think this decision had on the subsequent loss of Native American lands?

5. How can there be a "discoverer" when there are already people living on the land?

6. How did the issue of the assimilation of the Native Americans arise in *Johnson v. McIntosh*? Do you think the Court would have held differently if they believed the Native Americans could have been assimilated? What form would that assimilation most likely have taken?

7. What was the Court's view of what would happen to the land if they ruled differently? Review the following excerpt from the opinion. "But the tribes of Indians inhabiting this country were fierce savages, whose occupation was war, and whose subsistence was drawn chiefly from the forest. To leave them in possession of their country, was to leave the country a wilderness; to govern them as a distinct people, was impossible, because they were as brave and high spirited as they were fierce, and were ready to repel by arms every attempt on their independence." What imagery is being conveyed to the reader?

8. The Court documents what prevents oppression of those who are conquered. Describe the process. Why were the Native Americans oppressed?

JOSEPH WILLIAM SINGER

Legal Theory: Sovereignty and Property
86 Nw. U.L. Rev. 1, 41–43, 44–47, 50–51 (1991).

* * *

If "property is a set of social relations among human beings," the legal definition of those relationships confers—or withholds—power over others. The grant of a property right to one person leaves others vulnerable to the will of the owner. Conversely, the refusal to grant a property right leaves the claimant vulnerable to the will of others, who may with impunity infringe on the interests which have been denied protection.

Sometimes the state grants freedom to the general public to use particular valuable resources—land, for example, or an idea—without vesting exclusive control or possession in any particular person or group. The liberty to use or have access to those resources is a valuable property right which, if taken away, may significantly restrict a person's wealth or life possibilities. This is true even though the right of access is non-exclusive. At the same time, the fact that this kind of property right is non-exclusive means that it is a mere privilege to use the resources as long as no one else gets to them first; others have similar privileges to use the resources. To the extent those resources are scarce, the state leaves people vulnerable to having the things they need taken or appropriated by others. The freedom to use or possess limited resources implies a correlative vulnerability in others. The failure to assign an exclusive property right to a specific person leaves her at risk of having her interests infringed by others.

At other times, the state confers a property right by granting a specific person or group of persons the right to call on the aid of the state to keep others from using particular resources without the owner's consent. The right to exclude others entails a duty, enforceable by state coercion, to defer to the owner's will. To the extent the owner possesses resources needed by the non-owner, the law confers upon the owner a power that is "limited but real" to make the non-owner do what the owner wants. The creation of a property right therefore leaves some people vulnerable to the will of others.

Morris Cohen reminds us that "[t]he extent of the power over the life of others which the legal order confers on those called owners is not fully appreciated...." Conversely, the failure to protect a set of interests as exclusive property rights leaves the people who assert those interests vulnerable to others. Both the creation and the failure to create a property right leaves people vulnerable to harm, either at the hands of the state or at the hands of other persons. A central question, therefore, is how our legal system goes about defining and allocating property rights. Much has been written about this problem. I want here to address it from a new angle. What lessons can we learn about property rights, and the relation between property and state power, by focusing on the ways in which the rules in force deal with the property rights of American Indian nations?

American Indian legal issues are generally treated as a specialized field whose principles are irrelevant to the core of United States property law. To the extent the rules of Indian property differ from rules concerning non-Indian property, they are understood as exceptions to basic principles. These exceptions are thought to deal with an exceptional social context; they are not thought to affect the integrity of the core principles. But what happens if we take the law of American Indian property as a central concern rather than as a peripheral one? What happens if it is the first thing we address, rather than the last?

If we start our analysis of the relation between sovereignty and property by asking how the law treats the original possessors of land in the United States, we learn some valuable lessons about property law generally. We also learn some surprising facts about the basis and distribution of sovereign power in the United States.

Traditional property law casebooks and treatises generally ignore American Indian property law. The rules of non-Indian property law are developed in depth, but American Indian property law is either not mentioned at all, or is addressed only through discussion of Chief Justice John Marshall's opinion in the venerable case of Johnson v. M'Intosh. This case is often read (incorrectly) to hold that American Indian nations lost whatever property rights they may have had because they were conquered by the United States. Although Indian tribes had a right of occupancy to the lands they continued to possess, that right could be extinguished by the United States, which had conquered them. Regrettable as it may be, in this version of the law, conquest seems to be a phenomenon of the past which cannot be undone. This traditional approach touches on American Indian law only to emphasize its marginality. Conquest happened; it may have been wrong but it cannot be rectified—too much water has passed under the bridge.

Suppose we started our analysis of property by taking seriously the history of the legal treatment of American Indian nations. * * * If we took American Indian law seriously, it becomes clear, as I have argued in this article, that the legal system currently confers less protection on American Indian property than it does on non-Indian property. The rules about just compensation for takings of property either do not apply to Indian property (original Indian title may be taken without just compensation) or impose lesser constraints on the government than in the non-Indian context (recognized title may be taken without just compensation if the government, in good faith, is exercising its fiduciary power to manage Indian affairs for the good of the Indians under its trust relationship with Indian nations). Further, non-Indian property rights appear to be granted super-protection when they are located on Indian reservations (non-Indians appear to have a right to vote in the government which zones their property only if that property is located on an Indian reservation). This super-protection of non-Indian property inside reservations limits the sovereign power of Indian nations in a way that does not apply to non-Indian municipal governments, and infringes on the property rights of the Indians who are neighbors to the non-Indians.

* * *

Property in the United States is associated with a racial caste system. Nor is this a phenomenon of the past; the law continues to confer—and withhold—property rights in a way that provides less protection for property rights of American Indian nations in crucial instances than is provided for non-Indian individuals and entities. This means that if we want to help a client determine the extent of its property rights, the first thing we need to know is whether the client is an American Indian nation or, say, a business corporation. The law provides a certain level of protection for the interests of General Motors and a quite different level of protection for the interests of the Yakima Nation. Imagine having to explain this to a client, and being asked why.

This divergent treatment is not simply a minor fact of injustice that could be corrected by strategic changes in contemporary constitutional law doctrines. Rather, it means that the distribution of property rights in land in the United States has less than auspicious origins. Unless it is rectified—unless it can be rectified—the distribution of real property is inherently suspect. The history of United States law, from the beginning of the nation to the present, is premised on the use of sovereign power to allocate property rights in ways that discriminated—and continue to discriminate—against the original inhabitants of the land. Changing a few doctrines of law would not erase this history of injustice, nor undo its effects on the current situation of Indian nations. If the injustice cannot be easily rectified, then it places continuing obligations on the present and future generations to attend to the meaning of the past. If those who benefit from this history of injustice claim a vested right to its benefits, they should be aware that what they claim is a right to the benefits of a system of racial hierarchy.

Nor is this lesson confined to American Indian nations. Black Americans, torn from Africa, placed in slavery, and then "freed," were never given the land, education, and other resources that had been available to many other Americans. Unless we join the Supreme Court in calling a halt to history, we need to understand the current distribution of property in the United States as growing out of this history of injustice. We must see the ways in which the rules in force are implicated in the social construction of race. We need to understand the racial context in which property law developed and in which the distribution of wealth has been established and continues to be established. This context gives us no reason to feel confident that the distribution of wealth in the United States is just.

We learn from American Indian law that the rules in force identify certain interests that will be protected as property rights and other interests that will be denied protection as property. * * *

Suppose we dwell on the fact that promises made to municipal bondholders are enforceable as recognized property rights, but that promises made to Indian nations in treaties may be breached with impunity. We may be led to ask how the law draws distinctions among the interests it will protect and those it will not protect. What other interests are not recognized as property?

Consider that jobs are granted quite limited protection as property interests. It is possible to work for a company for many years and then be fired without being given a reason, despite the substantial personal investment which went into the job. On the other hand, if one is given a license to enter another person's property and to invest substantially in reliance on the license—for example, by building a road—then the doctrine of easement by estoppel makes the right of access irrevocable for whatever period is required by justice. What makes a monetary investment on someone else's property more worthy of legal protection than a lifetime commitment to an employer? What makes a personal investment in working for someone else less important than the financial investment of the employer?

Consider further that employers are granted wide power to hire replacement workers when their employees go out on strike. The law therefore allows employers to use workers against each other as strike-breakers; this right includes the liberty to attempt to attract workers away from other jobs. However, employees are not allowed to engage in secondary boycotts; attempts to persuade other employers to deal fairly with their employees by refusing to deal with those employers is unprotected by federal law. The law fails to protect workers who wish to band together against another employer to put economic pressure on that employer, while it protects employers who use other employees against its own employees. This means that employees are not protected if they refuse to deal with another company that is hiring strikebreakers. Why is the right to hire strikebreakers part of the employer's protected property rights while the right to refuse to deal with that employer is not a part of employees' protected property rights?

Consider that nuisance law prohibits property owners from unreasonably causing substantial harm to the use and enjoyment of neighboring property. Nuisances regulated by the common law include such harms as pollution or excessive noise. Yet corporations are allowed to close large factories that have been in existence for many years, putting thousands of people out of work, creating substantial misery and wrecking the local economy without any liability to the workers or the community.

Most work performed by men is done for pay. Yet historically many women have performed unpaid work in the home. Recent proposals to implement "workfare" are premised on the notion that women taking care of children in their homes are "not working" and that welfare payments are therefore handouts or gratuities which must be paid off. Why doesn't taking care of children count as "work"? Why is it that women's labor in the home does not count as labor sufficient to create property rights?

These examples show that property rights are not self-defining. Rather, the legal system makes constant choices about which interests to define as property. It also determines how to allocate power between competing claimants when interests conflict. And the pattern of protection and vulnerability is a result of a historical and social context which has created different opportunities based on such factors as race, sex, sexual orientation, disability and class.

* * *

Focusing on American Indian property thus gives us a rather different picture of the origin of property rights than that to which most of us are perhaps accustomed. The historical basis of original acquisition of property in the United States is not individual possession in the state of nature, with government stepping in only to protect property rights justly acquired. Rather, it is redistribution by the government from those who were thought not to need the property or to be misusing it to those who were thought to need it—a different picture, indeed.

Notes and Questions

1. Explain how *Johnson v. McIntosh* can be viewed as a takings decision?

2. Provide examples of how the "legal system makes constant choices about which interests to define as property" in a way that supports racial subordination.

3. How important are the rules governing property to the economic empowerment of people of color? *depends on what we define as "property."*

4. Professor Singer notes that "[f]ocusing on American Indian property thus gives us a rather different picture of the origin of property rights ..." Is he right?

5. Consider the next case for further support of Professor Singer's position.

TEE–HIT–TON INDIANS v. U.S.

348 U.S. 272, 75 S.Ct. 313, 99 L.Ed. 314 (1955).

MR. JUSTICE REED delivered the opinion of the Court.

This case rests upon a claim under the Fifth Amendment by petitioner, an identifiable group of American Indians of between 60 and 70 individuals residing in Alaska, for compensation for a taking by the United States of certain timber from Alaskan lands allegedly belonging to the group. The area claimed is said to contain over 350,000 acres of land and 150 square miles of water. The Tee–Hit–Tons, a clan of the Tlingit Tribe, brought this suit in the Court of Claims under 28 U. S. C. § 1505. The compensation claimed does not arise from any statutory direction to pay. Payment, if it can be compelled, must be based upon a constitutional right of the Indians to recover. This is not a case that is connected with any phase of the policy of the Congress, continued throughout our history, to extinguish Indian title through negotiation rather than by force, and to grant payments from the public purse to needy descendants of exploited Indians. The legislation in support of that policy has received consistent interpretation from this Court in sympathy with its compassionate purpose. *Paternalistic*

Upon petitioner's motion, the Court of Claims under its Rule 38(b) directed a separate trial with respect to certain specific issues of law and any related issues of fact essential to the proper adjudication of the legal issues. Only those pertinent to the nature of the petitioner's interest, if any, in the lands are here for review. Substantial evidence, largely documentary, relevant to these legal issues was introduced by both parties before a Commissioner who thereupon made findings of fact. The Court of Claims adopted these findings and held that petitioner was an identifiable group of American Indians residing in Alaska; that its interest in the lands prior to purchase of Alaska by the United States in 1867 was "original Indian title" or "Indian right of occupancy." *Tee-Hit–Ton Indians* v. *United States*, 128 Ct.Cl. 82, 85, 87, 120 F.Supp. 202, 203–204, 205. It was further held that if such original Indian title survived the Treaty of 1867, 15 Stat. 539, Arts. III and VI, by which Russia conveyed Alaska to the United States, such title was not sufficient basis to maintain this suit as there had been no recognition by Congress of any legal rights in petitioner to the land in question. 128 Ct.Cl., at 92, 120 F.Supp., at 208. The court said that no rights inured to plaintiff by virtue of legislation by Congress. As a result of these conclusions, no answer was necessary to questions 2, 5 and 6. The Tee–Hit–Tons' petition was thereafter dismissed.

Because of general agreement as to the importance of the question of compensation for congressionally approved taking of lands occupied in Alaska under aboriginal Indian use and claim of ownership, and the conflict concerning the effect of federal legislation protecting Indian occupation between this decision of the Court of Claims, 128 Ct.Cl., at 90, 120 F.Supp., at 206–207, and the decision of the Court of Appeals for the Ninth Circuit in *Miller* v. *United States*, 159 F.2d 997, 1003, we granted certiorari, *347 U.S. 1009.*

The Alaskan area in which petitioner claims a compensable interest is located near and within the exterior lines of the Tongass National Forest. By Joint Resolution of August 8, 1947, 61 Stat. 920, the Secretary of Agriculture was authorized to contract for the sale of national forest timber located within this National Forest "notwithstanding any claim of possessory rights." The Resolution defines "possessory rights" and provides for all receipts from the sale of timber to be maintained in a special account in the Treasury until the timber and land rights are finally determined. Section 3(b) of the Resolution provides:

> "Nothing in this resolution shall be construed as recognizing or denying the validity of any claims of possessory rights to lands or timber within the exterior boundaries of the Tongass National Forest."

The Secretary of Agriculture, on August 20, 1951, pursuant to this authority contracted for sale to a private company of all merchantable timber in the area claimed by petitioner. This is the sale of timber which petitioner alleges constitutes a compensable taking by the United States of a portion of its proprietary interest in the land.

The problem presented is the nature of the petitioner's interest in the land, if any. Petitioner claims a "full proprietary ownership" of the land; or, in the alternative, at least a "recognized" right to unrestricted possession, occupation and use. Either ownership or recognized possession, petitioner asserts, is compensable. If it has a fee simple interest in the entire tract, it has an interest in the timber and its sale is a partial taking of its right to "possess, use and dispose of it." *United States* v. *General Motors Corp.*, 323 U.S. 373, 378. It is petitioner's contention that its tribal predecessors have continually claimed, occupied and used the land from time immemorial; that when Russia took Alaska, the Tlingits had a well-developed social order which included a concept of property ownership; that Russia while it possessed Alaska in no manner interfered with their claim to the land; that Congress has by subsequent acts confirmed and recognized petitioner's right to occupy the land permanently and therefore the sale of the timber off such lands constitutes a taking pro tanto of its asserted rights in the area.

The Government denies that petitioner has any compensable interest. It asserts that the Tee–Hit–Tons' property interest, if any, is merely that of the right to the use of the land at the Government's will; that Congress has never recognized any legal interest of petitioner in the land and therefore without such recognition no compensation is due the petitioner for any taking by the United States.

I. Recognition.—The question of recognition may be disposed of shortly. Where the Congress by treaty or other agreement has declared that thereafter Indians were to hold the lands permanently, compensation must be paid for subsequent taking. The petitioner contends that Congress has sufficiently "recognized" its possessory rights in the land in question so as to make its interest compensable. Petitioner points specifically to two statutes to sustain this contention. The first is § 8 of the Organic Act for Alaska of May 17, 1884, 23 Stat. 24. The second is § 27 of the Act of June 6, 1900, which was to provide for a civil government for Alaska, 31 Stat. 321, 330. The Court of Appeals in the Miller case, *supra*, felt that these Acts constituted recognition of Indian ownership. 159 F.2d 997, 1002–1003.

We have carefully examined these statutes and the pertinent legislative history and find nothing to indicate any intention by Congress to grant to the Indians any permanent rights in the lands of Alaska occupied by them by permission of Congress. Rather, it clearly appears that what was intended was merely to retain the status quo until further congressional or judicial action was taken. There is no particular form for congressional recognition of Indian right of permanent occupancy. It may be established in a variety of ways but there must be the definite intention by congressional action or authority to accord legal rights, not merely permissive occupation. *Hynes* v. *Grimes Packing Co.*, 337 U.S. 86, 101.

[margin note: must be definite intention by Cong. action]

This policy of Congress toward the Alaskan Indian lands was maintained and reflected by its expression in the Joint Resolution of 1947 under which the timber contracts were made.

II. Indian Title.—(a) The nature of aboriginal Indian interest in land and the various rights as between the Indians and the United States dependent on such interest are far from novel as concerns our Indian inhabitants. It is well settled that in all the States of the Union the tribes who inhabited the lands of the States held claim to such lands after the coming of the white man, under what is sometimes termed original Indian title or permission from the whites to occupy. That description means mere possession not specifically recognized as owner-ship by Congress. After conquest they were permitted to occupy portions of territory over which they had previously exercised "sovereignty," as we use that term. This is not a property right but amounts to a right of occupancy which the sovereign grants and protects against intrusion by third parties but which right of occupancy may be terminated and such lands fully disposed of by the sovereign itself without any legally enforce-able obligation to compensate the Indians.

This position of the Indian has long been rationalized by the legal theory that discovery and conquest gave the conquerors sovereignty over and ownership of the lands thus obtained. 1 Wheaton's International Law, c. V. The great case of *Johnson* v. *McIntosh*, 8 Wheat. 543, denied the power of an Indian tribe to pass their right of occupancy to another. It confirmed the practice of two hundred years of American history "that discovery gave an exclusive right to extinguish the Indian title of occupancy, either by purchase or by conquest." P. 587.

* * *

In *Beecher* v. *Wetherby*, 95 U.S. 517, a tract of land which Indians were then expressly permitted by the United States to occupy was granted to Wisconsin. In a controversy over timber, this Court held the Wisconsin title good.

"The grantee, it is true, would take only the naked fee, and could not disturb the occupancy of the Indians: that occupancy could only be interfered with or determined by the United States. It is to be presumed that in this matter the United States would be governed by such considerations of justice as would control a Christian people in their treatment of an ignorant and dependent race. Be that as it may, the propriety or justice of their action towards the Indians with respect to their lands is a question of governmental policy, and is not a matter open to discussion in a controversy between third parties, neither of whom derives title from the Indians. The right of the United States to dispose of the fee of lands occupied by them has always been recognized by this court from the foundation of the government." P. 525.

In 1941 a unanimous Court wrote, concerning Indian title, the following:

"Extinguishment of Indian title based on aboriginal possession is of course a different matter. The power of Congress in that regard is supreme. The manner, method and time of such extinguishment raise political, not justiciable, issues." *United States* v. *Santa Fe Pacific R. Co.*, 314 U.S. 339, 347.

No case in this Court has ever held that taking of Indian title or use by Congress required compensation. The American people have compassion for the descendants of those Indians who were deprived of their homes and hunting grounds by the drive of civilization. They seek to have the Indians share the benefits of our society as citizens of this Nation. Generous provision has been willingly made to allow tribes to recover for wrongs, as a matter of grace, not because of legal liability. 60 Stat. 1050.

(b) There is one opinion in a case decided by this Court that contains language indicating that unrecognized Indian title might be compensable under the Constitution when taken by the United States. *United States v. Tillamooks*, 329 U.S. 40.

Recovery was allowed under a jurisdictional Act of 1935, 49 Stat. 801, that permitted payments to a few specific Indian tribes for "legal and equitable claims arising under or growing out of the original Indian title" to land, because of some unratified treaties negotiated with them and other tribes. The other tribes had already been compensated. Five years later this Court unanimously held that none of the former opinions in Vol. 329 of the United States Reports expressed the view that recovery was grounded on a taking under the Fifth Amendment. *United States v. Tillamooks*, 341 U.S. 48. Interest, payable on recovery for a taking under the Fifth Amendment, was denied.

Before the second Tillamook case, a decision was made on Alaskan Tlingit lands held by original Indian title. *Miller v. United States*, 159 F.2d 997. That opinion holds such a title compensable under the Fifth Amendment on reasoning drawn from the language of this Court's first Tillamook case. After the Miller decision, this Court had occasion to consider the holding of that case on Indian title in *Hynes v. Grimes Packing Co.*, 337 U.S. 86, 106, note 28. We there commented as to the first Tillamook case: "That opinion does not hold the Indian right of occupancy compensable without specific legislative direction to make payment." We further declared "we cannot express agreement with that [compensability of Indian title by the Miller case] conclusion."

Later the Government used the Hynes v. Grimes Packing Co. note in the second Tillamook case, petition for certiorari, p. 10, to support its argument that the first Tillamook opinion did not decide that taking of original Indian title was compensable under the Fifth Amendment. Thereupon this Court in the second Tillamook case, 341 U.S. 48, held that the first case was not "grounded on a taking under the Fifth Amendment." Therefore no interest was due. This later Tillamook decision by a unanimous Court supported the Court of Claims in its view of the law in this present case. *See Tee–Hit–Ton Indians v. United States*, 128 Ct.Cl., at 87, 120 F.Supp., at 204–205. We think it must be concluded that the recovery in the Tillamook case was based upon statutory direction to pay for the aboriginal title in the special jurisdictional act to equalize the Tillamooks with the neighboring tribes, rather than upon a holding that there had been a compensable taking under the Fifth Amendment. This leaves unimpaired the rule derived from *Johnson v. McIntosh* that the taking by the United States of unrecognized Indian title is not compensable under the Fifth Amendment.

This is true, not because an Indian or an Indian tribe has no standing to sue or because the United States has not consented to be sued for the taking of original Indian title, but because Indian occupation of land without government recognition of ownership creates no rights against taking or extinction by the United States protected by the Fifth Amendment or any other principle of law.

if so generous, why not interpret the law in their favor?

(c) What has been heretofore set out deals largely with the Indians of the Plains and east of the Mississippi. The Tee–Hit–Tons urge, however, that their stage of civilization and their concept of ownership of property takes them out of the rule applicable to the Indians of the States. They assert that Russia never took their lands in the sense that European nations seized the rest of America. The Court of Claims, however, saw no distinction between their use of the land and that of the Indians of the Eastern United States. *See Tee–Hit–Ton Indians v. United States*, 128 Ct.Cl. 82, 87, 120 F.Supp. 202, 204–205. That court had no evidence that the Russian handling of the Indian land problem differed from ours. The natives were left the use of the great part of their vast hunting and fishing territory but what Russia wanted for its use and that of its licensees, it took. The court's conclusion on this issue was based on strong evidence.

In considering the character of the Tee–Hit–Tons' use of the land, the Court of Claims had before it the testimony of a single witness who was offered by plaintiff. He stated that he was the chief of the Tee–Hit–Ton tribe. He qualified as an expert on the Tlingits, a group composed of numerous interconnected tribes including the Tee–Hit–Tons. His testimony showed that the Tee–Hit–Tons had become greatly reduced in numbers. Membership descends only through the female line. At the present time there are only a few women of childbearing age and a total membership of some 65.

The witness pointed out that their claim of ownership was based on possession and use. The use that was made of the controverted area was for the location in winter of villages in sheltered spots and in summer along fishing streams and/or bays. The ownership was not individual but tribal. As the witness stated, "Any member of the tribe may use any portion of the land that he wishes, and as long as he uses it that is his for his own enjoyment, and is not to be trespassed upon by anybody else, but the minute he stops using it then any other member of the tribe can come in and use that area."

?? valuing individual over tribal Cultural value going back to M'intosh

When the Russians first came to the Tlingit territory, the most important of the chiefs moved the people to what is now the location of the town of Wrangell. Each tribe took a portion of Wrangell harbor and the chief gave permission to the Russians to build a house on the shore.

The witness learned the alleged boundaries of the Tee–Hit–Ton area from hunting and fishing with his uncle after his return from Carlisle Indian School about 1904. From the knowledge so obtained, he outlined in red on the map, which petitioner filed as an exhibit, the territory claimed by the Tee–Hit–Tons. Use by other tribal members is sketchily asserted. This is the same 350,000 acres claimed by the petition. On it he marked six places to show the Indians' use of the land: (1) his great uncle was buried here, (2) a town, (3) his uncle's house, (4) a town, (5) his mother's house, (6) smokehouse. He also pointed out the uses of this tract for fishing salmon and for hunting beaver, deer and mink.

The testimony further shows that while membership in the tribe and therefore ownership in the common property descended only through the female line, the various tribes of the Tlingits allowed one another to use their lands. Before power boats, the Indians would put their shelters for hunting and fishing away from villages. With the power boats, they used them as living quarters.

— shows possession

In addition to this verbal testimony, exhibits were introduced by both sides as to the land use. These exhibits are secondary authorities but they bear out the general proposition that land claims among the Tlingits, and likewise of their smaller group, the Tee–Hit–Tons, was wholly tribal. It was more a claim of sovereignty than of ownership. The articles presented to the Court of Claims by those who have studied and written of the tribal groups agree with the above testimony. There were scattered shelters and villages moved from place to place as game or fish became scarce. There was recognition of tribal rights to hunt and fish on certain general areas, with claims to that effect carved on totem poles. From all that was presented, the Court of Claims concluded, and we agree, that the Tee–Hit–Tons were in a hunting and fishing stage of civilization, with shelters fitted to their environment, and claims to rights to use identified territory for these activities as well as the gathering of wild products of the earth. We think this evidence introduced by both sides confirms the Court of Claims' conclusion that the petitioner's use of its lands was like the use of the nomadic tribes of the States Indians.

? why, b/c it couldn't

The line of cases adjudicating Indian rights on American soil leads to the conclusion that Indian occupancy, not specifically recognized as ownership by action authorized by Congress, may be extinguished by the Government without compensation. Every American schoolboy knows that the savage tribes of this continent were deprived of their ancestral ranges by force and that, even when the Indians ceded millions of acres by treaty in return for blankets, food and trinkets, it was not a sale but the conquerors' will that deprived them of their land. The duty that rests on this Nation was adequately phrased by Mr. Justice Jackson in his concurrence, Mr. Justice Black joining, in *Shoshone Indians v. United States*, 324 U.S. 335, at 355, a case that differentiated "recognized" from "unrecognized" Indian title, and held the former only compensable. *Id.*, at 339–340. His words will be found at 354–358. He ends thus:

> "We agree with Mr. Justice Reed that no legal rights are today to be recognized in the Shoshones by reason of this treaty. We agree with

Mr. Justice Douglas and Mr. Justice Murphy as to their moral deserts. We do not mean to leave the impression that the two have any relation to each other. The finding that the treaty creates no legal obligations does not restrict Congress from such appropriations as its judgment dictates 'for the health, education, and industrial advancement of said Indians,' which is the position in which Congress would find itself if we found that it did create legal obligations and tried to put a value on them." *Id.*, at 358.

In the light of the history of Indian relations in this Nation, no other course would meet the problem of the growth of the United States except to make congressional contributions for Indian lands rather than to subject the Government to an obligation to pay the value when taken with interest to the date of payment. Our conclusion does not uphold harshness as against tenderness toward the Indians, but it leaves with Congress, where it belongs, the policy of Indian gratuities for the termination of Indian occupancy of Government-owned land rather than making compensation for its value a rigid constitutional principle.

only get money if they leave

The judgment of the Court of Claims is

Affirmed. * * *

Notes and Questions

1. John Lowndes argues that the Court in *Tee–Hit–Ton Indians* finds that the United States has superior title by the very presence of Whites in North America. Is that a reasonable interpretation of *Tee–Hit–Ton Indians*? *See* John P. Lowndes, *When History Outweighs Law: Extinguishment of Abenaki Aboriginal Title*, 42 Buffalo L. Rev. 77 (1994). For an additional discussion of the *Tee–Hit–Ton Indians* decision, *see* Stacy L. Leeds, *The More Things Stay The Same: Waiting on Indian Law's Brown v. Board of Education*, 38 Tulsa L. Rev. 73, 80–81 (2002).

2. Describe the Court's legal analysis in the *Tee–Hit–Ton Indians* decision. Does it extend the logic from *Johnson v. McIntosh?* Y

3. After the *Tee–Hit–Ton Indians* decision, it becomes clear that under the United States Constitution, sovereign Indian nations had no property rights that the judicial system was legally required to recognize. How did societal beliefs impact the court's analysis and shape this area of the law?

4. Where does the Court send the Native Americans to look for compensation? *Congress*

5. Professor Nell Newton describes how the United States government used the legal system to take land from Native American tribes "by methods both naked and subtle despite the high sounding words of the Fifth Amendment Takings Clause." Nell Jessup Newton, *Compensation, Reparations, & Restitution: Indian Property Claims in the United States*, 28 Ga. L. Rev. 453, 457 (1994). Would you agree?

ALFRED L. BROPHY

Integrating Spaces: New Perspectives on Race in the Property Curriculum.
55 J. Legal Educ. 319, 319–320, 322–324 (2005).

INTRODUCING THE PROPERTY COURSE: OF EVICTIONS,
NATIVE LAND RIGHTS, AND SLAVERY

Of Blackstone's Absolutism and Ellison's Questions

Many property classes begin with a statement from William Blackstone about the seemingly absolute rights associated with property:

This is nothing which so generally strikes the imagination, and engages the affections of mankind, as the right of property; or that sole and despotic dominion which one man exercises over the external things of the world, in total exclusion of any other individual in the universe.

Despite those broad rights, Blackstone observed the seeming fragility of the intellectual foundation of property rights:

Pleased as we are with the possession, we seem afraid to look back to the means by which it was acquired, as if fearful of some element in our title; or at best we rest satisfied with the decision of the laws in our favour, without examining the reason or authority upon which those laws have been built.

Indeed, Blackstone accepted the utility of refusing to interrogate the source of title. For, presumably, such an inquiry might destabilize respect for property. But Blackstone also thought it worthwhile for students of law to go further. "When law is to be considered not only as a matter of practice, but also as a rational science, it cannot be improper or useless to examine more deeply the rudiments and grounds of those positive constitutions of society."

* * *

On the Property Rights of Native Americans, Slaves, and Slave–Owners

I begin my property course with a segment on "property rights versus civil rights," an idea adapted from the Donahue, Kauper, and Martin casebook. We explore the competing rights of property owners to the exclusive use of their property with the interests of others. I assemble readings from several sections of the property book, so we explore Native American property rights (or non-rights); migrant farm workers' rights to have visitors at their homes; the right of the state to zone; and the limits on the right of others to govern use of property. One might also include the Civil Rights Act of 1964, which limited the right to exclude, as well as the Civil Rights Act of 1866, which prohibited discrimination in the selling or leasing of property. Property theorists have explored the right of exclusion and its implications for civil rights as well. I seek to illustrate the ways that property rights exist in a larger context of competing public and private rights. One might just as easily use Buchanan v. Warley, a 1917 United States Supreme Court decision *limitations on the power to exclude*

that struck down a racial zoning ordinance, to show <u>the limitations on the government's power to exclude,</u> although it implicitly accepts the power to zone.

The first case assigned in many property courses is Chief Justice John Marshall's opinion in Johnson v. McIntosh, which dealt with a conflict between grantees who had received title to the same land from the federal government and from Native Americans. The case presented a conflict between two white people regarding who had the superior claim: the man who traced his title from a grant from the Illinois and Piankeshaw Indians in 1775 or the man who traced his title to a grant from the United States in 1819. Marshall began his analysis by reciting the rule long followed by European nations that discovery gave a right to the "discovering" nation to confirm its title to the land by conquering (or purchasing from) the native inhabitants. Marshall recognized some of the seeming oddness, perhaps even injustice, of taking land from the Natives, for in announcing the rule, he acknowledged how "extravagant the pretension of converting the discovery of an inhabited country into conquest may appear." He further acknowledged how the conclusion that the Natives were merely occupiers, not owners of the land, "may be opposed to natural right, and to the usages of civilized nations." But he thought no other rule could be applied. For if a holding "be indispensable to the actual condition of the two people, it may, perhaps, be supported by reason, and certainly cannot be rejected by Courts of justice."

Marshall thus announced a two part rule: discovery plus confirmation of title, which might happen by conquest as well as by purchase. Conquest presented an imperative rule: "Conquest gives a title which the Courts of the conqueror cannot deny, whatever the private and speculative opinions of individuals may be, respecting the original justice of the claim which has been successfully asserted." He had no desire to issue a decision at odds with either long-term prescription or public opinion. As he concluded, "if a country has been acquired and held under it; if the property of the great mass of the community originates in it, it becomes the law of the land, and cannot be questioned."

There is much in Johnson that is useful in introducing the property course: the idea that property rules are dictated by the state and that they are confirmed by long-term usage; the respect given rights that are acquired under that usage; the extent to which courts will, of necessity, support property and long-term usage. Johnson can set many themes for a course, as well as teach about the power of the right of property. Johnson is worthy of sustained exploration and Lindsay Robertson's study is a fine companion to assign with the case. Johnson has a twentieth-century analog in Tee–Hit–Ton Indians v. United States, which suggests that, even in the absence of conquest, the sovereign's claim to property will prevail over the claim of Natives.

* * *

Notes and Questions

Is history relevant in current litigation of property rights? If so, how much of an influence should it be?

Assuming you agree that the original property rights of American Indians were unfairly "taken" without compensation by the U.S. Government and/or the judiciary, what should the remedy be?

Chapter 8

CRITICAL RACE THEORY AND CIVIL PROCEDURE

This Chapter looks at Critical Race Theory and Civil Procedure. Think of the various legal rights that people of color have gained through the judicial system. Although this Chapter is the last in the book, it arguably is the most important. If the judicial system is an avenue of protection of rights for people of color, the ability to have your case heard is of primary importance.

The Chapter begins with an excerpt that provides an overview of the various ways that you could incorporate a critical race theory perspective into a Civil Procedure course. The balance of the chapter discusses the variety of ways that civil procedure can be used as a bar to achieving racial equality. The Chapter considers two decisions: (i) *Dred Scott*; and (ii) *Conley v. Gibson* and concludes with an excerpt that prods us to consider the ways in which procedural rules lead to substantive results which may negatively impact people of color and their quest for racial equality.

SECTION 1. CRITICAL RACE THEORY AND CIVIL PROCEDURE: AN OVERVIEW

KEVIN R. JOHNSON

Integrating Racial Justice Into the Civil Procedure Survey Course.
54 J. Legal Educ. 242–247, 253, 259, 263 (2004).

Although I fear that the average law student might disagree, civil procedure is not simply a boring set of technical rules governing the litigation process. True, it can be taught that way, but any proceduralist knows that civil procedure can be much more. Indeed, it touches on some of the nation's most pressing social justice issues, ranging from full, fair, and efficient compensation of victims of mass torts to the democratic underpinnings of the system of trial by jury.

This article lays out the case for raising issues of race, as well as class and gender, in the civil procedure survey course—a class in which, surprisingly enough, they naturally fit. * * *

I. WHY INTEGRATE RACE, GENDER, AND CLASS INTO CIVIL PROCEDURE?

This section offers a brief justification for raising issues of racial justice, as well as more general issues of social justice, into the basic civil procedure course. Integrating race into class discussion broadens the students' focus beyond the doctrine outlined in the case at hand (without diminishing its importance). This will increase students' interest and raise their consciousness of how the law—even facially neutral doctrinal analysis—implicates social justice concerns.

A. The Undisputed Importance of the Issues

Any serious examination of modern U.S. social life must come to grips with race and class. Although race and class are discussed more frequently in connection with the criminal justice system, they influence the civil justice system as well. Students of civil procedure must learn to recognize their effects.

Analysis of civil rights and racial justice issues is important to legal education generally because those issues are central to a full understanding of U.S. social life. Race unfortunately constitutes a deep divide in the U.S. justice system—one that affects the legal profession as a whole. Social justice concerns have led to a proliferation of genres of legal scholarship, among them critical legal studies, which focuses on issues of class in the law; critical race theory, which analyzes the important role of race in the law, legal decision making, and law enforcement; and critical feminist theory, which studies the gendered nature of law and legal doctrine. Even if one does not buy into such theoretical frameworks, it is not easy to ignore the fundamental truth that race, class, and gender influence the judicial system in the United States.

B. Making Civil Procedure "Real" for the Students

Raising issues of racial justice breathes life into a topic that the average law student does not immediately latch onto. Especially in a course that spans the entire first year, it is important to maintain students' interest and to show them that civil procedure is more than an arcane set of rules with little bearing on public policy issues: in fact, it is relevant to the most pressing social controversies of the day.

Moreover, the course lets the instructor demonstrate how procedural rules have substantive impacts and implicate deep questions of social justice. Serious social divides cannot help but influence the allocation of justice in our court systems, civil as well as criminal—although not many law students know this intuitively. Discussion of the possible reflection of society's biases in the civil justice system can help students to be sensitive to such concerns in their future legal studies.

C. Civil Procedure as Neutral Territory for the Exploration of Social Justice Concerns

One distinct advantage of touching on issues of race in Civil Procedure is that, unlike Constitutional Law, the subject matter of the course is not seen as a natural hotbed of ideological controversy. Political lines are not etched in stone before the discussion begins. At the same time, important civil procedure landmarks raise fundamental issues of constitutional interpretation and individual rights.

* * * For many students, Civil Procedure is the first—and thus a very important—exposure to constitutional law in law school. It also can be an introduction to the complex issues of race and class implicated by the law, and can have a formative impact on a student's analysis, throughout law school, of these all-important issues.

D. Cautionary Notes

Of course, issues of race are not especially relevant to every area covered in Civil Procedure. * * * This article is not a covert (or overt) attempt to offer a critical race theory analysis of civil procedure. It does not offer a theory about how the law of civil procedure works with other bodies of law to subordinate racial minorities, women, the poor, and other groups. I simply argue for raising issues of social justice in the course. Such an approach is suggested by Rule 1 of the Federal Rules of Civil Procedure, which calls for the construction and administration of the rules "to secure the just, speedy, and inexpensive determination of every action" (emphasis added). It is easy for a class to fall into a pattern of focusing more on economy and efficiency concerns, which are often most obvious in the individual case and are more likely to be fully addressed by the courts, than on fairness and social justice.

One final cautionary note: integrating issues of racial justice, as well as gender and class, requires great sensitivity to the issues and to students' possible reactions to them. * * *

* * *

A. Subject Matter Jurisdiction: Citizens, Out-of-Staters, and Foreigners

Citizenship is a central concept in civil procedure. It is often said that racial minorities in the U.S. are afforded second-class citizenship. Civil procedure is one of the first places in the law school curriculum where conceptions of citizenship, and their connection with race, can be discussed. In examining citizenship, race and the nation's treatment of foreigners are topics worthy of discussion.

1. Conceptions of Citizenship

Citizenship, a touchstone of diversity-of-citizenship jurisdiction in the federal courts, is one of the areas of civil procedure in which race is relevant. Consider Dred Scott v. Sandford, a famous case brought in federal court on the basis of diversity-of-citizenship jurisdiction that brought the nation to the brink of civil war: the Supreme Court denied a freed African–American slave the ability to invoke the diversity jurisdiction of the federal courts because he was not a "citizen." Dred Scott is worth at least a passing reference in the discussion of diversity-of-citizenship jurisdiction. It is an important civil procedure milestone exemplifying institutionalized racism and the subordination of African–Americans, freed and enslaved. Because he was African–American, Dred Scott was denied citizenship under the law and denied access to the federal courts to resolve a claim to his very freedom. The Court's ruling was entirely consistent with the subordination of African–Americans—slavery being the most obvious example—in the United States. As Chief Justice Roger Taney wrote for the Court, "Blacks were so far inferior that they had no rights which the white man was bound to respect." The interpretation of citizenship raises the specter of race lurking in run-of-the-mill procedural doctrine.

2. The Justification for Diversity Jurisdiction

An introduction to the subject matter jurisdiction of the federal courts, with a focus on federal question and diversity-of-citizenship jurisdiction, is the bread and butter of most civil procedure survey courses. Diversity jurisdiction ostensibly offers litigants a "neutral" federal court alternative to the state courts if the litigants are from different states. In considering "citizenship" in modern times, one might reasonably ask students whether social divides other than bias against out-of-staters, the traditional justification offered for diversity-of-citizenship jurisdiction, are more significant in contemporary American social life.

Strong arguments can be made that race, national origin, immigration status, gender, and sexual orientation pose much more significant problems of discrimination and bias in the modern United States than bias against citizens of another state. Bias against African–Americans is generally viewed as a more pressing and prevalent social problem than bias against out-of-staters. Most observers, including first-year law students, would readily agree that other forms of discrimination dwarf any faced by citizens from other states. Diversity-of-citizenship jurisdiction, in this light, appears to be a historical anachronism, not a pressing modern need. It therefore can serve as the basis for fruitful class discussion.

* * *

D. Pleading

Pleading often raises issues of access to the courts, which are particularly important to litigants pursuing civil rights claims. Dioguardi v. Durning (1944), one of the earliest interpretations of the notice pleading requirements of the Federal Rules of Civil Procedure, dealt with an immigrant plaintiff's claim against the federal government. In an opinion written by one of the principal architects of the Federal Rules, Judge Charles Clark, the court found a barely intelligible pro se complaint drafted by an Italian immigrant to be sufficient to withstand a motion to dismiss.

A leading notice pleading case decided by the Supreme Court in 1957, Conley v. Gibson, involved a claim of racial discrimination against African–American railroad workers. The Court enunciated a frequently quoted—and quite liberal—approach to pleading: "[A] complaint should not be dismissed for failure to state a claim unless it appears beyond doubt that the plaintiff can prove no set of facts in support of his claim which would entitle him to relief."

Despite the clear liberality of notice pleading, beginning in the 1960s lower courts imposed stricter pleading requirements on many different types of suits, including civil rights actions, "fueled by concerns over burgeoning dockets and a perception of recurring frivolousness." One can only ask why civil rights, as opposed to personal injury, cases have been the focus of rigorous pleading standards in the lower courts.

Recent Supreme Court decisions have flatly rejected pleading requirements imposed by lower courts in civil rights and employment discrimination cases. The Court's continued adherence to notice pleading has made it easier to bring civil rights claims, a noteworthy point given that the Rehnquist Court is generally thought to be more conservative in rulings on civil rights and related claims.

Before it was amended in 1993, Federal Rule of Civil Procedure 11, which generally provided for mandatory sanctions for the filing of meritless actions, was criticized for its negative impact on civil rights litigants. A fair question to direct to the class is whether sanctions may disproportionately deter public interest groups from bringing cutting-edge civil rights litigation. Could, for example, the possibility of sanctions have inhibited civil rights advocates from bringing cases like Brown v. Board of Education, which called for the overruling of well-established precedent (Plessy v. Ferguson) and the "separate but equal" doctrine? This is an important question. Strict pleading requirements and frequent imposition of sanctions for bringing "frivolous" lawsuits may inhibit the filing of civil rights litigation designed to secure racial justice. Access to the courts, which is an issue governed by the federal pleading rules, is critically important to marginalized groups seeking to vindicate their civil rights.

* * *

G. Fairness for Racial Minorities in Civil Litigation

A more general question is whether racial minorities can expect to receive a fair trial in the United States. This question is discussed more frequently in connection with criminal cases in which an African–American is a defendant than in civil cases in which a racial minority is a party. Still, it is an issue well worth raising in class in connection with cases such as Edmonson v. Leesville Concrete Co. and Curtis v. Loether. Could the African–American plaintiffs in those cases reasonably expect to get a fair trial?

One can only wonder whether and, if so, how race may subtly influence the civil litigation process. For example, in a garden-variety automobile accident case in 1961, the Mississippi Supreme Court noted that a witness (Hal Buckley) was "a Negro man." This language was included in the excerpt of the case in the seventh edition of the Cound, Friedenthal, Miller & Sexton casebook but edited out of the eighth edition. Why did the Mississippi Supreme Court mention Buckley's race, and what does this tell us about the justice system in place in that state at the time? (And why did the casebook authors edit out that reference to race?) Do jurors, and perhaps courts, today silently consider a witness's race in deciding credibility? May unconscious racism or stereotypes influence the jury's credibility determinations? A teacher can raise questions about judging the credibility of witnesses and whether we should trust juries to make such difficult, and somewhat arbitrary, determinations.

* * *

Civil Procedure need not be a course in which students are only drilled in the nuts and bolts of the Federal Rules of Civil Procedure. Rather, because the subject implicates issues that go to the core of the U.S. justice system, it can offer students a law school introduction to some of the most important social issues of our time. A teacher who raises issues of race, gender, class, and immigration status can place the cases in their proper context and show how procedural doctrine implicates social justice concerns. * * *

Notes and Questions

1. Is Professor Johnson correct when he states that Civil Procedure touches upon some of the nation's most pressing social justice issues? If so, how?

2. How important was litigation in the advancement of civil rights for people of color?

3. How can rules be designed to encourage litigation? Discourage litigation? Are the rules the sole determinant of those rights or does the judiciary play a significant role in interpreting those rules?

SECTION 2. WHO CAN SUE: A PLAY IN TWO ACTS

SCOTT v. EMERSON

15 Mo. 576 (1852).

OPINION: SCOTT, J., delivered the opinion of the court.

This was an action instituted by Dred Scott against Irone Emerson, the wife and administratrix of Dr. John Emerson, to try his right to freedom. His claim is based upon the fact that his late master held him in servitude in the State of Illinois [where slavery was illegal], and also in that territory ceded by France to the United States, under the name of Louisiana, which lies north of 36 degrees 30 minutes, north latitude, not included within the limits of the State of Missouri.

It appears that his late master was a surgeon in the army of the United States, and during his continuance in the service, was stationed at Rock Island, a military post in the State of Illinois, and at Fort Snelling, also a military post in the territory of the United States, above described, at both of which places Scott was detained in servitude—at one place from the year 1834, until April or May, 1836; at the other from the period last mentioned until the year 1838. The jury was instructed, in effect, that if such were the facts, they would find for Scott. He, accordingly, obtained a verdict. [Scott argues that because he was in free country, he became free under the Somerset doctrine which holds that a slave became free upon setting foot in a free jurisdiction.]

The defendant moved for a new trial on the ground of misdirection by the court, which being denied to her, she sued out this writ of error.

Cases of this kind are not strangers in our courts. Persons have been frequently here adjudged to be entitled to their freedom, on the ground that their masters held them in slavery in territories or States in which that institution was prohibited. From the first case decided in our courts, it might be inferred that this result was brought about by a presumed assent of the master, from the fact of having voluntarily taken his slave to a place where the relation of master and slave did not exist. But subsequent cases base the right "to exact the forfeiture of emancipation," as they term it, on the ground, it would seem, that it is the duty of the courts of this State to carry into effect the constitution and laws of other States and territories, regardless of the rights, the policy or the institutions of the people of this State.

The States of this Union, although associated for some purposes of government, yet in relation to their municipal concerns have always been regarded as foreign to each other. * * * Every State has the right of determining how far, in a spirit of comity, it will respect the laws of other States. Those laws have no intrinsic right to be enforced beyond the limits of the State for which they were enacted. The respect allowed them will depend altogether on their conformity to the policy of our institutions. No State is bound to carry into effect enactments conceived in a spirit hostile to that which pervades her own laws. In the Conflict of Laws, sec. 36, it is said: "but of the nature, and extent and utility of this recognition of foreign laws, respecting the state and condition of persons, every nation must judge for itself, and certainly is not bound to recognize them, when they would be prejudicial to their own interests. It is, in the strictest sense a matter of the comity of nations, and not of any absolute paramount obligation, superceding all discretion on the subject." So in sec. 32, it is said, "it is difficult to conceive upon what ground a claim can be rested, to give any municipal laws an extra-territorial effect, when those laws are prejudicial to the rights of other nations or to those of their subjects; it would at once annihilate the sovereignty and equality of every nation, which should be called upon to recognize and enforce them, or to compel it to desert its own proper interests and duty to its own subjects in favor of strangers, who were regardless of both. A claim so naked of any principle or just authority to support it, is wholly inadmissible.''

* * * States in which an absolute prohibition of slavery prevails, maintain that if a slave, with the consent of his master, touch their soil he thereby becomes free. The prohibition in the act, commonly called the Missouri Compromise, is absolute. How is that to be interpreted? That act prevails along our entire western boundary; if our courts take upon themselves the task of enforcing the laws of other States, it is nothing but reasonable that they should take them as they are understood where they are promulgated. If a slave passes our western boundary, by the order of his master, and goes into the territory subject to the Missouri Compromise, does he thereby become free? Most of the courts of this Union would say that he does, if his freedom is sought to be recovered under the laws of that territory. If our courts undertake the task of enforcing that act, should they not take it as most of the other States would? Some of our old cases say, that a hiring for two days would be a violation of the constitution of Illinois and entitle the slave to his freedom. If two days would do, why not one? Is there any difference in principle or morality between holding a slave in a free territory two days more than one day? And if one day, why not six hours? The old cases say, the intent is nothing, the act is the thing.

Now, are we prepared to say, that we shall suffer these laws to be enforced in our courts? On almost three sides the State of Missouri is surrounded by free soil. If one of our slaves touch that soil with his master's assent, he becomes entitled to his freedom. Considering the numberless instances in which those living along an extreme frontier would have occasion to occupy their slaves beyond our boundary, how hard would it be if our courts should liberate all the slaves who should thus be employed! How unreasonable to ask it! If a master sends his slave to hunt his horses or cattle beyond the boundary, shall he thereby be liberated? But our courts, it is said, will not go so far. If not go the entire length, why go at all? The obligation to enforce to the proper degree is as obligatory as to enforce to any degree. Slavery is introduced by a continuance in the territory for six hours as well as for twelve months, and so far as our laws are concerned, the offense is as great in the one case as in the other. Laws operate only within the territory of the State for which they are made, and by enforcing them here, we, contrary to all principle, give them an extra-territorial effect Chancellor Kent says: "A statute, though not in the nature of a judicial proceeding, is, however, a record of the highest nature. But if a statute, though a matter of record, was to have the same effect in one State as in another, then one State would be dictating laws for another, and a fearful collision of jurisdiction would instantly follow. That construction is utterly inadmissible. While it is conceded to be a principle of public law, requisite for the safe intercourse and commerce of mankind, that acts, valid by the law of the State where they arise, are valid everywhere, it is at the same time, to be understood, that this principle relates only to civil acts founded on the volition of the parties, and not to such as proceed from the sovereign power. The force of the latter cannot be permitted to operate beyond the limits of the territory, without affecting the necessary independence of nations." 2 Kent 117–8.

This language is used when speaking in reference to the legislation of other States of the Union. It is conceived that there is no ground to presume or to impute any volition to Dr. Emerson, that his slave should have his freedom. He was ordered by superior authority to the posts where his slave was detained in servitude, and in obedience to that authority, he repaired to them with his servant, as he very naturally supposed he had a right to do. To construe this into an assent to his slave's freedom would be doing violence to his acts. Nothing but a persuasion that it is a duty to enforce the foreign law as though it was one of our own, could ever induce a court to put such a construction on his conduct. The present attitude of the parties to this suit is conclusive, as to an actual consent, and nothing but the foreign law or the aid derived from it, can raise an implied one. If the State of Missouri had prohibited slavery within her limits, and our courts were called upon to execute that law, some zeal might be tolerated in our efforts to execute it; but while slavery obtains here, there is no consideration which would warrant us in going such lengths against our own citizens, for having permitted their slaves to remain in the territory of a State where slavery is prohibited.

* * * An attempt has been made to show, that the comity extended to the laws of other States, is a matter of discretion, to be determined by the courts of that State in which the laws are proposed to be enforced. If it is a matter of discretion, that discretion must be controlled by circumstances. Times now are not as they were when the former decisions on this subject were made. Since then not only individuals, but States, have been possessed with a dark and fell spirit in relation to slavery, whose gratification is sought in the pursuit of measures, whose inevitable consequence must be the overthrow and destruction of our government. Under such circumstances it does not behoove the State of Missouri to show the least countenance to any measure which might gratify this spirit. She is willing to assume her full responsibility for the existence of slavery within her limits, nor does she seek to share or divide it with others. Although we may, for our own sakes, regret that the avarice and hard-heartedness of the progenitors of those who are now so sensitive on the subject, ever introduced the institution among us, yet we will not go to them to learn law, morality or religion on the subject.

As to the consequences of slavery, they are much more hurtful to the master than the slave. There is no comparison between the slave of the United States and the cruel, uncivilized negro in Africa. When the condition of our slaves is contrasted with the state of their miserable race in Africa; when their civilization, intelligence and instruction in religious truths are considered, and the means now employed to restore them to the country from which they have been torn, bearing with them the blessings of civilized life, we are almost persuaded that the introduction of slavery amongst us was, in the providences of God, who makes the evil passions of men subservient to his own glory, a means of placing that unhappy race within the pale of civilized nations.

Judge Ryland concurring, the judgment will be reversed and the cause remanded.

[Dissent omitted]

Notes and Questions

1. What was the court concerned about in deciding in favor of Mrs. Emerson?

2. Notice that Dred Scott won his freedom at the lower court level. Does that surprise you? As Professor David Thomas Konig has written "Between 1806 and 1857 the St. Louis Circuit Court heard more than 280 freedom suits, whose range of human experience reveals the complexity of a uniquely American struggle. This struggle, between those seeking freedom and those opposing it, reveals that the process that culminated in Dred Scott was a long one, consisting of hundreds of trials that tested the concept of the rule of law in a bitterly divided community." David Thomas Konig, *The Long Road to Dred Scott: Personhood and the Rule of Law in the Trial Court Records of* St. Louis Slave Freedom Suits, 75 UMKC L. Rev. 53 (2006) He continues: "The freedom suits thus presented many aspects to Antebellum Americans—most basically, one of hope for petitioners versus one of protected property rights for masters. They might arguably be seen, to be sure, as allowing the law to provide legitimacy for slavery by making a relatively insignificant concession to a statistically small number of successful petitioners—for providing, as Noonan explains, 'masks [that] made bearable the institution of slavery.' " Id. at 55. In fact, when the Missouri appellate court ruled against Dred Scott, it was reversing longstanding precedent. In other words, Dred Scott and his attorneys had every reason to believe their lawsuit would be successful.

DRED SCOTT v. SANDFORD
60 U.S. 393 (1857).

MR. CHIEF JUSTICE TANEY delivered the opinion of the court.

This case has been twice argued. After the argument at the last term, differences of opinion were found to exist among the members of the court; and as the questions in controversy are of the highest importance, and the court was at that time much pressed by the ordinary business of the term, it was deemed advisable to continue the case, and direct a re-argument on some of the points, in order that we might have an opportunity of giving to the whole subject a more deliberate consideration. It has accordingly been again argued by counsel, and considered by the court; and I now proceed to deliver its opinion.

There are two leading questions presented by the record:

1. Had the Circuit Court of the United States jurisdiction to hear and determine the case between these parties? [diversity jurisdiction question] And

2. If it had jurisdiction, is the judgment it has given erroneous or not?

The plaintiff in error, who was also the plaintiff in the court below, was, with his wife and children, held as slaves by the defendant, in the State of Missouri; and he brought this action in the Circuit Court of the United States for that district, to assert the title of himself and his family to freedom.

The declaration is in the form usually adopted in that State to try questions of this description, and contains the averment necessary to give the court jurisdiction; that he and the defendant are citizens of different States; that is, that he is a citizen of Missouri, and the defendant & citizen of New York.

The defendant pleaded in abatement to the jurisdiction of the court, that the plaintiff was not a citizen of the State of Missouri, as alleged in his declaration, being a negro of African descent, whose ancestors were of pure African blood, and who were brought into this country and sold as slaves.

To this plea the plaintiff demurred, and the defendant joined in demurrer. The court overruled the plea, and gave judgment that the defendant should answer over. And he thereupon put in sundry pleas in bar, upon which issues were joined; and at the trial the verdict and judgment were in his favor. Whereupon the plaintiff brought this writ of error.

* * *

[Court grapples with the question of whether a defendant can waive a defense of lack of subject matter jurisdiction if he fails to raise it below or to preserve it on appeal. The court makes it clear that the defendant did not waive it because subject matter jurisdiction can be raised at any point in the life of a case.]

This is certainly a very serious question, and one that now for the first time has been brought for decision before this court. But it is brought here by those who have a right to bring it, and it is our duty to meet it and decide it.

The question is simply this: Can a negro, whose ancestors were imported into this country, and sold as salves, become a member of the political community formed and brought into existence by the Constitution of the United States, and as such become entitled to all the rights, and privileges, and immunities, guarantied by that instrument to the citizen? One of which rights is the privilege of suing in a court of the United States in the cases specified in the Constitution.

It will be observed, that the plea applies to that class of persons only whose ancestors were negroes of the African race, and imported into this country, and sold and held as salves. The only matter in issue before the court, therefore, is, whether the descendants of such salves, when they shall be emancipated, or who are born of parents who had become free before their birth, are citizens of a State, in the sense in which the word citizen is used in the Constitution of the United States. And this being the only matter in dispute on the pleadings, the court must be understood as speaking in this opinion of that class only, that is, of those persons who are the descendants of Africans who were imported into this country, and sold as salves.

The situation of this population was altogether unlike that of the Indian race. The latter, it is true, formed no part of the colonial communities, and never amalgamated with them in social connections or in government. But although they were uncivilized, they were yet a free and independent people, associated together in nations or tribes, and governed by their own laws. Many of these political communities were situated in territories to which the white race claimed the ultimate right of dominion. But that claim was acknowledged to be subject to the right of the Indians to occupy it as long as they though proper, and neither the English nor colonial Governments claimed or exercised any dominion over the tribe or nation by whom it was occupied, nor claimed the right to the possession of the territory, until the tribe or nation consented to cede it. These Indian Governments were regarded and treated as foreign Governments, as much so as if an ocean had separated the red man from the white; and their freedom has constantly been acknowledged, from the time of the first emigration to the English colonies to the present day, by the different Governments which succeeded each other. Treaties have been negotiated with them, and their alliance sought for in war; and the people who compose these Indian political communities have always been treated as foreigners not living under our Government. It is true that the course of events has brought the Indian tribes within the limits of the United States under subjection to the white race; and it has been found necessary, for their sake as well as our own, to regard them as in a state of pupilage, and to legislate to a certain extent over them and the territory they occupy. But they may, without doubt, like the subjects of any other foreign Government, be naturalized by the authority of Congress, and become citizens of a State, and of the United States; and if an individual should leave his nation or tribe, and take up his abode among the white population, he would be entitled to all the rights and privileges which would belong to an emigrant from any other foreign people.

We proceed to examine the case as presented by the pleadings.

The words "people of the United States" and "citizens" are synonymous terms, and mean the same thing. They both describe the political body who, according to our republican institutions, form the sovereignty, and who hold the power and conduct the Government through their representatives. They are what we familiarly call the "sovereign people," and every citizen is one of this people, and a constituent member of this sovereignty. The question before us is, whether the class of persons described in the plea in abatement compose a portion of this people, and are constituent members of this sovereignty? We think they are not, and that they are not included, and were not intended to be included, under the word "citizens" in the Constitution, and can therefore claim none of the rights and privileges which that instrument provides for and secures to citizens of the United States. On the contrary, they were at that time considered as a subordinate and inferior class of beings, who had been subjugated by the dominant race, and, whether emancipated or not, yet remained subject to their authority, and had no rights or privileges but such as those who held the power and the Government might choose to grant them.

It is not the province of the court to decide upon the justice or injustice, the policy or impolicy, of these laws. The decision of that question belonged to the political or law-making power; to those who formed the sovereignty and framed the Constitution. The duty of the court is, to interpret the instrument they have framed, with the best lights we can obtain on the subject, and to administer it as we find it, according to its true intent and meaning when it was adopted.

In discussing this question, we must not confound the rights of citizenship which a State may confer within its own limits, and the rights of citizenship as a member of the Union. It does not by any means follow, because he has all the rights and privileges of a citizen of a State, that he must be a citizen of the United States. He may have all of the rights and privileges of the citizen of a State, and yet not be entitled to the rights and privileges of a citizen in any other State. For, previous to the adoption of the Constitution of the United States, every State had the undoubted right to confer on whomsoever it pleased the character of citizen, and to endow him with all its rights. But this character of course was confined to the boundaries of the State, and gave him no rights or privileges in other States beyond those secured to him by the laws of nations and the comity of States. Nor have the several States surrendered the power of conferring these rights and privileges by adopting the Constitution of the United States. Each State may still confer them upon an alien, or any one it thinks proper, or upon any class or description of persons; yet he would not be a citizen in the sense in which that word is used in the Constitution of the United States, nor entitled to sue as such in one of its courts, nor to the privileges and immunities of a citizen in the other States. The rights which he would acquire would be restricted to the State which gave them. The Constitution has conferred on Congress the right to establish an uniform rule of naturalization, and this right is evidently exclusive, and has always been held by this court to be so. Consequently, no State, since the adoption of the Constitution, can be naturalizing an alien invest him with the rights and privileges secured to a citizen of a State under the Federal Government, although, so far as the State alone was concerned, he would undoubtedly be entitled to the rights of a citizen, and clothed with all the rights and immunities which the Constitution and laws of the State attached to that character.

It is very clear, therefore, that no State can, by any act or law of its own, passed since the adoption of the Constitution, introduce a new member into the political community created by the Constitution of the United States. It cannot make him a member of this community by making him a member of its own. And for the same reason it cannot introduce any person, or description of persons, who were not intended to be embraced in this new political family, which the Constitution brought into existence, but were intended to be excluded from it.

The question then arises, whether the provisions of the Constitution, in relation to the personal rights and privileges to which the citizen of a State should be entitled, embraced the negro African race, at that time in this country, or who might afterwards be imported, who had then or should afterwards be made free in any State; and to put it in the power of a single State to make him a citizen of the United States, and endue him with the full rights of citizenship in every other State without their consent? Does the Constitution of the United States act upon him whenever he shall be made free under the laws of a State, and raised there to the rank of a citizen, and immediately cloth him with all the privileges of a citizen in every other State, and in its own courts?

The court think the affirmative of these propositions cannot be maintained. And if it cannot, the plaintiff in error could not be a citizen of the State of Missouri, within the meaning of the Constitution of the United States, and, consequently, was not entitled to sue in its courts.

It is true, every person, and every class and description of persons, who were at the time of the adoption of the Constitution recognized as citizens in the several States, became also citizens of this new political body; but none other; it was formed by them, and for them and their posterity, but for no one else. And the personal rights and privileges guarantied to citizens of this new sovereignty were intended to embrace those only who were then members of the several State communities, or who should afterwards by birthright or otherwise become members, according to the provisions of the Constitution and the principles on which it was founded. It was the union of those who were at that time members of distinct and separate political communities into one political family, whose power, for certain specified purposes, was to extend over the whole territory of the United States. And it gave to each citizen rights and privileges outside of his State which he did not before possess, and placed him in every other State upon a perfect equality with its own citizens as to rights of person and rights of property; it made him a citizen of the United States.

It becomes necessary, therefore, to determine who were citizens of the several States when the Constitution was adopted. And in order to do this, we must recur to the Governments and institutions of the thirteen colonies, when they separated from Great Britain and formed new sovereignties, and took their places in the family of independent nations. We must inquire who, at that time, were recognized as the people or citizens of a State, whose rights and liberties had been outraged by the English Government; and who declared their independence, and assumed the powers of Government to defend their rights by force of arms.

In the opinion of the court, the legislation and histories of the times, and the language used in the Declaration of Independence, show, that neither the class of persons who had been imported as slaves, nor their descendants, whether they had become free or not, were then acknowledged as a part of the people, nor intended to be included in the general words used in that memorable instrument.

It is difficult at this day to realize the state of public opinion in relation to that unfortunate race, which prevailed in the civilized and enlightened portions of the world at the time of the Declaration of Independence, and when the Constitution of the United States was framed and adopted. But the public history of every European nation displays it in a manner too plain to be mistaken.

They had for more than a century before been regarded as beings of an inferior order, and altogether unfit to associate with the white race, either in social or political relations; and so far inferior, that they had no rights which the white man was bound to respect; and that the negro might justly and lawfully be reduced to slavery for his benefit. He was bought and sold, and treated as an ordinary article of merchandise and traffic, whenever a profit could be made by it. This opinion was at that time fixed and universal in the civilized portion of the white race. It was regarded as an axiom in morals as well as in politics, which no one thought of disputing, or supposed to be open to dispute; and men in every grade and position in society daily and habitually acted upon it in their private pursuits, as well as in matters of public concern, without doubting for a moment the correctness of this opinion.

And in no nation was this opinion more firmly fixed or more uniformly acted upon than by the English Government and English people. They not only seized them on the coast of Africa, and sold them or held them in slavery for their own use; but they took them as ordinary articles of merchandise to every country where they could make a profit on them, and were far more extensively engaged in this commerce than any other nation in the world.

The opinion thus entertained and acted upon in England was naturally impressed upon the colonies they founded on this side of the Atlantic. And, accordingly, a negro of the African race was regarded by them as an article of property, and held, and bought and sold as such, in every one of the thirteen colonies which united in the Declaration of Independence, and afterwards formed the Constitution of the United States. The slaves were more or less numerous in the different colonies, as slave labor was found more or less profitable. But no one seems to have doubted the correctness of the prevailing opinion of the time.

The legislation of the different colonies furnishes positive and indisputable proof of this fact.

[Court goes on to cite statutes supporting its point.]

* * *

The language of the Declaration of Independence is equally Conclusive:

It begins by declaring that, "when in the course of human events it becomes necessary for one people to dissolve the political bands which have connected them with another, and to assume among the powers of the earth the separate and equal station to which the laws of nature and nature's God entitle them, a decent respect for the opinions of mankind requires that they should declare the causes which impel them to the separation."

It then proceeds to say: "We hold these truths to be self-evident: that all men are created equal; that they are endowed by their Creator with certain unalienable rights; that among them is life, liberty, and the pursuit of happiness; that to secure these rights, Governments are instituted, deriving their just powers from the consent of the governed."

The general words above quoted would seem to embrace the whole human family, and if they were used in a similar instrument at this day would be so understood. But it is too clear for dispute, that the enslaved African race were not intended to be included, and formed no part of the people who framed and adopted this declaration; for if the language, as understood in that day, would embrace them, the conduct of the distinguished men who framed the Declaration of Independence would have been utterly and flagrantly inconsistent with the principles they asserted; and instead of the sympathy of mankind, to which they so confidently appeared, they would have deserved and received universal rebuke and reprobation.

Yet the men who framed this declaration were great men—high in literary acquirements—high in their sense of honor, and incapable of asserting principles inconsistent with those on which they were acting. They perfectly understood the meaning of the language they used, and how it would be understood by others; and they knew that it would not in any part of the civilized world be supposed to embrace the negro race, which, by common consent, had been excluded from civilized Governments and the family of nations, and doomed to slavery. They spoke and acted according to the then established doctrines and principles, and in the ordinary language of the day, no one misunderstood them. The unhappy black race were separated from the white by indelible marks, and laws long before established, and were never thought of or spoken of except as property, and when the claims of the owner or the profit of the trader were supposed to need protection.

* * *

No one of that race had ever migrated to the United States voluntarily; all of them had been brought here as articles of merchandise. The number that had been emancipated at that time were but few in comparison with those held in slavery; and they were identified in the public mind with the race to which they belonged, and regarded as a part of the slave population rather than the free. It is obvious that they were not even in the minds of the framers of the Constitution when they were conferring special rights and privileges upon the citizens of a State in every other part of the Union.

Indeed, when we look to the condition of this race in the several States at the time, it is impossible to believe that these rights and privileges were intended to be extended to them.

It is very true, that in that portion of the Union where the labor of the negro race was found to be unsuited to the climate and unprofitable to the master, but few slaves were held at the time of the Declaration of Independence; and when the Constitution was adopted, it had entirely worn out in one of them, and measures had been taken for its gradual abolition in several others. But this change had not been produced by any change of opinion in relation to this race; but because it was discovered, from experience, that slave labor was unsuited to the climate and productions of these States: for some of the States, where it had ceased or nearly ceased to exist, were actively engaged in the slave trade, procuring cargoes on the coast of Africa, and transporting them for sale to those parts of the Union where their labor was found to be profitable, and suited to the climate and productions. And this traffic was openly carried on, and fortunes accumulated by it, without reproach from the people of the States where they resided. And it can hardly be supposed that, in the States where it was then countenances in its worst form— that is, in the seizure and transportation—the people could have regarded those who were emancipated as entitled to equal rights with themselves.

* * *

Now, the Constitution does not limit the power of Congress in this respect to white persons. And they may, if they think proper, authorize the naturalization of any one, of any color, who was born under allegiance to another Government. But the language of the law above quoted, shows that citizenship at that time was perfectly understood to be confined to the white race; and that they alone constituted the sovereignty in the Government.

Congress might, as we before said, have authorized the naturalization of Indians, because they were aliens and foreigners. But, in their then untutored and savage state no one would have thought of admitting them as citizens in a civilized community. And, moreover, the atrocities they had but recently committed, when they were the allies of Great Britain in the Revolutionary war, were yet fresh in the recollection of the people of the United States, and they were even then guarding themselves against the threatened renewal of Indian hostilities. No one supposed then that any Indian would ask for, or was capable of enjoying, the privileges of an American citizen, and the word white was not used with any particular reference to them.

Neither was it used with any reference to the African race imported into or born in this country; because Congress had no power to naturalize them, and therefore there was no necessity for using particular words to exclude them.

It would seem to have been used merely because it followed out the line of division which the Constitution has drawn between the citizen race, who formed and held the Government, and the African race, which they held in subjection and slavery, and governed at their own pleasure.

* * *

Undoubtedly, a person may be a citizen, that is, a member of the community who form the sovereignty, although he exercises no share of the political power, and is incapacitated from holding particular offices. Women and minors, who form a part of the political family, cannot vote; and when a property qualification is required to vote or hold a particular office, those who have not the necessary qualification cannot vote or hold the office, yet they are citizens.

So, too, a person may be entitled to vote by the law of the State, who is not a citizen even of the State itself. And in some of the States of the Union foreigners not naturalized are allowed to vote. And the State may give the right to free negroes and mulattoes, but that does not make them citizens of the State, and still less of the United States. And the provision in the Constitution giving privileges and immunities in other States, does not apply to them.

Neither does it apply to a person who, being the citizen of a State, migrates to another State. For then he becomes subject to the laws of the State in which he lives, and he is no longer a citizen of the State from which he removed. And the State in which he resides may then, unquestionably, determine his status or condition, and place him among the class of persons who are not recognized as citizens, but belong to an inferior and subject race; and may deny him the privileges and immunities enjoyed by its citizens.

But so far as mere rights of person are concerned, the provision in question is confined to citizens of a State who are temporarily in another State without taking up their residence there. It gives them no political rights in the State, as to voting or holding office, or in any other respect. For a citizen of one State has no right to participate in the government of another. But if he ranks as a citizen in the State to which he belongs, within the meaning of the Constitution of the United States, then, whenever he goes into another State, the Constitution clothes him, as to the rights of person, with all the privileges and immunities which belong to citizens of the State. And if persons of the African race are citizens of a State, and of the United States, they would be entitled to all of these privileges and immunities in every State, and the State could not restrict them; for they would hold these privileges and immunities under the paramount authority of the Federal Government, and its courts would be bound to maintain and enforce them, the Constitution and laws of the State to the contrary notwithstanding. And if the States could limit or restrict them, or place the party in an inferior grade, this clause of the Constitution would be unmeaning, and could have no operation; and would give no rights to the citizen when in another State. He would have none but what the State itself chose to allow him. This is evidently not the construction or meaning of the clause in question. It guaranties rights to the citizen, and the State cannot withhold them. And these rights are of a character and would lead to consequences which make it absolutely certain that the African race were not included under the name of citizens of a State, and were not in the contemplation of the framers of the Constitution when these privileges and immunities were provided for the protection of the citizen in other States.

* * *

In the case before us, we have already decided that the Circuit Court erred in deciding that it had jurisdiction upon the facts admitted by the pleadings. And it appears that, in the further progress of the case, it acted upon the erroneous principle it had decided on the pleadings, and gave judgment for the defendant, where, upon the facts admitted in the exception, it had no jurisdiction.

We are at a loss to understand upon what principle of law, applicable to appellate jurisdiction, it can be supposed that this court has not judicial authority to correct the last-mentioned error, because they had before corrected the former; or by what process of reasoning it can be made out, that the error of an inferior court in actually pronouncing judgment for one of the parties, in a case in which it had no jurisdiction, cannot be looked into or corrected by this court, because we have decided a similar question presented in the pleadings. The last point is distinctly presented by the facts contained in the plaintiff's own bill of exceptions, which he himself brings here by this writ of error. It was the point which chiefly occupied the attention of the counsel on both sides in the argument—and the judgment which this court must render upon both errors is precisely the same. It must, in each of them, exercise jurisdiction over the judgment, and reverse it for the errors committed by the court below; and issue a mandate to the Circuit Court to conform its judgment to the opinion pronounced by this court, by dismissing the case for want of jurisdiction in the Circuit Court. This is the constant and invariable practice of this court, where it reverses a judgment for want of jurisdiction in the Circuit Court.

* * *

The case before us still more strongly imposes upon this court the duty of examining whether the court below has not committed an error, in taking jurisdiction and giving a judgment for costs in favor of the defendant; for in Capron v. Van Noorden the judgment was reversed, because it did not appear that the parties were citizens of different States. They might or might not be. But in this case it does appear that the plaintiff was born a slave; and if the facts upon which he relies have not made him free, then it appears affirmatively on the record that he is not a citizen, and consequently his suit against Sandford was not a suit between citizens of different States, and the court had no authority to pass any judgment between the parties. The suit ought, in this view of it, to have been dismissed by the Circuit Court, and its judgment in favor of Sandford is erroneous, and must be reversed.

It is true that the result either way, by dismissal or by a judgment for the defendant, makes very little, if any, difference in a pecuniary or personal point of view to either party. But the fact that the result would be very nearly the same to the parties in either form of judgment, would not justify this court in sanctioning an error in the judgment which is patent on the record, and which, if sanctioned, might be drawn into precedent, and lead to serious mischief and injustice in some future suit.

We proceed, therefore, to inquire whether the facts relied on by the plaintiff entitled him to his freedom.

[The court again recites the facts surrounding Dred Scott's argument that he's a free man.]

In considering this part of the controversy, two questions arise: 1. Was he, together with his family, free in Missouri by reason of the stay in the territory of the United States hereinbefore mentioned? And 2. If they were not, is Scott himself free by reason of his removal to Rock Island, in the State of Illinois, as stated in the above admissions?

We proceed to examine the first question.

The act of Congress, upon which the plaintiff relies, declares that slavery and involuntary servitude, except as a punishment for crime, shall be forever prohibited in all that part of the territory ceded by France, under the name of Louisiana, which lies north of thirty-six degrees thirty minutes north latitude, and not included within the limits of Missouri. And the difficulty which meets us at the threshold of this part of the inquiry is, whether Congress was authorized to pass this law under any of the powers granted to it by the Constitution; for if the authority is not given by that instrument, it is the duty of this court to declare it void and inoperative, and incapable of conferring freedom upon any one who is held as a slave under the laws of any one of the States.

* * *

But in considering the question before us, it must be borne in mind that there is no law of nations standing between the people of the United States and their Government, and interfering with their relation to each other. The powers of the Government, and the rights of the citizen under it, are positive and practical regulations plainly written down. The people of the United States have delegated to it certain enumerated powers, and forbidden it to exercise others. It has no power over the person or property of a citizen but what the citizens of the United States have granted. And no laws or usages of other nations, or reasoning of statesmen or jurists upon the relations of master and slave, can enlarge the powers of the Government, or take from the citizens the rights they have reserved. And if the Constitution recognizes the right of property of the master in a slave, and makes no distinction between that description of property and other property owned by a citizen, no tribunal, acting under the authority of the United States, whether it be legislative, executive, or judicial, has a right to draw such a distinction, or deny to it the benefit of the provisions and guarantees which have been provided for the protection of private property against the encroachments of the Government.

Now, as we have already said in an earlier part of this opinion, upon a different point, the right of property in a slave is distinctly and expressly affirmed in the Constitution. The right to traffic in it, like an ordinary article of merchandise and property, was guarantied to the citizens of the United States, in every State that might desire it, for twenty years. And the Government in express terms is pledged to protect it in all future time, if the slave escapes from his owner. This is done in plain words—too plain to be misunderstood. And no word can be found in the Constitution which gives Congress a greater power over slave property, or which entitles property of that kind to less protection than property of any other description. The only power conferred is the power coupled with the duty of guarding and protecting the owner in his rights.

Upon these considerations, it is the opinion of the court that the act of Congress which prohibited a citizen from holding and owning property of this kind in the territory of the United States north of the line therein mentioned, is not warranted by the Constitution, and is therefore void; and that neither Dred Scott himself, nor any of his family, were made free by being carried into this territory; even if they had been carried there by the owner, with the intention of becoming a permanent resident.

We have so far examined the case, as it stands under the Constitution of the United States, and the powers thereby delegated to the Federal Government.

But there is another point in the case which depends on State power and State law. And it is contended, on the part of the plaintiff, that he is made free by being taken to Rock Island, in the State of Illinois, independently of his residence in the territory of the United States; and being so made free, he was not again reduced to a state of slavery by being brought back to Missouri.

Our notice of this part of the case will be very brief; for the principle on which it depends was decided in this court, upon much consideration, in the case of Strader et al. v. Graham, reported in 10th Howard, 82. In that case, the slaves had been taken from Kentucky to Ohio, with the consent of the owner, and afterwards brought back to Kentucky. And this court held that their status or condition, as free or slave, depended upon the laws of Kentucky, when they were brought back into that

State, and not of Ohio; and that this court had no jurisdiction to revise the judgment of a State court upon its own laws. This was the point directly before the court, and the decision that this court had not jurisdiction turned upon it, as will be seen by the report of the case.

So in this case. As Scott was a slave when taken into the State of Illinois by his owner, and was there held as such, and brought back in that character, his status, as free or slave, depended on the laws of Missouri, and not of Illinois.

It has, however, been urged in the argument, that by the laws of Missouri he was free on his return, and that this case, therefore, cannot be governed by the case of Strader et al. v. Graham, where it appeared, by the laws of Kentucky, that the plaintiffs continued to be slaves on their return from Ohio. But whatever doubts or opinions may, at one time, have been entertained upon this subject, we are satisfied, upon a careful examination of all the cases decided in the State courts of Missouri referred to, that it is now firmly settled by the decisions of the highest court in the State, that Scott and his family upon their return were not free, but were, by the laws of Missouri, the property of the defendant; and that the Circuit Court of the United States had no jurisdiction, when, by the laws of the State, the plaintiff was a slave, and not a citizen.

Moreover, the plaintiff, it appears, brought a similar action against the defendant in the State court of Missouri, claiming the freedom of himself and his family upon the same grounds and the same evidence upon which he relies in the case before the court. The case was carried before the Supreme Court of the State; was fully argued there; and that court decided that neither the plaintiff nor his family were entitled to freedom, and were still the slaves of the defendant; and reversed the judgment of the inferior State court, which had given a different decision. If the plaintiff supposed that this judgment of the Supreme Court of the State was erroneous, and that this court had jurisdiction to revise and reverse it, the only mode by which he could legally bring it before this court was by writ of error directed to the Supreme Court of the State, requiring it to transmit the record to this court. If this had been done, it is too plain for argument that the writ must have been dismissed for want of jurisdiction in this court. The case of Strader and others v. Graham is directly in point; and, indeed, independent of any decision, the language of the 25th section of the act of 1789 is too clear and precise to admit of controversy.

But the plaintiff did not pursue the mode prescribed by law for bringing the judgment of a State court before this court for revision, but suffered the case to be remanded to the inferior State court, where it is still continued, and is, by agreement of parties, to await the judgment of this court on the point. All of this appears on the record before us, and by the printed report of the case.

And while the case is yet open and pending in the inferior State court, the plaintiff goes into the Circuit Court of the United States, upon the same case and the same evidence, and against the same party, and proceeds to judgment, and then brings here the same case from the Circuit Court, which the law would not have permitted him to bring directly from the State court. And if this court takes jurisdiction in this form, the result, so far as the rights of the respective parties are concerned, is in every respect substantially the same as if it had in open violation of law entertained jurisdiction over the judgment of the State court upon a writ of error, and revised and reversed its judgment upon the ground that its opinion upon the question of law was erroneous. It would ill become this court to sanction such an attempt to evade the law, or to exercise an appellate power in this circuitous way, which it is forbidden to exercise in the direct and regular and invariable forms of judicial proceedings.

Upon the whole, therefore, it is the judgment of this court, that it appears by the record before us that the plaintiff in error is not a citizen of Missouri, in the sense in which that word is used in the Constitution; and that the Circuit Court of the United States, for that reason, had no jurisdiction in the case, and could give no judgment in it. Its judgment for the defendant must, consequently, be reversed, and a mandate issued, directing the suit to be dismissed for want of jurisdiction.

* * *

[Omitted concurring and dissenting opinions]

Notes and Questions

1. Why didn't res judicata prevent the case from being heard? There is reason to believe that had res judicata been argued, it would have prevented the case from being heard by the federal courts. *See* Eric T. Dean, Jr., *Reassessing Dred Scott: The Possibilities of Federal Power in the Antebellum Context*, 60 U. Cin. L. Rev. 713, 715–731 (1992). Why didn't issue preclusion prevent the case from being heard? Consider the penultimate paragraph of the court's opinion. Couldn't the decision have been much shorter?

2. Notice how the court purports to describe how Native Americans had superior rights than African–Americans. Recall Chapter 7 *supra* and the description of the court's treatment of Native Americans property rights. Were their rights superior or were both groups subordinated by the use of different legal doctrines?

3. Recall after September 11, 2001 there was some discussion of requiring national identification cards for those of Arab descent—including Arab–Americans. *See* Sam Howe Verhovek, *A Nation Challenged: Civil Liberties; Americans Give in to Racial Profiling*, N.Y. Times, Sept. 23, 2001, at 1A "A CNN/USA Today/Gallup poll taken a few days after the attacks showed that Americans were supporting special measures intended for those of Arab descent. In the survey, 58 percent backed more intensive security checks for Arabs, including those who are United States citizens, compared with other travelers; 49 percent favored special identification cards for such people, and 32 percent backed 'special surveillance' for them." *Id*. Is it too

far a stretch to suggest that certain groups could have their citizenship taken away given the "right" national security crisis?

4. Once the Court finds that it lacks subject matter jurisdiction, why didn't the opinion end? Why did the court continue to analyze the question of whether Dred Scott was free and declare the Missouri Compromise unconstitutional? Was this judicial activism by the court?

SECTION 3. WHAT DO YOU HAVE TO PLEAD?

CONLEY ET AL. v. GIBSON ET AL.

355 U.S. 41, 78 S.Ct. 99, 2 L.Ed.2d 80 (1957).

MR. JUSTICE BLACK delivered the opinion of the Court.

Once again Negro employees are here under the Railway Labor Act asking that their collective bargaining agent be compelled to represent them fairly. In a series of cases beginning with *Steele v. Louisville Nashville R. Co.*, 323 U.S. 192, this Court has emphatically and repeatedly ruled that an exclusive bargaining agent under the Railway Labor Act is obligated to represent all employees in the bargaining unit fairly and without discrimination because of race and has held that the courts have power to protect employees against such invidious discrimination.

This class suit was brought in a Federal District Court in Texas by certain Negro members of the Brotherhood of Railway and Steamship Clerks, petitioners here, on behalf of themselves and other Negro employees similarly situated against the Brotherhood, its Local Union No. 28 and certain officers of both. In summary, the complaint made the following allegations relevant to our decision: Petitioners were employees of the Texas and New Orleans Railroad at its Houston Freight House. Local 28 of the Brotherhood was the designated bargaining agent under the Railway Labor Act for the bargaining unit to which petitioners belonged. A contract existed between the Union and the Railroad which gave the employees in the bargaining unit certain protection from discharge and loss of seniority. In May 1954, the Railroad purported to abolish 45 jobs held by petitioners or other Negroes all of whom were either discharged or demoted. In truth the 45 jobs were not abolished at all but instead filled by whites as the Negroes were ousted, except for a few instances where Negroes were rehired to fill their old jobs but with loss of seniority. Despite repeated pleas by petitioners, the Union, acting according to plan, did nothing to protect them against these discriminatory discharges and refused to give them protection comparable to that given white employees. The complaint then went on to allege that the Union had failed in general to represent Negro employees equally and in good faith. It charged that such discrimination constituted a violation of petitioners' right under the Railway Labor Act to fair representation from their bargaining agent. And it concluded by asking for relief in the nature of declaratory judgment, injunction and damages.

The respondents appeared and moved to dismiss the complaint on several grounds: (1) the National Railroad Adjustment Board had exclusive jurisdiction over the controversy; (2) the Texas and New Orleans Railroad, which had not been joined, was an indispensable party defendant; and (3) the complaint failed to state a claim upon which relief could be given. The District Court granted the motion to dismiss holding that Congress had given the Adjustment Board exclusive jurisdiction over the controversy. The Court of Appeals for the Fifth Circuit, apparently relying on the same ground, affirmed. 229 F.2d 436. Since the case raised an important question concerning the protection of employee rights under the Railway Labor Act we granted certiorari. 352 U.S. 818.

We hold that it was error for the courts below to dismiss the complaint for lack of jurisdiction. They took the position that § 3 First (i) of the Railway Labor Act conferred exclusive jurisdiction on the Adjustment Board because the case, in their view, involved the interpretation and application of the collective bargaining agreement. But § 3 First (i) by its own terms applies only to "disputes between an employee or group of employees and a carrier or carriers."[3] This case involves no dispute between employee and employer but to the contrary is a suit by employees against the bargaining agent to enforce their statutory right not to be unfairly discriminated against by it in bargaining. The Adjustment Board has no power under § 3 First (i) or any other provision of the Act to protect them from such discrimination. Furthermore, the contract between the Brotherhood and the Railroad will be, at most, only incidentally involved in resolving this controversy between petitioners and their bargaining agent.

Although the District Court did not pass on the other reasons advanced for dismissal of the complaint we think it timely and proper for us to consider them here. They have been briefed and argued by both parties and the respondents urge that the decision below be upheld, if necessary, on these other grounds.

As in the courts below, respondents contend that the Texas and New Orleans Railroad Company is an indispensable party which the petitioners have failed to join as a defendant. On the basis of the allegations made in the complaint and the relief demanded by petitioners we believe that contention is unjustifiable. We cannot see how the Railroad's rights or interests will be affected by this action to enforce the duty of the bargaining representative to represent petitioners fairly. This is not a

---

3. In full, § 3 First (i) reads:

"The disputes between an employee or group of employees and a carrier or carriers growing out of grievances or out of the interpretation or application of agreements concerning rates of pay, rules, or working conditions, including cases pending and unadjusted on the date of approval of this Act [June 21, 1934], shall be handled in the usual manner up to and including the chief operating officer of the carrier designated to handle such disputes; but, failing to reach an adjustment in this manner, the disputes may be referred by petition of the parties or by either party to the appropriate division of the Adjustment Board with a full statement of the facts and all supporting data bearing upon the disputes." 48 Stat. 1191, 45 U. S. C. 153 First (i).

suit, directly or indirectly, against the Railroad. No relief is asked from it and there is no prospect that any will or can be granted which will bind it. If an issue does develop which necessitates joining the Railroad either it or the respondents will then have an adequate opportunity to request joinder.

Turning to respondents' final ground, we hold that under the general principles laid down in the *Steele, Graham*, and *Howard* cases the complaint adequately set forth a claim upon which relief could be granted. In appraising the sufficiency of the complaint we follow, of course, the accepted rule that a complaint should not be dismissed for failure to state a claim unless it appears beyond doubt that the plaintiff can prove no set of facts in support of his claim which would entitle him to relief. Here, the complaint alleged, in part, that petitioners were discharged wrongfully by the Railroad and that the Union, acting according to plan, refused to protect their jobs as it did those of white employees or to help them with their grievances all because they were Negroes. If these allegations are proven there has been a manifest breach of the Union's statutory duty to represent fairly and without hostile discrimination all of the employees in the bargaining unit. This Court squarely held in *Steele* and subsequent cases that discrimination in representation because of race is prohibited by the Railway Labor Act. The bargaining representative's duty not to draw "irrelevant and invidious" distinctions among those it represents does not come to an abrupt end, as the respondents seem to contend, with the making of an agreement between union and employer. Collective bargaining is a continuing process. Among other things, it involves day-to-day adjustments in the contract and other working rules, resolution of new problems not covered by existing agreements, and the protection of employee rights already secured by contract. The bargaining representative can no more unfairly discriminate in carrying out these functions than it can in negotiating a collective agreement. A contract may be fair and impartial on its face yet administered in such a way, with the active or tacit consent of the union, as to be flagrantly discriminatory against some members of the bargaining unit.

The respondents point to the fact that under the Railway Labor Act aggrieved employees can file their own grievances with the Adjustment Board or sue the employer for breach of contract. Granting this, it still furnishes no sanction for the Union's alleged discrimination in refusing to represent petitioners. The Railway Labor Act, in an attempt to aid collective action by employees, conferred great power and protection on the bargaining agent chosen by a majority of them. As individuals or small groups the employees cannot begin to possess the bargaining power of their representative in negotiating with the employer or in presenting their grievances to him. Nor may a minority choose another agent to bargain in their behalf. We need not pass on the Union's claim that it was not obliged to handle any grievances at all because we are clear that once it undertook to bargain or present grievances for some of the employees it represented it could not refuse to take similar action in good faith for other employees just because they were Negroes.

The respondents also argue that the complaint failed to set forth specific facts to support its general allegations of discrimination and that its dismissal is therefore proper. The decisive answer to this is that the Federal Rules of Civil Procedure do not require a claimant to set out in detail the facts upon which he bases his claim. To the contrary, all the Rules require is "a short and plain statement of the claim" that will give the defendant fair notice of what the plaintiff's claim is and the grounds upon which it rests. The illustrative forms appended to the Rules plainly demonstrate this. Such simplified "notice pleading" is made possible by the liberal opportunity for discovery and the other pretrial procedures established by the Rules to disclose more precisely the basis of both claim and defense and to define more narrowly the disputed facts and issues. Following the simple guide of Rule 8 (f) that "all pleadings shall be so construed as to do substantial justice," we have no doubt that petitioners' complaint adequately set forth a claim and gave the respondents fair notice of its basis. The Federal Rules reject the approach that pleading is a game of skill in which one misstep by counsel may be decisive to the outcome and accept the principle that the purpose of pleading is to facilitate a proper decision on the merits. Cf. *Maty* v. *Grasselli Chemical Co.*, 303 U.S. 197.

The judgment is reversed and the cause is remanded to the District Court for further proceedings not inconsistent with this opinion.

It is so ordered.

Notes and Questions

1. How can the rules on notice pleading be interpreted to disadvantage certain plaintiffs?

2. Why are courts more suspicious of civil rights claims than personal injury claims?

3. *See* Emily Sherwin, The Story of Conley: Precedent by Accident in Civil Procedure Stories (Edited by Kevin Clermont) 281–306 (Foundation Press 2004) for a detailed description of the background events of the case. Justice Black who wrote the majority opinion "was born and raised in Alabama . . . . [and] had been an active member of the Ku Klux Klan." *Id*. at 294. He did however sign the unanimous opinion in *Brown vs. Board of Education*. *Id*. I would argue this proves a recurring theme in this course, namely, the complexity of race.

4. Can procedural rules "discriminate" on the basis of race? From a CRT perspective are procedural rules as important as substantive rules? Are they more important? Consider the following Brooks' excerpt.

SECTION 4. CONCLUDING THOUGHTS

ROY L. BROOKS

Critical Race Theory: A Proposed Structure and Application to Federal
Pleading, 11 Harv. BlackLetter J. 85, 102–112 (1994).

2. *FEDERAL PLEADING*

The federal pleading system is set forth in the Federal Rules of Civil
Procedure. Drafted in 1934 and taking effect in 1938, the Federal Rules
of Civil Procedure (FRCP) provide the most modern and liberal set of
procedural rules available in American courts. Many states have adopted
them in whole or in part.

* * *

This latter feature of federal pleading—notice pleading—is perhaps
the most important reform, because it illustrates the basic pleading
philosophy of the federal pleading system. Notice pleading under Rule
8(a)(2) requires only that a pleading make a "short and plain statement
of the claim showing that the pleader is entitled to relief." Elaborating
on Rule 8(a)(2), the Supreme Court in *Conley v. Gibson* provided a more
complete statement of notice pleading and its relation to other pleading
functions:

> all the Rules require is a 'short and plain statement of the claim'
> that will give the defendant fair notice of what the plaintiff's claim
> is and the grounds upon which it rests. The illustrative forms
> appended to the Rules plainly demonstrate this. Such simplified 'no-
> tice pleading' is made possible by the liberal opportunity for discov-
> ery and the other pretrial procedures established by the Rules to
> disclose more precisely the basis of both claim and defense and to
> define more narrowly the disputed facts and issues.

Notice pleading not only eliminates the need to distinguish between
"ultimate facts," "evidentiary facts," and "conclusions of law," it also
underscores the basic philosophy of federal procedure as a whole—
namely, a lawsuit should be tried on the merits, not on the pleadings.

Rannels v. S.E. Nichols, Inc. provides an excellent illustration of
notice pleading. * * *

In rendering its decision, the court of appeals explicitly stated what
it believed the FRCP "do not require a claimant to set out in detail the
facts upon which he bases his claim." The court reasoned that "[all rule
8(a) requires] ... is 'a short and plain statement of the claim' that will
give the defendant fair notice of what the plaintiff's claim is and the
ground upon which it rests." Additionally [sic], the court of appeals
pointed out that whether a pleading satisfies the "ultimate facts"
requirements of code pleading is irrelevant for federal pleading, and "a
court is ill-advised to rely on a chimerical distinction [between 'ultimate
facts,' 'evidentiary facts,' and 'conclusions of law'] extinct since 1938

[the year the federal rules became effective]." The court concluded that it would run afoul of "the spirit of the Federal Rules of Civil Procedure for decisions on the merits to be avoided on the basis of . . . mere technicalities."

Rannels not only illustrates the liberality of federal pleading rules but also the practical difference between federal and code pleading. The plaintiff's pleadings were not detailed enough to reach trial under code pleading but were sufficient under federal pleading. In federal pleadings, the parties rely upon discovery for disclosure of the facts, the pretrial conference for formulation of the issues, and the motion for summary judgment to dispose of sham claims. The Rule 12(b)(6) motion to dismiss for failure to state a claim can also be used to dispose of sham or insubstantial claims. And Rule 12(e) gives the trial judge discretion to require more detailed pleading in a particular case. Notwithstanding this maze of interlocking pretrial procedure, the central point of federal pleading is clear: *a motion to dismiss a complaint for failure to state a claim should not be granted solely because the claim in question is defectively stated; the motion should be granted only when no claim exists.*

With this general background, we can now turn to a consideration of how CRT might respond to some of the issues raised by federal pleadings.

B. A CRT Critique

Necessarily, a CRT critique of federal pleadings begins with the subordination question. This question presents a two-pronged inquiry: whether federal pleadings law, in concept or implementation, gives low or no priority to the concerns of people of color or otherwise disadvantages them; and, if so, what can be done to correct the problem. The first part of the question seeks to deconstruct federal pleading, and the second part searches for reconstructive measures.

1. First Prong of the Subordination Question

Federal courts have applied the federal pleading rules in a manner that has resulted in the early dismissal of many civil rights cases; not on the merits but on procedural grounds. Most of the dismissals have taken place in the context of cases brought under Section 1983. * * *

In essence, Section 1983 permits individuals to sue local governments and governmental officials for civil rights violations.

Some federal courts have construed Section 1983 to require that a complaint, at the very least, "outline the facts constituting the alleged violation." Thus, whereas a federal complaint normally need only "set forth enough information to outline the elements of a claim or to permit inferences to be drawn that these elements exists," Section 1983 actions are subjected to a less liberal form of pleading, one that is more analogous to fact pleading under the codes.

In *Leatherman v. Tarrant County Narcotics Intelligence and Coordination Unit,* the Supreme Court unanimously rejected the application of a "heightened pleading standard" to Section 1983 claims brought against municipalities. The Court reasoned that "it is impossible to square [such a standard] . . . with the liberal system of 'notice pleading' set up by the Federal Rules." However, the Court left open the door for the Rules Advisory Committee to adopt a heightened pleading standard for Section 1983 claims.

Significantly, lower federal courts adjudicating Section 1983 claims do not agree on the scope of *Leatherman.* Some have held that *Leatherman* applies only to certain types of Section 1983 claims. Others have held that the rationale of the decision applies to all Section 1983 claims. Still others have held that *Leatherman* applies to all claims outside of Rule 9, which would include Section 1983 and other civil rights claims. Thus, the scope of heightened pleading standard for Section 1983 and other civil rights claims is still an unsettled area of civil procedure.

From a CRT perspective, application of any heightened pleading standard to civil rights cases constitutes racial subordination. The heightened pleading standard disadvantages the civil rights plaintiff by imposing the difficult, if not impossible, burden of making specific factual allegations about events known only to the defendant. The defendant is not required to disclose this information to the plaintiff until discovery, yet the plaintiff is forced to plead such unknown facts to prevent the dismissal of her civil rights claim. The heightened pleading standard, therefore, means that civil rights plaintiffs are required to plead facts that non-civil rights plaintiffs are not expected to know prior to discovery.

Admittedly, an argument can be made that the heightened pleading standard is not race-specific—that it applies to whites as well as minorities. Anyone who sues under the civil rights statutes must comply with this standard. Ergo, the heightened pleading standard subordinates everyone equally, which is to say it does not subordinate any particular race.

This argument, however, ignores the racial subordination inherent in the heightened pleading standard, because it looks at the rule in the abstract rather than contextually. Analyzing the heightened pleading standard from the standpoint of the litigation experiences of people of color, it is clear that the subordination is not race-neutral. For people of color, litigation has always been the most essential governmental resource in the protracted struggle for racial equality in America. Not surprisingly, then, the plaintiff in a civil rights case is ten times more likely to be a person of color than a white person. The result of this disparity is that the heightened pleading standard limits access to the courts for people of color far more than it does for whites. In so doing, the standard disadvantages people of color.

Notwithstanding its disparate impact on people of color, proponents of the heightened pleading standard advance four arguments to justify its application in federal courts: (1) a lower standard would encourage frivolous civil rights litigation in federal courts; (2) civil rights cases should be litigated in state courts (3) civil rights cases can create unnecessary harassment and embarrassment, tarnishing the defendant's reputation; and (4) "[i]n recent years there has been an increasingly large volume of cases brought under the Civil Rights Act"—for example, while during the twelve month period ending June 30, 1967, plaintiffs filed only 2131 civil rights cases, in the twelve-month period ending June 30, 1987, these filings increased to 43,359, a twentyfold increase in twenty years.

* * *

There are several responses to these arguments, however. First, while there are undoubtedly frivolous civil rights complaints filed each year, there is no way of knowing whether the percentage of frivolous civil rights lawsuits is greater than or less than the percentage of other types of frivolous lawsuits. Moreover, if the sham lawsuit is the evil that courts and legislatures seek to eliminate, then why not simply abolish notice pleading for all federal pleadings—why single out civil rights cases? Or why not rely, as the Supreme Court envisioned in *Conley v. Gibson,* on other features of the pretrial process to weed out sham claims, civil rights-based or otherwise?

Second, the claim that civil rights cases should be litigated in state rather than federal courts ignores the extent to which civil rights issues are national issues, which are what the federal courts were designed to address. If state courts had exclusive jurisdiction over civil rights claims, they would be responsible for determining what pleading would be sufficient to sustain such claims. This would result in a person's access to court hinging at least in part on whether she resides in one part of the country or another.

Third, the fact that a defendant in a civil rights action may be harassed or embarrassed does not take us very far. Surely the civil rights defendant's discomfort is no greater than that of defendants in most other types of civil litigation. In fact, it may be even less than that of certain types of civil litigation such as insider trading cases, or criminal prosecutions. If the defendant's level of discomfort were a criterion for deciding whether to curtail litigation, our society would have to disallow a great number of civil claims and perhaps all criminal prosecutions. Indeed, the defendant's discomfort adds to the deterrence value of litigation.

Fourth, the increase in the number of civil rights filings in recent years does not justify the heightened pleading requirement. The annual percentage of civil rights filings is not substantially greater than the annual percentage of other types of cases filed in federal court. For example, civil rights cases accounted for approximately eighteen percent of all cases filed in federal court in the fiscal year ending June 30, 1987. For that same period, contract cases represented nineteen percent of federal filings. It is also important to recognize that the increase in the number of civil rights cases filed may be warranted by the inertia of discriminatory traditions in our society and by the increased knowledge of legal rights people of color are continuing to gain.

Clearly, the heightened pleading standard is not completely groundless. Some arguments lodged in its support are indeed logical and empirically sound (although no more so than the race crits' opposing arguments). While federal judges have not adopted the standard blindly, a race crit would still question the judges' rationale, given the fact that the rule ultimately results in racial subordination. Policy considerations that weigh in favor of racial domination and the disempowerment of people of color must indeed be questioned. When a court shows more concern for a defendant's reputation than for vindicating a plaintiff's civil rights, it would seem that the existing legal order is not objective and value-neutral but rather slants in favor of whites. Race crits would point out that the heightened pleading standard seems to reveal a judicial bias against civil rights cases (especially when considered in light of the amount of Rule 11 sanctions granted against plaintiffs in such cases). A race crit would characterize this phenomenon as "procedural racism" at the least.

2. Second Prong of the Subordination Question

In contemplating solutions to the problem of racial subordination in federal pleading, one must keep in mind the basic objective of CRT—to use law as a tool for social transformation. In the context of federal pleading, this means that the federal pleading regime must be reconstructed to facilitate civil rights plaintiffs' access to federal courts.

* * *

Other than an outright prohibition against granting motions to dismiss in civil rights cases, perhaps the rule of the law is that most acceptable to race crits—most compatible with racial empowerment—is the following: *No civil rights complaint shall be dismissed unless the plaintiff has had an opportunity to engage in discovery.* Thus, race crits would adopt a special pleading rule applicable to civil rights cases that essentially precludes pre-discovery dismissal.

* * * [A] race crit would argue that the special pleading rule is specific and attentive to the inability of the civil rights plaintiff to obtain specific facts about her claim at the pleading stage. The rule is also cognizant of the fact that much of the information necessary to establish or disestablish a civil rights claim (e.g., intent) remains in defendant's possession.

* * * [A] race crit would defend the special pleading rule on the ground that it is needed to counterbalance racism. Society and its institutions, including its legal system, express a white world-view, a perspective that necessarily operates to the benefit of whites at the expense of people of color. The federal courts' treatment of civil rights claims, including Rule 11 sanctions, is merely further evidence of this built-in bias. Rules of law that are more explicitly oriented toward nonwhites, that are more affirming of nonwhite experiences, that are more empowering of nonwhites are therefore needed to right this wrong.

The assimilationist would undoubtedly criticize the special pleading rule. * * * [S]he or he would argue that the rule allows civil rights plaintiffs to plead less facts than ordinary plaintiffs. Therefore, the lower pleading rule is inconsistent with notice pleading and the general scheme of federal pleading. To the race crit, of course, the assimilationist is either hopelessly and dangerously naive or callously insensitive to the plight of minorities.

The pluralist as well as the assimilationist would offer yet another rationalist challenge to the special pleading rule. They would argue that the lower pleading rule for civil rights plaintiffs promotes racial inequality, the very condition race crits seek to avoid, because the rule stigmatizes minority plaintiffs. The rule reinforces social stereotypes about the abilities of minorities and constructs victim-centered identities of such groups. For this reason alone, the argument continues, the lower pleading rule, like any other asymmetrical rule, should be rejected.

Race crits have a quick counterargument * * *—namely, racial stereotyping predates and exists quite apart from the special pleading rule. One cannot, therefore, realistically pin racial stereotyping on any asymmetrical rule of law favoring minorities, least of all a special pleading rule.

Notes and Questions

1. How feasible is Professor Brooks' suggestion that civil rights cases cannot be dismissed before discovery has occurred. Are there any unintended consequences of such a rule that Professor Brooks hasn't considered? Would this rule make it more difficult for employees of color to get hired? Or could you argue that the reason why employees of color are not hired pre-dates any such special pleading rule?

2. Can pleading rules have a racially disparate impact?

3. Do you agree with Professor Brooks statement that "litigation has always been the most essential governmental resource in the protracted struggle for racial equality in America?"

4. Would you agree with Professor Johnson that "the possibility of sanctions [could] have inhibited civil rights advocates from bringing cases like Brown v. Board of Education, which called for the overruling of well-established precedent (Plessy v. Ferguson) and the 'separate but equal' doctrine?"

5. The Supreme Court has recently stated in a case involving prisoner's rights, that heightened pleading will not be required and the regular notice pleading rules apply. Jones v. Bock, 549 U.S. ___, 127 S.Ct. 910, ___ L.Ed.2d ___ (2007). In civil rights cases, the Supreme Court has repeatedly held that notice pleading is all that is required, yet lower courts have still applied the higher "heightened pleading" standard. *See generally* Christopher M. Fairman, Heightened Pleading, 81 Tex. L. Rev. 551 (2002). Profes-

sor Fairman states: "Despite . . . the Supreme Court's endorsement of notice pleading in Conley v. Gibson, federal courts have embraced heightened pleading burdens in a variety of situations. Nowhere has the squeeze been tighter than in civil rights cases."

*

Index

References are to Pages

339

†